WASHINGTON's
China

A volume in the series

Culture, Politics, and the Cold War

Edited by Christian G. Appy

THE NATIONAL
SECURITY WORLD,
THE COLD WAR, AND
THE ORIGINS OF
GLOBALISM

JAMES PECK

WASHINGTON'S
China

University of Massachusetts Press AMHERST & BOSTON

Copyright © 2006 by University of Massachusetts Press
All rights reserved
Printed in the United States of America

LC 2006003166
ISBN 1-55849-536-3 (library cloth ed.); 537-1 (paper)
Designed by Richard Hendel
Set in Charter and The Serif Black types by
BookComp, Inc.
Printed and bound by
The Maple-Vail Book Manufacturing Group

Library of Congress Cataloging-in-Publication Data

Peck, James, 1944–
  Washington's China : the national security world, the Cold War, and the
origins of globalism / James Peck.
        p. cm.—(Culture, politics, and the cold war)
  Includes bibliographical references and index.
  ISBN 1-55849-537-1 (pbk. : alk. paper)—ISBN 1-55849-536-3 (library cloth :
alk. paper)
  1. United States—Foreign relations—China. 2. China—Foreign
relations—United States. 3. Cold War. 4. United States—Foreign
relations—1945–1989. I. Title. II. Series.
  E183.8.C5P395 2006
  327.7305109'045—dc22

                                                    2006003166

British Library Cataloguing in Publication data are available.

For Laurie

CONTENTS

Acknowledgments ix

Note on Transliteration and Sources xi

Abbreviations xiii

Introduction 1

1 ★ Visionary Globalism and the National Security Community 17

2 ★ China as Puppet 48

3 ★ Containing China before Korea 83

4 ★ Isolating China 110

5 ★ From Monolithic to International Communism 140

6 ★ Taiwan and the Uses of Tension 173

7 ★ Revolutionary China and Containment without Isolation 195

8 ★ Modified Containment plus Subversion 226

Notes 261

Index 323

ACKNOWLEDGMENTS

Over the years I've greatly benefited from many conversations here and in China about the issues explored in *Washington's China*. I want to thank Sol and Pat Adler, Helen Daniells, Israel Epstein, J. William Fulbright, Susan Gyarmati, Hao Wang, Huang Youyi, Lin Wusun, Harry Magdoff, David and Nancy Milton, Moss Roberts, Franz Schurmann, John S. Service, Laurie Sheck, Paul Sweezy, and James C. Thomson Jr. I particularly want to express my appreciation to Tom Engelhardt and Marilyn Young, who were instrumental in so many ways in bringing this book to fruition.

A number of people contributed to the final work on this book. Chris Appy, series editor for Culture, Politics, and the Cold War, provided excellent editorial advice and asked numerous probing questions. The text benefited enormously from the sensitive and skillful editing of Craig Seligman. Clark Dougan, senior editor at University of Massachusetts Press, provided unstinting support and encouragement throughout the years needed to complete the book. Carol Betsch, managing editor, combined good spirit and technical savvy while both working on and shepherding the book through editing and production. A special thanks also goes to the manuscript's two copy editors, Nancy Raynor and Patricia Sterling.

My wife, Laurie, was a source of enormous support and encouragement. Conversations about China and America have been woven into the fabric of our daily lives for almost three decades, and nourished this book in innumerable ways. And my daughter, Maia, lived through various incarnations of this book with enormous good will and spirit.

NOTE ON TRANSLITERATION AND SOURCES

Chinese personal names, place names, and sources are given in the text in pinyin. Thus Mao Tse-tung is Mao Zedong, Chou En-lai is Zhou Enlai, Chiang Kai-shek is Jiang Jieshih, and Kuomintang is Guomindang, except in quoted passages, where Wade-Giles is retained. Spelling is often inconsistent in national security documents throughout these years; sometimes they follow political guidelines (such as Peiping, Red China). Quoted materials are left as they appear in the original; explanatory interpolations are provided only if essential to clarify meaning.

When I first began working on this book, many of the declassified documents were on microfiche as part of the Declassified Documents Reference System. Today, many of them are part of the Declassified Documents Reference System Database. In the notes, references to a source from the microfiche are cited as *ddc*. When the document was used from the database, it is cited as *DDC*. For *ddc* I have included the date of the document, the year it was declassified, and its filing number. This is no longer necessary for *DDC* in most cases, though I have often provided this additional information when available. Many of the CIA's NIES and SNIES are available online at the CIA website, www.foia.cia.gov/ or on CD-ROMS released by the CIA, as cited in the notes.

ABBREVIATIONS

The following abbreviations are used throughout, in both text and notes.

CCP	Chinese Communist Party
CIA	Central Intelligence Agency
DOD	Department of Defense
DOS	Department of State
DOSC	*Confidential U.S. State Department Central Files*, microform (Frederick, Md.: University Publication of America, 1981–86)
FRUS	U.S. Department of State, *Foreign Relations of the United States* (Washington, D.C.: Government Printing Office, 1948–63)
GATT	General Agreement on Tariffs and Trade
GMD	Guomindang
GRC	Government of the Republic of China (Nationalist China)
JCS	Joint Chiefs of Staff
KMT	Kuomintang (retained in quotations)
NATO	North Atlantic Treaty Organization
NIE	National Intelligence Estimate
NSC	National Security Council
NSW	the national security world
OCB	Operations Coordinating Board
ORE	Office of Reports and Estimates (CIA)
ORI or OIR	Office of Research and Intelligence (DOS)
PPS	Policy Planning Staff of the State Department
PRC	People's Republic of China
PSB	Psychological Strategy Board
ROC	Republic of China
SEATO	South East Asia Treaty Organization
SNIE	Special National Intelligence Estimate
USIA	United States Information Agency

WASHINGTON's China

INTRODUCTION

This book had its origins in the early 1960s when the Kennedy administration was rapidly expanding its war against Vietnam and justifying the escalation by heralding the image of a frightening, expansionist China. Coming from an educated upper-middle-class moderate Republican family, I was not particularly critical of Kennedy's policies at first. Yet I had been uneasy with the militant Cold War tone of his presidential campaign—so uneasy that at the age of sixteen I had stuffed envelopes for Richard Nixon at the local Republican campaign headquarters. Though I really understood little of the emotionally charged exchanges between the two candidates over the offshore Chinese islands of Jinmin and Matsu in the 1960 campaign debates, the intensity of Kennedy's hostility to China haunted me and undoubtedly influenced my decision to take undergraduate courses in Chinese history. Had it not been for the Cuban Missile Crisis in October 1962, my interest in China and the Vietnam War might have remained low-key for several more years. But that event shook my faith in the rationality of the American government (although Khrushchev's rashness appalled me just as much). And I was taken aback by the fervent, unquestioning support in my college for Kennedy's actions—except on the part of a few teachers who guided me to I. F. Stone's newsletters.

I had always found it hard to sympathize with Washington's unrelenting anxiety over communism. The Chinese revolution struck me as an intensely nationalistic upheaval—a desperate effort to build a new society from the devastation of a collapsing civilization, its leaders drawn to communist ideology largely as a means of asserting their independence and finding ways to rebuild their society. The Vietnamese struggle seemed just as obviously nationalistic, with leaders unlikely to subordinate their country's interests to China's or to anyone else's, whatever their shared ideology. The Soviet Union had imperial ambitions, as the Eastern Europeans (and others) could attest. And the United States? It seemed just as fiercely nationalistic—its acclaimed exceptionalism part of an ardent faith, its globalism a way of asserting its power, its proclaimed universalism a mask for a pervasive provincialism. Power tends to create its own justifications, I thought, and great power all the more so. Such reflections found little support amid the ideological ferocity of the Cold War. Washington was disconcerted and sometimes terrified by almost every strong nationalism, except its own.

In 1966, when I entered Harvard's graduate program in East Asian studies, the Vietnam War still had its supporters on the faculty, but most of my teachers spoke of it as a costly mistake. Yet what, exactly, was the mistake? They discussed Chinese and Vietnamese nationalism and recounted the historic enmity between the two nations but would then quickly veer off into lurid predictions about the spread of communism, assertions about the necessity of defending the global order or American credibility, or expressions of the need to support nonviolent methods of modernization. Yet even though my teachers did not think "a billion nuclear-armed Chinese" (as Vice President Hubert Humphrey used to put it) were likely simply to spill over into Vietnam and the rest of Asia, their fear of China was palpable in their repeated assertions that the United States was combatting "wars of national liberation" or the "Maoist model of revolution," that "Maoist measles" was threatening to spread across the Third World, and whole peoples needed inoculation against it. The very same George Kennan who as early as 1964 was challenging aspects of the Vietnam War was simultaneously writing of a China led by "embittered fanatics," "ruthless" men "consumed with ambition"; a China threatening to expand over Asia, and permeated with "hatred" toward the utterly blameless United States.[1] If such words could issue from the critical Kennan, what could one expect from the hawks?

By 1966, the virulent and mind-numbing hostility toward an abstract China had persisted for almost two decades. *Washington's China* reflects some of the questions I began asking myself in those years. Why did the United States seek to isolate China for so long? Why did it continue to recognize Jiang Jieshih's rival regime on Taiwan as the legitimate government of China and block Beijing from taking China's seat in the United Nations? Why the years of economic blockade, the ongoing support for Jiang's covert war against the mainland, the numerous CIA operations within China and around its periphery? Why the early and prolonged commitment to fighting insurgency movements throughout Southeast Asia under the guise of "containing" China? And why the virulence of Washington's language—the Manichaean cosmology of good and evil that typically infused so many official statements?

"Hostility" is an emotionally charged word but an elusive one. It involves intense anger, whether concealed in the cool, abstract language of geopolitics or overtly exposed in ideological warfare and in racial and cultural stereotypes. China's revolution, its communism, its radical nationalism, its model of development from the late 1940s on—all these were anathema to the United States and the global order it was determined to establish. The pervasive combination of fear and condescension remains, in varied ways, to this day.

Washington's China thus began as an examination of the character of American hostility toward China from the late 1940s to the late 1960s, focusing particularly on the ways it was fueled and sustained by American objectives in Asia. Domestic interests aggravated that hostility, but they never fundamentally shaped the policy or accounted for the ideological intensity behind it. American historians have offered various explanations for this hostility, the most common being that the Korean War "froze" relations. Some have argued that the American decision to place the Seventh Fleet in the Taiwan Strait on June 27, 1950, turned Taiwan into a contentious and more or less unresolvable issue thereafter. Others have maintained that the fear of communism combined with domestic politics (particularly the China lobby and McCarthyism) to preclude a more flexible policy. The explanations are many, and several have validity.

Few, however, grapple fully with the most striking aspects of America's China policy. By the late 1940s, containment had come to be largely accepted as the best way to deal with the Soviet Union, but not many advocated isolating the USSR in the way that China was isolated. There were always contacts and discussions with the USSR; it is hard to see how without them the emerging bipolar world could have been quite so compatible with the interests of the two great powers. In the months after Stalin's death in March 1953, the Eisenhower administration began a debate over expanding contact with the USSR, which the new Soviet leadership eagerly sought. Endless discussions weighed the pros and cons of cultural exchange and of negotiation, their urgency fueled in part by increasing concern over the Soviet Union's new nuclear capability. How could the Cold War ethos be maintained and the requisite American mobilization sustained, asked Secretary of State John Foster Dulles, amid "peaceful coexistence"? Others lauded the benefits of cultural exchange and its potential for loosening the Soviet grip on Eastern Europe, arguing that contact could become a sophisticated weapon in America's armory.

None of this was true of relations with China. American policy was to remain far harsher and more extreme toward that country. Even cultural contact was feared likely to contaminate those who came in touch with China, thus weakening the American position. The United States monitored in enormous detail the contacts of its own citizens and those of other nations with China. American diplomats followed the movements of the overseas Chinese community: who went to China and why, and what they did and said upon their return. They reported on the trips of countless Europeans and Asians, examining their statements and writings and local press coverage on their return, and called for propaganda campaigns to counter any potentially positive image of China.

Even in internal discussions, government officials rarely suggested that drawing Chinese leaders into any diplomatic discussions would serve any purpose other than the negative one of legitimizing the communists; even vague nods in that direction were attacked as undermining American support for Taiwan.

Few business contacts were permitted, either. Again, compare the checkered but persistent history of American businesses with the Soviet Union after November 1917. Businessmen suspected of dealings with the People's Republic of China (PRC) were carefully monitored, and the Treasury Department reported in detail on financial transactions in Hong Kong as part of the ongoing American embargo against trade with China. No journalist was granted permission to enter China on an American passport until Edgar Snow made it in 1959. Nor did any literary image of China ever match the Soviet Union of John Le Carré's novels, challenging the West in a deadly "game" with its own intricate rules. The Chinese seemed to be beyond such games, beyond rules. Hence John Foster Dulles's refusal to shake Zhou Enlai's hand at the Geneva Conference in 1954, a minimal civility that had not been denied even the Soviets.

Many Western historians argue that Beijing was at least as hostile to Washington as Washington was to Beijing. Their reasons are varied: the revolutionary inflexibility of the triumphant communists; the reinforcement of communist dogmatism by American intervention in the Chinese civil war after 1945; resentment over centuries-long humiliation at the hands of the West (now symbolized by American power); a lack of experience in dealing with other states as equals (the center-of-the-world syndrome); China's pride (its xenophobic nationalism); the very nature of the communist system, which requires a demonizable enemy to promote internal unity and the pursuit of domestic revolutionary goals, and so on. Yet, whatever one makes of these arguments, they all tend to ignore the obvious: that Beijing would have responded to recognition by Washington, that it would have taken its seat in the United Nations had it not been blocked, that it would have willingly traded (on however limited a basis) with the United States and its allies.

Washington's strategy of containing China through isolation created an extraordinary situation for many years: the United States was almost completely cut off from the People's Republic. The discussions held in Warsaw between Chinese and American diplomats rarely went anywhere. The Chinese repeatedly rejected a baldly drawn-up "peaceful" settlement of the Taiwan issue, arguing that the terms amounted to a legitimization of direct American involvement in the ongoing Chinese civil war and thus flagrant violation of Chinese sovereignty. Unlike with Eastern Europe in the 1950s, there was little sense in the decade or so following June 1950 that China should be drawn into the international community and that contact with the West would alter it.

My contention in *Washington's China* is that American hostility was driven by a fear of China's attaining a great-power status capable of allowing it to challenge an Asian system shaped by America. Four critical factors suggest the nature of this hostility. First, from the late 1940s on, the United States was seeking to shape a new Asian order. Isolating China went hand in hand with reshaping the rest of Asia; the former provided the most effective ideological justification for the latter. As I explain in chapters 3, 4, and 5, only isolation could effectively "contain" China, and such a policy became possible only in the wake of the Korean War. Throughout the 1950s, "containment without isolation" was ideologically unable either to assist in the attainment of key U.S. objectives in Asia or to contain China; only isolation combined with intense hostility would work.

Second, isolating China was not simply a response to the enormity of the Chinese revolution, the Sino-Soviet alliance, the radical Chinese model of development, or the model for "wars of national liberation" in the Third world. All these were involved, but they were inseparable from a profound aversion to China's intensely asserted independence and its impassioned nationalistic determination to find its way to great-power status. At the root of American hostility throughout these years was opposition to a China that would not accept the new Asian capitalist order that the United States was shaping.

Third, for all this hostility to Beijing, China was never Washington's central strategic or immediate ideological preoccupation. Washington's main concerns were the Cold War with the Soviet Union and the economic organization of the core areas of the capitalist world in ways that would firmly tie the underdeveloped world to their needs. But this hostility to Beijing does bring into focus certain American objectives far more clearly than does American policy toward the Soviet Union. China seemed to challenge Westernizing and later modernizing visions of the world; it embodied what was most dangerous in Third World nationalism and revolutionary change. Its size, its cultural density, its potential power, and its looming presence in Asia made it a challenge to the world the United States was seeking to build far different from the kind posed by the Soviet Union. There is another aspect that haunts these documents, though rarely evident in the formal documents—race. Eisenhower commented in his memoirs that "no matter what differences in culture and tradition, values or language, the Russian leaders were human beings, and they wanted to remain alive."[2] The Chinese, according to Eisenhower, were different, often fanatical, irrational, and caring little or nothing for human life. "We are always wrong when we believe that Orientals think logically as we do," Eisenhower said, his words often echoed by other leaders throughout these years.[3] In the National Security Council (NSC), the Soviet Union was white and still part of Western civilization; China was very much the other. In the National Security World (NSW), "otherness" is as often as not the racial codeword.

Fourth, if Washington feared the emergence of an independent, powerful China capable of challenging it in Asia and elsewhere, national security officials spoke of it this way only indirectly in policy debates. What emerged in the late 1940s—the belittling of the revolution's independence, the dismissal of the profound nationalism of the Chinese communists, the refusal to accept the legitimacy of China's quest for great-power status—underlines the condescending attitude that has continued in various forms ever since. Such denigration served to sustain and promote key American global and regional Asian strategic objectives; it was never simply a misperception that distorted American strategy.

Washington's Chinas

The American commitment to containing China by isolating it is just part of the story. Hostility to China was deeply embedded in Washington's public and private simplifications and its crude ideological formulations. In the 1940s, Washington labeled China a "puppet"; in the years of the Sino-Soviet alliance, the early to mid-1950s, Beijing was Moscow's "independent junior partner"; in the 1960s, it became an expansionist force and a feared "revolutionary model." Other Chinas followed: China the skilled geopolitical player in the Soviet-American-Chinese triangle of the 1970s; the human rights violator with economic development potential of the 1980s and 1990s; and now China the uneasy ally against terrorism and, at last, economic behemoth.

In this book I focus on three Chinas—the puppet, the junior partner, and the revolutionary model—to explain how and why such simplifications emanated from the national security bureaucracy. None were ever really accurate. They were assessments of China not as it was but as Washington needed it to be in order to pursue specific strategies. The Chinese communists were no less independent minded in the 1940s than they were in the 1960s. They were no more revolutionary in 1965 than they were in 1949. Their calculations of national self-interest were as strong in the late 1940s as they were at any other time.

China as Puppet

Starting with the triumph of the Chinese revolution in the late 1940s, in chapter 2 I look at the way American policy makers radically denied the possibilities of nationalistic independence. In debates over U.S. global policy, China was seen as a mere puppet of Kremlin-directed "monolithic Communism." In arguments now often downplayed or dismissed by historians as too embarrassingly crude for Secretary of State Dean Acheson and others to have actually believed, Chinese nationalism was placed in opposition to Chinese communism and the Chinese communists characterized as subordinate to Moscow—that is, willing to sell out their country, willing to allow Soviet domination of key Chinese provinces, and willing to pursue Soviet objectives that subordinated China's national interests to those of Moscow.

National security managers created an ideological framework that diminished or denied Chinese communism's roots in Chinese nationalism, the revolution's passionate commitment to Chinese independence, and its potential challenge to a bipolar, Eurocentric world. Chinese communism, they claimed, was neither independent nor nationalistic; rather, it was an alien, manipulative force insidiously infiltrating nationalistic movements with agents loyal to Moscow. Acheson and other American officials claimed that they were siding with Chinese nationalism against communism—justifying in this way almost all forms of American intervention in the revolution. Opposing communism meant defending China's true interests. A Chinese communist was profoundly un-Chinese, just as an American communist was un-American. No patriotic nationalist could really be a communist. As Dean Rusk said, the new government in Beijing was "not Chinese."[4]

China the puppet reflected the adamant ideological belief in a bipolar, Manichaean, communist/noncommunist world that characterized Truman's Washington. The conflict was, first and foremost, an East-West battle, and Washington's challenge was, in part, to persuade others at home and abroad to see it that way too. China's dramatic assertion of independence was thus twisted into a form of subordination to Moscow; a propaganda campaign ridiculed Chinese claims to independence, insisting that its "standing up" by asserting its independence was blatantly contradictory with its "leaning to one side" by establishing friendly relations with the Soviets. Washington's intensifying bipolar Cold War ethos preferred not to see, let alone accept, China's fiercely asserted nationalistic independence.

Washington's Asia was a tumultuous, war-torn continent being fought over by two white powers that embodied the ideological, economic, and strategic keys to the future. Though Washington dominated Japan in far more apparent ways than even the most rabid "cold warriors" could come up with to prove Soviet domination of China, the contrast of an independent China and a subordinate Japan was, of course, unpalatable ideologically and unacceptable.

China as Junior Partner

In the early months of the Eisenhower administration, a different vision of China emerged, that of international communism's "junior partner." Nationalism and communism were less often directly contrasted except by Jiang Jieshih on Taiwan; now both Chinese communism *and* Chinese nationalism were anathema to the United States. Beijing was no longer Moscow's puppet; it was its ideological ally, but still very much a part of the Sino-Soviet bloc and of "international" (rather than monolithic) communism.

The vision of a Sino-Soviet bloc encapsulated the changes Washington saw in the world after the late 1940s. The global threat was still overwhelmingly Soviet, but the Asian challenge came increasingly from China. Asia, far more than Europe, was the front line, nowhere more so than in the Taiwan Strait and Southeast Asia. The Soviet Union, with its growing nuclear capabilities and its newly assertive role in the "underdeveloped world," remained *the* enemy, the leader of international communism. Moreover, the Soviets' strategy of "peaceful coexistence" and their calls for lessening tensions struck a responsive chord among allies and neutrals alike, thus making them, in Washington's eyes, a far more sophisticated ideological foe than they had been in the early years of the Cold War.

Meanwhile, the danger of the Chinese enemy was increasingly played up. Leaders of the Eisenhower administration saw a deepening long-term split in the communist world between the Soviet Union (an imperial, expansive power but one that calculated its national interests coldly and carefully) and China (more violent, more revolutionary, more nationalistic, more irrational and anti–status quo). To a considerable degree, their perception reflected the relative stabilization of relations in Europe, the weakness of "containment" in Asia, and their preoccupation with the more fervent expressions of nationalism around the globe.

In the Bandung era, when China proclaimed the five principles of peaceful coexistence and Asian leaders met at their 1955 summit, Moscow's and Beijing's models of development often blurred together, their industrialization and state planning systems seen as growing threats (the India-versus-China development model). Yet there were differences. Nationalism as potential neutralism was interwoven with the Russian threat; nationalism as verging toward a radical and more revolutionary path was increasingly associated with China. In both cases, Washington fought against "extreme nationalism" under the rubric of anticommunism.

The differing implications of containment in Europe and Asia had become striking by the advent of the Eisenhower administration. In Europe, containment meant drawing a line across the continent. Though the issue of Germany and Berlin remained highly contentious, what was being contained and how were nonetheless relatively clear. Not so in Asia. There, containment proved inseparable from nation building. It meant drawing lines through social groupings and classes and in some countries between a large overseas Chinese community and a local non-Chinese population. It called for American involvement in the most intricate internal affairs of Asian countries, to help approved governments or local forces shape and channel indigenous nationalism in acceptable directions. And it came to depend for its success on the rigid isolation of China from the rest of Asia—an isolation embodied in the American recognition of Taiwan as a rival government to Beijing. The contrast between China and the USSR was quite useful, serving to simplify and shape Washington's concern with its quite different though complementary strategies in Europe and the core capitalist countries, on the one hand, and in the "underdeveloped world" on the other.

China as Revolutionary

After 1958, at first slowly and then more forcefully under the Kennedy administration, a full-blown "revolutionary China" came to the fore—a radical society threatening to galvanize a discontented, often distraught Third World. By the end of the Eisenhower administration—with the threat of radical nationalist movements in the Middle East, symbolized by Nasser's leadership in Egypt; with the shadow cast by the 1958 revolution against the pro-Western leadership in Iraq; with the looming spread of revolutionary sentiment in Latin America following the 1958 recession and the rise of Castro; with the rapid movement toward African decolonialization and radical developments in Indonesia and Vietnam—the notion of a Third World in upheaval and desperately in need of modernization had taken hold. In this context, China increasingly alarmed Washington as *the* revolutionary power, the embodiment of the most radical and disturbed forces on the globe, bitterly anti–status quo and, after 1964, armed with nuclear weapons. The USSR might still present the preeminent nuclear threat, but China increasingly appeared to be the more serious independent threat to a U.S.-centered world order.

The long-anticipated split between Beijing and Moscow had become a reality, though the full ideological demise of "international communism" was still to come. Chinese nationalism was now viewed as a revolutionary blend of communism and radical nationalism that required an almost pathological fanaticism and hatred for the United States and the Western world. The Vietnam War was one step in "containing" China.

The new view stood in stark contrast to the bipolar Manichaean world most sweepingly articulated in the National Security Council analysis widely known as NSC 68. In the mid-1960s the administration undertook a major interdepartmental study of China. By then, the imperial threat from the Soviets had diverged considerably from the revolutionary threat presented by the Chinese. Beijing, the study announced, "stands for revolutionary change leading ultimately to a Communist world"; the most likely peril to peace in Asia, Africa, and Latin America was the "whole range of militant dissidence, fomented, encouraged, or supplied by Communist China. . . . The weakness and frustration of many nations and groups in the underdeveloped world . . . make them turn away from sober, unsatisfactory realities towards Chinese solutions for their problems."[5]

Hence China was now a double threat: as the leader of revolutionary forces throughout the underdeveloped world, and as a great-power rival of the USSR and the United States. In both roles it was inimical to the goal of an effective capitalist order encompassing Asia and the Third World, and even to basic stability there. Modernization and its deadly discontents had now become the battleground; Washington trumpeted modernization theory as the means of effecting major change without revolution. Yet Washington's vision of a revolutionary China also produced a surprising twist: the first stirrings of an official quest for ways to bring China into the "family of nations." Even as the Johnson administration rapidly escalated the Vietnam War, it was beginning to rethink China policy. The element that had for so long formed its core—China's isolation—finally lost its tenacious grip; the reasons for this change are the subject of chapters 7 and 8.

Visionary Globalism and the National Security World

For years I underestimated the ideological ferocity of the national security bureaucracy at the center of American foreign policy. The visionary globalism that I analyze in chapter 1 required a remarkable leap of faith: the belief that Washington could continually restructure the United States and the globe in ways that would ensure American centrality in world affairs. Such faith passionately held that American foreign policy strategists really did think globally (as opposed to asserting American interests globally—a quite different proposition). They easily transformed local disputes and contexts into "global" issues whose complexity and importance only they could truly understand. In other words, ideology is not simply the purple prose that adorns policies (as I once thought); rather, American globalism is itself a profoundly ideological formulation that is part and parcel of Washington's thinking and strategizing about the world. Thus Washington's China is part of Washington's world and is fundamentally shaped by Washington's global strategies.

Debates over these global strategies after the mid-1940s, particularly in the executive branch, addressed, broadly speaking, four consistent long-term global goals: (1) to retain the paramount position of American military power, through both alliances and nuclear preeminence; (2) to dominate the new international order in such a way as to ensure the economic centrality of the United States, to prevent trade restrictions on its goods and the flow of its capital, and to undermine any and all ways of development and state planning that it considered autarkic; (3) to defeat in the long run and contain in the shorter run the power and appeal of mass-based nationalisms and to counter communism, Soviet power, and the revolutionary transformation of societies; and (4) to construct a world order that would both sustain and acknowledge certain American values and accept the central role of the United States in implementing them.

At times these goals engendered bitter controversy at the highest levels of the American government (including heated debates over how best to use the American domestic market to build the international economic system), but there was considerable agreement on the *global* character of the strategies and the ways of thinking it would take to place the United States at the center of a new global order. The formulators of these strategies rarely recognized that they were encumbered by ideological thinking. The national security bureaucracy and its leader, the president, prefer seeing themselves as dealing with the brutal realities and specific interests of American power. They might "scare the hell out of the American people" by invoking the horrors of communism (or, today, terrorism) and championing the defense of freedom everywhere, as Senator Arthur Vandenberg urged Truman to do if he wished to meet the goals of the Truman Doctrine. But the national security bureaucracy is usually portrayed as an ideology-free place where hardheaded, even cold-blooded men make their decisions reasonably, practically, and unemotionally.

It was not—not at all. The American historian Louis Hartz once wrote that Americans are so steeped in ideology that they do not even know they have one. Nowhere is the truth of this observation more evident than in the case of visionary globalism. To enter into the workings of the national security bureaucracy in the late 1940s is to confront a world in which strategies designed to order the postwar world belonged to a deeply visionary quest. As I explain in chapter 1, American globalism did not simply fall into Washington's lap by accident. Washington's world strategy came out of an enormous ideological undertaking, an act of faith that saw a world where American power was the central reality and where all aspects of American life that could be reorganized to achieve this end were to be brought into play for decades to come. The national security bureaucracy exists at the center of this faith; its true believers stand at the apex of the American state, where their unrelenting effort to persuade (or "educate" or—as they sometimes simply say—"indoctrinate") Congress and their fellow citizens as to the virtues of this globalism parallels their own fervent process of self-indoctrination, wherein they internalize the language—the code words, the analogies—and the ways of thinking that they then insist are utterly non-ideological means of strategizing about an American-centric world.

Only by appreciating this dynamic is it possible to understand Washington's China. In the following pages, I analyze national security documents to show how they provide the ideological explanations and justifications for American strategies toward the entire communist bloc throughout the Cold War, as well as toward Europe and Japan. Thus, while my main focus in this book is China, I dissect the world in which American policy is formulated—a world where strategy, language, propaganda, and self-indoctrination ultimately blend to create the mind-set of the national security managers.

Words have consequences; the limits of our language, as Ludwig Wittgenstein wrote, are the limits of our world. My aim is thus to zero in on the ways that policy, and the depictions of China that flow from it, draw so widely on words and images that are not derived per se from analyses of China at all. Officials debating China used the key code words and the same language in which they debated other parts of the world. This language changed, to some degree, as administrations changed. In each administration one finds this inculcation of terminology from the top of the foreign policy world down. Histories of American policy on China rarely examine in depth the means by which ideologically molded strategic orientations at the highest levels colored the way every area of the world was seen. They tend to focus on the changes in policy that came from changing bilateral assessments of China. Yet to examine effectively what is going on here leads into a world where objective analysis and belief blend together in the formation of government policies. Such a world is misunderstood when critics focus only on how "misperceptions" led to unwise policies. For American power seeks not so much to understand the world as to order the world around its own interests, and its language of power requires that perception and analysis and faith come together. "Misconceptions" there may have been in analyzing China and the rest of the world. But they do not begin to explain why American power operates as it does.

Enduring Hostility

Today, as Beijing and Washington sometimes share an antiterrorist language and American business investments in China are at record levels, hostility and fear seem far less. And certainly, overt hostility has never been as great as before President Nixon's trip to Beijing in 1972. Yet, in *Washington's China,* I caution that the basic reasons for continued eruptions of hostility and fear toward China (and elsewhere) remain embedded in America's visionary globalism. There is little reason to believe that the current depictions of China are any less ideological than their predecessors, or that hostility is really that far from the surface.

The depth of this hostility became more real to me in the late 1960s, when I began to look at how the field of Chinese studies had developed in the United States after the destructive rampage of Senator Joseph McCarthy. Though it had been massively rebuilt—thanks to a hundred million dollars from the Ford Foundation and defense-justified expenditures—something still seemed to have gone terribly wrong. The writings of an earlier generation, in the 1930s and 1940s, on an intensely nationalistic, revolutionary China were all but dismissed or ignored. When I entered graduate school in 1966, Edgar Snow's *Red Star over China* (1938) was on only the supplementary reading list of a few courses. It has been said that we Americans are people who do not wish to keep much of the past in our heads. But this is not really an accurate way to put it. There are reasons why certain attitudes toward the Chinese revolution and China itself were discredited, and reasons that this discrediting was then explained away as a temporary aberration, called McCarthyism, in American politics. What most struck me was the fear and angry incomprehension that had replaced the empathy of those earlier writers, who had looked at both the staggering human costs and the possibilities in the vast revolutionary changes sweeping China in the 1940s—and had not turned against them. In addition to Edgar Snow, there were John S. Service, the foreign-service officer whose dispatches constitute the finest American diplomatic writings to come out of China; Jack Belden, an iconoclastic, anarchistically inclined recorder of the lives of the down and out, whose hatred for the corrupt machinations of leaders was matched by his empathy for the daily efforts of the Chinese people to survive; Agnes Smedley, who traveled extensively throughout the country seeking to join the Chinese in their struggle; William Hinton, whose writings about the Chinese peasantry would become influential in the late 1960s; and Graham Peck, who dissected Jiang's brutal Guomindang.

Here were Americans who, face to face with the most momentous revolution in history and often unsure of its implications and critical of its course, did not recoil—as so many Americans did then and later. Here were Americans who, encountering a society profoundly different from their own, both recognized and lived with their differences and saw something of value in each society. And here were Americans whose writings were to make them outcasts in their own land. Snow, Belden, and Service returned from China knowing that they were truly American—that, as Jack Belden wrote, one could be for the cause of the Chinese people but never, never once be one of them,[6] only to find that their own country had turned on them, denying in practice the very values to which they had believed it was committed. They hoped that the American government could learn to live with the Chinese revolution and a radical transformation of a world that could not simply become part of a greater American design.

Damned both by McCarthy and by many liberals as romanticizers of revolution or, worse, communist dupes, these writers were, in fact, the ones who grasped truths that would be ignored for decades. They not only knew China well; they understood that the revolution was a fiercely nationalistic—and often frightening—force. But they weren't afraid, and they argued that fear could bring no understanding. They tended to see the Chinese revolution as a desperate attempt at survival in a country where so many other ways had so miserably failed. As Mao told Snow (and others), no people would voluntarily choose such a harsh path unless the most extreme conditions had driven them to it. Understanding this, they argued that the Chinese revolution was not something to "contain" or "isolate"; empathy with its vast problems, rather than hostility, was closer to their way of coming to terms with this revolutionary China. Their knowledge was bound up with the deep conviction that China would be neither American nor Soviet but Chinese. They felt the depths of China's struggle for independence, for standing up, for finding its own way. And they approved.

In the 1940s, they hoped that the United States could find a way to live with China. They argued that America should have recognized the Chinese communists early on—beginning a relationship with them during the war years with General Joseph Stilwell, and certainly by the late 1940s. They saw recognition as a step the United States should take both because it kept possibilities open and because it was a recognition of reality. They believed that China should be in the United Nations, not outside it, and that China would not become bitterly and irrevocably hostile unless American actions pushed the Chinese revolution relentlessly in that direction.

In 1968, when I led a year-long seminar at Harvard's Kennedy Institute of Politics, these targets of McCarthyism would join us—one each month—to talk about his or her experiences in China and to reflect on American foreign policy. Lyndon Johnson was then president, and Sino-American relations were at an abysmal point, with Mao being vehemently attacked as a slightly mad revolutionary who was blocking the possibility of improved relations with Washington. That it was, above all, Mao who would turn out to be the Chinese leader most responsive to an alternative American policy was simply dismissed. Yet John Service and Edgar Snow bluntly said that any such change would come from Mao—the same Mao who had been perfectly capable of establishing diplomatic relations both in the pre–Korean War period *and* at the time of the Bandung Conference, in 1955. More startlingly, they were just as certain that Mao would prove open to a new relationship if the United States government offered him the option. In 1970, when the *People's Daily* published a photograph of Mao standing on Tienanmen with Edgar Snow at his side, Service pointed it out to me with the words, "The change is finally coming, if only Washington responds." As Henry Kissinger wrote in his memoirs nearly a decade later, "The inscrutable Chairman was trying to convey something"—but we had "missed the point."[7] Indeed, one searches in vain through decades' worth of CIA estimates and volumes of diplomatic reports for such an insight. Snow and Service had no doubts, from the 1930s on, about the commitment of China's new leaders to a revolutionary transformation of China's domestic order, but they never believed that this commitment needed to stand in the way of diplomatic ties or of China's rightful seat in the United Nations—if only Washington proved willing to live with the Chinese revolution. That Washington was not willing, and why, is largely the subject of *Washington's China.*

Over the decades, national security documents occasionally hint at a recognition of the reasons Washington's policies aggravated Chinese hostility or offended Beijing's "nationalist pride," particularly on the issue of Taiwan. The "threatening" character of the American military buildup in East Asia, especially after the Korean War, does not go entirely unremarked. Yet in the end it is always the Chinese who are said to be really hostile. American officials soothed whatever uneasiness they might have had over past policies with an "even if" mind-set—even if the United States assisted the Nationalists in the Chinese civil war; even if Taiwan remained the linchpin of American containment policy up to this very day; even if the Chinese communists were justified in bitterly resenting the embargo, their exclusion from the United Nations, and the American pressure that kept many nations from recognizing their regime; even if the rapid American military buildup in East Asia in the early 1960s understandably worried Beijing, which had lived under the nuclear threat for two decades—still, the *fundamental* reasons for China's policies and its bitter denunciations of American policies are *never* fundamentally explainable by United States policy. As NSC 166/1 bluntly put it in 1953, "Even if particular Far Eastern issues were resolved to the satisfaction of Peiping, the Chinese Communists, as communists, would continue to maintain a basic hostility to the West in general and the US in particular."[8] The basic reasons for hostility lay on the Chinese side: their communism, their revolutionary ethos or, later, their intense nationalism, their xenophobia, their cultural messianic streak, and their drive for regional, possibly global hegemony.

What I describe in *Washington's China* is this systemic, inculcated inability to come to terms with the virulence and pervasiveness of American visionary globalism underlying Washington's strategic policy. In October 2004, the CIA released thirty-seven National Intelligence Estimates (and accompanying

Special National Intelligence Estimates) on China. Not surprisingly, the intro-duction provided does not dwell on American intelligence lapses: failure to fore-see China's intervention in the Korean War; the part American hostility played in generating the Sino-Soviet relationship and then in undermining it through a combination of limited détente with the Soviet Union and American military escalation in Asia; the failure to recognize Mao as the key to a new foreign policy with the United States, and so on. Instead, the introduction praises the estimates as "well-grounded in reality" and criticizes Chinese statements in the 1950s and 1960s as "remarkably negative, shrill, and hostile," with nothing at all in them or China's situation that could be seen as "even vaguely desirous of improving bilat-eral relations." There is a caveat, however: the estimates are not "able (author-ized) to evaluate fully the impact of U.S. policy choices on the foreign affairs decisions of the People's Republic of China."[9] And, of course, there's the rub.

1 VISIONARY GLOBALISM AND THE NATIONAL SECURITY COMMUNITY

Since the National Security Council (NSC) was created in 1947, its operations have provided the best entrée into the workings of the national security world and, in particular, into United States policy toward China. From the beginning, the NSC was a fervent apostle of an American visionary globalism. What this globalism entailed—its formulations, its characteristics—underlay specific U.S. policies toward China. Globalism was always an ideological vision, a way of perceiving and shaping the world to achieve American objectives. Globalism brought a kaleidoscope of American interests into some order, balancing different regions against one another, assessing priorities, assigning short- and long-term objectives. It offered a vision of the world that demanded ways of integrating ideological, economic, political, and military concerns with overall "strategic thinking."

This globalism was inseparable in the end from Washington's depiction of China. Its view of China (as variously a puppet, a junior partner of the Soviet Union, a revolutionary threat, a ruthless geopolitical manipulator, and, today, an ally in the war on terrorism) was inextricably interwoven with American global objectives—objectives that come into greater focus when viewed from a greater distance.

Visionary Globalism

In 1945, the United States—its technologies and science unsurpassed, its economy unequaled, its aspirations global—abruptly emerged as the most powerful nation in a charred and leveled world. With the victory of American power over all the nation's enemies, the virtual collapse of its allies, and the settlement of the Pacific war largely on its own terms, America saw World War II as a kind of culminating event in its ascendancy.

And yet its leaders were uneasy. Europe had been decimated. Though the Soviet Union had suffered the savagery of the Nazi onslaught, its armies were now in Eastern Europe, and communist parties appeared strong in Western Europe. Elsewhere, the conclusion of the war had set in motion a process of social upheaval and decolonialization that was reshaping the world. The specter of civil war, revolution, and chaos loomed everywhere.

Domestically, the fear of economic crisis gripped the Roosevelt and Truman administrations. Just as the ghost of Munich haunted Washington's foreign-policy makers, so did the shadow of the Great Depression haunt its economic-policy makers. They feared that the peace so many had fought for might, after all, lead to another crisis of capitalism. And so their policies had to deal with both upheaval abroad and the possibility of depression at home.

The international economic crisis of the 1930s had dealt a shattering blow to the American economy. The Depression accentuated the division of the world into increasingly self-sustaining trading blocs, with the U.S. share of world trade plummeting by almost half and the negative balance of trade lasting for most of the decade. The nation's vast agricultural surpluses found no markets. Trading zones threatened to tie up raw materials that were critical to the deficient American economy. In the view of many New Dealers, as well as corporate leaders, this destruction of the international economic system was a prime cause of the rise of fascism (with its concomitant militarism and economic nationalism) in Germany and Japan.

By itself, the New Deal provided no solution to the economic disaster of the 1930s. In offering sometimes sweeping but essentially defensive domestic measures to shore up American capitalism and alleviate the suffering of some of the hardest-hit victims, it may have soothed the rough edges of the Depression, but neither a process of "normal recovery" nor governmental measures had restored the system's health. The temporary upswing of the economy after 1933 had ended with the sharp recession of 1938, and before the onset of massive, war-induced spending, some 9 million people had been unemployed.

Franklin Roosevelt's vision of the postwar world has often been interpreted as an extension of his New Deal to the world at large. More accurately, it was an answer to the New Deal's weaknesses at home, an attempt to counter domestic depression and the resulting social turmoil by restructuring the capitalist world system through "international" institutions to answer the needs of a globe-spanning American capitalism. For the economic leaders of the Roosevelt administration, the reform of a ferociously nationalistic world racked by depression, war, economic trading blocs, and revolution was an absolute precondition for the long-term prosperity of the United States.

During the war the debate over the new economic order was intense, but almost without exception government spokesmen agreed that the world financial system had to be restructured, with trading blocs eliminated and financial barriers lifted. The challenges included maintaining America's high wartime profits, rapidly expanding its share of world trade, opening markets for its goods and farm products, obtaining the necessary raw materials, and putting the labor force that had been temporarily absorbed into its military and its defense industries to work. American officials were frank about the links between this transformation of the world economy, American exports, the availability of cheap raw materials, and full employment with the utmost clarity. The United States needed foreign markets in which to sell the products pouring out of its factories, the materials and cheap oil to fuel the factories, and the competitive edge against its rivals.

Two developments, one international and one domestic, were crucially important to this transformation. Internationally, the war had left Britain— previously the center of the largest trading bloc—broke and vulnerable to American pressure; Germany and Japan, the two great industrial powers in their respective parts of the world, were defeated, occupied, and subject to an American-directed transformation of their economies; the Soviet Union was still weak economically and facing the immense task of rebuilding; and the old colonial empires were crumbling. Domestically, meanwhile, the New Deal and the war had given rise to a system of executive, corporate, and bureaucratic power that was capable of administering a global order.

The model of the state that emerged from the New Deal and the war— autonomous, innovative, and powerful—became the foundation for Washington's most impressive Cold War ideological achievement: the visionary globalism that came to flourish within the national security world (NSW). The NSW was pivotal for the emerging U.S. global role, and the global role reinforced the pivotal role of the NSW. The two became inseparable.[1]

After 1945, visionary globalism became the most powerful ethos at the pinnacle of American state power. Anticommunism was the popular faith for waging the Cold War, containment was the geopolitical strategy, but visionary globalism shaped them both. It was an outlook far more elitist and less widely held than the other two, and although it had its roots, variously, among Wall Street financiers, lawyers, corporate CEOs, defense industries, and press leaders, its real home was in the secret corridors of the national security world that was taking shape under the aegis of the American presidency. From the beginning, visionary globalism was most at home at the apex of the American state—the White House. The country's leaders believed in the centrality of the state in ordering a new world, with "wise men" to run it; theirs was a vision that they knew would take the full power of the U.S. government to achieve. Out of Zeus's head came the goddess of war and wisdom; out of the American presidency came the power to create a world with "wise men" to manage it.

That ideologically driven elites at the apex of the American state shape long-term policy is not just a tendency of recent days. What these leaders set out to do after 1945 was unprecedented in its scale. Empires have risen and fallen; states had organized parts of the globe over the millennia. But at the apex of U.S. state power, enshrouded in its utmost secrecy, labored men whom Dean Acheson described without embarrassment in biblical language—in the beginning was chaos, and out of it the Americans would create a new global order unlike anything ever before seen.[2] The Achesons, McCloys, Lovetts, and Harrimans were anything but moderates; their views reflected no emerging consensus in America about the nation's post–World War II international role. They well knew that there were opposing conceptions of the national interest. They saw their situation as precarious and perilous, as a minority undertaking, as something that was not widely popular at home or abroad. Their triumph, to themselves and others, was the claim that they actually embodied *the* national interest for the presidents they served. What they sought, and with remarkable success succeeded in doing, was to capture the heights of the American state for a distinct vision of the world, one that has continued to evolve ever since.

Their attitude was fervently visionary—using anticipation and prediction as a way of shaping forces and bureaucracies toward objectives. Though sometimes inchoate as a source of policy, visionary globalism nevertheless offered a cohering faith that would provide the context for almost all international policy discussions over the next fifty years. The visionary globalism of the NSW was so successfully transmuted into policies and so deeply believed by the "wise men" that its core elements were not regarded as ideological at all. They were simply the national security world's common sense—its wisdom about American power and American needs.

The vision was never a simple one. It comprised economic and military dimensions, including the faith that a new economic order could be built and American power promoted to protect it. Initially, it imbibed aspects of New Deal progressivism in the belief that American power could end the old colonial systems and meet the "rising tide of expectations" the war had unleashed. More than this, though, visionary globalism was a way of seeing the world as one, of always seeing specific situations, events, and crises vis-à-vis the global needs of American power and policy. It was a faith that the world would become one *if* America played its global role, a way of thinking that reinforced American power and the role of the national security managers: America was No. 1, they were at the center, and the president was at *their* center.

Neither anticommunism nor containment fully accounts for the animating vigor of the vision that seized American policy makers after World War II. And although America's dynamic capitalism, with its never ending search for more capital, land, and labor, was and remains expansionist, there is an important difference between expansionism and visionary globalism. Expansionism proceeds incrementally, with the state adding on pieces of territory and military bases. But there is no direct path from expansionism to a doctrine of organizing the globe from the top down; nor did American expansionism engender the faith to undertake this task or the ideology to overpower its critics at home. Visionary globalism was not simply the natural extension of American expansionism, which had begun when the country did; nor was it the natural outgrowth of the capitalist world market system that America helped to revive after 1945. The globalism whereby America undertook to dominate, organize, and direct the "free world" was the product of a worldview held by the leaders of the American state. Thus visionary globalism is not simply a projection of corporate America or a vision of capitalism per se; it is a vision of American-centric state globalism using capitalism as a key to its global reach, integrating everything that it can into such an undertaking. It is not a vision of a marketplace that operates without state power but a vision of state power ordering the structures of the global economic order. It is a vision not of a world of ever freer competition but of competition designed to serve the needs of that center.

And here is one of the anomalies of visionary globalism. Domestically, it was not a widely shared faith, yet it was held as beyond contention in the national security community. In fact, globalism was harshly and repeatedly criticized in the United States. Right-wing anticommunists, national capitalists, political leaders such as Senator Robert Taft—all opposed it. It had no popular constituency; instead, it was the province of powerful special interests. The visionary globalism that underlay the next half century of American power was the innermost faith and conviction of the few. Only anticommunism was to overcome this great divide.

Yet even if anticommunism worked to mobilize the public and, in private, to sharpen the fighting focus of the national security managers, it is not a sufficient key to American foreign policy after 1945, for it did not supply the underlying vision of the new world. It provided the ideological alarm to rouse the

American populace, but it was visionary globalism that mobilized business, financial, military, and political leaders to construct the new global order. Anticommunism provided a mobilizing vision of the evil enemy, but it was visionary globalism that saw beyond the worldwide battlefield of anticommunism to an economic, cultural, and political interdependency that had to be nourished to win the ideological war. Whereas anticommunism offered a superb rationale for the central role of state power, visionary globalism laid out the global order it was to realize. Anticommunism donned the mantle of freedom against the horrors of the "non-free world." Visionary globalism held that American ways were universal and that a transformed world capitalist system would implement them.

These visionary qualities of an American-centric globalism were in no way moderate. The need for a cohering ideology at the apex of the American state, the Manichaean temptation and crude simplifications, the us-versus-them rhetoric—all are deeply nourished by this American-centric vision. Anticommunism and antiterrorism, the American state's two great fighting faiths, can wage the specific ideological battles against the "enemy," but they do not fuel the deepest faith. These fighting faiths drew on the sweeping tenets of the deeper faith—in an American-centric world order, modernity, the marketplace, the emancipatory power of American freedom, capital, and the implicit universality of American ways. Visionary globalism is a form of ideological total war against all who stand apart from an American-centric world, a war waged endlessly at the apex of the American state. Like Antaeus, both of the fighting faiths are grounded in this relentless visionary globalism.

Anticommunism was particularly effective in weakening conservative domestic critics of globalism, and the national security managers knew it. They waged ideological war at home by indirection, which was to be the master key to their success. For beneath the bitter anticommunist controversies of the McCarthy period lay a subtle consensus about globalism. While liberals and many Republican leaders in the 1950s committed themselves to globalism, the most vehement elements of the right spoke the language of an *inverted* globalism that saw the international struggle reflected on the home front. Both sides fully accepted the notion of America as the leader of the "free world," the only alternative to Soviet despotism and the spread of communism. Both sides endorsed all but unlimited American power, with the right insisting that loyalty at home would guarantee sweeping victories abroad.[3] The national security world and the right wing both saw the world in Manichaean terms, with the former favoring an international crusade and the latter a domestic one. Globalism abroad and McCarthyism at home proved compatible—if not quite complementary.

The Wise Men of the NSW

As members of the NSW have long insisted, "In the American political system, only Presidents have incentives to think of the national interest."[4] The wise men and their descendants fervently believed that their task was to rise above warring bureaucratic interests, advising the chief executive and formulating the *real* national interest for him. Others in government and the public, representing particular interests, could not grasp the global picture from their limited perspectives. The national security managers were there to help the president stand above such limited ways of thinking. As Dean Acheson said, "Foreign policy is the whole of national policy looked at from the point of view of the exigencies created by 'the vast external realm' beyond our borders. It is not a 'jurisdiction.' It is an orientation, a point of view, a measurement of values—today, perhaps, the most important one for national survival."[5]

For two decades these managers made up a remarkably cohesive, consistent, and powerful elite. America had never before seen such a group, and nothing else quite like it can be found to this day. Before 1940 a small and somewhat ineffective foreign policy bureaucracy had served under the president as Foreign Service officers, Commerce Department officials, and so forth. But after 1940, with increasingly centralized presidential authority to back them up, the national security managers, working with the military, began to redefine national U.S. interests. They were men who had been recruited by Henry Stimson and James Forrestal, plus a few others with similar backgrounds, such as Dean Acheson, William Clayton, and Averell Harriman. They came from the great banking houses and law firms of New York and Boston. They knew one another. They had a feel for power and how to use it, and they believed that history had summoned them. No one else, they thought, so unselfishly embodied the national interest: they knew what was right for the country and what was wrong. In later years they wrote about how they had laid the foundations for a new world and triumphed over isolationism. But despite the adulation that still surrounds their names (Robert Lovett, John McCloy, Dean Acheson, John Foster Dulles, Douglas Dillon, James Forrestal, and so forth), their actions displayed an unmistakable mixture of public interest and self-interest—a commitment to "public duty" and "civic responsibility" that barely masked a naked grasp for power.

The wise men took the bureaucratic transformation that the American war effort had effected and codified it into the concepts, the rhetoric, the ideology, the alliances, and the military networks that shaped the American side of the Cold War. After Roosevelt's death, they stepped in to shape the Truman administration's world picture.[6] In later years, the Bundys, Maxwell Taylor, Walt Rostow, Brent Scowcroft, Henry Kissinger, and Zbigniew Brzezinski sought to extend and at times transform these structures, providing some semblance of continuity amidst the momentous changes in American globalism since the 1960s. Much has been made of the breakdown of the foreign policy establishment beginning with the Vietnam War. Yet even as the partisan wars became more evident and the politics of party erupted with the collapse of the Cold War consensus, visionary globalism remained unchallenged. As other debates raged, it underlay an increasingly public vision of an American-centric global order.

The National Security Council and Its Codes

The National Security Council, which was expressly designed to stand at the policy center of the American security state, offers the most revealing window onto this community. From its inception in 1947, its task was to make policy coherent and ensure that it was based on a comprehensive knowledge of the global picture.[7] The NSC was to "assess and appraise the objectives, commitments, and risks of the United States in relation to our actual and potential military power"; was "to advise the President with respect to the integration of domestic, foreign, and military policies relating to the national security," while serving as his "highest level policy advisor staff arm"; and was also to have "responsibility for general direction of the Central Intelligence Agency." It was to draw on the latest intelligence to formulate its recommendations, seeking a consensus within the national security bureaucracy where possible, or laying out alternative positions when necessary, and forecasting likely developments.[8]

As the NSC evolved over the years, its initial mission—to coordinate political and military questions—"quickly gave way to the understanding that the NSC existed to serve the President alone," and the "view that the Council's role was to foster collegiality among departments quickly gave way to the need by successive Presidents to use the Council as a means of controlling and managing competing departments."[9] In the past fifty years, the national security advisor has morphed from the largely administrative executive secretary serving the council's needs in the early Truman years into a powerful presidential advisor. In the Kennedy years, under McGeorge Bundy, the NSC became a "truly Presidential foreign policy staff" acting as the president's eyes and ears in the foreign policy bureaucracy. Its members, appointed at his pleasure, are expected to view foreign policy from his perspective. Its power is largely unwritten: even though some presidents downgraded its formal role, the system of centralization of power in the president's key advisors tended to cluster around the NSC, thus shifting foreign policy–making power from the cabinet departments to the White House.[10]

In its formative years the NSC was a center of both analysis and ideological warfare, a place where policies were shaped ad hoc in moments of crisis amid a deep commitment to a specific global order, an environment where the making of policy and the propagation of a faith became inseparable in the formulation of American foreign relations.[11] What emerges from a study of the NSC documents is a consciously shaped and reshaped point of view that valued in the council itself the order, continuity, reasonableness, and moderateness it so often failed to find in the world it analyzed. The way documents were drafted and redrafted, the words that codified the interpretations of opponents, the definitions, the explanations of momentous events—all these things grew out of the ethos of the emerging national security bureaucracy wherein analysis and ideology fell into a symbiotic relationship. The evidence lies in the ways the statements were produced and how they were discussed. As one NSC advisor wrote to a colleague:

> It is very difficult to digest these papers without losing their sense. They present their conclusions in broad settings and historical perspectives which really must be read along with the conclusions in order that the latter be fully understood. . . . The story does not stop here, however. In order to get a reasonable grasp of the United States undertaking in the Cold War, other NSC papers must be read. These include the area and country papers, e.g., China, Southeast Asia, Turkey. It seems to me that these can be digested. The program papers and progress reports in the NSC 68 and 114 series must be included. These can be digested. After the audience has read these papers and digests of papers, I would then suggest that it be exposed to three statements which attempt to present the U.S. position in summary form. . . . He will now be in a position to clothe these cold statements with the background and implications drawn from his previous reading.[12]

At the beginning of each policy statement or study stands "a clear, sufficient statement of the problem to which the proposed statement of policy is addressed."[13] Most assessments begin with a ringing reaffirmation of the values of the American way—its freedoms, its virtues, and its irreconcilable opposition to communism. This is often followed by an equally strong statement in support of the globalist perspective—encoded in the language of credibility, prestige, the interrelatedness of events, the domino theory. In addition, there are often definitions of key NSW concepts. The formulation of global policy required bureaucratically shared tenets and concepts, which were continually being espoused. The code words do not emerge from the dynamic of American relations with individual countries but quite the reverse: they frame the understanding of them. Consider, for example, this early (March 30, 1948) definition of the Cold War:

> The defeat of the Axis left the world with only two great centers of national power, the United States and the USSR. The Soviet Union is the source of power from which international communism chiefly derives its capability to threaten the existence of free nations. The United States is the only source of power capable of mobilizing successful opposition to the Communist goal of world conquest. Between the U.S. and the USSR there are in Europe and Asia areas of great potential power which if added to the existing strength of the Soviet world would enable the latter to become so superior in manpower, resources and territory that the prospect for the survival of the U.S. as a free nation would be slight. In these circumstances, the USSR has engaged the U.S. in a struggle for power, or 'cold war', in which our national security is at stake and from which we cannot withdraw short of eventual national suicide.[14]

Such definitions not only succinctly explained to officials what was at stake but also gave them the vocabulary to use in discussing U.S. foreign policy—with foreign diplomats, with Congress, in public statements, and among themselves. The list of definitions and concepts is long: *neutralism, fifth columnist, dominoes,* and *credibility, containment, nationalism, the free world, covert operations, propaganda warfare, modernity and modernization, nation building, colonialization, Kremlin-dominated communism, international communism, insurgency, the international marketplace,* and so on. National Security Council documents not only define (and when necessary redefine) these terms but also provide a capsule history of key events and ideas—the Russian Revolution, decolonialization, the appeal of communism. That the shaping of a policy language and the education (and self-education) of the policy formulators and readers are inseparable is evident all the way down the line, from presidential discussions and NSC debates to intelligence analyses and Department of State reports from the field. Such terminology was understood as a much-needed way of simplifying complex events in order to formulate and justify policy. Code words become the touchstones for their analysis. As Dean Acheson explained, "Qualification must give way to simplicity of statement, nicety and nuance to bluntness, almost brutality in carrying home a point."[15] Unless reality is conceptually oversimplified to allow the underlying globalist imperatives to emerge, there is nothing but a "bloomin' buzzin' confusion." Or, put another way: "Conflict, whether it be hot or cold, is a great simplifier, reducing issues to their fundamentals."[16]

Each new administration since Truman's has begun with a reassessment of U.S. foreign-policy objectives. In later years, departing administrations have been allowed by law to take their detailed NSC files with them. When President Johnson left, so did the NSC files under his command; President Clinton's files went with him as well. Sometimes foreign governments have confronted an administration with documents from an earlier one that were unavailable to the American officials.[17] Yet this lack of institutional continuity actually reinforces the ideological element in the formulation of policy. "Every new administration begins with a review of developments and U.S. policies around the globe"[18]—a matter of both necessity and desire. And so shifts in policy and ideology are not evident only in moments of crisis, when decisions are quickly being pushed up through the chain of command; they are most sweepingly apparent at the creation of an administration—a circumstance that offers one of the most useful ways of tracking ideological shifts during the Cold War.

The "Enemy"

"To establish a tradition is to forget its origins," the philosopher Edmund Husserl often said. The NSC's most neglected origins are rooted in a concentrated and highly conscious mobilizing for propaganda warfare. From the beginning, the NSC took an active role in mobilizing the American populace, in coping with opposition at home and among recalcitrant allies abroad, and in shaping (for the world and for itself) a convincing rationale for overcoming whatever stood in the way of American global strategy. Ideas, concepts, and arguments were fine-tuned for their propaganda value. Hence the creation of the Psychological Strategy Board, which brought together high-level officials from the NSC, the Departments of State and Defense, and the CIA to shape the American message and American policies for the ideological cold war.[19]

In his 1947 lectures at the National War College, George Kennan lamented U.S. weakness in this area: "All you have to do is to realize the enormous importance, perhaps the almost overriding importance, of the propaganda weapon, and to take a look at our propaganda apparatus as it exists today. It is pitiful."[20] To Kennan, as to many others, "political warfare" was alien to the American tradition, but it was something that Americans had to master, and quickly.

They had to learn—as C. D. Jackson, special assistant to President Eisenhower, put it in 1953—that "psychological warfare . . . does not exist apart from the policies and above all the acts of governments." Policies and propaganda had to be tightly bound together, the former shaping the latter. Here the communists had an advantage.[21] The United States, Jackson observed, did not have "the monolithic potential that the enemy had and has. They are able to indulge in push-button cold warfare, because they control all the instruments of communication from top to bottom on an instant basis and we do not, and we would not want to if we could."[22] But all American acts and policies, he argued, should be analyzed in terms of their propaganda implications and orchestrated into an effective ideological position—which was President Eisenhower's aim in establishing the Jackson Committee and reorganizing the Psychological Strategy Board into the Operations Control Board (OCB).[23]

The communist enemy quickly became the touchstone for envisioning what had to be done. The communists took a global view, subordinating their diverse objectives to the requirements of a global strategy. They kept their allies and supporters in an almost rigid battlefield formation that American officials often sadly regretted as alien to their ranks (though they often lauded this "weakness" as a testament to the American commitment to freedom). The same officials noted that communist doctrine provided their opponents with a view of the world and a political line that shaped their policies.[24] From this observation followed several more. First, the line entailed a clear formulation of ultimate long-range goals—in this case, the radical weakening of the free world and, ultimately, world conquest. Second, the strategy for achieving these goals involved a set of opportunistic tactics that could shift flexibly according to time and place; the trained eye, however, could discern the global thread. Third, these tactics were consciously interconnected; Soviet political, ideological, cultural, military, and economic strategies were all part of a total dynamic, and thus to focus on just one aspect would be to miss the underlying strategic thinking and its dynamic force. The communists, in other words, were masters of ideological warfare and propaganda, waging the battle for hearts and minds with astonishing tenacity and perseverance.[25] As one NSC statement put it, "Organized like an army they attack, retreat, zigzag, attack again, relentlessly pushing forward in accordance with the strategy of their world plan of operations based on the principles of Marxism-Leninism. They are unified in thought, unified in command, unified in action and unified in the goal they are seeking. But they are very flexible in tactics and strategy as they move forward like a far-flung army against the non-Communist world which is neither unified in thought, command, action nor goal and which is especially lacking in unanimity insofar as combating the expansion and entrenchment of Communism is concerned."[26]

NSC documents consistently assert the "globalism" and "sense of history" that made the communists the "rival center," the counterpoint to the United States. These enemies carefully calculated the balance of force before they acted, skillfully linking events in one part of the world with those in another, and knew how to prioritize, to subordinate one objective to another. In addition, they came well armed with effective categories of analysis: class struggle, the united front, imperialism, revolution, the logic of capitalism. They offered appealing imagery of redistribution of wealth and power and a model for rapid industrial development.[27] As NSC 20/4 put it:

> After the revolution, the Bolshevik leaders succeeded, through clever and systematic propaganda, in establishing throughout large sections of the world public certain concepts highly favorable to their own purposes, including the following: that the October Revolution was a popular revolution; that Soviet power was in some way connected with ideals of liberalism, freedom, and economic security; and that it offered a promising alternative to the national regimes under which other peoples lived. A connection was thus established in the minds of many people between Russian communism and the general uneasiness arising in the outside world from the effects of urbanization and industrialization, or from colonial unrest."[28]

Furthermore, the Communists combined ruthless cynicism with high-sounding idealism. They were shrewd propagandists who appeared to be both believers and cynical operators at the same time.[29] When a line or position changed, the Communists could quickly espouse the new one with every bit as much conviction.

American officials often spoke with awe of such an enemy—though whether this picture ever truly fit the Soviets is very much open to question. But a preoccupation with one's enemy can reflect—and shape—one's own assumptions. The NSC was, in part, a means for fitting diverse interests and policies into an overall framework of basic strategies, ideological formulations, code words, and priorities in ways that take on considerable significance when they are viewed as a mirror image of the communist world. Facing a ruthless, amoral opportunistic foe, the NSC had no doubt that the United States needed to learn to wage war with dirty hands and good intentions.[30] Covert warfare, propaganda warfare—these were essential strategies.[31]

Mobilizing the Mobilizers

In studies of the NSC, ideological fervor is often viewed more as an obsessive preoccupation with the idea of "Communism" and an embarrassing eruption of purple prose than as an ethos inextricably underlying the formulation and execution of policy—that is, as a matter oddly irrelevant to the drafting of the documents themselves. As H. W. Brands asks, "Who were the authors preaching to? NSC 68 was a top-secret document that would remain classified for almost a quarter-century. Only persons near the center of the policy process would read it. Presumably, such persons didn't need to be convinced of the superiority of the American way of life over that of the Soviets."[32] John Lewis Gaddis, after quoting several examples of the "rhetorical" prose of

NSC-68, concludes in similar fashion: "This is not what one would expect in a top secret document destined not to be made public for a quarter of a century."[33]

But why should we expect otherwise? Why should we presume that the formulators themselves needed no ideological orientation or justification? Why shouldn't we expect to find in the most secret documents of American policy the articulation of an ideological faith, a vision within which strategy and tactics are understandable, formulated, and legitimized? Instead of attempting to understand why officials are urged on by hortatory calls in policy documents, historians have too often viewed these calls as marginal. They have seen American leaders using ideology to manipulate others without acknowledging how deeply the tenets of the faith gripped these leaders themselves.

Yet it is critical to recognize this mobilizing of the mobilizers in order to understand how they dealt with China. Ideology was always seen as central to the great battle of "ideas" being waged. Acheson wrote of bludgeoning the bureaucratic mind with "clarity greater than truth" as though he himself were immune to the process, but in fact, a "fighting faith," a counterideology to communism, was crucial.[34] The geopolitical, economic, and military strategies and vision of the national security community rested upon ideological foundations.

Ideology served many functions: it shaped the notion of globalism itself. It provided a structure for debates among military, geopolitical, economic, and ideological interests and offered a context for relating their diverse strategies; it mobilized opinion at home and among allies abroad. While mobilizing others, it also mobilized the ideological mobilizers themselves. Ideology was the linchpin holding the global aspects of policies together. The discussions of containment, credibility, dominoes, and communism reveal a community for whom policy formulation was, in part, an act of faith.

Policy formulation, it is often argued, is more rational the less ideological it is. But this distinction does not really fit the national security community. The issue is a basic one: can the fundamental formulation of interests in these years be stripped of the ideological waging of the Cold War? Do the "strategies of containment," for example, really make sense if not seen as inherently ideological formulations? For John Lewis Gaddis, they do. He prefers to see NSC policy memos as fundamentally nonideological—that is, as nonideological analyses wrapped in a lamentable purple prose that can be stripped away without altering what lies beneath. "They can, in themselves, stimulate further action," he writes. "They provide otherwise myopic bureaucracies with a sense of perspective, visible goods, and most important, standards against which to detect contradictions and anomalies."[35] The standards and the sense of perspective are, for him, not ideological either—in fact, they provide a way of avoiding its ideological pitfalls. In Gaddis's view, ideology distorts policy; emotionalism, moralism, and misplaced idealism all breed misperceptions. He does not deny the presence of ideology but rather laments it, viewing it as separable from rational policy formulation—as though an American global vision could have existed in these years without an enormous ideological mobilization.

The NSC as a Community of Faith

If the NSC involved a system of faith, what might we expect an investigation of its documents to uncover?[36] First, not only a vision of the world but also a deep reverence proclaiming that vision unassailable and universal. And so in document after document we find countless paeans to the uniquely well-intentioned and, above all, free America. As one preamble goes: "The genius, strength and promise of America are founded in the dedication of its people and government to the dignity, equality and freedom of the human being under God. These concepts and our institutions which nourish and maintain them with justice are the bulwark of our free society, and are the basis of the respect and leadership which have been accorded our nation by the peoples of the world."[37] Though NSC 68 is often singled out for its "hortatory" prose, it is hardly atypical, nor is George Kennan's reference, a year earlier, to the United States' "ideological integrity—that is, . . . the heritage and philosophical concepts which are inner reasons that we are, for all our shortcomings, not only great but good, and therefore a dynamic force in the mind of the world."[38]

We would further expect that high priority be given to propagating the faith—that great effort be committed, as these documents phrase it, to the "development throughout the world of positive appeals superior to those of communism."[39] We would expect to find a call to arms—a mobilization of the faithful and a further mobilization of the mobilizers. And NSC documents are, in fact, often strident in their proclamation of a sacred trust, their exhortation to remain resolute and steadfast. Many of them begin apocalyptically: any place can become a single domino, threatening a chain reaction. If Tonkin falls, Indochina will fall. If Indochina goes, Southeast Asia goes. The expanding "doubt and fear" require that the United States stand tall and resist aggression. Neutralism, acceptable in isolated cases, can spread like wildfire, becoming unstoppable, and could produce a "relatively swift alignment of the rest of Asia." Nor would it end there. The Middle East could then "go to Communism, thereby endangering the stability and security of Europe." Japan would have to accommodate the "Soviet bloc." The rubber of Indonesia would become unprocurable, the sea and air lanes between the Western Pacific and the Near East inaccessible.[40] The documents sound a similar alarm for every country, every region. Every place is a microcosm of the larger conflict. This, too, is what one would expect of such a fighting faith.

It is hardly surprising that such a militant faith should divide the world into forces of good and evil. In this respect, the NSC and the public hold fast to the same opposition: the forces of "communism" versus the forces of the "free world." No value is more stressed in these documents than freedom. The contrast with communism is a total one. The NSC saw the United States as a unique power whose motives (if not always its actions) were good and its role central to the betterment of humanity—the last, best hope of Earth.[41]

Freedom means unceasing "opposition to the communist goal of world conquest." International communism, whatever its local variations, is the enemy, "the most voracious and evil imperialism in history."[42] Freedom is qualitatively different, and multiple in its manifestations—military, economic, political, and cultural. The concept of freedom is, in fact, the key ideological weapon in the U.S. arsenal. Though it becomes shaped into anticommunism, it is not quite the same thing. It is what everyone wishes for, but NSC documents rarely place it in the context of such values as equality, fraternity, and community.[43] It has great emancipatory powers—from repressive regimes, from poverty—but it remains elusive, abstract. There is something cold, austere, and demanding about this concept of freedom. If we are not eternally vigilant, it will be lost.[44]

Freedom is the supreme value for a good reason: American-style capitalism is inseparable from it. Freedom and the market cannot be separated in NSC, and the international market is the only force really capable of promoting freedom's further development.[45] This is the NSC's sole vision of freedom; it is "pure," so to speak. Max Weber once described the emancipatory freedom of capital, breaking the bonds of tradition and using whatever it can on its quest for profit, which it must, by its nature, carry out.[46] Freedom committed to cooperative ventures would restrict itself, and so such ventures are anathema to it (except, perhaps, as ordering devices that capital might need in order to function.) The question "To what end freedom?" remains unasked in these documents, since they cannot speak easily of any values that limit such freedom. That is why balancing values, such as equality, fraternity, and community, so often appear threateningly communistic. Communism, in these documents, is a galaxy of liberally acclaimed values that have been twisted to attack freedom.

Freedom, moreover, is inseparable from "good intentions." Americans have good intentions because they are free and believe in freedom—and these good intentions can be challenged, the NSC documents suggest again and again, only when there has been some kind of ideological lapse on the American side, some failure of communication that calls for renewed vigor. Regardless of any unpleasant action the United States feels called upon to undertake, its good intentions must be acknowledged. (Backing a reactionary foreign government, for example, may be regrettable, but it is only a short-term expedient.) A deep foreboding, however, haunts these documents. Underneath all the self-congratulation runs the constant worry that the ideology is not well packaged, that something is missing, that because anticommunism is, so to speak, a negative ideology, the message has not been packaged positively enough.

Yet anticommunism is the mobilizing factor. And what is the public, at home and abroad, being mobilized for? The answer is clear to those in the national security community: for an integrated global economic system under American leadership. The National Security Council understood that this required a total effort in every area—waging total war culturally as well as politically, militarily as well as economically, psychologically as well as socially. The NSC was created just as the use of state power to shape the new global economic order was gaining credence. This task, however, was not the same as defeating communism, and the NSC scrupulously distinguished between the two.

The ideological dilemma was a deep one: the quest to build an integrated global economic system under U.S. leadership engendered no such compelling faith for the rest of the world.[47] Anticommunism supplied the mobilizing passion and sense of direction that the economic dimension, on its own, could not. Freedom might stand as a central value in fighting the enemy, but it could not convincingly call up the faith when it stood alone before the rest of the world. In the end, it was anticommunism that provided the mobilizing sense of unity, confidence, and coherence. In the NSC documents, no other value is held to be even remotely so effective—and perhaps that, too, is what one would expect.

We might further expect the self-images of two nations in conflict to take on some similar features. Each adversary speaks of itself as peaceful, the other as aggressive. Each regards the motives of the other as bad, its own as good. The enemy's actions are evil; one's own are morally neutral.

We would further expect to find little tolerance for those who deviate too far from the faith; those cast outside the bounds of humanity would be tarred with the enemy's brush. The communists appeared to have an uncanny ability for subverting free societies via the manipulation of gullible idealists, altering the thought processes of free people without their victims' even knowing it.[48] "In this way," Kennan wrote, "Moscow's doctrine became to some extent a domestic problem for every nation in the world . . . more than just another problem in foreign affairs. They are facing also an internal enemy in their own countries."[49] Worst of all were the "fifth columnists"—an "enemy committed to the undermining and eventual destruction of their respective national societies"—against whom harsh internal security measures were necessary. Constant vigilance was essential.[50] According to NSC 20/1, drafted by George Kennan:

> We must recognize that ONLY A PORTION of international communism outside Russia is the result of environmental influence and subject to correction accordingly. Another portion represents something in the nature of a natural mutation of species. It derives from a congenital fifth-columnism with which a certain small percentage of people in every community appear to be affected, and which distinguishes itself by a negative attitude toward the native society and a readiness to follow any outside force which opposes it. This element will always be present in any society for unscrupulous outsiders to work on; and the only protection against its dangerous misuse will be the absence of the will on the part of great power regimes to exploit this unhappy margin of human nature.[51]

NSC documents repeatedly restate the seriousness of the subversive threat to the United States and its institutions, calling for the nation to "urgently develop and execute a firm and coordinated program (to include legislation if necessary) designed to suppress the communist menace in the U.S. in order to safeguard the U.S. against the disruption and dangerous subversive activity of communism."[52]

And of course we should not be surprised that the members of the national security community regarded themselves as absolutely central to the nation's global task—a role they emphasized with their belief in the primacy of the executive in foreign policy. They held a passionate conviction that America's global role depended on the kind of forceful, effective leadership that only a president could provide. Control required centralization. And if there was always a global dimension to their economic and ideological goals, the prospect of nuclear warfare bespoke this dimension with a special immediacy. The well-being of the country—its very existence—depended on these players. Few other bureaucrats could be expected to understand the full range of the issues involved or the steady hands essential to deal with continual crisis. They were thinking about the unthinkable long before Herman Kahn labeled it such.

A faith that bifurcates its world also divides something in its holder, projecting onto the "enemy" what it prefers to avoid dealing with closer to home.[53] If nations, like people, can come to resemble what they hate, the obsessions with the communist "enemy" may suggest an element in the national security managers' own agenda. They needed a vision of the world that would provide a proper context for their actions—and justification for their means. In contrast to the communists' "logic of history," they saw the world as a vast, intricate battlefield on which everything had become of importance to the United States. Confronted with an amoral enemy obsessed only with expediency and driven by a will to power, they advocated a tit-for-tat battle to be waged with equally ruthless force. Challenged by an enemy so unified and so centralized, they urged the need to organize and counterattack.

An "evil other" can involve much more than being shaped by the "other." What was projected onto the communists manifested deep preoccupations at the heart of visionary globalism. The corollary of an American focus on communist infiltration was an American call for a "total penetration approach"— cultural, military, economical, and psychological (or, in the language of later years, via human rights, culture, the economic marketplace, educational training of foreign elites, and so on). The national security officials' attacks on Soviet (and Chinese) expansionism conveniently deflected attention from the more intense expansionism of the United States. The advantages a Manichaean worldview might provide for American policy could be left unexamined, since this was the world the Soviets (they believed) had created. The zero-sum-game mentality may have locked in globalist thinking on each side, but the expansion of American power that the game required was defensive, they felt. The Soviets were portrayed as opponents of nationalism in Eastern Europe—and cynical manipulators of it elsewhere. National Security Council documents from the earliest years insist again and again that no communist (including Mao Zedong, Kim Il Sung, and Ho Chi Minh) could be an authentic nationalist leader.

The Language of Power

We might expect to find, as we do in other faiths in conflict, an arcane, austere language for dealing with realities (nuclear war, mega deaths, covert operations, guerrillas, communists, modernization) that the populace at large cannot be expected to understand fully or to bear. Both the world and the enemy become abstract: countries turn into dominoes, their histories and cultures paling next to the strategies of global politics and ideological warfare. The term *vital interests* has the ring of hard realism about it, connoting something clear-cut, calculated, and down-to-earth.[54] Yet few groups have transformed specifics into abstractions more effectively than did the national security community. The essence of evil, Sartre wrote, is to make the concrete abstract. In the NSC, power and such abstractions locked together to further the global reach of American interests.[55] A small conflict in a faraway country was not simply a local situation sometimes involving outside powers: it was a historic battle, a test of American power and credibility. Hence Acheson's assertion that

Korea was "not a local situation . . . it was the spear-point of a drive made by the whole Communist control group on the entire power position of the West."[56] In national security documents, Berlin, Quemoy, Vietnam, and the Plain of Jars all became invested with symbolic importance and turned into causes worth dying for.

The national security community created an artificial terrain of danger and crisis that emphasized strategy, defense, and the balance of power. Its senior officers saw themselves as generalists by necessity—global thinkers, first and foremost, specialists in power but not experts in local histories and cultures. They might consult such experts, but what they learned from them was only one of their tools. They believed that to serve the president, they had to be able to shape the often chaotic rush of events into a coherent pattern that he could understand. "The bureaucratic search for 'understanding' does not begin in wonder," it has been aptly said, "but in the reduction of the world to the ordinary and the manageable."[57]

Throughout the Cold War, nothing reduced a complex and chaotic world better than anticommunism. Seeing communism everywhere was a way of seeing American global interests in any particular situation; obscure events and areas assumed their places in a familiar ideological landscape. American diplomats might appear astonishingly insensitive when confronted with local specifics that challenged a U.S. position, as though they were misperceiving local realities. But there is a difference between a misunderstanding and a necessary illusion. The perceived threat of communism was never really useful as a means of understanding immediate historical and cultural contexts; rather, it was a way of placing them amid American global concerns. Washington had to grasp nationalism and revolution—local realities par excellence—through this global perspective, or ultimately, Washington could not grasp them at all. One finds here a peculiar combination of cynicism and true belief: cynicism because the officials knew that what they were trying to convey was not always what they perceived, and true belief because they could sincerely claim that what they were conveying was, to paraphrase Acheson, clearer than truth.

Thus, obfuscating generalizations at the highest level of the American government were not anomalies; they were the rule. Experts often challenged them. One can find nearly as many CIA analyses contesting the domino theory as supporting it—but not at the highest levels of government, and certainly not at the level of presidential speech writing. The higher one climbs in the national security community, the greater the need one finds for generalization and encoded, official language. These were the mobilizing simplifications for both the security elite and the public.

Yet NSC officials saw themselves as moderates at heart, forced against their inclination into a ferocious war of "dirty hands" and agonizing choices.[58] The true extremists were their opponents,[59] whose advantage lay in "the extent to which totalitarian Communist leadership is able to act ruthlessly and rapidly and to repudiate agreements without being subject to moral restraints."[60] American officials could thus wash their hands of the consequences of their own acts: "We are entirely within our rights, and need feel no sense of guilt, in working for the destruction of concepts inconsistent with world peace and stability and for their replacement by ones of tolerance and international collaboration. It is not our business to calculate the internal developments to which the adoption of such concepts might lead in another, nor need we feel that we have any responsibility for those developments."[61]

The public language of these officials differs markedly from the private. Whereas in public they cited the Sino-Soviet alliance and the indivisible threat of "World Communism," in private they recognized the differing interests of Russia and China and spoke of expecting and even provoking long-term conflicts between the two countries. In public, fearing widespread disapproval, they mostly denied the existence of the covert operations they endorsed in private. In public they spoke of the free movement of peoples and ideas; in private they were frank about linking such proclamations with covert operations and a rollback ethos. In public they promoted self-determination and nationalism; in private they blanched at any immoderate manifestations of these phenomena and often opposed their economic and at times political and ideological expression. In public they espoused a willingness to negotiate, whereas in private they saw negotiation as a propaganda trap to be avoided if possible. In public they portrayed containment as defensive.[62] In private they acknowledged its often highly offensive and provocative nature, as in NSC 141, which called attention to the "extremely grave threat to the United States" that a Soviet thermonuclear capacity would entail: "It would tend to impose greater caution on our cold war policies to the extent that these policies involve significant risks of general war."[63]

Key Concepts

Three concepts significantly defined in NSC documents—bipolarity, domino theory, and nationalism—are central to any attempt to situate and analyze the national security world's attitude toward China.

Bipolarity

Initially formulated in starkly black-and-white, either/or terms, bipolarity lay at the heart of the NSC vision of the world until the early 1960s. It kept the center of the struggle to two white-ruled nations,[64] fighting it out ideologically over the continent of Asia.[65] This belief in the existence of two orders, two ways, two directions pervades the writings of officials, scholars, and journalists from the late 1940s onward.[66] It legitimized and reinforced a deeply felt conviction that the United States bore the preeminent responsibility for shaping the newly emerging global system, by mobilizing allies and neutrals alike in the conflict with communism. This simplistic bipolarity had the advantage of making it far more difficult for Washington's allies to evolve strategies of their own.[67]

Tension, not its relaxation, was the way to justify and reinforce U.S. policies. Neutralism, which in Washington's eyes denied the necessary centrality of the bipolar conflict, risked vitiating the intensity of and removing the emotional glue from American alliances and policies in Europe as in Asia.[68] Perpetual pressure on the Soviet Union, a critical aspect of containment, was inseparable from perpetual pressure on allies and neutrals.

The Cold War is so often depicted in NSC documents as a titanic struggle between the United States and the Soviet Union that it is important to note the Chinese use of the term *cold war* as a depiction not of global circumstances but of a U.S. strategy and policy for dealing with those realities. As I will show in chapter 2, this Cold War bipolarity profoundly shaped China analysis—so much so that Mao's late-1940 statement that "China stands up" is usually regarded as contradicting the notion of a China that "leans to one side." The very ease with which American officials spoke of the Chinese communists as puppets offers a highly useful key for assessing their conception of bipolarity.

Domino Theory

The image of the domino suggests the way that a problem, an issue, or a country might quickly acquire worldwide ramifications. Sometimes American officials conceded that an area might be of no great value except, as John Foster Dulles said, "from the point of view of prestige." But if the country is seen as a domino, it then takes on "paramount" importance.[69]

In a May 1954 press conference, Dulles defended the domino theory as the basis for the Southeast Asia Treaty Organization (SEATO): "This is the whole theory of collective security. You generally have a whole series of countries that can be picked up one by one. That is the whole theory of the North Atlantic Treaty. As they come together, then the 'domino theory,' so-called, ceases to apply. And what we are trying to do is create a situation in SEA where the domino situation in SEA will not apply."[70]

Even those who discounted the theory's most sweeping implications invoked it when it was useful for their arguments.[71] George Kennan, for example, challenged the scope of the Truman Doctrine in its call for defending "free peoples" whenever they were challenged by communism. But in his 1947 lectures at the National War College, he utilized the apocalypticism of domino thinking in a manner strikingly similar to what can be found in almost every major NSC statement from 1947 to 1968:

> I believe that to deliver up the Middle East to Russian political penetration, even though that penetration might itself be inconclusive and eventually unsuccessful, would have a highly unfavorable reaction in Western Europe itself. It would render a tremendous impetus to "bandwagon" adherence to the communist movement at precisely the moment when that has become almost the only type of further adherence the communists can hope for. Russian penetration of the Middle East might well be sufficient to push both Italy and France across that fateful line which divides the independence of national life from the catastrophe of communist dictatorship. It might mean the final loss of our positions in North Africa; and then the Iberian peninsula could not hold out long. It might make hopeless the position of other non-communist countries in northwestern Europe. As for England, the resulting situation would present a cruel and crushing dilemma. It would necessarily paralyze the political will of that country and would probably make it impossible for England to do anything but cling to a precarious and unhappy neutrality in the hope that times would eventually change. And to this would have to be added the shattering blow which American prestige would suffer in the Far East; a blow which would certainly complete the dissipation of United States influence in all areas other than those which we were prepared to hold and to police by force of arms.[72]

Kennan's argument echoes and incorporates the NSC's notion of dominoes—the fear that under foreseeable conditions the entire global edifice might come tumbling down. Even if "semi-barbaric Moscow" and its force could not permanently dominate all the areas in question, the "damage they can do may take years to repair. Let us remember that the barbarians who sacked Rome were also not strong enough to consolidate their conquest of Italy. Nevertheless, their advent spelled the virtual end of the Roman Empire—and the beginning of many centuries of ignominy for the city which was its heart and soul."[73]

There was an internal version of dominoes as well; should the communists join a government, it might soon succumb to them. Beginning with the alarm sounded by one very early NSC document over the 1948 Italian elections—should the communists join a coalition, they would "thereafter, following a pattern made familiar in Eastern Europe, take over complete control of the government and transform Italy into a totalitarian state subservient to Moscow"—this fear remained omnipresent.[74]

Domino thinking strongly reinforced the regard for the United States as the ultimate arbiter of the West's global vision: "Domino thinking by its very nature implied that the parts were unable to act for failure to see the whole. Effective internationalism thus depended not so much on democratization as on the diffusion of the proper global historical framework," writes Frank Ninkovich.[75] No single country, not even the entirety of Europe, could really be trusted—a skepticism encouraging a sense that "the fate of Europe was far too important a matter to be left to Europeans alone to decide."[76]

Should other nations ever come to doubt the U.S. commitment to its global role—its credibility—then the falling dominoes could rapidly reach a cataclysmic end.[77] If American credibility was challenged, if others saw it as gravely weakened, aggression would soon follow (the Munich analogy). Credibility restrained the aggressor. The hovering presence of American determination to stand strong if the "peace of the world" was threatened was what made the United States powerful in areas where its actual presence was weak.[78] Containment could not work without it.

Nationalism

The NSC saw nationalism among allies and neutrals as a potential threat, a precursor to economic controls limiting the influence of the international marketplace, even without any immediate Soviet presence.

Everywhere, nationalism threatened to raise its worrisome head. French nationalism became an onerous burden as Washington was trying to design policies that incorporated Germany into European economic and defense arrangements. Elsewhere in Western Europe, nationalism presented a disruptive challenge to immediate policies as well as an impetus toward economic state planning. (The attitude toward Eastern Europe was, of course, precisely the opposite: there, American policies, both covert and overt, were designed to point up the exploitive character of Soviet domination and to encourage indigenous nationalism.)

Beyond Europe, rising nationalism appeared more and more threatening as the Cold War progressed. In South America it embodied forces hostile to North American wealth and power, and what had elicited concern during the Truman years became a pervasive preoccupation under Eisenhower. According to a March 1953 NSC document, "There is a trend in Latin America toward nationalistic regimes maintained in large part by appeals to the masses of the population. . . . It is essential to arrest the drift in the area toward radical and nationalistic regimes."[79] In the late 1950s, developments in Cuba suggested that such nationalism might combine with revolutionary movements of even more frightening potential—both in themselves and as models for others.

In the Africa of the 1950s, though nationalism was initially a quiescent force, it was an emerging threat to the heavy-handedness of the European powers, particularly the French in North Africa and the British in Egypt. The Truman administration had fretted over North African anticolonialism, especially as it affected European bases in the region, and the Eisenhower administration grew increasingly alarmed at the situation: "Nationalism versus Colonialism is the great issue in Africa today," an NSC analysis declared. "At the moment, all others, no matter how important, are subordinate to it. Our policies in any field will be of little or no value if we ignore this issue."[80] Washington sought both to discourage "premature" independence and to promote continued links between former African colonies and their European "partners."[81]

In Asia, revolutionary overtones inflamed the issue of nationalism from the beginning—in China, Vietnam, Indonesia, the Philippines, and Korea. There, more than anywhere else, nationalism veered toward "anti-imperialism" and radical upheaval. In the late 1940s the United States sought to paint itself as an ideological supporter of nationalism—or at least, as Kennan put it, its "healthy" version. Anticolonial but not anti-imperial attitudes were the NSC's markers of "independent" and "healthy" nationalism; anti-imperialism reflected an inclination toward communist propaganda (or "thought patterns") that had to be exposed and opposed.

In NSC documents the battle against communism was often yoked with the goal of suppressing a nationalism that was taking an unpalatable direction. Concern over anti-imperialism gave way in the 1950s to fear of "extreme nationalism" or "ultra nationalism" and, in the 1960s, of radical and revolutionary nationalism. While supporting nationalism might be effective in certain cases, the phenomenon remained a source of great uneasiness, especially when it was tied to an assertive economic state sector and nationalistic mobilizations of the population.

Containment as Defensive

The mind-set that emerges in NSC documents is that of a government which saw its actions as defensive and responsive. Soviet hostility and aggression arose from the USSR's innermost nature and the designs of communism—not in response to American actions. Chinese policies reflected the nation's ideologically driven expansionism and thirst for power—not a response to American actions. The dissolution of the Sino-Soviet alliance would ultimately come about, if it did come about, from antagonisms in the Sino-Soviet relationship—not as a result of American actions.[82]

Nevertheless, however insistently NSC officials depicted the American role, both to the public and to themselves, as defensive—as containing, as holding the line—they were, in fact, relentlessly pursuing covert war, psychological warfare, and the economic reorganization of the globe. So it was that NSC statements often expressed alarm with "defensive" strategies: what was needed was the "organization of a world-wide counter-offensive against Soviet-directed world communism." As a March 1948 NSC document stated, "A defensive policy cannot be considered an effectual means of checking the momentum of communist expansion and inducing the Kremlin to relinquish its aggressive designs."[83]

World Capitalism

Though the ideological enemy was communism, the great task the NSC had set for itself was the creation of an integrated, cooperative world capitalism under American leadership.[84] About this task there was no ambiguity: it was never far from the calculations of policy makers, and it remained a remarkably fundamental and consistent objective, so pervasive and unchallenged as to require little in the way of overall analysis.[85] As Task Force "A" of the Solarium Project (set up by Eisenhower at the beginning of his administration to study overall Cold War strategy and headed by George Kennan) stated in its 1953 report to Eisenhower, "Economic expansion is the driving force upon which U.S. strength is based, and is basic to our concept of successfully coping with the Soviet Union."[86] Leaders of the NSC rarely stepped back to consider how such an economic system might benefit some at the cost of others. There was no sense that some nations profit as others lose out in the international marketplace or that decisions by rich nations might damage the development of poor ones. *All* nations could develop economically—if only they could find the will to do so.

The most critical, most unquestioned belief of the Cold War years was that the United States, at the center of the international marketplace, stood to profit in the long term; but then so did the world as a whole, not just elites or corporate centers. Though the United States had an ideological rival in the USSR, there was never to be more than one center of capitalism. The task—a huge one—was to remove the impediments to its proper functioning. Yet this goal did not suggest any obvious way of dealing with the enormous economic problems already existing. The efforts of the Truman administration in the late 1940s to solve the dollar gap and to revitalize the economies of Western Europe and Japan, even with all the economic stimulus resulting from the Korean War expenditures, still seemed very much in doubt.[87]

The Eisenhower administration worried about the failure of underdeveloped nations to develop or attract sufficient capital. The task, particularly in Asia, was to build up local economies enough to withstand the perils and attractions of the communist model. The budgetary riskiness of American policies, evident in Secretary of the Treasury George M. Humphrey's constant injunctions to hold costs down, was just one manifestation of debates over economic priorities. The Kennedy-Johnson years saw the increasing use of selective foreign access to the domestic American market as a tool for shifting the global priorities of developed and underdeveloped nations alike; the aim was to use the domestic American economy to both build up selected allies and to lock in their economies with America's advancing capitalism.

For the NSC, U.S. interests were inseparable from the goal of internationalizing the global economy. As NSC 141 put it in a major reexamination of American policy in early 1953, "The success or lack of success of the free world in dealing with certain long-term economic problems may well be the most important single factor affecting the development of the long-term relationship between the Soviet system and the free world."[88] Indeed, when the NSC began operating in 1947, it saw itself as a vital tool in coordinating the up-to-then disparate and unintegrated efforts to commit Japan and Europe to the course of multilateralism and interdependence.

Several major implications follow from such a policy orientation. First, NSC documents repeatedly concluded that nationally organized economies were ultimately inconsistent with long-term American interests and were thus to be opposed—even if, for tactical reasons, temporary accommodation was useful. Economic internationalism was a constant preoccupation in the core capitalist areas. American debates about European recovery and, later, European unification revolved around how, not whether, to overcome national economies. "The problem is that there is little real enthusiasm in Europe for energetic action to expand economic activity," Solarium Project's Task Force "A" reported. "Part of the apathy concerning expansion comes from traditional European economic and political thinking with its high Socialistic content."[89] Trade liberalization to break down existing European barriers and to reduce "economic nationalism" and prevent the rise of a third force were urgently required.[90] Japan had to be opened up to American investment (though in the 1940s and 1950s the greater focus was on opening American markets to Japanese goods). In West Germany, economic integration (with its remilitarizing implications) was never quite fast enough.[91]

The NSC, insisting that this course required lower U.S. tariffs, saw domestic opposition to lower tariffs as a serious impediment to global American interests.[92] The United States had to "endeavor to remove barriers to trade . . . [and] resist pressure of small groups for legislation which make it more difficult for Latin American countries to trade with us. Discriminatory trade practices must be recognized as dangerous to hemispheric solidarity." In return, American capital had to be allowed to move freely into these countries. Not that the United States no longer promoted its own forms of protectionism; the issue at hand was the lowering of other countries' barriers to capital and the need for the United States to at least appear to take a stand strong enough to allow successful negotiation of tariff and investment issues. However inconsistent the United States could be at times, the ideological line remained clear: "U.S. tariffs and other U.S. restrictions on imports are clearly incompatible with the position of the U.S. as the overwhelming force in the free world economy."[93]

The world economic order, moreover, required that the trading patterns between the Europeans and their colonies be restructured so that a new "political, psychological, and sociological community of purpose" could connect the industrialized and underdeveloped nations. The United States had to take the lead in the development of such "economic interdependence," thus ensuring that a substantial investment of capital was made in the underdeveloped countries and their natural resources made available for the capitalist centers.[94]

"Capital" was really brought up only in discussing one major problem—the lack of it.[95] American officials discovered that there was too little capital to go around and too little flowing where it needed to flow—into Europe and Japan in the 1940s and early 1950s and into underdeveloped areas thereafter.[96] This insufficiency could invite the strengthening of local state sectors as an all too plausible short-term remedy for the absence of needed capital.[97] How should the United States deal with such a threat? Aid had a role, but the NSC increasingly took the view that international organizations (the World Bank, the General Agreement on Tariffs and Trade, the International Monetary Fund, and so forth) needed to fund or control those areas where the state might step in and, in so doing, build in restraints on the state's economic nationalism. Such an international approach offered a further advantage: it would defuse hostility to the United States while encouraging corporate investment and private capital ("pioneering efforts to take a more multilateral approach to economic problems involving outside pressure on national economic policies, while preserving control over essential U.S. interests").[98] But the problem remained: too little capital and too many demands on it.

This is not just a question of capital flows but one of how NSC officials saw capital working and the problems in how it was working. They did not much explore why capital went where it did, why it seemed so inadequate in the places they wanted it to go in the Third World. Of course, the problems of a decimated Europe and Japan could be understood in terms of the war and its aftermath. But as NSC 141 put it, in words that echoed through most of the documents, "The classical remedies should be utilized as fully as possible, but it should be recognized that extraordinary measures will also be necessary."[99]

Even "Keynesian militarism" was never seen as an answer for Latin America and the Third World.

The fear that key natural resources in the Third World might be lost was another consistent theme.[100] Numerous reports delineate which areas have which materials and which Western companies have invested (and how much) in which countries. The question was not simply of access but of privileged access. Specific industries, naturally, looked to specific needs, but the reports placed these immediate needs in their international economic context, clarifying the real reason resources would be "lost" if a government turned to economic nationalism or communism: not because rubber or oil could no longer be bought, but because the ways in which it would have to be bought would be radically altered.

Political Economy and the NSC

Why was the struggle for global power and against communism waged openly, whereas the struggle to shape an international economic order remained subterranean? National Security Council documents suggest that aggressive anticommunism functionally furthered the American global economic goals that, in turn, were critical for achieving American political and military objectives. They repeatedly indicate that the struggle against communism most easily galvanized popular and congressional support when the issues were not portrayed as global economic ones. Yet the NSC considered the two struggles inseparable and saw itself as the body responsible for making the international system work.

But how did anticommunism connect the two levels—the quest for an international economic order with political/military policies? First, the NSC was preoccupied with the effort to shape an international economic order outside of and surrounding the communist world. The political/strategic dimension of the struggle was a lever for forcing reluctant noncommunist powers to change their economic and trade patterns in ways palatable to the United States. The lengthy discussions over Germany and Japan provide prime illustrations. The greatest threat to an integrated world capitalism under American auspices lay in the existence of rival centers of national capitalism—particularly Germany, Japan, and Britain. (The Soviet Union was not a threat on this level.) The NSC brought careful focus to reconstructing these potential economic rivals within the newly shaped international economic order.

Second, in the NSC documents, hostility to communism is inseparable from hostility to all forms of, or even hints of, closed economies. State planning and autarkic development were anathema in principle, whatever the tactics immediate political expediency might sometimes require.

Third, discrediting the communist model in all its socialist degrees was an important and highly charged ideological task. Efforts to impede China's industrialization and development and to discredit Chinese methods may or may not have had much actual effect, but that those efforts were legitimate and moral means for defeating communism, with its planned economies, was never in doubt. "Communist China's rate of economic growth," one document concluded, was "a fundamental source of danger" to the United States in the Far East.[101]

In the view of the NSC, violence and conflict in the world were most frequently and fundamentally eruptions of the political, not the economic, realm. A smoothly operating marketplace would not be violent—it would be orderly and productive. What was particularly disruptive and divisive was politics: the nationalist resurgences that threatened economic improvements, and communism, which demonically took advantage of the shortcomings of capitalism so as to manipulate the injustices of the past against the economic hopes of the present. Capitalism could not shape the world by itself. It needed the help and power of the NSC's political strategies.

In short, communism versus freedom was the central ideological conflict defining the world of the NSC. The marketplace and capital could not provide any cohering vision or faith on their own; only anticommunism gave coherency to the American view of the world. And yet an effective ideological formulation proved elusive, even though it was repeatedly assigned the "highest priority."[102]

"Modernization" and Revolution in the Third World

In the Truman years, NSC references to underdeveloped nations acknowledged the need to be responsive to anticolonialist sentiments and to "aspirations" for social and economic change. But by the early years of the Eisenhower administration, "ultra-" or "extreme" nationalism, with its demands for radical change, had come to be viewed as a threat. Underdeveloped nations turned into a battle zone between the Soviet Union and the United States, which, to its frustration, all too often found itself cast as the "defender of the 'so-called exploiters' in opposition to the interests of the common people."[103] The Soviets had been quick to exploit the vast dissatisfaction of the "so-called world-wide 'sociological revolution'"—"an inchoate force which, if not recognized and taken account of, can seriously weaken Free World strength and cohesion."[104]

Up through the mid-1950s, the NSC's word for this change-seeking discontent, which so needed channeling, was *Westernization*. Its focus was often the intellectual leaders of the movement who were believed susceptible to communist appeals. By the late 1950s the word had changed to *modernization*, and it accompanied a growing concern with revolution, which was to become central in the Kennedy and Johnson years. But the challenge was always "Communism's appeal to the Asian intellectual," rooted in its "proven ability to carry backward countries speedily through the crisis of modernization and industrialization."[105]

The most striking omission from the documents in the first decade of the NSC is any sustained discussion of revolution. Even when revolutions were mentioned, the revolutionary process rarely was.[106] Revolution as a means of change was all but unacknowledged, except as a matter that communists could exploit; "extreme nationalism" remained the greater concern. Not even the Chinese revolution provoked any significant analysis of the phenomenon itself. The focus on communism and the Soviet Union ignored the potentials of liberation movements and revolutionary ideologies. The belief that revolutions could be controlled from the outside, by Kremlin-dominated communism, permeates these documents.

Gradually there comes a shift, from discussion of the problems of European colonialization and the need for a gradual transition to independence (often while remaining under the tutelage of the European colonial power) toward discussion of development and, by the later 1950s, of "modernization" and its discontents. But the phenomenon of revolution itself was not examined carefully until the late 1950s. When at last it erupted as a looming threat, a very different vision of China emerged, along with a sense of the way that revolutions themselves, as national wars of liberation, might imperil the visionary globalism that had asserted itself with ever greater boldness since 1945.

2 CHINA AS PUPPET

Washington's view of China as a Kremlin-dominated satellite goes to the heart of the Cold War ethos that was emerging in the late 1940s. Global policy, ideological warfare, self-indoctrination, and contempt for China went hand in hand. China was very much understood through Washington's prevailing globalizing strategic thinking and ideological formulations; the key terms, the tone, and the frameworks for understanding China flowed from this NSC perspective far more than they ever did from events in China. This perception comprised several dimensions: the dismissal of Chinese nationalism and the acquiescence of the Chinese communist leadership to the dismembering of their nation: an understanding of the Chinese communist leadership as "more Commie than Chi"; a vision of Stalin as puppeteer; and a view of China as an "Asian Tito," which, ideologically, worked against the opening that American officials sometimes said they sought. By late 1949, these themes had grown pervasive, constituting not just the assumptions underlying policy discussions but also the core of the developing propaganda war against the Chinese communists. Policy and ideology, analysis and propaganda warfare, merged at times almost indistinguishably.

By October 1, 1949—the founding date of the People's Republic of China—the United States was deep into an ideological war with Beijing. But neither the bipolar Cold War ethos nor the notion of China as Soviet puppet provided a clear and coherent policy toward the Chinese revolution. From the late 1940s to the beginning of the Korean War, American policy in Asia was torn by a series of contradictions that left Washington unable to shape or implement a strategy fully compatible with its emerging ideological goals. Just as it took the Korean War to enable the views set forth in NSC 68 largely to triumph in Washington, so, too, did the Korean War work to resolve the profound gap between the means and the ends of American policy in Asia.

Why containment in Asia came to differ from its European counterpart sets the context for the policies and attitudes that emerged toward China. In Asia, a policy of containment without isolation could not work, whereas in Europe, containing the Soviet Union never required a similar kind of isolation. In Europe, containment meant a divided Germany and a divided continent, a line down the middle as a way of eventually attaining some stability. But no such line could be drawn in Asia. Washington sought to integrate both Germany and Japan economically and politically into their regional contexts through a fundamental reshaping of the global economy centered in the United States. These two "workshops," with their economic might, were at the core of American economic and strategic policy. "Containing them" and containing "Communism" proved inseparable. But Japan could not play the pivotal role in Asia that Germany did in Europe. The "reverse course" that emerged in Japan by 1947 did not carry the same sweeping implications for stabilizing Asia that German policy did for Europe.[1] Germany was contiguous with a number of important capitalist countries with which it could be integrated in many ways. Japan was relatively isolated from other capitalist powers. And China and much of Asia, unlike Europe, were in the midst of enormous revolutionary upheaval and in fierce conflict with the declining European colonial powers.[2]

Once Washington had decided to rehabilitate Germany economically (and militarily) and had attained the means to do so, "a moment of temporary deadlock and stocktaking seems to have been reached" in Europe, the CIA stated in its 1949 *Review of the World Situation*. Both the United States and the Soviet Union had "pretty well exhausted the strategic courses of action earlier initiated and . . . come to a temporary deadlock." Situations "that have been previously noted are being developed tactically rather than strategically."[3] Though Washington worried about the tenuous economic basis of its European policies, and recessionary developments in 1949 suggested "fundamental economic weaknesses of the West," containment remained a coherent policy: a line could be drawn, with Germany at the center. Containment, in this sense, was well under way.[4]

As a CIA review of January 1950 stated, "While European strength and stability will remain of prior strategic importance to the U.S., most of the immediate crises during 1950 will probably arise in Asia. There the urgent question is whether Soviet-oriented China-based Communism can continue to identify itself with nationalism and sweep into power elsewhere in Asia."[5] East Asia had become "the center of the world's most immediate and urgent international tensions." The danger of Soviet aggression had "receded in Europe and the Near East," where a "revolutionary situation" no longer existed.[6] As Dean Acheson told Ambassador Philip Jessup in July 1949 in requesting a reevaluation of Washington's Asian policies in the light of the Chinese communist triumph, "You will please take as your assumption that it is a fundamental decision of American policy that the United States does not intend to permit further extension of Communist domination on the continent of Asia or in the Southeast Asia area."[7]

The resulting document (NSC 48/1)called for the containment of communism in Asia, though the meaning of this policy was bitterly debated. Sharp differences arose over how to deal with communist China in regard to a variety of issues: recognition, Taiwan, the United Nations, trade, and so forth. The year 1949 was not an open moment with the United States divided over seeking "accommodation" with Beijing. Rather it was a period when the United States had no way to shape or implement a coherent policy toward Asia and China—even as the ideological desire to contain China and its revolution was becoming more and more virulent.

A Slavic Manchukuo: Nationalism versus Communism

Dean Rusk's depiction of the Chinese Communists—that they were "not Chinese," not truly nationalistic but somehow alien and external to the real China—had become a widely expressed view among senior NSC officials by the late 1940s. As Acheson put it, the communists had "captured" the revolutionary processes; while neighboring nations were "at last achieving true national independence, China, with its long, proud history, is now becoming a mere dependency in the Soviet orbit."[8] Acheson saw a profound conflict between Chinese nationalism and Chinese communism. The communists had captured and manipulated Chinese nationalism; they were traitors, subservient to the Kremlin but cynically aware of the need to co-opt the nationalistic wrath of the Chinese people. Such a stark contrast between nationalism and communism was central to the global NSC strategic analysis during these years, and it was applied to China with stunning consistency.

In late 1947 and early 1948, this conflict dominated assessments of China. As was predicted in NSC 34 in October 1948, nationalism would become an increasingly "thorny problem for the Communists": having risen to power on a "ground-swell of nationalism," even Chinese Communist Party (CCP) members, not to speak of their "collaborators," were becoming "infected" with patriotism. So long as they fought with Soviet support, first against Japan and then against Jiang, they could equate nationalism with loyalty to the Soviet

Union. But when the fighting stopped, the "mantle of rationalization" would fall to the ground and the ties between the Kremlin and the Chinese Politburo would—perhaps suddenly, perhaps gradually—be revealed for what they really were. And if the Chinese Politburo should be revealed as subservient in any way to the Kremlin, the CCP leadership would face serious difficulty with powerful sentiments of nationalism and xenophobia from the Chinese public and within the party itself. But by "a nice piece of irony . . . at precisely the time the Chinese Communist leadership is most likely to wish to conceal its ties with Moscow, the Kremlin is most likely to be exerting utmost pressure to bring the Chinese Communists under complete control."[9] This analysis was predicated on two key assumptions: first, that the Chinese communists could be distinguished from authentic Chinese nationalists and, second, that the CCP was vulnerable to nationalism's full emergence. Acheson's letter of transmittal for the white paper excoriated the Chinese communists for having forsworn "their Chinese heritage and having publicly announced their subservience to a foreign power, Russia."[10]

George Kennan offered a similar assessment, arguing in February 1949 that "the full force of nationalism remains to be released in Communist China" and a few months later that the Chinese communists were "inducing" the Chinese people to accept "a disguised form of foreign rule."[11] A September 1949 CIA study concluded, more broadly, that communist movements and regimes were "vulnerable principally to the force of nationalism."[12] American officials repeatedly used this line of argument with foreign diplomats and with one another; it would be hard to overstate its pervasiveness. In July of 1948, Ambassador Stuart warned that the triumph of the Chinese communists would be tantamount to the loss of China's national independence: "China was now facing . . . the loss of her national independence after the Communist triumph. It had ceased to be merely an issue of Kuomintang factional politics as against Chinese Communists but was also part of a struggle between the fundamental principles of democracy and freedom on the one side and the domination of a minority controlled by Moscow on the other. Their revolution and the war against Japan had been fought to win national independence which was now again jeopardized."[13]

As Acheson concluded in his memoir, "Those who proclaimed their loyalty to Moscow proclaimed loyalty to an enemy of China." "Communism," he believed, was the "subtle, powerful instrument of Russian imperialism, designed and used to defeat the very interests we shared with the Asian peoples, the interest in their own autonomous development uncontrolled from abroad."[14] True nationalism as a form of "autonomous development" was ultimately inseparable from an open, international market system; false "nationalism" turned away from such openness—a contrast Acheson frequently stressed. Or as General George Marshall added: "phony nationalism" was mouthed by "demagogic leaders" who promised to redress and revenge past so-called wrongs and inequalities.[15] The divide between communism and "real nationalism" had become total and clearly reveals a world where ideology and policy, detailed analysis and the application of an ideological line, had become inseparable.[16]

When in 1950 the Soviet Union recognized the Democratic Republic of Vietnam, Acheson argued that this communist solidarity belied Ho Chi Minh's "nationalism," revealing "Ho in his true colors as the mortal enemy of native independence in Indochina."[17] Kennan, skeptical though he was of the degree of support Acheson accorded the French, nonetheless shared his underlying assumptions, arguing that if the French withdrew, "the basic conflict then would be between nationalism and Stalinism. Nationalist elements would thereupon tend to gravitate away from the present Viet Minh popular front and coalesce in a nationalist anti-Stalinist organization." Resistance to Soviet and Chinese influence would lead in time to "the triumph of Indochinese nationalism over Red Imperialism."[18] But the difficulties in encouraging this nationalism, Kennan noted, were many—beginning with the condescension of the Europeans toward Asian cultures, which combined with the "bitter hatred on the part of the colonial peoples" to create an "essentially psychopathic relationship." Unfortunately, "maneuvering between these two shores remains the only channel lying between polarization and Stalinization."[19]

Kremlin domination of the Vietnamese communist movement was an article of faith in Washington, but finding examples of it was another matter. One OIR report stated, "To date the Vietnam press and radio have not adopted an anti-American position," making Indochina an "anomaly." Either Moscow had issued "no rigid directives" or "a special dispensation for the Vietnam government has been arranged in Moscow."[20] Either way, it was possible that the ties might be so subtle that only communist insiders could really see them. In other words, the very absence of evidence supported the case for the Kremlin's diabolical cleverness.

Diplomatic cables from these years read like a combination of reportage and ideology—strikingly so in the exchanges between American diplomats and Prime Minister Jawaharlal Nehru of India. The Chinese, Nehru argued, were both communists and nationalists. They were pursuing their own interests, and given continued U.S. hostility, they might well align themselves with the Russians. The same, he thought, was true of the Vietnamese—a position that led W. Walton Butterworth, the Assistant Secretary of State for Far Eastern Affairs, to accuse him of obfuscation. "In a single sentence [Nehru] acknowledges Ho Chi Minh to be a Communist" and yet in the very next one "generally takes the attitude that he is primarily a Nationalist." Obviously, this is nonsensical, Butterworth concluded, because accepting that Ho was a communist means that he is working toward extending Soviet domination.[21] Nehru refused "to recognize this imperialism because it is being carried out by Indochinese instead of foreigners."[22] Other Indian diplomats strongly reiterated Nehru's opinion. The chief of the Indian mission in Japan, for example, argued to an American official that he "did not believe Soviet Russia would find Communist China a willing servant of Moscow nor that the Soviet Government would be happy to have a vast and potentially powerful but non-compliant state, even though communist, as an eastern neighbor." The Chinese, he concluded, were both genuine communists and sincere adherents to communist principles and philosophy, and he expected them to manifest strong political independence from Moscow. He "had no doubt that they would remain Chinese," citing the strong force of Chinese culture.[23] What to American officials was an "essential question"—"whether Chinese communists can operate independently of Kremlin"[24]—was not even an issue. Nor did the Indians find it reasonable to argue over whether the Communists were more or less Chinese. The racial overtones in the question were obvious to them and hardly worthy of consideration.

The British shared the Indian view. "For Communism to succeed in China it must be Chinese," a 1950 aide-mémoire to Washington stated. "It is difficult to believe that Mao Tse-tung and his followers are any less Chinese than their compatriots, or that the xenophobic tendencies of the Chinese people disappeared in the white heat of Communist fervor."[25] British documents are filled with references to Chinese "xenophobia" and its strong anti-British and anti-imperialist outlook. British policy post-1945 favored a weak, divided China in which British interests, mainly in South China and Hong Kong, could be protected. Confronted instead with a unified, intensely nationalistic China, the British still sought to keep a foot in the door, hoping to reinforce their position in Hong Kong.[26]

British diplomatic writings do not intimate that Mao and the Chinese communists had the slightest intention of subordinating themselves to Moscow: "Such information as is available suggests that so far the Peking Government, while generally taking the Moscow line on matters which are not vital to China, has not in any way committed itself to policies which are inconsistent with the independence of China. . . . [I]t is far more likely that they intend to create a Communist China in their own concept; admittedly a Communist China which will be a friend and ally of the Soviet Union, but certainly not its satellite."[27]

The United States, on the other hand, a nation locked in a bitter argument over American and un-American activities, found the incompatibility of Chineseness with communism entirely in line with its own ideological outlook.

As NSC internal security memorandums demonstrate, in the national security bureaucracy, American communists were not considered truly American; their thoughts and their beliefs were un-American.[28] The notion that no one could be both a communist and an American was hardly confined to McCarthyites. And since communism was so alien to what any patriotic nationalist could believe, sweeping actions to expose, contain, and isolate it were entirely justified.

In Washington's China, the Chinese communists' readiness to give up the nation's independence made it possible for the Soviets to dismember China. In his January 12, 1950, speech to the National Press Club, Acheson offered a chilling vision of Soviet imperialism: "The Soviet Union is detaching the northern provinces of China from China and is attaching them to the Soviet Union. This process is complete in Outer Mongolia. It is nearly complete in Manchuria, and I am sure that in Inner Mongolia and Sinkiang, there are very happy reports coming from Soviet agents to Moscow. . . . [T]hat the Soviet Union is taking the four northern provinces of China is the single most significant, most important fact, in the relation of any foreign power with Asia."[29]

The "process of bringing the Chinese Communists and their collaborators under Kremlin control," NSC 34 stated, "leads to the drive to reduce the territory under the direct control of the Chinese Communists—the Bolshevik adaptation of the classic doctrine of divide and rule."[30] Joint economic ventures offered a further way for the Soviets both to exploit local resources and "to penetrate and gain control over Sinkiang."[31] As Dean Rusk put it in 1951, "The territorial integrity of China is now an ironic phrase." Sinkiang, Inner Mongolia, Manchuria—China "is losing its great northern areas to the European empire which has stretched out its greedy hands for them for at least a century."[32]

Stalin as Puppeteer

National security managers believed Stalin's imperial ambitions and drive for control would almost certainly create an acute Chinese nationalist backlash, resulting in either widespread opposition to the communists or divisions within the CCP. George Kennan was one of the earliest spokesmen for this view—a view, once again, that was in complete conformity with the global NSC line about Stalin and nationalist movements everywhere else. He observed in January 1946 that the Soviet Union was trying to become the "predominant influence in China. It does so because, by revolutionary tradition, by nationalist ambition and by kinetic nature, Russia is an expansionist force." Influence alone was not enough—a "neutral" China was unacceptable to Stalin. Nor would he be satisfied with a "friendly" China, in the sense that Canada and Mexico were friendly to the United States. Stalin, Kennan argued, believed that under stress such friends were "politically, economically, and militarily undependable." The only relationship the Kremlin wanted was one based "on the recognized ascendancy of one to the other"; thus Stalin and the Kremlin "can be satisfied only with influence eventually amounting to effective control."[33] The Chinese Communist Party was Stalin's chief tool for consolidating Russian control over China.[34] The CCP "has been and is an instrument of Soviet policy," the CIA concluded.[35]

This vision of Stalin prevailed during the Truman administration and was meticulously applied to China.[36] American officials never seriously entertained the possibility that Stalin might eventually have to deal with the Chinese communists as a partner or an ally or that China simply could not be dominated. Nor did they sense that Stalin's calculation of Soviet interests had less to do with communist globalism than with the intensely Eurocentric attitude that the Far East was of secondary importance.[37]

The national security bureaucracy saw Stalin as a calculating master of power and realpolitik pushing relentlessly to dismember and weaken China— with a divided CCP the likely result. "The greater the success of the Chinese Communists, the greater will be the Kremlin's disposition to interfere in China in order to assure 'internationalist' control and the greater will be the difficulty of reconciling this interference with Chinese nationalism and anti-imperialism. In the end, Chinese nationalism may well prove stronger than international communism."[38] The signing of the Sino-Soviet Treaty, in February 1950, put a temporary damper on the optimism. "If the USSR proceeds gradually, it will probably be able to minimize Chinese dissidence until such time as the Russians can deal with it effectively."[39] Admittedly, this might be a "long and involved process," a CIA analysis concluded in early June 1950, but "current trends and circumstances clearly favor consolidation of Soviet control." Because China needed Soviet aid, "the Peiping regime will not resist Soviet penetration."[40] China, once again, was viewed through NSC formulations that delineated how Stalin and Kremlin-dominated communism operated *in general*, and few modifications are evident in its applications. If sufficient evidence of Soviet machinations to control such areas as Manchuria was often lacking, wrote one American consul, the "magnificient Manchurian prize" was so "inspiring" it should be regarded as "axiomatic" that the Soviet Union would make a "determined effort" to dominate it.[41]

In the NSC's view, Stalin did not even trust other communist parties unless they had been infiltrated by operatives loyal to him. The satellite imagery that dominated discussions of Eastern Europe ignored the revolutionary dynamic of the Chinese communists. NSC 58/2 laid out the criteria for a satellite: "the

Stalinist penetration of the government and mass organizations" as "reinsurance against ideological corruptibility"; the espousal of the "common body of Communist ideology" in such a way as to provide the rationale for the "imposition of Soviet imperialism in all of its aspects, political, economic and cultural, and for satellite acceptance of a colonial status; the working formula for totalitarianism. . . . [T]his channel of influence and control appears well nigh invulnerable." Since its only real weaknesses were its self-destructive purges and its violation of nationalist sentiment, "the reverse of the Stalinist dogma—nationalism—should be encouraged," overtly and covertly.[42] Eastern European satellite imagery pervaded almost all the prognostications about China. "The extent to which Moscow will succeed in dominating China" depended on "various unfavorable factors peculiar to the complex China scene. This combination is different and apparently more formidable than any which Moscow has yet surmounted elsewhere."[43]

Kennan doubted that the Chinese communists would in the end prove subservient to Moscow: they had little reason to be grateful to Stalin; the CCP had already ruled a sizable area of China for more than a decade and had established a de facto regime; it had come to power on its own; and it had taken on "nationalist coloration."[44] He concluded: "The men in the Kremlin would suddenly discover that this fluid, subtle oriental movement which they thought they held in the palm of their hand had quietly oozed away between their fingers."[45]

Other factors might inhibit Russian control. Ambassador Stuart pointed to the contradiction between Chinese individualism and communism, and to the "deep-rooted friendship for the United States" particularly among educated Chinese, whom the communists ultimately could not afford to alienate.[46] The health of the Chinese economy depended on trade with the West, which would require the Chinese communists to moderate their hostility and establish some autonomy from Moscow. Moreover, China was simply too big and too populous to be controlled for long from the outside.

Such arguments, however, were all predicated on the same questionable assumption: that Stalin sought to dominate, divide, or dismember China, and that by the late 1940s his implement for doing so was the Chinese Communist Party.[47] To challenge such a pervasive conviction would open up a Pandora's box of related questions—such as whether Stalin really meant for Kremlin-dominated communism to dominate the world and whether he ever had any practical global strategy comparable to that of the United States.

Kennan was skeptical when baldly presented with some of the more extreme implications of his own arguments. In regard to Soviet control over Eastern Europe, it was "unlikely that approximately one hundred million Russians will succeed in holding down permanently, in addition to their own minorities, some ninety millions of Europeans with a higher cultural level and with long experience in resistance to foreign rule."[48] At the same time, he was among the leading formulators of the notion concerning the Soviets' single-minded pursuit of domination, without much discrimination as to where: "To the old conspirators of the Kremlin the questions to ask about any foreign communist party are: who controls the party apparatus; who controls the secret police; who controls (if they exist) the armed forces; and does the foreign leader love power more than he fears the Kremlin. . . . The primary concern of the Kremlin with regard to China is . . . how to ensure complete and lasting control over them and their collaborators. No one is more keenly aware than the Kremlin of the skill, subtlety and patience necessary to accomplish this."[49]

A debate flourished in Washington as to how to characterize the bond between the Kremlin and the Chinese communists. Were ideology and doctrine sufficient to prove subservience? Many thought they were. As Butterworth observed in 1947: "It is not necessary to establish proof that there is direct connection and liaison between the Chinese Communist Party and the Soviet Union. The ideological affinity between the Chinese Communists and their brethren of the Soviet Union is in itself sufficient to create a probable menace to the internal security of China."[50] This perspective resolved the knotty issue of proof. Diplomats found it hard to cite significant examples of concrete Soviet assistance to the Chinese communists; however much they tried, the CCP appeared to be operating independently enough: most of its supplies came from American equipment captured from the Guomindang. Some American officials pointed to assistance the Soviets had given the Chinese communists in Manchuria, but it had been slight in comparison with U.S. aid. And Soviet actions in stripping Manchurian industries had hardly generated popular support in China itself for the communists.

In the end, the "proof" of Chinese subordination was almost always centered in ideology—just as it was true for all other areas of the world in the strategic mind-set of the NSC. "The Kremlin," wrote Ambassador Stuart in January 1947, "must be aware that . . . no one has yet been able to prove that [the CCP] has direct ties with the Soviet Party." Perhaps, he added, the "only direct link with the Soviets is ideological affinity." However, if it was hard to decipher actual subservience, it was helpful to remember that apparent independence might be "a useful vehicle for spreading the Communist line."[51]

"More Commie than Chi"

The idea that communist ideology made the Chinese communists less nationalistic carried over into the analysis of potential divisions among Chinese communist leaders. Such analysis reflects only minor variations in the ardent

NSC strategic guidelines for understanding this dynamic. Ambassador Stuart described a CCP statement lauding the Soviet Union as a "reaffirmation of loyalty to USSR and world Communism that seems far more Communist than Chinese."[52] As the Consul General John Cabot in Shanghai put it, "We do not know whether and to what extent the Chinese Communist leaders are more Chinese than Communist."[53] Among the party leaders, wrote Cabot, who had come from a post in Yugoslavia, there appeared to be "a good many who are one hundred percent Moscow stooges, and a good many others who, although orthodox Communists, are thinking in terms of Chinese rather than Soviet interests." The rank and file, he added, "think of themselves as Chinese before thinking of themselves as Communists."[54] The Kremlin, he noted in a cable, needed local agents and ideological kinsmen to consolidate its control of the CCP. "Soviets will endeavor through Chinese international Communists on top levels . . . to keep potentially dissident elements satisfied until time Soviet power in Chinese Communist ranks judged sufficient to permit purge of 'betrayers of the revolution.'" Although it was admittedly difficult to assess how well the Soviets had carried out this policy, Cabot believed their progress was "palpable."[55]

This understanding of inner Chinese Communist Party dynamics suggested that, as an alternative to a need to lure the Chinese leadership away from the Soviets, a split between nationalistic elements and those holding a pro-Soviet line—that is, between those more Chinese and those more communist—might occur on its own. As was argued in one Policy Planning Staff of the State Department (PPS) paper in February 1950, "The pressure of . . . events will tend to inspire nationalistically-inclined leaders in the CCP to break with those elements in the leadership who have sold themselves out completely to the Kremlin . . . We should, of course, be ever on the alert for symptoms of such a break-away and should judiciously do all within our power to foster such a split."[56] In other words, the United States might be able to cooperate in a limited way with some of the Chinese communists. As Cabot argued, "By using our aid program to exert steady pressure on the Communists to get rid of the extreme Kremlin ring while cooperating within limits with any truly Chinese elements, I feel we might get somewhere."[57]

A CIA memorandum reasoned that in consolidating power, "Party unity may encounter the most severe test through the CCP's subservience to the USSR."[58] The issue was always seen as subservience versus independence. Arguments among Chinese communist leaders over how best to pursue the nation's interests rarely served as the prism through which American diplomats assessed developments in China. Cabot, for example, called for using U.S. aid to oust pro-Kremlin elements in the Chinese communist leadership. In negotiating for aid programs in communist areas, he suggested, "we would be in a position to say, in effect, 'We should like to extend aid in accordance with our traditional friendship for the Chinese people. We have nothing against the adoption of Communism as an economic doctrine by the Chinese people if they so choose. But do you think we are going to extend aid while that Moscow stooge ———— is in a position of authority?'"[59]

And both overt and covert American policy could exacerbate the division in the CCP. Reports to this effect were innumerable. A typical one reads, "While congen Shanghai doubts that Gen Chen Yi is at present QTE potential Tito UNQTE, rumors persist that Chen QTE more Chi than Commie UNQTE, ambitious, at odds with strict partly liners Jao Shou-shih and Chen Yun, in disfavor with Mao who fears his popularity and susceptibility to bourgeois temptations."[60]

American manipulation of internal Chinese processes was entirely justified, of course, by the looming Soviet presence and by the very communism of the Chinese communists. Often the debate involved a carrot versus a stick. Cabot recommended the carrot—aid and possible recognition. Others advocated "assertive political warfare" to promote division and conflict among factions in the communist areas and to isolate the "minority Stalinist": the denial of recognition and aid, they believed, would be a useful stick.[61]

The distinctions made between pro- and anti-Moscow groups, often placing specific leaders in one camp in one report and in the opposite camp in another, are perhaps most noteworthy for the assumptions they exclude. Few reports if any examine how and why particular Chinese leaders might assess Soviet objectives and their relation to Chinese interests. The notion of debates among intensely nationalistic Chinese leaders over policy and the course of their own revolution virtually never came into play.[62] Nor is this surprising, following as it does the lines of the formulations and language in NSC directives and strategic assessments of the world.

An Asian Tito?

Titoism, it is often argued, demonstrated that American officials were more flexible, sophisticated, and nuanced in their approach than these ideological formulations might suggest: look how quickly Washington supported Marshal Tito of Yugoslavia when he proclaimed his independence from Moscow in 1948. Yet a careful examination of Titoism shows that the United States used the phenomenon far more as an ideological weapon against the Chinese communists than as an opening to which they could respond. And it reveals once again the ways in which general NSC formulations set the fundamental frameworks for analyses of China.

The dispute between Tito and Moscow became public in July 1948, and it quickly colored debate about China. Could Mao be an Asian Tito, and if so, what did that mean? Was an Asian Tito ideologically acceptable to the United States? And if so, what could the United States do to encourage such a development?

For John Lewis Gaddis, Titoism showed "first, that nationalism could serve as an antidote to communism; second, that the creation of a Soviet 'empire' was as likely to cause difficulties as advantages for the Russians; and third, that as a result not all communists everywhere need be considered enemies of the United States." Gaddis quotes Walter Bedell Smith, writing in March 1949 when he was ambassador in Moscow: "The United States does not fear communism if it is not controlled by Moscow and not committed to aggression."[63] Thus after Tito's break and with the imminent victory of the CCP, Truman authorized plans to "exploit through political and economic means any rifts between the Chinese Communists and the USSR and between the Stalinist and other elements in China both within and outside of the communist structure."[64]

Stalin and the Cominform's denunciation of Tito for nationalism added fuel to this strategy. "If proof were needed" of the severity of the split, Butterworth argued, "the Kremlin's characterization of Tito's activities as embodying the high crime of nationalism would have provided it."[65] Butterworth does not pause, however, to see Tito as a communist *and* a nationalist; he uses him as an example of the contradiction confronting all communists: their necessary hostility towards nationalism. They use and manipulate it, but fundamentally, they attack it.

Both Tito and Mao had come to power without Stalin's assistance; both commanded a powerful army. The factors pointing to Titoism were, if anything, stronger in China than in Yugoslavia, given China's greater size, its historic culture, and its huge population. Hence, American diplomats in China quickly applied the "lesson" of Tito to the Chinese, including the Chinese communists. "I am confident," John Cabot wrote, "that most of the present top Communist leaders know in their souls that they're not 100% satisfactory to the Kremlin. By hammering on the theme that the Kremlin will sooner or later liquidate them . . . I think we might get somewhere."[66] Some saw splits in the communist Chinese leadership along Titoist versus non-Titoist lines. Consul General O. Edmund Clubb cabled from Beijing the possibility that "Chou [En-lai] and his group" were "seriously at odds with so-called radical wing and may be straining towards Titoism . . . [but] he and other potential Titos would assuredly lose out in any attempt palace coup."[67] At brief moments, another possibility emerged, as in a note from Director Roscoe Hillenkoetter of the CIA to Truman: "Chou En-lai stated the CCP has to have allies, and if Chiang and the reactionaries are all allied with the U.S. the CCP must ally with the USSR. It would be a dream on the part of the American government to expect the CCP to split with the USSR, but they can expect the CCP will not always be anti-American. The CCP can't afford two enemies at one time, but there is nothing to keep them from having more than two friends."[68]

But Zhou's comment was ignored. The consensus was that real independence would come with the intensity of Tito's break—an animus matching Martin Luther's against the Pope. Tito had been "excommunicated";[69] the quarrel was a heretical schism "between the Kremlin and the Communist Reformation."[70] As George Kennan put it, Tito was "as important for Communism as Martin Luther's proclamation was for the Roman Catholic Church."[71]

Implicit in the Titoist model for American officials was virulent hostility toward the Soviet Union. Tito did not arise as a neutral between East and West but as a heretical enemy of the Kremlin, a reaction to Stalin's insatiable urge to dominate. As Dean Acheson wrote in *Present at the Creation*, any American policy that had hopes of detaching China from Moscow first required "that the Chinese Communists follow Tito in stopping active abuse of us."[72]

The Policy Planning Staff, and particularly George Kennan, had immediately zeroed in on the intensity of the break between Yugoslavia and the USSR. That this "new factor of fundamental and profound significance" came as such a surprise reveals much about the ideological climate of these years. Despite Tito's having come to power largely on his own and his having fought next to the Allied forces in World War II, the ideological bond with Moscow had given him the appearance, as Kennan put it in late 1946, of "a bird dog which has been so well trained that it has been taught to heel and no longer needs to go on the leash."[73] Little in European diplomatic history justified this view, but in the face of such objections American officials only insisted that much more on the unique character of the communist enemy they faced. Historian Robert Blum analyzed the U.S. failure to foresee Tito's clash with Stalin, but his careful study in one sense reinforced the ideological character of the American outlook with the subtitle "The Anatomy of an Intelligence Failure."[74] An intelligence failure perhaps, but more fundamentally it was the outcome of the axiomatic American conviction embodied in NSC strategic thinking that Kremlin-dominated communism was a stronger force than any nationalism.

The Soviet-Yugoslav break was seen as an effect of Soviet-Yugoslav relations—with American policy an unrelated factor. It was discussed—in terms similar to those applied to China[75]—as a response to Kremlin leaders who were "so inconsiderate, so relentless, so overbearing and so cynical in the discipline they impose on their followers that few can stand their authority for very long."[76] The firm belief in Stalin's drive to dominate all indigenous communist forces and to oppose any national autonomy fit easily with the argument that as long as the Chinese communists in their "public statements and propaganda . . . follow the Kremlin line," there was no basis for the Americans to pursue a Titoist solution with China or a policy based on China's immediate self-interest.[77]

Tito was not widely labeled a nationalist in U.S. diplomatic dispatches of the 1940s. On the contrary, "Tito rose to power and now retains it by a sedulous application of the Leninist-Stalinist blueprint for totalitarianism. It is only in the third ideological stratum—that of subservience to the interests of the USSR—that Tito openly deviates ideologically from the satellites."[78] Kennan sharply differentiated long-term "healthy nationalism" from the "Tito virus," a rival Stalinism, which used national pride and resistance to the Soviets as a means of consolidating power.[79] Kennan's contribution was to distinguish a deep hostility to Titoism—a socioeconomic system that was still communism—from short-run realpolitik that could accommodate it for the sake of weakening the Soviets.[80] He acknowledged the difficulty of dealing with Tito while seeking to prevent the emergence of independent communism in other parts of the world.[81] In time it might be possible to work for the transformation of the Yugoslav system, but too quickly sought, this goal risked undercutting the very dictatorial powers that Tito needed in order to fight Stalin.

But the idea of an independent communist government was not popular with other American policy makers or the public at large. Truman was willing to go along with any development that appeared to weaken Russia, but his *Memoirs* suggest an absence of enthusiasm: out of more than one thousand pages, he devotes a single sentence to the break between Tito and the Kremlin: "Their strongest satellite, Yugoslavia, had suddenly developed a taste for independent action, and the European Recovery Program was beginning to succeed."[82]

In his memoirs Acheson suggests another problem: while crediting Kennan with quickly recognizing "this break within the Soviet monolith as the awakening of national independence and self-interest," he adds that it would have been "bad politics and bad morals" for the West to ally itself with Tito. And, indeed, support for aid to Yugoslavia proved nearly fatal to James Richards, chairman of the House Committee on Foreign Relations, who almost lost his safe seat over the issue in 1950.[83]

Officials in the United States saw Tito as an enormous asset in their efforts to break up the "satellite model" of Soviet control over Eastern Europe. His independence was most evident in his *hostility* to Moscow. Washington supported Tito for other than merely ideological reasons, of course. He was willing to end his support for the guerrilla movement in Greece and, in time, see the conflict over Trieste resolved. Titoism, moreover, did not pose the threat of social revolution—an issue of growing concern in Asia.

Pushing to One Side

The most widespread argument for a more "flexible" policy toward the Chinese communists grew out of what diplomats bemoaned as a "tragic dilemma": that American backing of Jiang by late 1948 was driving Chinese nationalism into the arms of the communists and, ultimately, the Soviets. Supporting Jiang's regime, they held, inflamed anti-American feelings in almost every sector of Chinese society.[84] Underwriting the Nationalists on Taiwan "plays directly into hands of Moscow." Even appearing to assist Jiang's blockade of Shanghai was pushing middle-of-the-roaders toward the Soviets. A refusal to recognize the Chinese communists was "just what Russia wants"; an "embargo" would serve "Moscow's goal of extending its influence in China."[85] This line of argument is epitomized by an ORI analysis of "what we could assume would be the preferences of the Kremlin if they could dictate U.S. policy in China" which covered the following issues: recognition of Beijing; economic policy; the status of Taiwan; the status of Tibet; support of the anti-communist underground in China, and containment.

These findings, however, were intensely debated—for example, by Philip Sprouse of the State Department. The ORI concluded that the Soviets opposed immediate recognition of China by the United States but would favor it by late 1950, whereas Sprouse believed that Moscow would "prefer to have the United States declare its intention never to recognize the Peiping regime." The ORI thought Moscow wanted the United States to impose "moderate restrictions" on its exports to China; Sprouse thought Moscow preferred "aggressive economic warfare." The ORI thought Moscow wanted the United States to continue "military advice and logistic and economic aid to Nationalist Government" but opposed a "military occupation"; Sprouse argued that Moscow favored an occupation that would antagonize China and drive it toward Moscow. The ORI thought Moscow secretly wanted Washington to recognize Tibetan independence and "extend economic and logistic aid," and also that Moscow favored "indirect logistic support of underground [by the U.S.], via Nationalist Government," as well as "moral condemnation of Communist aggression." On these points Sprouse essentially agreed—the USSR, he thought, "would be gratified to see U.S. strength directly engaged in hostilities with indigenous Communist forces throughout Asia."[86]

But whatever the disagreement about specifics, the crux of these arguments was always the foreboding that American actions were pushing the Chinese communists toward the Soviets. Yet when it came to changing policy, from 1947 on nothing happened. A July 1947 memorandum prepared for Walter Butterworth illustrates the dilemma. After noting Jiang's failure as a leader and the perilous weakness of the Guomindang, the memo saw no way either to win or to disengage. American commitments elsewhere precluded the kind of military force it would take to make a real difference against the communists—and such all-out aid would heighten the tension with the Soviets in the Far East, compromise American positions and commitments in Western Europe, destroy Asian confidence in American "integrity and political objectivity," antagonize noncommunist Chinese opinion, "freeze the manifestly unpopular government" in power, and set the stage for a civil war even worse than Spain's. Cessation of aid, however, was just as unpalatable. Withdrawal was incompatible with the American effort to establish a viable global position; it would lead to an early if not immediate collapse of the Nationalist government and in all likelihood a communist victory, and it would bolster communist prospects elsewhere in Asia, particularly Korea and Southeast Asia, thus removing a serious obstacle to Soviet expansionism.[87]

The choices were stark. In the worst case, the government would disintegrate; in the best, a "middle group might be able to restore a modicum of stability." Such a possibility was "fairly remote" but it could not be dismissed, because "it offers for the United States a constructive middle course between the extremes of all-out aid to the present Government and cessation of all aid thereto." Drawing back from his stark alternatives, it advocated "a reasonable and coordinated program of conditional aid . . . to foster the emergence of a regime with an inclination to move along lines satisfactory to American political concept and which would thus offer a reasonable risk for a larger scale public and private financial and economic aid while at the time engaging in a holding operation against the progressive spread of the Chinese Communism and its corollary, Soviet political expansionism." Aid to Jiang's government could at least give the middle groups inside and outside the government a chance to embark on a program of "national self-help," facilitate projects that would assist the Chinese people, and support the rationale for comparable U.S. policies in Southeast Asia.[88]

A cable from Ambassador Stuart dated October 22, 1948, reiterated that "the present regime has lost confidence of people." Stuart nonetheless recommended that "we continue to support present regime to the utmost feasible in light of our commitment elsewhere and of our total resources."[89] With this continuing if reluctant support for Jiang went bitter laments that it offered the Chinese communists a "means of deflecting Chinese attention and wrath from the USSR to the U.S. at the very time when the attention of all Chinese should be directed to the newly announced treaty and agreements with the Kremlin and Soviet encroachments in the peripheral Chinese provinces."[90] The Chinese, in short, were failing to recognize Soviet imperialist aims in China. "Communist propaganda has been extraordinarily successful in stirring up

Chinese nationalistic sensibilities against the United States and the other Western powers," John Cabot wrote. "In the light of Russia's record, this is amazing to me, but it is the fact."[91]

The Ideological War

American diplomats often wrote as though an ideological war were being waged in China—and they were losing. Yet lamentations in Washington about the failing global ideological crusade were equally fervent, and China, despite the extremity of the situation, is largely portrayed through these Washington-based NSC preoccupations. Despite the obvious reasons for the widespread Chinese anger over continued American support for and diplomatic recognition of Jiang, these diplomats tried to argue that, somehow, the course of events should be reversible. "We must use every available fact and all our energies to paint real picture of Communist menace, citing events in U.S.S.R., Yugoslavia and elsewhere behind Iron curtain," Ambassador Stuart cabled to Acheson. "Our information media must forcefully explain . . . and prove great evils and loss of freedom communism holds in store for China."[92]

"The deep emotion on which the anti-American feeling is based makes it impossible for the students to view the problems with objectivity," wrote Angus Ward, consul general at Mukden. "They cannot forgive the United States for continuing to deal with a government from which they have withdrawn all loyalty." Nor could they see that the United States desired a democratic government and was just as critical of Jiang's corrupt government as they were or that American aid was "prompted by humanitarian motives rather than by sinister design." They "cannot understand the American aversion to Communists."[93] The problem was much the same throughout Asia: how could the United States gain the support of "moderate nationalists" instead of pushing them over to the communists? With the French, Dutch, and British efforts to reestablish their colonial influence in Southeast Asia as a backdrop, the dilemma was often put in ideological terms: how could the United States avoid being labeled an imperialist power?

Kennan's writings suggest some of the nuances involved in the NSC's assessment of nationalism. He distinguished between the "sentiment of nationalism (anti-imperialism)" and nationalism itself. The sentiment was what the communists mobilized against the Western colonial system—and against the United States, insofar as it could be perceived as supporting that system. Anti-imperialism was thus little more than a propagandistic means for communists to seize nationalist movements against Americans' "bad intentions." Thus Kennan, in drafting NSC 34, rejected "all-out aid" to Jiang not on the grounds that it would not work ("It might, but only if the U.S. would provide as much as was necessary for as long as was necessary") but primarily because it would amount to "overt intervention," which "multiplies resistance to the intervener. The ramified forces of new nationalism and traditional Chinese xenophobia would be likely to rally to the Communists, whose ties with the USSR are obscured in Chinese eyes by the Communists' violent anti-imperialism." Overt U.S. intervention might strengthen Jiang militarily, but it would "tend politically to strengthen the Communists." The more the United States assisted Jiang militarily, "the more the National Government would tend to be regarded in Chinese eyes as a puppet . . . and the more the intervention would cost."[94]

Acheson agreed. The only thing that could obscure "the true function of Communism as an agent of Russian imperialism" in China, he said in his January 12, 1950, speech at the National Press Club, "is the folly of ill-conceived adventures on our part." The United States must "not undertake to deflect from the Russians to ourselves the righteous anger, and the wrath, and the hatred of the Chinese people which must develop. It would be folly to deflect it to ourselves."[95]

Yet this was precisely what American diplomats saw their government doing in China: supporting a reactionary regime and thus acting the part of the imperialist. American diplomats reported countless instances of the way American involvement with a loathed regime was engendering hatred among a wide variety of Chinese (including Nationalists). Why had the United States ended up trying to "foist a rotten, unpopular government on the Chinese people?" John Cabot asked in a long report to Butterworth. It "would be worse than a crime, it would be stupid, to pursue our present aid policy. . . . Let us not persist further in a course which is to my mind both unwise and immoral. If the Chinese want peace, are prepared to accept Communism, and feel that China will absorb Communism as it has so many conquerors, can we be certain we know better than they what is good for them?"[96]

Cabot acknowledged what most American diplomats understood all too well: that it was the United States, not the USSR, that had massively intervened in the civil war. He described the transportation of thousands of Nationalists by U.S. transport to strategic points being surrendered by the Japanese "in order that the Nationalists might get to them ahead of the Communists." Marines had been used to keep the Tianjin-Beijing railway open and were stationed in the naval base in Tsingtao. Large amounts of military and economic aid had been given to the Nationalists "and practically nothing to the Communists." The United States maintained military advisory groups in China and had given Jiang's government $125 million. "On the other hand, the most serious allegation of Russian interference I have heard is that they turned over large quantities of Japanese arms and munitions to the Communists when withdrawing from Manchuria; against this, if I remember rightly, General Marshall has stated that we turned over large quantities of surrendered Japanese arms and munitions to the Nationalists"—who "botched the job" and pursued a "tortuous and unappreciative course towards the United States."[97]

Then Cabot pinpointed the grimmest irony. If the Chinese communists turned out not to be subservient to Moscow, then the whole U.S.-aid program would have been a ghastly mistake. The United States would not only have failed to maintain in power "the rotten and unpopular government" that it favored and have jeopardized its entire position in China unnecessarily, but it would also have intervened in China's internal affairs, would have blocked much-needed and long overdue reforms, and, moreover, would have driven into Moscow's arms a new government with which we might have enjoyed reasonably normal relations. In the end there was only one possible ideological defense: "If we had any right to aid Nationalist China against the Chinese Communists, it could only be on the basis of defense against Soviet aggression, for otherwise it would be intervention in Chinese internal affairs."[98]

But where were the signs of Soviet aggression? Cabot warned against the "naive oversimplification of the problem." Yet when he began to break down the notion of "Russian aggression" into its components, he could point only to some very limited concrete military assistance on their part. He argued that the Chinese communist subservience to Moscow should not simply be assumed, and urged flexibility toward the emerging communist government, knowing full well that his suggestions might be "poison ivy from the domestic political viewpoint."[99]

In the end, however, the vague omnipresence of the Soviet threat prevailed. Thus, even if in the weeks before V-J Day the United States had not been planning to aid Jiang in his struggle with the Communists; even if the United States had not launched the greatest airlift of troops up to that time to place Jiang's soldiers in North China and key ports; even if the United States had not sent sixty thousand marines to Manchuria and North China; even if the Marshall Mission itself had been predicated upon ultimately siding with Jiang if a compromise could not be found—even if all these things had not been so, Washington believed, the Chinese communists would have acted no differently once they came to power: such was the ideological framework that enshrouded American policy debates. Though Washington did not (or could not find a way to) commit massive military force to achieve its objectives in China, it was never willing to "accept the verdict of the struggle in China"; it never sought to abstain from involvement in China's civil war, and it never ceased expressing its deep ideological hostility to the Chinese communists and the revolution they led.[100]

Psychological Warfare and Kennan's Critique

By 1948, NSC calls for an effective program of global psychological warfare against the Soviets had reached fever pitch, and efforts to deal with the Chinese communists were a natural concomitant. But the best possible propaganda weapons with which American officials spoke of arming themselves were all but indistinguishable from the assumptions underlying their own policy debates. Where conviction stops and propaganda starts is all but impossible to sort out in NSC documents of these years.

The refusal to acknowledge the independence-minded nationalism of the Chinese revolution was the center of the propaganda onslaught against China. That propaganda served two broad purposes. By insisting that China had not "stood up" but had leaned to one side, it once again accentuated the primacy of the Soviet foe. At the same time, it demeaned and diminished the anti-imperialist, intensely nationalistic revolution itself. This universalizing of the ideological war reflected the growing frustration over Moscow's apparent capacity to attract local nationalisms: it became vital to insist that China's was not a nationalistic revolution, that it was not a model to be emulated by nationalist elites but rather an object lesson in a process that turned on genuine nationalists and in time destroyed them.

Throughout the Truman years Washington officials bitterly criticized the "efforts by India and other Asian nations to rationalize the communist revolution in China as a basically nationalist movement." Communism had appeared in Asia "in the form of Asians preaching nationalism and promising Utopia to the poverty-strickened masses."[101] But as Butterworth frankly stated, "In promoting nationalism, we, of course, must be careful not to encourage the native peoples to feel resentment towards colonial powers."[102] Few officials could figure out how to steer such an arduous path.

The campaign against China assumed a contemptuous tone that had rarely been applied to the Soviet Union. The very idea of China as a satellite was a deeply insulting one. Russia at least was viewed as a credible global opponent. China was not. In the prevailing bipolar, ideological outlook, Asians could not be the prime shapers of their own destiny; two white Western powers were directing Asia's course and they were the two models, the two rival ideologies, for the foreseeable future. In this context, Washington's repeated insistence that the Chinese were subordination to Moscow takes on a deeper meaning. The emphasis on the Soviets justified another non-Asian power's intervention in a fashion just as intricate and forceful as the communists were accused of. Communism, in this sense, was always a mirror image of American actions: the negative counterpoint to American positive intervention.

Washington's ideological response to the Chinese revolution, therefore, was not simply to seek to contain the USSR but also to seek to contain China and communism in Asia. Hence containment and "nation building" came to be inseparable aspects of the same process in Asia. Seeing the proudly independent Chinese communists as puppets provided the rationale for a deepening involvement of the United States in almost every aspect of the economic, social, intellectual, cultural, political, and psychological affairs of other Asian nations.

As John Paton Davies Jr. wrote, it was time to open up a new front in the "battle for the minds, emotions, and loyalties" of Asian peasants who were "the water element in which the guerrilla fish swim." The United States needed to combat the idea that "communism was the wave of the future"—a task that required leading the forces of change and learning how to succeed in "fomenting, or fostering, or combating, or preventing Asiatic revolutions."[103]

The long-term hope that the United States could assist poor countries to develop remained in the late 1940s more a hope than a policy. By the end of the Truman years, these efforts had come into greater focus, but the communists still seemed better able than the Americans to harness nationalism.[104] They had effectively appealed to the "two great revolutionary movements which have dominated the recent history of Asia—the national revolution against western imperialism and the social revolution against the poverty and distress of the people." The Chinese communist's success in land reform, it was feared, would be repeated elsewhere in Asia if "the field of agrarian reform is left by default to Communist propaganda."[105]

But no one really had any concrete notions of how to proceed. The outpouring of psychological warfare materials during these years suggests some embryonic ideas, but until the Korean War broke out, the means were terribly limited. Repeatedly, diplomats fell back on the old tack of invoking nationalistic sentiment to combat communism, unable as yet to see a step beyond, into a convincing program of nation building. China specialist O. Edmund Clubb called for renewed efforts to arouse military resistance among the Tibetans, the Mongols, and the Muslims of western China and other minority groups, even as he called for intensifying American denunciations of aggressive Soviet imperialism. Davies called for greater efforts to "cause a revolt against Soviet influence and control in China," regretting that it was not yet the time to incite a "revolutionary movement which would challenge the entire Chinese communist apparatus." If China remained in the "Soviet camp," then efforts should be made to split off southern China under a regional government.[106]

Underlying the preoccupation with Soviet domination lurked another concern that vividly colored the ideological warfare of the years to come. China was clearly "the most 'have-not' of all the 'have-not' countries," George Kennan warned. "If we can find the answer with regard to China I am sure we have found 3/4ths of the answer with respect to any other areas of the world. . . . The Chinese Communists represent a potentially politically successful 'have-not psychology' that will have huge emotional appeal. . . . Two-fifths of our problems with respect to the rest of the world today is to determine what is really the desirable and advisable stance of a 'have' nation to 'have-not' nations, because a very large part of the world is composed of "have-nots," not just in Asia but elsewhere, and that is a very, very bitter problem."[107] Anti-imperialism was the psychological temptation of the world's have-not nations, and in the anticolonialist struggles in Asia it was threatening to get out of hand. For men like Kennan, Marshall, and Acheson, China became the archetype of anticolonialist upheaval in the underdeveloped world.

Yet outside of appeals to anticommunism and "moderate" (and thus genuine) nationalism, these leaders had little sense of how they might shape a broadly popular message for Asia. Kennan had a bleak vision of the alternatives. Psychological warfare, he argued, might be appropriate for Europe, but its efficacy in Asia was far less clear. The "essence of our struggle with the USSR is ideological," he wrote, but Asia was not going to develop in "a liberal or peaceful" way. Its adaptation to modern technology, its population problems, its backwardness would "require new forms of life and social organization." When others saw the lesson of the Chinese revolution as the need for programs designed to encourage American economic assistance, Kennan was dubious. He was particularly wary of any long-term mainland commitments in Southeast Asia. The process of upheaval, he warned, would be "long and violent," and in its course some peoples would be likely to fall temporarily under the influence of Moscow, since communist ideology had "greater lure for such peoples, and probably greater reality, than anything we could oppose to it."[108]

The United States, Kennan asserted, could not hope to deal with such a challenge without committing resources far beyond what was prudent. Thus Washington should "dispense with the aspiration to 'be liked' or to be regarded as the repository of a high-minded international altruism. We should stop putting ourselves in the position of being our brothers' keeper and refrain from offering moral and ideological advice. We should cease to talk about vague and—for the Far East—unreal objectives such as human rights, the raising of the living standards, and democratization. The day is not far off when we are going to have to deal in straight power concepts. The less we are then hampered by idealistic slogans, the better."[109] Americans needed to recognize their limitations "as a moral and ideological force among the Asiatic peoples."[110] The Soviets had a clear advantage here, but Kennan disagreed with the notion that their proximity in Asia was what gave them the upper hand in fostering local communist movements: "By the nature of international communism the USSR enjoys this advantage all over the world irrespective of the Soviet Union's relative strength in any particular area."[111]

But what if the issue was viewed in terms, again, of the haves versus the have-nots? The problem was far greater than a mere geopolitical challenge. "We have about 50% of the world's wealth but only 6.3% of its population," Kennan wrote in 1948: "This disparity is particularly great . . . between ourselves and the peoples of Asia. In this situation, we cannot fail to be the object of envy and resentment. Our real task in the coming period is to devise a pattern for relationships which will permit us to maintain this position of disparity without positive detriment to our national security. To do so, we will have to dispense with all sentimentality and day-dreaming; and our attention will have to be concentrated everywhere on our immediate national objectives. We need not deceive ourselves that we can afford today the luxury of altruism and world benefaction."[112]

Kennan's overall view of Asia in late 1949 was not quite so bleak. He thought a viable balance of power could emerge, with Japan playing a critical role, but he acutely felt the ideological disadvantages under which Washington labored.[113] Other officials took issue with Kennan's pessimism toward ideological warfare. They had no doubt that China was an enemy, its revolution an immediate threat, and the issues it posed central to the economic and strategic future of Asia. The challenge had to be met at all levels, and they vowed to wage ideological warfare throughout Asia.

While Washington thought Moscow likely to control China for years to come, it fretted over the revolutionary dynamic. Could China lead the "revolution in Asia"? Would the Kremlin assign it this role? The CCP would certainly seek to control the large and influential overseas Chinese community and to provide direct assistance to Asian communist movements; a few observers, looking into the more distant future, wondered whether China might one day "choose to compete with the USSR for leadership of the Communist movement in Asia."[114] In the meantime, though, American officials outdid themselves in expressing their ideological disdain for the CCP, knowing full well that their comments were an insulting way of framing the coming triumph of the Chinese communists. Here propaganda and ideological convictions blend to propagate a virulent image of Chinese Communism.[115]

The Wedge

Beginning in 1948, the NSC advocated efforts to promote a split between the Soviet Union and China and within the CCP itself. NSC 48/1 made it national policy: "The United States should exploit through appropriate political, psychological, and economic means any rifts between the Chinese Communists and the USSR and between the Stalinists and other elements in China, while scrupulously avoiding the appearance of intervention. Where appropriate, covert as well as overt means should be utilized to achieve these objectives."[116] Here, as elsewhere, policy, ideology, and propaganda warfare were interwoven.

In its various forms, the "wedge theory" rested on a series of convictions I have already noted, all of which became part of the propaganda warfare program: (1) that American actions were not a decisive factor in the shaping of Chinese communist policies or Chinese-Soviet relations; (2) that the Chinese communists were neither independent nor nationalist; (3) that Soviet imperialism was the main threat to Chinese independence; (4) that in the long term differences would emerge between the USSR and China; (5) that China would have to demonstrate ideological hostility to Moscow in order to pursue improved relations with the United States;[117] and (6) that the Kremlin was unable to pursue any but its own inflexibly driven interests.

John Lewis Gaddis, among others, had noted some of the contradictions in the American approach. The United States was maintaining relations with Jiang even as it was leaving open the possibility of providing military and political support to various regional anticommunist resistance groups, in Tibet, Taiwan, Szechwan, and southern China—as though these challenges to China's effective unity would not be perceived as a gross insult to Chinese nationalism. But "it is clear, nonetheless, that the State Department, with the approval of the President himself, had by the spring of 1949 come to rely on the long-term possibility of a Sino-Soviet rift as the best hope for minimizing the damage to American interests that was sure to follow the final Chinese Communist consolidation of power."[118] What is perhaps even clearer is that U.S. officials thought they could take such highly provocative steps without affecting this "long-term possibility," even as they had ready excuses for failing to take short-term steps.

Those who suggested carrots shared the main assumptions of the hardliners. Their carrots, however, were at best bite size, while the sticks were enormous. Those who advocated flexibility rarely ever mentioned more than modest trade, usually between Japan and China, and as often as not this policy was understood more in terms of U.S.-Japanese interests. The carrot approach never required either breaking relations with Jiang or toning down the propaganda war. There was simply no interest in opening up relations with a Communist China until it displayed hostility toward the Soviet Union.

The Great Divide

The emerging emphasis on ideological warfare contrasts markedly with the views of a small but highly articulate group of American diplomats, military officers, and reporters who had come to know China in the 1930s and had contact with the Chinese Communists in Yanan in 1944 and 1945.[119] In the late 1940s and early 1950s, the writings of diplomats who had been with the communists in Yanan—in particular, those of John S. Service—were brutally assailed.[120] So, too, were the writings of various journalists, among them Edgar Snow, whose *Red Star over China* had first revealed to Americans the extraordinary depths of the movement for social revolution in China.[121] In this classic, written as Japanese armies swept over the country in 1937, Snow reported on a China strikingly different from that of the late 1940s. In the backwaters of north China, he described the dedication of the communists to resisting the Japanese and to creating a social revolution. Never before had Snow seen a Chinese force of such potential magnitude, so deeply rooted in the peasantry, so capable of changing their lives, or so guided by a meaningful vision of society.

Not until 1944 were Americans again able to observe the Chinese communists so closely. President Roosevelt had repeatedly pressured Jiang Jieshih to allow an American military mission into Yanan, on the grounds that it was necessary to the war against Japan. Jiang had bitterly acquiesced. The intense criticisms of the American reports from Yanan by both politicians and scholars in the 1950s all but obscures the reports' remarkable accuracy on the most fundamental issues—the intense nationalism and independence of the Chinese communists, their drive to win the civil war, their likely turn toward the Soviet Union if the United States supported Jiang, the depth and scope of the Chinese revolution, and the almost certain triumph of the communists over the corrupt and decadent Guomindang.

For Service and others, including General Joseph Stilwell, it had made sense to give arms to everyone willing to fight the Japanese, including the communists. By late 1944, Service was convinced that the communists were the most dynamic if not yet the most powerful force in China. Jiang *and* the Communists should receive arms—a policy that seemed to him both practical and realistic, because the attitudes of the Chinese Communist Party would be partly shaped in response to American actions; because reforming the Guomindang appeared hopeless; and because, with Soviet participation in the war likely, it was essential to deepen American contacts quickly, building a basis of trust and establishing American interest in an independent China. The paramount fact was that China was in the midst of an enormous revolutionary upheaval.

Guomindang China emerges in graphic detail in Service's concise, unemotional, but never bureaucratic dispatches: the archaic social system unable to die, weighing down on a people barely able to live; the exploitation by landlords of the peasantry; the deaths of tens of thousands of peasants in the endlessly corrupt Nationalist system of conscription ("regarded in the minds of the people as a sentence of death"); the famines induced as much by man as by nature.[122] In the 1950s and early 1960s, American historians and political scientists asked how it was that the United States could not have forced Jiang Jieshih either to make the reforms essential for his survival or to back a leader who would. Since Jiang was "utterly dependent on American support for victory in the war against Japan and for survival after the war in his struggle with the Communists," American power should have sought to rebuild the "social and political foundations of the Nationalist Government through a series of sweeping reforms." The vast forces demanding change should have been molded by American hands, set in motion according to American plans, supervised by American personnel, and justified on grounds of the military urgency of the war against Japan.[123]

That had been General Stilwell's inclination. After Pearl Harbor, President Roosevelt had assigned him to increase the effectiveness of U.S. aid to the prosecution of the war and to improve the combat efficiency of the Chinese army, but since Washington had little intention of diverting military supplies needed elsewhere to China, Stilwell's mission became the organizing of the one resource China had in quantity: manpower. After his years as military consul during the 1930s, he had an enormous faith in the capacities of the Chinese peasants, but his attitude toward Jiang and his corrupt military system echoed General Erich Ludendorff's estimate of Austria's fighting potential in World War I: "We are allied to a corpse."

Service knew that the Chinese army could only mirror the regime; to tackle its weakness was to become entangled in the very structure of the Guomindang. Creating an effective fighting force would have destroyed Jiang's political world. In the fall of 1944 the situation reached a crisis. As Jiang's armies crumbled before a Japanese advance, Roosevelt demanded Stilwell's appointment as commander in chief of the Chinese armies. Jiang refused; Roosevelt relented, and Stilwell was recalled. To later critics, FDR's weakness of will was catastrophic. It meant that the United States would not promote the reforms among the noncommunist groups needed to prepare them to compete successfully with the CCP.

Service, who advised Stilwell, had hoped that Stilwell's appointment would successfully reduce the American commitment to Jiang. He did not advocate promoting a particular direction to China's changes, holding that America should offer no hard-and-fast solutions, that unity was a Chinese problem for the Chinese to solve themselves. Washington had to be willing to adjust to the tidal wave of events in China—but nothing was possible until Jiang was stripped of unconditional American support.

"There may be a collapse of the Kuomintang Government," Service wrote, "but it will not be the collapse of China's resistance" to Japan. He cited the parallel with Yugoslavia, where the British came to support Tito.[124] But he argued just as strongly that the Guomindang "cannot crush these militant people now" and that their armed forces would fail in the future. The communists "cannot be eliminated," and efforts by the Guomindang to do so "will strengthen the ties of the Communists with the people: a Communist victory will be inevitable." The Guomindang was doomed without sweeping reforms ("the Communists will be the dominant force in China within a comparatively few years"), and a policy of continued support with pressure was useless.[125] "Encouraged by our support, the Kuomintang will continue in its present course, progressively losing the confidence of the people and becoming more and more impotent." Nor should the United States hold to its hope "that China under the present Kuomintang can be an effective balance to Soviet Russia, Japan, or the British Empire in the Far East" after the war.[126] Service saw no dichotomy between nationalism and communism and had no sense that the Communists were somehow alien or exploiting discontent to further insidiously imposed alien objectives. And certainly he never suggested that the CCP was planning to sell out its country to the Soviets.

On all these basic points, Service's accounts—along with those of Davies and others—proved highly accurate. Yet by early 1946, every one of these insights was being obfuscated by and subordinated to ideological concerns. Gone in the diplomatic and NSC documents is the radical independence of the communists and their roots in an enormous rural revolution, replaced by a growing preoccupation with whether their ideological affinity meant they were subordinate to Moscow. Service and the others had never posed the issue as a *pivotal* one, and they knew that Chinese communist subordination to the Soviets, given the power of the revolutionary movement, was out of the question. The speed with which such views were swept aside, as the ideological formulations of the NSC dichotomized nationalism and communism, was stunning. The enormity of the Chinese revolution slipped into the background.[127]

What was left in the diplomatic dispatches after 1945 were dissections of the failure of the Guomindang, its rottenness, the hopelessness of its reform, an anguished questioning as to how the United States could continue to support such a reactionary and brutal regime—and the conclusion that, nonetheless, the United States had to continue its support because of the communists. Stilwell, Service, and the others had been willing to cut the tie with Jiang if it came to that. Their successors never were.

John F. Melby: The Diplomat as Diarist

Missing in these post-1945 dispatches, moreover, was a persuasive sense of why the communists were so likely to win. But in private papers, some diplomats, such as John F. Melby, demonstrated a far more profound understanding. On Averell Harriman's suggestion, Melby had been shifted from the Moscow embassy to serve in China. His "primary job," as he later wrote, "was to keep track of what the Russians were up to in China." Though until then he had had no interest in China, he soon began to wonder whether "as much of the answer to the riddle might be found in China as in the Kremlin." Melby quickly concluded that "the Communists have absorbed an incredible amount of punishment, have been guilty of their own share of atrocities, and yet still have retained a kind of integrity, faith in their destiny, and will to prevail." The Guomindang, by contrast, "has gone through astonishing tribulations, has committed its excesses, has survived a major war with unbelievable prestige, and is now throwing everything away at a frightening rate because the revolutionary faith is gone and has been replaced by the smell of corruption and decay."[128]

It is rare to find in the State Department's *Foreign Relations of the United States* volumes the kind of criticisms that Melby delivered, unvarnished by any ideologically protective coating. Taking a fifty-mile trip into a remote rural area, where, he wrote, "we dropped back 1,000 years," he found that the communists, "as much through necessity as wisdom," were penetrating the villages and "finding a response where for a long time no one cared what happened." They were neither dominating the rural revolution nor simply shaping it to their own ends—they were having to "mount and ride the same mammoth social revolution which is still and will be for a long time the story of Asia." In the end, "only that government which can satisfy minimum peasant aspirations will secure and retain peasant loyalty. Herein lies the greatest failure of the KMT."[129]

Ties to the Guomindang, Melby concluded, were Washington's greatest failure; we are "aligned with a faction that is losing the Mandate of Heaven." He noted how pervasive among Americans was the "absence of any idea of what to do about China. All anyone knows is that disaster is not far off." After accompanying a group of American journalists on a visit to China, he wrote that "they did not like what they saw, but they also could not figure out anything else to take its place that they would like any better and that had a better chance of coming to pass." When he asked them why they never reported on the peasants revolts, "they just shrugged their shoulders and said that there is no use doing it since the American public is not interested in China and no paper at home would print the story."[130]

Although the repressive brutality of the GMD was reported in State Department documents, it was always placed in the either-or context of the communist alternative. Melby, like others, noted that the deeply nationalistic Chinese were becoming infuriated by American support for Jiang. And he did not think that the Chinese communists were subordinate to Moscow. "Not since 1927 have they taken orders from anyone," he wrote, "and they are hardly likely to do so when they are the victors." He dismissed "the Kremlin satellite theory" about China. "Whatever weaving they may do through necessity, [the Chinese Communists] will in their ideas, attitudes and actions be guided by their own years of struggle and experience, not by the struggles and experiences of anyone else."[131] Melby, unlike Ambassador Stuart at times, saw no hope for a transformed Jiang, and he saw no credible alternative (as other diplomats sometimes did) in a third force of intellectuals sympathetic to American ideals and professionals who could pressure the government—people more inclined to the "modern" world. American journalists in China, who were less immediately preoccupied with policy decisions, liked the idea of this middle way but saw no means of achieving it. Those Chinese who believed in it lacked weapons, and Jiang would brutally suppress them. There was no way to counterbalance these circumstances with any conceivable use of American power.

This reality directly challenged the key justifications for a continued American presence. The United States regarded itself as instrumental in building up the "modern" classes of China. Melby noted the great gap between modern, Western-educated Chinese intellectuals and professionals and those carrying out the revolution. "Having been Western educated, they had lost touch with their own people. They could know what had to be done and still feel more at home in the Faculty Club at Harvard or the International Club in Shanghai than they could in the villages where the work of China is done." [132]

A similar theme sometimes emerges in State department documents:

The U.S. had trained large numbers of Chinese in American universities but the wide disparity between the standards of living in the U.S. and China had made these American-trained Chinese good for running industries, teaching, banking and similar pursuits, but not for leading a revolution. The Chinese revolution had been led by Chinese trained in China and Japan. American returned students tended to think of baths and flush toilets and wooden floors. Chinese trained in Russia and Russians who came to China were unlike Americans in that they could all live under poor conditions. Chinese now being trained in the U.S. would never become the leaders of a new revolution and they would exert no decisive influence on developments in China.[133]

Communism, Melby concluded, "has come to China for a long time to come. Western democracy, especially the American brand, is an unfamiliar idiom to the Chinese, far more alien than Communism. . . . The American system is something the Chinese do not understand, have never had, and do not now want."[134] Rarely do such views appear in U.S. diplomatic dispatches, and Melby himself did not offer them publicly; he understood "the realities of diplomatic reporting during these years." Later on he observed that "stating the need for the U.S. to accept by 1947 or 1948 the evident likely outcome of the Chinese revolution was simply an unacceptable message, even by diplomats in the field who believed it." But, he added, few did believe it: "It was simply too disquieting and unpalatable to not only accept that the U.S. did not have the answers, but that the Chinese Communists had a right to run China if they attained the Mandate of Heaven." Melby sympathized with the plight of Ambassador Stuart and others who had deep roots in China: "Like others of his persuasion, he can see a lifetime going down the drain."[135] They could not cut themselves loose from their China—and neither in a different way could the United States.

The 1949 White Paper and Walter Lippmann

A white paper issued by the State Department in August 1949 concluded that the United States did everything it could to sustain Jiang but that the collapse of Nationalist China was, in the end, his own failure. The civil war was ultimately beyond American control. And this analysis was substantially correct: the United States did all that it practically could to assist Jiang for as long as it could. But Walter Lippmann, responding to the white paper in his newspaper column, raised a pertinent question: if Jiang was so inept and so corrupt, then why had the United States poured $3 billion into a lost cause? To claim justification for such a policy and then to justify its failure on the grounds that the outcome was beyond our control, he charged, was "tantamount to saying that there was no such thing as a sound or an unsound, a right or a wrong, a wise or an unwise policy toward the Chinese civil war." The outcome of the war, he continued, may well have been beyond American control, but "America's own actions were very much under its control." Why did the United States put its prestige behind a government that its own documents showed was "hopelessly corrupt"? The administration, he concluded, did not have to answer for the "loss" of China; it had to answer for its persistence in a policy it now admitted had been doomed from the start.[136]

Lippmann's three-column dissection of the white paper focuses on this persistence and the government's overwhelming support for Jiang's lost cause. Lippmann, unlike Acheson, regarded the Chinese communists as "independent nationalists." But their differences went far deeper. Lippmann accepted the revolution; he did not like it, but he held that Washington, upon realizing that it could not alter the situation, should not have kept attempting to do so. And almost as bad was that ideologically, Washington remained just as committed to its old course as it always had been. That, he concluded, is what Acheson had really meant in his cover letter for the white paper when he said there was nothing wrong with the policy—events just overwhelmed it.

Lippmann recognized that even the traces of alternative approaches mentioned in the white paper lacked any strategic clarity, and not just out of fear of right-wing domestic critics, though they were one element. The deeper problem was ideological: the inability of the diplomats in the field to write, in their dispatches to Washington, in ways that were not already part and parcel of the enormous policy failure that the white paper embodied.

Edgar Snow's Dissent

Among those who challenged official Washington's view of China in the late 1940s, no dissenter stands out more than Edgar Snow. In the late 1940s, as an associate editor of the *Saturday Evening Post,* Snow wrote two relevant articles: "Will China Become a Russian Satellite?" and "Will Tito's Heretics Halt Russia?" That the *Post* understood how controversial Snow's views were is clear from the highly unusual editorial disclaimers it ran with both articles. And the *Post* was correct: the articles challenged almost every assumption then prevalent about China, communism, nationalism, and revolution.

In the China article, Snow posed a series of questions: "Will a communist-led government inevitably mean that China must fall under the absolute domination of the Kremlin? Will Moscow plant 'specialists' in the Chinese police force, the army, the party Politburo, the state apparatus, to constitute a government above government, as in East Europe? Will China fall into the orbit of Soviet economic planning, with powers held by Russian commissars to operate mines and industries to meet Russia's strategic demands? Will the Kremlin be able to dictate internal policy to Chinese Communists, as well as control China's vote in the United Nations?" According to the dominant view, the obvious answer to all these questions was *yes*; even to raise them was ideologically bold. But Snow argued emphatically that China would *not* become a satellite: "Soviet Russia would not hold effective domination over the extremely nation-conscious Chinese Communists."[137] In the Tito article, he chided those, like Kennan, who had expressed "surprise" at Tito's "defection" since "a number of people who studied communist growths in various countries had long believed that a development such as the Belgrade schism was certain to come." Snow himself had entertained that possibility a full decade earlier when he concluded that the Chinese were "the first foreign communists openly to place their national interests on a level with those of Russia." Moreover, he believed that the Chinese Communist Party had so deeply penetrated the social fabric that the nation would be resentful of any Soviet effort to control its internal affairs, which is why Stalin had not dispatched as many agents to China as he had to Eastern Europe.[138]

Snow scoffed at the notion that China's shared adherence to a communist ideology constituted prima facie evidence of subordination. "Is the party ideology of the moment of greater permanent importance than the nation's whole past? . . . Or greater than its vital economic requirements and exchanges with the rest of the world?" China was an immense country with a civilization stretching back three thousand years. The Chinese revolutionaries had come to power on their own—indeed, at times, in conflict with the Soviets. To grasp the country's revolutionary process was simply not possible, he argued, without understanding how they had come to embody a decades-long struggle to regain China's independence. In essence, the communists "have been nationalists continuing an independence movement."[139]

Snow rejected the search for policies predicated on divisions within the Chinese leadership. "Virtually all the veterans who form the hard core of this party, men now in their fifties and sixties, are products of more than twenty years of common history *made in China*. They could not now be seriously divided by outside critics."[140] Though these men might have policy disagreements, Snow rejected the ideological foundation of the nationalism-versus-communism dichotomy, noting its derogatory implication that some members of the leadership were willing to sell out to the Kremlin.

He acknowledged the potential conflicts between China and Russia. Moscow was going to have to learn to deal "with a major foreign power run by communists possessing all the means of maintaining real equality and independence." But to imagine that the Kremlin would simply repeat the mistakes it had made with Yugoslavia, or that it lacked any ability to operate otherwise than as Kennan and others had portrayed it was "highly illusory." The Russians were likely to proceed "with extreme caution, hopefully waiting for the Americans to make the blunders on which their own success could be improvised."[141] Snow agreed that any Soviet effort to deprive Beijing of economic, political, and military control over Manchuria would lead to an explosion in China, but it would be an explosion of anger from the Chinese Communists against the Soviets, not a split within the CCP. Stalin almost certainly understood these realities.

It was true that the Chinese resented the Soviet looting of Manchurian industry and stocks. The methods and attitudes of Soviet bureaucrats in Manchuria had not gone over well with the Chinese communists. Nor was it likely that importing Russian-speaking Chinese to run Soviet-Chinese enterprises would be a popular move. But to argue that the Chinese communists would tolerate the dismemberment of their country (or that the Soviets any longer sought it) had no basis in reality. The Chinese communists had led a revolution that satisfied urgent needs of the peasantry and released an "energy aroused by anti-foreign slogans of a nationalist movement." Its success would come by redeeming the most important promises of internal progress, popular reform, and true national independence, not by breaking them.

Snow conceded that serious contradictions existed between Chinese communism and Soviet expansionism. "But such differences are a very minor matter compared to the 'contradictions' between the 'national aspirations of the Chinese Communists' and the aims of continued American intervention against them!" The great question confronting American policy, he wrote, was whether to go on intervening in China's civil war. Would Washington continue to listen to those who insisted that normal relations with the Chinese communists were impossible, that it was necessary to "fight them by all means available, short of war"?

He believed that even if the United States had remained neutral in the civil war, the communists would still have cancelled certain treaties the United States had made with the Guomindang and ended any special Western rights in China. Much hostility would still have existed. But the reality that the "good old days" are gone, he argued, should not condemn the Chinese revolutionaries or mark them as "enemies of China's freedom." It in no way justified aid to anticommunist elements in southern China or aid to the tottering remnants of the European colonies in Southeast Asia. "So long as it is true that the United States is the main support of the old regime in China, and of any or all anticommunist parties, groups, politicians, or war lords prepared to continue what is now clearly a lost war, Americans will easily hold their present position as Foreign Enemy No. 1."

But once the Chinese communists had shattered all opposing military forces, what then? Would they allow the Soviets to use China as a base for their actions in other areas of Asia or to make it into a subordinate ally in some global design for war? Snow thought not: "China is a nation that is bankrupt—its cities ruined, its railways wrecked, its machinery antiquated or useless, its river and canal systems broken down, its people hungry, weary, and ragged, eager to work but lacking the tools and other means. Chinese Communists are not so stupid as to think, once they begin to carry the full responsibility of national power, that they can solve all those internal problems and simultaneously launch a war, or help Russia to launch a war, against the United States."

But if the United States continued its interventionist policies, a Chinese-Soviet alliance might well result; still, such an alliance would be unlikely to persist if the United States did not "intend to hold onto any part of China, nor to try to impose its will there in alliance with anticommunists of all varieties."

The issue was not the Soviet Union but whether and how the United States would learn to live with the "struggle of Asia for equality and independence." The "entire colonial system is close to an end," he concluded. "It is an era of 'Asia for the Asiatics'—and of government of, by and for Asiatics. . . . It is much too late to restore any empires in this part of the world. Too late for Russia as well as for any other power."

Once in power, Snow wrote, China would become "the first communist-run major power independent of Moscow's dictation." He suggested a possible scenario:

China might eventually become a kind of Asiatic Moscow. . . . As such, it would come to constitute the symbol of the overthrow of the European colonial system in Asia. . . . On the other hand, it might also set up a frontier against the expansion of communism *as an extension of Russian nationalism* in the East. China under Communist leadership [might become] the center of a new system of independent Asiatic states, might eventually prove to be a principal factor in the stabilization of world peace. Given the opportunity to develop its own resources at arm's length co-operation with other nations, such a new Asia might form a bloc of powers important enough to maintain a stable balance between the Russian and American spheres of influence.

Snow was deeply impressed by just what American officials were so vehemently denying: China's intense nationalism, its independence, and its commitment to finding its own way. Unlike others in Washington, he neither demeaned, ridiculed, nor feared the effort. But by late 1949 he was almost alone in his views, which, along with those of a few others, were swept away in the rapidly escalating ideological war.

*The real issue, therefore, is not which
side started the cold war. It is rather
the far more subtle one of which side
committed its power to policies which
hardened the natural and inherent
tensions and propensities into bitter
antagonism and inflexible positions.*
—William Appleman Williams

3 · CONTAINING CHINA BEFORE KOREA

The outbreak of the Korean War on June 25, 1950, enabled Washington to shape, with astonishing speed and determination, an Asian policy that was to last for almost two decades. Critical aspects of that policy had emerged by early that year: the containment of China, the reverse course in Japan, the reorganization of the Asian economy, the intense ideological hostility to the Chinese revolution, and a deepening commitment to fighting communism in Southeast Asia. But it was Korea that abruptly cut through the host of controversies and problems that had been plaguing American policy for several years and brought together a policy of isolating the Chinese revolution with strategies for reshaping Japan and the rest of Asia in the context of a massive escalation of American power. As much as the United States had sought to contain China, that policy became tactically and strategically viable only with the possibility—which the Korean War opened—of significantly isolating it.

Three critical factors formed the foundations of America's China policy. First, by the late 1940s, Washington was deep into the ideology of global struggle against "Kremlin-directed monolithic Communism." This bipolar globalism permeated both debates within the NSC and regional and bilateral ones. The widespread acceptance of China as a Soviet satellite and the "wedge strategy" testify to its ideological pervasiveness.

Second, although NSC 48/2 in December 1949 defined the U.S. objective for Asia as the "containment of Communism," the means to achieve it proved elusive and the subject of acrimonious debate until the outbreak of the Korean War. Some historians, assessing the intensifying ideological animosity toward

China in these years, have concluded that there was no chance of accommodation.[1] Others think there was a lost chance and that Acheson himself kept an open mind on the issue of Taiwan during the months before the Korean War and was waiting for the "dust to settle."[2] Very few, however, have acknowledged just how contradictory U.S. policies were in the late 1940s: the hostile commitment to containment neither provided the strategies nor attracted the international support to put it in place. The bitter disputes in Washington grew out of a rift between what was practical and what was ideologically acceptable. Washington felt itself on the defensive, both tactically and diplomatically. It had never thought it would end up isolated on issues related to China—an enormous setback for U.S. policy throughout Asia. The refusal to recognize Beijing even as others were doing so; the UN's China seat going to Beijing even though Washington was not speaking to that government; an American embargo on China even as its allies carried on trading and American officials argued that Japan needed to trade with Beijing in order to reduce its financial burden on the United States: all these unsettling practical considerations were far more pressing before the Korean War than ideological discussions about developing a wedge between China and the Soviet Union.

The year 1949, then, was a time of considerable turmoil and deep frustration over the inability to envision how—not whether—to contain China. A virulent hostility to the Chinese Communists pervaded both hard-line and more moderate approaches to China policy. In Washington the issue of recognition was advocated by no significant official; no one considered any advantages of China's assuming its rightful seat in the United Nations; and no one seriously proposed accommodation with Beijing. Essentially, these months before the Korean War were a period when the United States despaired of finding a coherent policy toward Asia and China, even as the ideological desire to do so was becoming more and more adamant. The Truman administration wavered for months, buffeted between its own ideological predispositions, its domestic critics, and its inability to envision an effective hard-line strategy.

Third, the Korean War provided a significant way to resolve these disputes, enabling the United States to pursue a strategy far more in keeping with its ideological hostility to the Chinese communists. The war immediately reshaped the context of a number of highly contentious issues: Taiwan; recognition; the Chinese seat in the United Nations; trade, Japan, and the economic embargo; containment and the wedge strategy; and the understanding of the Chinese revolution itself. With the war, the United States could undertake to isolate and thus contain China through a rapid and massive escalation of power in East Asia.

The Perennial Subject of Taiwan

Before the Korean War the question of defending Taiwan from the communists was one not of principle but of costs. Washington had practically no support in either Asia or Europe for the steps it most desired. Acheson well knew that to block the efforts of the communists to invade Taiwan was to preclude the possibility of recognizing Beijing, and this was a step he hesitated to take, once it became clear how few other countries would support it.

From 1948 on, discussions of the "definition" of American interest in the island fill the diplomatic documents. Was it strategic? moral? limited? expansive?[3] As the communists swept over southern China, many despaired of a way to hold the island. Should the United States support an independent Taiwan? A UN trusteeship? By the fall of 1949 the military favored using limited military means to hold Taiwan. They opposed a major troop commitment but did not want Taiwan to be lost. Acheson, among others, questioned the wisdom of a military commitment: if Taiwan was not vital to American security, then force would put American prestige and credibility on the line far beyond what was rational.[4] On January 5, 1950, Truman stated that the United States would refrain from using military force to hold Taiwan "at this time," though economic assistance would continue: "The resources on Formosa are adequate to enable them to obtain the items which they might consider necessary for the defense of the island."[5] The consensus was clear that Taiwan should be denied to the communists,[6] the problem was one of means.

Historians have pointed to the disgust that Truman, Acheson, and other American leaders were feeling for Jiang and his corrupt regime. CIA studies of Jiang's future were bleak: the greatest imminent danger was from groups within that might seek accommodation with the communists. Various officials analyzed the prospects for a Taiwan independent from the mainland *and* free of Jiang. Acheson briefly considered the possibility. Others considered—not very hopefully—ways to reform the GMD. Perhaps Jiang could be persuaded (or forced) to ask for UN trusteeship and the Seventh Fleet be moved into the Taiwan Strait. With time, perhaps, better possibilities might emerge. No high-level American official argued that the United States should simply stay out of Taiwan; neither did many lower-level officials, and those who did so knew that they were bucking official policy.[7]

Although some historians believe that Acheson himself opposed separating Taiwan from the mainland, a closer look at his argument shows up inconsistencies. "We cannot afford to compromise an emerging new U.S. position in China by overtly showing a pronounced interest in Formosa," he told the NSC on March 1, 1949; to the Joint Chiefs of Staff he bluntly said that in Taiwan "we must face the fact that there is no Chinese basis for resistance to Communism," which would now seek to expand its dominion throughout Southeast Asia. "Above all," he declared, "we must get ourselves on the side of Nationalist movements." Was it worth it, he asked, to delay the fall of Taiwan by a year or so? It had yet to be demonstrated that "the loss of Formosa really breaches our defense." To acquire "additional time" at this price was too high a political cost, Acheson argued, but with a caveat. The real danger would not come from Communist assault, which "seems unlikely. The real danger is the continued decay within."[8] On January 5, 1950, he told Senators William Knowland and Alexander Smith that as "distasteful as the possibility was that the island might well be occupied by the Communists at some point in the future, we must concede the possibility and not compromise our entire position in the Far East by doing deeds that would give the lie to our words."[9]

Some historians see Acheson as having been sensitive to Asian nationalism and meaningfully open to relations with the People's Republic of China. Few other Asian leaders thought so. And his concern that the United States was up against the potential threat of irredentism was in no way incompatible with his support for political and economic efforts to keep Taiwan separate, or for allowing others to explore the prospects of an independent Taiwan, or for continuing aid to Jiang, or for continuing to recognize Jiang's government. Ideologically, Acheson fervently held to the familiar axioms that nationalism and communism were incompatible and that China was becoming dominated by the Soviets.

Acheson argued throughout 1949 that "if our present policy is to have any hope of success in Formosa, we must carefully conceal our wish to separate the island from mainland control."[10] An internal history of the JCS states that "the United States, according to the Secretary of State, had to conceal behind the Economic Cooperation Administration and China aid programs its efforts to separate Formosa from continental domination."[11] Yet by late 1949 it was no longer clear to him how to accomplish this goal. Neither he nor American military officials thought that Jiang could pull together a competent government on Taiwan; the regime was likely to fall from within. How, then, could American military power be effectively committed to Taiwan short of an occupation? To assign the fleet to holding Taiwan risked direct conflict with the PRC or an embarrassing internal collapse. Either result would further diminish American prestige and credibility.

Even those ready to invoke the perils of irredentism could flip-flop on the issue with amazing speed. George Kennan invoked this peril repeatedly in PPS and NSC documents, only to turn around and advocate the seizure of Taiwan. In a particularly impassioned and strident June 1949 memorandum, he declared that "we should take the plunge" and announce "a temporary unilateral reassertion of authority over the islands on the grounds that subsequent events had invalidated all the assumptions underlying the 1943 Cairo Declaration"—under which Taiwan was to be returned to China—"and that U.S. intervention was required by the interests of stability in the Pacific area as well as by the interests of the inhabitants of the islands." Kennan told the British the same month that even though the United States was dubious of Jiang's ability to hold Taiwan, Washington might move to support Taiwanese independence along with other "resistance elements in China."[12]

In other words, concern over irredentism and sensitivity to Chinese nationalism were just two more arguments to throw into the fray of disagreements about American policy. Acheson was unwilling to risk isolation on an issue with such wide international reverberations. To seize Taiwan would almost certainly preclude American recognition of China for a long time, and in ways that would "seriously hamper the achievement of general U.S. aims in Asia." It was a Rubicon that Acheson had no desire to cross.

Great Britain opposed any American attempts to hold Taiwan. Military efforts "would be fatal to the position of any foreign power in China which used such means to detach Formosa from China." London also opposed bringing the issue to the United Nations and was proceeding with recognition.[13] As W. Walton Butterworth noted, holding Taiwan would "almost inevitably lead to frictions and complications with the British and other friendly powers who will recognize the Communist regime without holding out any real possibility of a re-conquest of China itself."[14] Acheson warned that a military seizure would "risk giving the Soviets a chance of bringing us before the Security Council and throughout all Asia we would be represented as the supporters of this discredited, decayed KMT Government."[15] Intervening in the Chinese civil war on behalf of Jiang (or whoever came to power in Taiwan) could lead to a situation in the UN in which the United States faced certain defeat. It was one thing for the United States not to recognize the Chinese communists, but to support Jiang in the Security Council when he obviously was not in control of the country was quite another: a position that not even allies, let alone neutrals, were likely to back.

As a CIA analysis noted, such a position "would diminish U.S. prestige and opportunities for leadership in the UN"; in addition, "probably it would prevent the newly independent governments of India and Pakistan from cooperating with the US in South Asia."[16] During his visit to the United States in late 1949, Nehru strongly dissented from the American policy of nonrecognition, and he was particularly critical of U.S. support of a separate Taiwan—a blatant and dangerous intervention, he argued, in the internal affairs of China.

The issue was also critical in U.S. relations with Japan, for whom trade with China was then considered crucial. At this point, American policy makers were deeply concerned about the long-run economic viability of Japan and its probable continuing financial dependency on the United States. Japanese leaders made it clear that being cut off from China itself would be immensely unpopular in Japan.

In the light of these highly practical matters, it is striking how persistent the national security bureaucracy was in its push for a separate Taiwan, whether under the Nationalists, some other government, or the United Nations. In November 1949, Acheson's Far East consultants warned him that seeking to detach Taiwan from the mainland, either by force or through a trusteeship, would outrage the Chinese elements and destroy Washington's standing with the smaller countries of the world. Yet a key caveat followed: "However, should another nation bring the conflict involving Formosa before the United Nations as a threat to peace, we might join with other members in supporting a cease-fire resolution and the application of the principle of self-determination."[17] No one explored whether such a step would be regarded throughout Asia as nothing more than an American strategy to separate Taiwan from the mainland, or said anything about the complexities of bringing into the United Nations an issue involving a permanent member of the Security Council. This recommendation once again betrays the American determination to find a "middle course" that would produce a separate Taiwan without letting the United States appear to be responsible for engineering it.

Ideologically, irredentism was not a terribly effective argument; the real domestic restraint on U.S. policy was the lack of support for committing American forces to protect Taiwan; everything else up to that commitment was considered permissible.[18] The Joint Chiefs were willing to go even further, moving, by the summer of 1949 toward limited military assistance. If the issue was resisting communism, and if Southeast Asia was at risk, then, as General Omar Bradley, Chairman of the Joint Chiefs, argued, even a considerable delay in the fall of Taiwan would "affect the ability of the Chinese Communists to consolidate their regime."[19] General J. Laughton Collins, the Army Chief of Staff, seconded him, stressing in the NSC 48/1 debates in December 1949 the "diversionary value" of Taiwan: the "Chinese Communist expansion to the south might be deflected so long as they had Formosa to contend with or subdue."[20]

During these months, Acheson proved reluctant to accept his own aides' advocacy of force. He also refused to call Taiwan's status "undetermined." At the time of Truman's January 5, 1950, rejection-of-military-force statement, with numerous State Department officials arguing that Taiwan's status still had to await the peace conference with Japan—there were grounds, they insisted, for its independence—Acheson concluded otherwise: "Whatever political or legal quibbles others might wish to raise, as far as the United States Government was concerned, Formosa was Chinese."[21]

Truman and Acheson's position was not quite the heroic stance it is sometimes portrayed to be. Republican senators, though vehemently attacking Truman and Acheson for appeasement of communism in China, certainly did not wish the rug pulled out from under Jiang as *the* representative of China (the position Jiang would adamantly proclaim for several decades); to do so would have caused a political firestorm in both Washington and Taipei.[22] They wanted military intervention in the strait, not a statement that Taiwan was separate from China. For Acheson to say Taiwan's status was "undetermined," therefore, would have brought vehement criticism from practically all sides and risked extraordinary controversy with America's allies.

Truman's January 5 statement did not put the issue of Taiwan to rest. Nor did it lead to any serious advocacy of recognition within the State Department. Paul Nitze, the director of the State Department's Policy Planning Staff, supported recognition but only as part of a two-China policy whereby the United States would recognize both the Nationalist government in Taipei and the People's Republic in Beijing. Acheson's response to his oral presentation and report, as Nitze later recalled, was unambiguous: "Destroy them all [the written reports] but one; this is political dynamite!"[23]

The documents overwhelmingly suggest that if Jiang had been capable of defending himself with the weapons he had, the United States would have continued to recognize him. Whatever Acheson's distaste for supporting an utterly discredited leader, he encouraged telling Jiang that he had sufficient weapons and supplies if he would use them effectively. "The injunction under which we operate, to deny Formosa to the Communists and to continue recognition to the Nationalists," Livingston Merchant wrote to Acheson, "obviously requires that we give the Nationalists support in the UN and elsewhere; that we provide economic aid to Formosa; and that in other ways, such as permitting them to buy weapons and munitions, we support them in their war against the Mainland with the blockade and bombs."[24] In conjunction with the ECA, the State Department quietly increased nonmilitary funding to Taiwan by more than 90 percent.[25]

Few in the State Department had any real confidence that Jiang could save himself, but, as Merchant said in May 1950, the United States was "not prepared [to] take steps which might contribute to earlier collapse"—such as recognzing the PRC.[26] During the high pressure MacArthur hearings, Acheson asked his aides what to say about Formosa:

Would something along the following lines do: From the time the matter became a question, which was the fall of 1948 to the present time, so far as he [Acheson] knows the policy of this Government has been that the control of Formosa by a power hostile to the United States—or one that might disturb the peace of the Pacific—would be inimical to our interests and that we took, or were to take, whatever steps were possible in economic and diplomatic fields to maintain Formosa as it was and prevent its fall into hostile hands. It was not the policy of the Government until the 26th of June 1950 to commit or promise to commit American forces to bring that about.[27]

Acheson's summary is substantially correct, particularly in the light of Dean Rusk's and John Foster Dulles's actions in the months prior to the outbreak of the Korean War. As Assistant Secretary for the Far East, O. Edmund Clubb wrote, "Rusk is still working toward raising the question of Formosa. . . . Formosa presents a plausible place to 'draw the line' and is, in itself, important politically if not strategically."[28] Clubb himself was not persuaded, but he accepted Rusk's formulation of the problem: "At some time and place the issue with International Communism must be joined, but the present question is whether Formosa is the time and the place, whether our existing military resources are to be committed to that sector in the international arena."[29]

Rusk was one of those who sought to overcome Jiang's ineptitude and the dangers of direct intervention by placing Taiwan under UN protection and then intervening under its rubric. The United States should cut the Gordian knot and occupy the island, then work to create a new nation. A plebiscite strategy would in time blunt the immediate geopolitical costs from both outraged Communists and angered allies.[30] Rusk, drawing on Dulles's May 18 memorandum, proposed to approach Jiang through Dulles, offering a variant of a one-China, one-Taiwan policy or a two-China policy: "(a) the fall of Formosa in the present circumstances was inevitable, (b) the U.S. would do nothing to assist the Gimo [Generalissimo Jiang] in preventing this, (c) the only course open to the Gimo to prevent the bloodshed of his people was to request UN trusteeship."[31]

Meanwhile, a possible U.S.-engineered anti-Jiang coup was also in the air with Rusk a central figure in the discussions. "So long as the Generalissimo and his group of followers remain on Formosa, they will be a source of embarrassment and trouble to the U.S.," he wrote in May 1950. "By experience we know that they will be ready enough to make promises of action desired by the U.S. and equally ready to fail in fulfillment of such promises." The United States could offer the Nationalists massive new military and economic aid if Jiang would agree to resign, if they ceased air raids on the mainland, and if a new government were created and run by "such Chinese and Formosan leaders as the U.S. may designate." A UN trusteeship might then be arranged to offer the new regime protection.

Rusk, however, favored a second option which, "if successful, offers the better long-range possibilities." The United States was to inform General Sun Li-jen, long a U.S.-favored Nationalist military leader, that

> the U.S. government is prepared to furnish him the necessary military aid and advice in the event that he wishes to stage a *coup d'état* for the purpose of establishing his military control over the Island. Sun should also be given ample funds (the total might run into several million dollars) to assist him in buying over the other commanders necessary to such an undertaking; he should be given firm assurances of whatever additional funds he might need in this connection during the early stages. Urgent preparations would have to be made to arrange for the shipment from Guam or some other nearby U.S. base of the arms and ammunition necessary for meeting Sun's military requirements at the outset of such an undertaking. . . . Sun would thus become a more important figure in relation to the scene on the mainland without the handicaps of the Generalissimo and discredited Kuomintang leaders.[32]

A blunt memorandum by Philip Sprouse, who then worked on the State Department's China desk, enumerated the problems. Rusk's argument was that "the political cost to the U.S. arising from charges, within China, of violating China's territorial integrity and within the rest of Asia of a new American imperialism would be largely eliminated by the device of a [local] plebiscite to determine the wishes of the native Formosans." Admittedly, wrote Sprouse, the principle of self-determination had "abstract appeal," but "it is seldom that a nation has willingly given up part of its national domain as a result of a plebiscite and almost never has this occurred with a country in the throes of intense nationalism, as is China." To assume that the Chinese would find any course more palatable because it was accomplished by plebiscite was "unrealistic." Sprouse pointed out that "our sudden interest in Formosan rights at a time when Nationalist control of the island is in jeopardy and when the strategic importance of Formosa to the U.S. has been so warmly discussed, would hardly impress a cynical Asia." Neither the United States nor any of its Western allies had "moved to safeguard the rights of the Formosa people while Chinese Nationalist control of the island was secure, notwithstanding the oppression and atrocities of the Nationalist regime during the past years and notwithstanding the obvious fact that the Formosans hate the Nationalists fully as much as they hate the Communists." As for any moral obligation, "We have no more moral obligation to insure self-determination in Formosa than we have to insure self-determination in . . . Tibet, Bessarabia or Timbuktu." But the United States did have "the clearest kind of obligation, arising from Cairo and Potsdam not to attempt to separate Formosa from China." Moreover, "it is evident that the proposed Formosan state could not co-exist side by side with China without strong and continuous external support and that responsibility for this support would rest with the United States." Mainland Chinese, communist or not, "would not become reconciled to the separation of Formosa from China." Having fathered such a state, "we could never abandon it to China even if developments in China made closer relations with that country highly desirable." It would become "a permanent obstacle to improving relations with China."[33]

Sprouse had put his finger on precisely the point that had failed to move most American officials: the damage that the establishment of a separate Taiwan was likely to do for American long-term relations with China. Acheson had not wished to tie the United States militarily to a bankrupt lost cause, but he did not flinch from pursuing an independent Taiwan, even knowing how strongly European and Asian nations opposed it and how high were the possibilities for its failure.

In a May 30, 1950, memorandum, Rusk proposed steps to neutralize Taiwan (calling for a UN trusteeship and then protecting Taiwan during discussions) which would go further than many officials wished to go. Invoking the domino theory, he insisted that the issue was "within our power to solve . . . if we have the resolute will."[34] American will was not yet resolute, and the hurdles still seemed insurmountable; given a change in context, however, military commitments, dealings with allies and neutrals, and long-term China policy could radically shift gears.

The receptivity of Washington's policy makers to the various plans to separate Taiwan from China forms the essential background for understanding why the decision to place the fleet in the Taiwan Strait on June 27, 1950, created so little controversy among American officials. That decision cut through the contradictions that had lain at the core of U.S. policy by closing off any possibility of recognizing Beijing in the foreseeable future. It ended the intense frustration over the likelihood of Taiwan's being taken over by the Chinese communists. To see Truman, as some historians have, as "reflexively" intervening "in the nearby Chinese struggle" with the outbreak of the Korean War neglects both this drawn-out debate over Taiwan and the reasons the United States found itself acting without support from any of its allies.[35] The Korean War opened an opportunity to shape a new configuration of power in Asia and to shift decisively the context in which the issue of Taiwan had been argued for so many months. Washington then seized the opportunity to use Taiwan as the linchpin of its containment policies—then and ever since.

Recognition

The immediate dilemma facing the United States in 1949 was that few Western powers and few independent Asian countries were willing to withhold recognition of Beijing. Part of the difficulty for the United States was that recognition was inseparable from questions of its broader Asian policy. Recognition of Beijing required breaking with Jiang, and it would have meant ending American efforts to detach Taiwan from the mainland—a step practically no official was ready to take. Acheson and others warned against early recognition (though they never explained what they meant by it) as a move that would only raise the prestige of the Chinese communists at the expense of the United States.

How could the United States combine recognition with the NSC's policy of containing communism? How could containment work unless China was isolated? How could the appeal of China in Japan be countered, especially given continued trade between the two? More immediately, how should the United States proceed with the Japanese peace treaty, now recognized as an agreement that would be central to American power in Asia and the Pacific? All these questions touched on the shaping of the postwar order in Asia, and the answers the United States preferred were not often shared by others. It was not simply domestic opposition that restrained Truman and Acheson, who shared with their critics a deep ideological animus against the Chinese communists. The issue was how to shape a coherent policy.

Before the establishment on October 1, 1949, of the People's Republic of China, the United States had expended considerable effort in deterring other governments from rushing to recognize Beijing and in persuading them to act in concert. Many of the U.S.-proposed conditions for recognition had more to do with setting ground rules for discussions with allies and neutrals than with the Chinese. Now Washington was in an awkward position, as a CIA analysis outlined a few weeks later. Even the NATO countries, it warned, would "react according to widely divergent interests and opinions on the best course to follow." The British might follow the U.S. lead in the short run, but recognition would likely come soon. Southeast Asian governments would recognize Beijing unless the United States gave them "assurances of protection" from the "greatly increased threats to their security" that would follow if they refused to regularize their relations with the new regime. The Soviets, of course, would aggravate the situation by pushing for the PRC to take its seat on the Security

Council, a step that would become more and more likely with the continued decline of the Nationalists.[36]

By November 1949, Britain and India were moving toward recognition; Burma, Switzerland, Canada, Ceylon, Italy, Portugal, Denmark, Norway, Sweden, and Pakistan were expected to follow suit. The United States could no longer speak of moving in concert over the recognition issue; only in South America did the United States appear likely to hold the line.[37] Some American diplomats warned, as Ambassador Alan Kirk cabled from Moscow, that an "indefinite delay followed by ultimate recognition" would have the effect of further ceding "initiative to Soviet policy in China."[38] It was particularly worrisome that the newly elected members of the Security Council—India, Yugoslavia, and Ecuador—were to take their places on January 1, 1950, and Washington calculated that the Chinese communists might then be seated. India, Norway, the Soviet Union, the United Kingdom, and Yugoslavia were likely to vote for unseating the Nationalists; Egypt was wavering, and France was unpredictable. Only Nationalist China itself, the United States, Ecuador, and Cuba could be counted on to support the Nationalists.[39]

For years the official American arguments against recognition are treated with great respect and almost entirely at face value. Harry Harding writes that "discussions of the possibility of diplomatic recognition of the People's Republic within the U.S. government in 1949–50 *invariably* raised the question as to whether the new government in Peking was prepared to meet its international obligations."[40] Why invariably? What international obligations that other governments found largely irrelevant to the issue of recognition were so important to the United States?

Acheson laid down three criteria for recognition in his telegram to Ambassador Leighton Stuart in May 1949 (later the list expanded or contracted as was useful):

a. *de facto* control of territory and administrative machinery of State, including maintenance of public order;
b. ability and willingness of govt to discharge its international obligations;
c. general acquiescence of people of country in govt in power.[41]

These apparently innocuous criteria actually signaled an underlying hostility to recognition. De facto control was an obvious prerequisite, but from the beginning the United States, as the British and Indian governments repeatedly pointed out, had been willing to quibble over the consolidation of Chinese communist government control. Withholding recognition from "a government in effective control of a large part of China" was "legally objectionable," the British stated in August 1949. "Recognition was . . . the correct course in accordance with International Law."[42]

After October 1, 1949, with the Communists clearly in control of most of the mainland, the United States shifted its emphasis. In May 1950, Washington told the British that it was "not at present considering recognition," nor was it likely "to do so in any immediate future," even in the "event of the loss of Formosa," envisioning that such an event would result in "the absence of all relations with China, possibly for some considerable period."[43] There comes a point "where recognition can become symbol of humiliation rather than beacon."[44] Acheson's first criterion had been fully reversed: the United States was refusing to recognize the government in de facto control while recognizing the one that clearly was not.

The second criterion—the ability of the government to discharge its international obligations—was the subject of intense discussion among American officials. A relatively extensive literature documents incidents and acts by the Chinese communists that American officials considered so hostile as to betray profound hatred for the United States. According to Harry Harding, "These perceptions were . . . significantly shaped by the maltreatment of American citizens in China by the CCP in 1949 and the early 1950s. The incidents included the house arrest of consular officials in Shenyang in 1949, the invasion of the embassy residence in Nanjing some months later, the requisition of military barracks in Peking in January 1950, the harassment of diplomats seeking to leave China later that year, and the arrest of missionaries at about the same time."[45]

The United States certainly was quick to label such actions as a failure of the Chinese communists to "observe even minimum standards of international conduct, as evidenced by their treatment of U.S. consular officials in China."[46] A few officials noted that the Chinese communists had reason to challenge the hypocrisy of Western diplomats who insisted on diplomatic immunity even while remaining in a nation whose government their own refused to recognize. Other governments, including those of Britain and India, pointed to the evident problems in the American insistence upon claiming diplomatic immunity in the PRC while continuing both to recognize and in multiple ways to support the Nationalist government. A few even placed this attitude in the context of the old treaty port system, pointing out how such diplomatic claims resonated with the old imperial system of extraterritoriality. Some officials in China were not very impressed by Washington's stress on the Ward incident either (see below). "Communists have shown they respect diplomatic immunities in Ward, Soule, and Olive cases," cabled the consul general from Nanking in January 1950, "and their respect for agreement by [their] treatment [of] UNICEF rep and supplies."[47] And some years later, Japanese officials were still insisting to their American counterparts that the "United States erred in withdrawing its diplomatic and consular officials from China on so relatively small a provocation."[48] But by then the line was set. As Acheson cabled to the U.S. embassy in Djakarta in 1950, the "Chin Commies have had every opportunity to explore our intentions in talks with Amer officials, but have chosen instead to subject them to most brutal treatment and drive them from China."[49]

The few incidents affecting American officials were taken outside the context of the revolutionary upheaval and magnified into attacks on U.S. policy so hostile as to raise questions about recognition itself. In contemporary histories one finds an occasional comment on the difficulties of the Chinese communist leadership in controlling local groups and organizations that might have been acting autonomously or pursuing their own agendas. Yet what struck some contemporary observers was the opposite: the relative absence of disorder, given the enormity of the revolution and the civil war. Consul General Walter McConaughy wrote in early 1950 from Shanghai: "Deplorable incidents have occurred in China during recent months . . . but in this connection it must not be overlooked that real revolution has taken place, and viewed in this light it would appear to me that present revolution in China on whole has been much more orderly than similar revolutions in other countries."[50]

The house detention of the American consul general Angus I. Ward at Mukden in late November 1948, however, still looms large in the assessment of Sino-American relations during these years. "It is our belief that recognition by the U.S. of a Communist regime while the Mukden case is outstanding would be a tactical impossibility," became a diplomatic mantra.[51] Acheson insisted in his memoirs "that the treatment of Angus Ward . . . by the Chinese Communists and their attitude toward our rights and Chinese obligations were precluding recognition."[52] Rusk concurred: the Chinese communists had "not only arrested Angus Ward, they roughed him up pretty badly. So when the Chinese started seeking recognition . . . they did not really seek, and did not so much prepare the way for, recognition by the United States. They selected us as the dragon, enemy number one."[53]

Acheson told the British in December 1949 that it was essential to know whether the Chinese Communists would be acting "in conformity with international law and usage as a civilized power, or as an uncivilized or semi-civilized entity."[54] They had to be taught to respect both "international norms" and the United States—though the two were not always distinguished. If education did not work, John Paton Davies Jr. of the Policy Planning Staff suggested, then "a decisive form of pressure" might. The "dominant faction" in the leadership of the Chinese Communist Party was "unaware of power realities in the world and uncurbed by any manifestation of effective counter-force," and thus their "fanaticism can feel free to engage in the dangerous game of mounting provocation." Davies maintained that the security and safety of some 2,500 Americans residing in Communist China required the United States to prove that it was not a "paper tiger," and for him "the only feasible aim" was "a limited and flexible one—coercion by punitive action or the threat thereof," by which he meant "the highly selective bombing of such installations as arsenals, railroad roundhouses and factories." It was not the few offenses against diplomats and the bitter anti-American propaganda attacks that drove Davies to propose this message; it was the profound loss of American prestige and credibility, along with an inability "to make our influence felt in China."[55]

What was going on here? Sprouse, Chief of the Division of Chinese Affairs, noted on the Davies memo, "Maybe I'm old-fashioned, but this has to be read to be believed."[56] Davies had his own reservations: "George," he wrote Kennan, "I hope this won't seem too extreme. I have misgivings myself."[57] Yet O. Edmund Clubb, who in late 1949 had strongly recommended that the United States explore diplomatic recognition of the PRC, also expressed deep anger over what he perceived as irrational Chinese obstacles to improved American relations: "The Chinese political frenzy is as perverted in some respects as that of Hitlerite Germany, but is less intelligent in even a Machiavellian sense, and there is no reasoning with that madness born of xenophobia and infatuation (contradictorily enough) for the Soviets."[58] Exaggerated and angry fulminations are not policy, of course, but they are evidence of official incomprehension in the face of the anti-imperialism of the Chinese communists. America and the West's traditional forms of involvement in China—economic, diplomatic, educational, religious—were all under attack. As Bacon, the second secretary of the embassy in China wrote, the Ward case struck at the very root of centuries of Western status in China.[59]

Insistence that China honor its international obligations was soon widely evoked as a way of deflecting critics of the U.S. nonrecognition policy. Declared one official, for example, "Chinese Communist leaders have publicly announced their intention to abrogate or not to recognize a number of the international obligations contracted by the present Chinese government including specifically, most of the recent treaties and agreements between the U.S. and China."[60] One looks in vain in these documents for any careful study of what U.S. officials thought this meant, but it didn't really matter; the specifics were not the point. Two issues were key: how to deal with Western allies and Asian nations preparing to recognize Beijing, and the insistence that the Chinese be denied any acceptance as a revolutionary regime.

American officials who were fully aware of the actual CCP stands argued that the international community should reject them.[61] They opposed any dealings with a revolutionary regime, but the Chinese communists pointed to the earlier negotiations with the Soviet government over the Czarist treaties as a precedent. Few other powers took serious exception to the CCP position. The Canadians were expected to extend recognition "without any assurances of respect for international obligations or of minimum standards of conduct on the part of the Chinese Communist regime." They, like the British, argued that the "criteria of control of territory and acquiescence of the people seemed to be fulfilled and that no reference had been made to the question of obtaining commitments from the Chinese Communist regime."[62] Among the Asian countries, some fully sympathized with the Chinese position. Others, like India, raised the obvious question: why should the United States withhold recognition of communist China while continuing to recognize the USSR? After all, the Soviet Union had not lived up to the obligations made by the previous regime; why should the United States insist that the PRC assume the obligations of the Guomindang? For India, the point of recognition was not friendship but the ability to interact, and it was quite acceptable for this interaction to be based on "sound unfriendliness."[63] As the Indian ambassador to China commented, he did "not expect friendship from Communist government China through fact of recognition," but India would be in a position to "protect its interests" and proceed on a basis of "sound unfriendliness."[64]

Acheson's third criterion—the "general acquiescence" of the people to the government in power—also proved highly elastic. Acheson himself slightly rephrased it in a meeting with Senator Alexander Smith: acquiescence alone was not sufficient; there also had to be "an evident will on the part of the people to accept the government that had been established."[65] But then, popular support of the government was not sufficient either, as Under Secretary of State James Webb told Indian officials; it was also important to consider whether the new Chinese government "would act in the interests of the people of China."[66]

Yet in the late 1940s even some American consular officials in China were having difficulty figuring out who was acting in the people's interests—not to mention who was acting legally. Was the United States? The continuing American alliance with the GMD and the flagrant American approval of and even assistance in such acts as its bombing of Shanghai (among other targets), the blockade of the coast, and the massacres in the cities from which the Guomindang was withdrawing raise serious doubt about the legality of American policy.

The consul general's dispatch on the 1949 killings in Chongqing, the old wartime capital, was not viewed as anything unusual by Washington officials, who were well aware that the GMD was acting similarly in a great many other places. "Mass killings of Communist suspects, leftists, 'dissidents' . . . refired public hatred of KMT. . . . Corpses thus far recovered. . .at least 975 persons killed, mostly innocent. . . . Total killings exceed by many times total persons executed by Communists [in] Shanghai since takeover. Chinese popular opinion here regards killings as senseless butchery." In this case, though, there was at least some acknowledgment of American dirty hands: "Owing to America's continued recognition 'support' of KMT and failure to voice any official or popular disapproval of [its] killings, the affair has helped to . . . prove that American policy in China is cold-blooded, tyrannical. . . . [S]imilar bloodbaths . . . will achieve nothing but more hatred for the KMT and hostility toward U.S. for 'condoning' such actions."[67]

The Nationalists' bombing of Shanghai and other cities was equally damning. Bombing had been launched from Taiwan for months; the attack of February 6, 1950, the consul reported, resulted in more than one thousand civilian casualties. These measures were being carried out with American military equipment and American bombs, and given this obvious support of Jiang and the GMD, it didn't require "communist propaganda" to inflame the Chinese people. At a minimum, the consul general implored, the United States should take "vigorous and effective steps to dissuade the Chinese authorities on Formosa" from further attacks; moreover, the United States should publicly deplore them. The United States did neither, protesting only that some of its own property and interests had been hurt in the bombing, and the attacks continued.[68] The British repeatedly protested to Washington.[69] As late as May 1950, the United States was still supporting the bombing. And while acknowledging that the Nationalists' blockade of the Chinese coast created an opportunity for negative propaganda, Washington justified continuing it on the grounds that it caused a "multiplication of economic and administrative difficulties" for the Chinese communists.[70]

Some historians note that U.S. military assistance to the Nationalists had been suspended by this time, though the Nationalists retained the right to purchase needed military goods on the open market. In Washington, those requests led to continued debates; for example, should the U.S. sell them Napalm? (Yes, but the worry was that it might fall into Communist hands.) As with the bombings and the blockade, the United States had little intention of decisively limiting the GMD. As Sprouse said to the British consul, Hubert Graves, "The Chinese Government would not lift its 'blockade' unless it were told that all U.S. aid would be stopped immediately unless it did so. This . . . was not a measure which, in my opinion, the U.S. government would take."[71] In Washington, officials belabored the unfulfilled criteria for recognition; in China, American consular officials, insecure in their ambiguous diplomatic standing, were less worried by the restraint imposed on Angus Ward than about the consequences of the continuing

GMD brutality. While Acheson kept pounding Chinese communist infringements of international law, the British pointed out that Washington was flouting it in the areas of recognition and the blockade.

Increasingly alone, the United States insisted that it would not be pushed into recognition. In September 1949, Charles Yost spoke for most of the State Department when he wrote that since "prompt recognition" would signify American weakness, recognition "would presumably not take place for a considerable period and only after hard and prolonged bargaining." The delay would be useful, providing the United States with more time for its new containment measures to take effect. Trade should be restricted, and the United States needed to undertake "strenuous propaganda operations in China designed to discredit them [the communists] in the eye of their own people." He also called for various covert operations.[72] By February 1950, as the Office of Far Eastern Affairs put it, "The United States continues to recognize the National Government of China and is giving no serious consideration to recognition of the Communist regime."[73]

Washington, in other words, had invoked Acheson's three essential criteria for normalizing relations with China and then refused to apply any of them to its own actions. It refused to recognize a regime that controlled most and eventually (except for Taiwan) all of China, and it recognized a regime that obviously did not control the country. It invoked international norms that were vague and contradictory, and even though it was fully aware of GMD brutality, it never conceded any illegality in its support of the GMD. It spoke in rhetorical defense of Chinese territorial integrity while ensuring the division of the country.

However bitter the Chinese communists felt toward the United States, if Washington had recognized them as the government of China and as the legitimate occupant of the Chinese seat in the United Nations, it is hard to imagine that they would have refused recognition or threatened American diplomats.[74] The United States concluded that the Chinese communists wanted recognition.[75] What it did not acknowledge was the extent to which it refused to separate recognition from other issues. Although most historians treat American policy of the period as though the issue were about recognition of a government (albeit a measure bedeviled by domestic pressures from the right), it was not that simple. Recognition was just one aspect of a broader strategy the United States was developing for dealing with the Chinese revolution, and that is why it took so long to come.

Isolating China and the Remaking of Asia

More than any other factor, the isolation of China was the essential ideological and geopolitical touchstone for shaping a multilateral global capitalist system in Asia. Though the economic reorganization of Japan was an immediate issue, equally critical for American policy makers was the collapse of the European colonial systems and of traditional trading Asian patterns. That issue was inseparable from the Japanese one but not reducible to it. Because it was not yet clear how to move effectively toward a new order, the problem was less a matter of what U.S. objectives were than of how to achieve them. Seeking to isolate China would have profound consequences—some intended, some not—for the development of international capitalism throughout Asia.

In the face of the enormous upheaval and rising nationalisms sweeping the continent, the resources at hand seemed far too limited to cope with the discontent: the enormous expense that a Marshall Plan for Asia would entail made it economically and politically impracticable.[76] The Marshall Plan, it was argued, had addressed an already existing European industrial basis that had interdependent economies, with the result that the aid funds spurred the economies. Capitalist restructuring, not nation building, had been the basis.[77] Despite the consensus, then, that the Asian economic order had to be reshaped, the resources at hand were meager and the hurdles staggering.[78] The issue of China's relationship to Asia's economic reordering was a pivotal one, but until June 25, 1950, there was very little hope that it could be effectively resolved.

Asia presented a further economic problem. Whereas governments there considered themselves "more or less self-contained units," the United States was committed to "integrating that region into the world trade pattern."[79] Socialism was a powerful aspiration among nationalist leaders in Asia, "closely associated with the desire, however unrealistic, to industrialize and achieve some degree of autarchy"—an understandable enough response to the vulnerable state in which European development of export economies had left things but still one inimical to U.S. interests. Concluded one State Department official, "The U.S. with its evaluation of private enterprise runs squarely against the state socialism of Southeast Asian leadership."[80]

Although American leaders sometimes advocated a kind of Asian regionalism, NSC documents reflect a deep uneasiness with any regionalism not economically interwoven with U.S. global priorities. In the late 1940s there were also ongoing arguments over a possible embargo against China. Would such an embargo push China further toward the waiting Soviets? Would it "worsen Chinese Communist economic prospects"?[81] The most pressing problem was that other nations made it evident that they would not go along with an embargo. "It is of course clear," Merchant concluded in a memo to Acheson, "that we could not expect the support of any other major Western nation for a program of economic warfare against China."[82]

That lack of support went even further, of course; it was understood as rooted in deep-seated historical grievances elsewhere. Nehru's views were deeply unpopular in Washington because he challenged the globalism underlying Washington's efforts to contain China. "Looking again at the historical perspective," he wrote in November 1950, "it is to the interest of Western Powers to prevent China and India getting too friendly. Oddly enough, I think that such friendliness is not to the liking of the Soviet Union also. Therefore, a certain encouragement is given by these Powers to anything which may spoil our relations."[83]

Among Washington's allies unenthusiastic about an embargo, Britain was concerned with its investments and its position in Hong Kong and was eager for Japan to have markets in China so that it would not move into the sterling area of Southeast Asia.[84] Other nations had their own reasons for keeping their distance. A draft report for the NSC on trade policy with China concluded, "It is difficult to see how the necessary degree of concerted action could be obtained."[85] As one official noted, "If we should cut off trade while the others permit theirs to go freely, it is likely that we would not impede in any significant way the progress of restoration of the economy, while we would at the same time put our people . . . in a very difficult position."[86]

Japan

Without a tenacious U.S. effort to isolate China, it is hard to imagine how Japan could have been brought so successfully into an alliance with the United States and its economic relations with China largely severed. The embargo of China shaped Japan's options, requiring the United States to open its own markets and to grant concessions to Japan on patents that would have been extremely difficult to push through without the Cold War ideology that drowned out the domestic opposition. The outbreak of the Cold War led to offshore procurement programs and other massive military expenditures that opened up new possibilities for Japan.

Japan's relation to Asia and the viability of its economy had preoccupied American officials since 1947. Of special concern was Japan's growing dependence on expensive raw materials, its politically restive population, its weak export potential vis-à-vis the United States, and, above all, the cost of supporting its stagnant economy. The Chinese revolution, the decolonialization struggles throughout much of Asia, the loss of Japan's empire and its merchant fleet, the efforts of European nations to retain control in Southeast Asia, the bitter memory of Japanese aggression: all these factors had left Tokyo in an extremely tenuous position. Though there was no consensus in Washington, the fear was widespread that Japan's exclusion from trade with Northeast Asia and China "would so drastically distort Japan's natural trade pattern that economic stability could be maintained only if the U.S. were prepared to underwrite substantial trade deficits on a continuing basis"—assistance Washington felt it could not afford.[87]

By late 1949, despite various discussions and plans, little headway had been made in developing Japanese trade with Southeast Asia and the United States. An NSC analysis that saw in trade between Japan and China a mild hope for a wedge between the Soviet Union and the Chinese communists became strong and unequivocal on more immediate economic matters: "Japan's economy cannot possibly be restored to a self-sustaining basis without a considerable volume of trade with China, the burden of Japan on the United States economy cannot be removed unless Japan's economy is restored to a self-sustaining basis and U.S. interference with natural Japanese trade relations with China would produce profound Japanese hostility."[88] Kennan's own assessment was stark: "China is . . . inextricably intertwined with the problem of Japan," and without trade between the two the problems of the Japanese economy would remain.[89] General Marshall agreed: "I don't think you can call the Japanese-Chinese trade exactly a 'must', but it comes pretty close to being that."[90] The alternative for the United States was to continue to pour money into Japan, an unacceptable long-term policy. Trade thus had to be permitted.

"Having made various projects for the development of Japanese trade over the future," concluded one state department official, "Japan must trade with North China and Manchuria and Korea and Formosa if it is to become self-supporting again. . . . Our feeling in the short run is that Japan stands probably more to gain from a continuation or a resumption of trade relations with China than through attempting at this time to get along without China and continue to depend exclusively upon the United States subsidy."[91]

In documents assessing Chinese-Japanese trade relations, two major points emerge. First, the viability of the Japanese economy far outweighed the significance of the wedge strategy.[92] Second, trade would certainly resume unless the United States prevented it, and over time it was "dubious" that the U.S. *could* restrict trade. Japanese leaders did not believe that trading with China would give the Chinese political leverage over their internal affairs, but they did think that "Sino-Japanese trade was indispensable to the economic well-being of both countries."[93] What worried NSC officials was the matter of long-term political orientation: Japan "would undoubtedly wish to maintain normal political and economic relations with the Communist bloc, and in the absence of open hostilities, would probably resist complete identification either with the interests of the United States or the Soviet Union."[94] Keeping Japan from adopting this neutral position was a critical issue for the Japanese peace treaty talks and inseparable from discussions of trade and relations with China.

These arguments took on new meaning with the outbreak of war in Korea on June 25, 1950. In the short run, to be sure, even after an American embargo on Chinese goods was put into place in 1951, there still lingered questions of Sino-Japanese trade, the role of Southeast Asia in the Japanese and European balance-of-payments problems, and the role the American market would play for Japanese goods. But underlying those questions was now an adamant American determination to avoid any risk of an independent Japanese foreign policy—which meant cutting off any possibility of trade between Japan and China. The key to controlling Japan (unlike China) lay in Washington's shaping the international environment in which the Japanese economy functioned. What emerged was a determined American effort to seize the opportunity offered by the war to pursue its economic vision of Asia's (and above all Japan's) role in a global order.[95]

British Imperial interests verses American Globalism

British governmental debates over colonial policy in the early Cold War years stood in striking contrast to the sweeping ideological and economic globalism of the NSC documents.[96] Britain's great difficulty was that its policies, as Anthony Eden put it, placed "a burden on the country's economy which it is beyond the resources of the country to meet."[97] By the early 1950s the country had essentially opted to rely on the United States to protect its declining colonial system.[98] The dilemma was that American multilateral trade arrangements seemed to pay little heed to British economic needs: hence the appeals within Britain to retain what was left of its empire as a means of propping up its share of the international market.[99]

Strong American opposition to the British sterling bloc and London's doubts about rapid trade liberalization both formed part of the background for British efforts to retain some independence over the handling of communism, particularly in Southeast Asia.[100] Singapore was of great strategic significance as a naval base and communications hub. Malaya, with its tin and rubber, was critical to the British economy, and any communist successes in French Indochina, Burma, Thailand, or Indonesia would make the struggle in Malaya all the harder. Lack of access to rice-growing areas would also complicate Britain's relations with its colonial territories.

Yet even as the British were pursuing a multilateral regional defense pact, they were criticizing Washington's ideological hostility toward China.[101] London favored containing China, not isolating it. This was, simply put, the great difference between the American and British positions on almost every issue—a difference with significant implications. From the British perspective, containment without isolation made sense. Such a policy would enable Britain to hold on to Hong Kong and thus protect its remaining economic interests in China.[102] Britain's advocacy of Sino-Japanese trade (and of recognition) reflected its concerns over Japanese expansion into its sterling areas in Southeast Asia and over the competitiveness of Japanese goods in British markets.[103] London was furious at Washington's continued undercutting of its sterling trade areas, whereas Washington insisted on its role as global arbiter, balancing Southeast Asia between the needs of its European allies and those of Japan.[104] Meanwhile, London sought to conciliate the major neutralist countries of the Colombo powers group, especially India. The problem, as the British commissioner-general in Southeast Asia warned, was not just to protect the area from communist insurgents but to deal with the growing "misunderstanding and hostility" between Asia and the United States before their differences became "irreconcilable."[105]

Britain and the United States also differed over the significance of nationalism, which the British perceived as a far greater threat to their empire than communism. As stated in one paper prepared by the Permanent Under Secretary's Committee for Colonial Affairs, "Since on the one hand nationalism almost invariably contains an actual or potential element of xenophobia, while on the other Great Britain has wider interests in the world than any other nation, we are bound to be the worst sufferers from nationalist activities." Like the Americans, the British distinguished between "intelligent and satisfied nationalism" and "exploited or dissatisfied nationalism," the latter reflecting a state of mind in which, as one analysis phrased it, "any sense of grievance, injustice or inferiority is magnified out of all proportion. This can lead to a state of unbalance amounting in the worst cases to hysteria. This state of mind is highly infectious."[106]

But in distinguishing between acceptable and anti-imperialist nationalist movements, American officials were trying to moderate anticolonialist sentiments in ways the British could not; to the British, Washington's approach was part of the problem. They recognized that nationalist movements had drawn great impetus from World War II and the withdrawal of Western powers from various areas. But as far as they were concerned, the ascendancy of the United States, "whose own origins were in successful revolution against Great Britain, and whose attitude towards 'colonialism' is, to say the least of it, equivocal," surpassed even "International Communism in encouraging revolt against the Western powers."[107]

Not that the British were not deeply concerned about Communism. They considered it "obvious that when an area falls into Communist hands its economic and trading value to the Western world becomes greatly reduced while Western capital assets are liquidated with little or no compensation."[108] Communist here refers to nations that have opted out of the international capitalist system, and in this sense the issue was international. But as far as London's preoccupation with nationalism as a threat to its colonial interests went, the unsettling image of a monolithic communism (or of China as a satellite) was ideologically not very useful.

For the Americans, the British position on China was hopelessly inadequate. The British government, an American official wrote in July 1950, based its approach on the position that "Communist China cannot now be described as a police state. To use this term would be to compromise 'our most valuable asset'—a strict regard for the truth. Communist China does not engage in the arrest and forceful suppression of political opposition; rather it deals with opposition largely on the intellectual and psychological plane through the use of propaganda, inspired popular movements, and personal persuasion." The U.S. position, in contrast, stressed the violent, tyrannical use of force. The Americans regarded Chinese communism as an externally imposed doctrine; the British pointed to the great popular movement led by Mao and the CCP. American reports stressed the bloodiness, brutality, and manipulativeness of land reform; in British reports land reform was "still the most potent weapon in the Communists' armory, and the basis of their appeal to the peasantry."[109]

What was most disturbing to Washington was that the British argued that "the main lines of Chinese policy, as its external manifestations are likely to affect the West, are those that would be (or have been) followed by any strong Chinese government." The British "information policy" drew back from placing "too great an emphasis on the Chinese Communists' large standing Army."[110] Taiwan and Tibet would require many of China's available troops, and others were already tied up in agricultural production and public works projects and would be for years to come. The idea of a China poised to overwhelm its neighbors was thus misleading. The great majority of its troops would continue to be engaged in agricultural pursuits.

And whereas American propaganda highlighted every example of Soviet involvement, the British insisted that "it is not wise to play up Russian domination and penetration in Communist China. The Chinese are not likely to take kindly to attacks upon their Government as an alleged victim of Soviet imperialism. Propaganda of this type would not serve the purpose of drawing the Chinese away from Russia."[111]

The Americans responded in frustration. In the words of one diplomat, the British had "overlooked the real danger which Chinese Communism poses— conquest of the rest of Asia," and in attempting "to be fair in evaluating the

Chinese Communist regime as it now exists," they were "prone to lose sight of its future potentialities." Most questionable of all was Britain's "apparent belief that the Chinese communist leaders, provided the West does not hopelessly alienate their affections, may some day turn away from Moscow."[112]

Kennan's Skepticism and the Ideological Triumph of Containment

By 1949, George Kennan was feeling increasingly out of step with several tendencies in American foreign policy. His contrasting views on Germany, his objection to the building of the H-bomb, and his reservations about NSC 68 have all been far more extensively examined by historians than has his growing uneasiness over U.S. policy in Asia, at the core of which was the question of how to evaluate the Chinese revolution.

As head of the Policy Planning Board, Kennan had argued that the communists could "not make a dangerous military power out of China."[113] There were five major industrial centers of power in the world, and in Asia only Japan was critical. Japan, not China, was vital to American national interests: "Japan and the Philippines will be found to be the cornerstones of such a Pacific security system and . . . if we can contrive to retain effective control over these areas there can be no serious threat to our security from the East within our time."[114] In balance-of-power terms, Kennan thought China was not likely to become important for some time. He further argued that the very enormity of the problems facing the Chinese communists once they came to power would keep them from becoming militarily expansionist—the country's economic backwardness, its "uncontrollable crude birth rate," its subsistence level of living.[115] He challenged the conclusions of NSC 48, which he thought placed too much stress on military factors and "implicitly imputes to the USSR a perhaps unjustified capability speedily to dominate the mainland areas of Asia and to develop these industrially backward, poverty stricken, disease ridden regions to a level of strength in the modern military sense which would constitute an early threat to the security of the U.S."[116]

Kennan saw a weak China that was likely to be a drain on Russia's immediate strength. The two nations had long histories of conflict; the Kremlin could not live with an "equal" China; and the incompatibility of their two economies would provide fuel for disagreement. In any case, there was not much the Soviets would—could—do for the Chinese economy, nor did they want to see China become a strong military power.[117] With the Chinese communists having risen largely through their own efforts, he saw a basis for a Chinese Titoism.

Initially, various CIA reports echoed Kennan's views, and military strategists, with some exceptions, agreed. Those views were to predominate, in one form or another, until the success of Chinese armies in the Korean War. But in another sense the notion of a weak China was blended into the notion of China as a Soviet satellite—thus justifying a strong American presence in Asia to contain communism. By early 1950, however, the State Department saw China emerging with a pronounced agenda of its own:

> The Chinese Communists show an exceptionally strong interest in Southeast Asia. In their evident intention to exert domination in the area they are doubtless egged on by the Soviets. Hong Kong, northern Indochina and Burma are all objects of Chinese irredentism. Their propaganda, however, is aimed at the whole area. They clearly hope to use the Chinese merchants in the various Southeast Asia countries as instruments in their policy, apparently believing that they can win over the merchants despite their bourgeois background.[118]

Kennan, too, was concerned about the impact that the triumph of the Chinese communists might have on Southeast Asia, particularly Indochina. But he did not consider a noncommunist Indochina as absolutely critical to American security, and he was equally cautious about any firm commitment to South Korea. If Washington could come up with a viable policy toward Japan, he insisted, it could attain its basic security objectives in Asia.

But by the early 1950s, such a view was no longer considered adequate—even to the extent that it ever had been. The triumph of the Chinese communists had not resulted in Washington's finding immediate practical steps to implement a sweeping strategy to contain China, but that was now the pronounced ideological direction of its policy. The debate was almost entirely over means and their regrettable paucity: with military power limited and economic priorities elsewhere, there seemed little possibility of creating an effective containment policy, because containment without isolation seemed to raise insurmountable problems. Ideologically, Washington had no doubt at all that China was an enemy or that its revolution was a threat to the economic and strategic future of Asia.

Noting the revolutionary changes sweeping Asia, NSC 48/1 had called for the containment of communism there. The JCS may have been in conflict over weighing the priorities of Asia versus Europe and the nature and kinds of military commitment that were called for, but by early 1950 they were firmly committed to a highly activist position: China "is the vital strategic area in Asia," they concluded, and they were "firmly of the opinion that attainment of United States objectives in Asia can only be achieved by ultimate success in China." The JCS urged recognition of the Nationalist "port closure" of communist China as a de facto blockade, called for covert operations in Southeast Asia, stressed the imperative need to hold the region, and appealed for early implementation of military aid programs in Indochina, Burma, the Philippines, Indonesia, and Thailand.[119]

American policy was not really one of "letting the dust settle" during these years. Yes, there was an intense effort to hold the line, waiting to see what opportunities might open for implementing the widely agreed-upon containment. But the ideological intensity of those times belies the imagery of *passive* waiting. As General Marshall noted in a discussion of China policy at an October 1949 round table: "I always want to move in first. On the other hand, it is equally dangerous that the first doesn't get you in before it is the proper time to get in. So timing is a vital consideration in this."[120]

The unexpected war in Korea provided his proper time.[121]

4

ISOLATING
CHINA

General MacArthur described the difference between the attitude towards death of Westerners and Orientals. We hate to die; only face danger out of a sense of duty and through moral issues; whereas with Orientals, life begins with death. They die quietly, "folding their arms as a dove, folding his wings, relaxing, and dying." With that, MacArthur folded his arms, and sighed.
—Averell Harriman, Memorandum of a Conversation with General MacArthur, June 8, 1951

Nothing indicates the direction of Washington's Asia policy more strikingly than its decision to send the Seventh Fleet into the Taiwan Strait during the first forty-eight hours of the Korean War. With the resolution of the debate over whether (though not necessarily how) to defend Taiwan came a renewed determination not to recognize the People's Republic of China and to keep it out of the United Nations. The decision's far-ranging implications were evident by the summer of 1950 in Washington's refusal to consider any resolution of the Korean conflict in those months that involved discussions of Taiwan, the China seat in the UN, or recognition of the PRC. Even though the United States was well aware how unpopular its actions were in Asia and Europe, its intransigence on Taiwan was merely the precursor to its adamant opposition to any general settlement of Asian issues.

The tenacity with which the United States refused to withdraw from the Chinese civil war became, in the following years, the strategic linchpin of its Asia policy. Isolating mainland China served both immediate and long-term goals. Taiwan could not now be "abandoned," and in this context a two-China policy came to look "moderate" in Washington (though not in Asia). Although Congress did influence the administration's China policies at times, there is little to suggest that it deeply affected basic American strategy.

Supporting Taiwan became the single most useful way of containing China *and* integrating Japan and other Asian countries, economically and militarily, into an American security system in Asia. No matter how India and other Asian countries might disapprove, nothing gave Washington greater immediate leverage in the region than its commitment to a rival Chinese government. For all of Acheson and his colleagues' disgust with Jiang, Taiwan offered a costly and difficult but indispensable way to isolate Beijing diplomatically and sustain Washington's efforts to promote containment and nation-building policies throughout Asia. After the outbreak of the Korean War, isolating China and remaking Asia—economically, ideologically, and militarily—became inseparable goals.

No other major power shared America's ideological preoccupation with China because no other nation had similar Asian and global concerns—but once the Korean War began, Washington became far less concerned about standing alone. Allies and neutrals alike understood the implications of Washington's massive commitment and the uselessness of raising any direct challenge. Before the clashes between UN and Chinese troops in November 1950, the United States had found it difficult to hold the line on Taiwan.[1] Afterward, it became confident that it could get its way.

Ernest Bevin, the British foreign minister, told the British cabinet in August 1950, "In the Far East . . . the United States have tended to be a law unto themselves since the end of the war, with results which have been far from happy"—an assessment few Asian governments would have disagreed with. The U.S. Defense Department flatly argued, in fact, that "the United States is now the dominant power in the Western Pacific," and in "any conflict of interest arising between the United States and other Western Powers" it would be essential to "insist that the United States security considerations in that area be overriding."[2] Although the administration might not broadcast this conviction, few ever doubted Washington's belief in its right to act on it.

With the start of the Korean War the United States noticeably heightened its ideological attacks on China—as puppet, as co-conspirator, as threat to Southeast Asia. "Peiping is at present time co-conspirator with Kremlin on Korean aggression and is actively engaged in plot against Indo-China," Acheson wired the U.S. ambassador in Britain on August 13. "If internatl Commie orbit has in fact decided to wage war by all convenient means against non-Commie world, our problem is to alert non-Commie world to nature of danger and not of trying to buy off Commies by token appeasements which cld only increase their prestige without reducing their appetites in slightest degree."[3] With the ideological line now tightly drawn and new means at hand, other elements in the isolation of China were quick to fall into place.

The Korean War: The Wedge and the Puppet

The Korean conflict initially reinforced, rather than challenged, American officials' conviction that China was subordinate to the Soviet Union, and they spoke of the war as part of an international Kremlin design. Their prism was still nationalism versus communism, and Beijing was, potentially or actually, a satellite. "The North Korean venture," a CIA review stated, "amounts to a laboratory test of the advantages the USSR might gain by fighting a war of limited objectives and limited liabilities through the medium of puppet troops."[4] In this "war by proxy," a State Department cable suggested, "centrally directed Communist Imperialism has passed beyond subversion in seeking conquer independent nations and now resorting to armed aggression and war."[5] It was "a Soviet move" that had been "decided on after the most minute examination of all factors involved in the Far Eastern situation"; the objective was "called for by the Kremlin's global strategy, as distinct from North East Asian strategy"; and there was "no possibility that the North Koreans acted without prior instruction from Moscow."[6] The Koreans themselves were all but dismissed as insignificant actors, and as for the Chinese, senior American officials initially found it difficult to understand how the war involved their national interests or to believe that they might have committed troops on their own initiative.[7]

The Joint Chiefs—though not MacArthur[8]—agreed (as a September 6, 1950, report concluded) that the Soviet Union was the "true enemy." The USSR had apparently entered "a new phase, which involves military operations on the Soviet perimeter in Eurasia by the armed forces of its satellites." Evaluating the situation in Korea required focusing on Soviet, not Chinese, intentions. "Although the Chinese Communists undoubtedly resent United States interference in Formosa and our position with respect to their desire for membership in the United Nations, Chinese Communist large-scale intervention in Korea would have to be considered as motivated by the USSR." China itself had "relatively little interest in Korea"; Chinese intervention, therefore, "would indicate a pattern of aggression, dictated by the USSR, in which Communist China would have subordinated its immediate interests to those of the USSR." From China's perspective, the JCS noted, Taiwan was a far more critical issue. But Communist Chinese control over Taiwan would pose a direct threat to Okinawa and the Philippines and, indirectly, to the American military position throughout the Far East. Taiwan, therefore, must be held "irrespective of the situation in Korea"—it could not become part of the bargaining over Korea.[9] The JCS, as well as the State Department, also saw the Soviet Union seeking to draw China more firmly into its embrace by encouraging conflict with the United States. "It would be greatly to the interest of the USSR for the United States to become involved in a general war with China," one JCS study concluded.[10]

The nationalism-versus-communism belief is directly reflected in the initial American opinion that China would not intervene in Korea. In the first few hours of the war, American officials suggested the efficacy of making China suffer for the Soviet Union's act by intervening in the Taiwan Strait. If Washington stiffened its position to "include effective measures to forestall Chinese Communist capture of Formosa the Chinese Communists might come to view the Korean adventure as a move by the USSR in disregard of Chinese Communist interests" and the challenge from a "newly militant posture of the U.S. in the Far East" as "a threat that had all but been created by Soviet blundering."[11] It was not yet clear "whether the USSR [would] force the Chinese Communists to give open military support to the Korean operations or to start a new operation elsewhere in the area." China "was unlikely to commit military forces to operations outside China on its own initiative, but would almost certainly comply with a Soviet request for military action."[12]

This initial response defined Washington's attitude toward China in the following months. The nature of the wedge, however, was changing.[13] The hopes of weakening the Sino-Soviet alliance now rested on escalating American hostility toward China and rapidly expanding the U.S. military presence in East Asia. ("Skillful manipulation might drive a wedge between the Chinese Communists and the Kremlin.")[14] Soviet global aims—not Chinese concerns over the security of its borders or Taiwan—remained the primary focus.[15] As for recognition or a Chinese seat in the UN, they were dismissed as beyond consideration.[16]

In September 1950 a CBS interviewer asked Acheson whether the Chinese might intervene in Korea. Pointing to a map of Asia, Acheson explained that Manchuria, Xinjiang, and Outer Mongolia were all objects of Soviet imperialism, and sending Chinese troops to Korea would only weaken the Chinese presence in those areas. "Now, I give the people in Peiping credit for being intelligent enough to see what is happening to them," Acheson said, and added:

> Why they should want to further their own dismemberment and destruction by getting at cross purposes with all the free nations of the world who are inherently their friends and have always been friends of the Chinese people as against this imperialism coming down from the Soviet Union I cannot see. And since there is nothing in it for them I don't see why they should yield to what is undoubtedly pressure from the Communist movement to get into the Korean War.[17]

The tendency to interpret signs of Chinese independence and China's pursuit of its national interests as expressions of hostility toward Moscow made Washington particularly inept when it came to evaluating China's reaction to the Korean War. The wedge was never anything but a way of dismissing the Chinese emotionally, writing off hostility to the United States as a sign of communism and hostility to the Soviet Union as a sign of Chineseness. It was a wholly ideological construct that could stress now one aspect, now another, neither one rooted in reality. In moments of enormous anger the communist aspect flared up, which is why, when the Chinese entered the war, Acheson and Truman so furiously invoked puppet and satellite imagery.[18]

In their meetings with Clement Atlee in December 1950, at a moment when American forces were reeling from the Chinese attack, Truman and Acheson once again dismissed British views on Chinese nationalism: "The Chinese Communists were not looking at the matter as Chinese," Acheson insisted, "but as communists subservient to Moscow. All they do is based on the Moscow pattern, and they are better pupils even than the Eastern Europe satellites." Though the Soviets and the Chinese might have some differing interests—"The Russians are no doubt pleased with the idea that we might be fully engaged in war with the Chinese Communists who are acting as their satellites"—Truman agreed that the Chinese "were complete satellites. The only way to meet communism is to eliminate it."[19] Atlee, in his turn, reiterated the British position that the Chinese could "be Marxists and yet not bow to Stalin. . . . Chinese civilization is very old and is accustomed to absorbing new things. They may wear the Red Flag with a difference."[20]

The wedge theory could never account for the Chinese communists' defense of China's immediate national interests.[21] There was rarely any sense that China might see itself threatened by U.S. actions in Taiwan, Indochina, or in Korea, and so, "barring a Soviet decision for global war," a CIA memorandum concluded, Chinese Communist intervention in Korea "is not probable in 1950."[22] Few issues facing Washington that summer and fall were more critical. As UN forces crossed the 38th parallel and moved rapidly north, Washington had to concede privately that China did in fact have motives for intervening: to enhance its prestige and contribute to a "major gain for World Communism"; to retain electric power along the Yalu; to prevent a "Western-type democracy" from establishing a common boundary; to encourage anti-Western trends in Asia; and to find an excuse in the war for its "failure to carry out previously announced economic reforms" and justify claims for "maximum Soviet economic aid to China." On the other hand, the motives against intervening included the damage it might do to rebuilding the Chinese economy; the renewed hope that opponents of the regime might take from a war with the United States; the loss of any possibility of entering the United Nations; and, of course, the military costs. But once again—perhaps above all—intervention would "make Peiping more dependent" on the Soviets and "increase Soviet control in Manchuria." It would risk opening China up to the accusation of "act[ing] as a Soviet cats paw."[23] It would be a pattern of aggression "dictated by the USSR, in which Communist China would have subordinated its immediate interests to those of the USSR."[24]

A JCS staff study conducted early in the war concluded that even though some thought had been given to China's coming to North Korea's aid, such considerations were "overshadowed by the far graver consequences that could derive from Russian action." The study points to numerous reports devoted to the intentions and capabilities of the USSR, "in contrast to the very few that even touched upon the question of Chinese entry." On June 30 the JCS considered a report prepared by the Joint Strategic Survey Committee (JSSC), titled "United States Courses of Action in Korea." Of the four possible developments that were contemplated, "all were based on various actions that might be taken by the Soviets; none were concerned with Red China."[25]

Not even after the Chinese entry did this vision of a Kremlin-controlled international communist movement change. In part, this ideological conviction worked to limit the war's expansion: the USSR was the enemy; European interests had to be protected and remained a far higher priority. It was MacArthur who most passionately disagreed, arguing that the Chinese commitment of troops "was largely motivated by the Chinese themselves," not the USSR, and was a further example of "Chinese imperialistic aspirations."[26] Implicit in his arguments was the conviction that Asia should carry a far greater weight in American strategic thinking.

John Paton Davies Jr. thought the Chinese communists might simply "be on the rampage, . . . reckless." In a comparison that would be used more frequently over the next fifteen years, he argued that unlike the "adept and practiced" provocateurs in the Kremlin, "Mao and company are bigots and novices."[27]

Generally, though, China's entrance into the war did not challenge the Truman administration's insistence on the preeminence of the USSR. Since the real issue was Soviet communism's global interests, dealing with China's national interests—recognition, the United Nations, Taiwan, the security of its borders—would only fuel the "aggressor's appetite." And since Korea did not involve legitimate Chinese national interests, there was no need to deal with Beijing, only Moscow. American negotiators similarly justified the exclusion of the PRC from the Japanese peace talks in 1951: "The Peiping regime had no views of its own and . . . its views were those of Moscow."[28]

Unless this ideological context is taken into account, it is difficult to explain the reaction of Acheson and others when—as Acheson wrote in his memoirs—"on October 3 Zhou [Enlai] summoned Pannikar [the Indian ambassador to Beijing] to the ministry to inform him that if American troops crossed the [38th] parallel China would enter the war. . . . Zhou's words were a warning not to be disregarded, but, on the other hand, not an authoritative statement of policy."[29] Various reasons have been given for the dismissal of such a stark warning. U.S. officials received the warning through several channels, including copies of Pannikar's own dispatches to the Indian prime minister.[30] But Washington tended to regard the Indian ambassador as pro-Chinese and thus "untrustworthy."[31] Some thought Zhou's comments marked nothing more than a "war of nerves" between India and China.[32] Jawaharlal Nehru, who thought this attack nonsense, urgently appealed to London and Washington not to regard Zhou's statement as a bluff. As he wrote a few days *after* the Chinese intervention, what China said "at the time, she meant. . . . [S]he felt that her own security was threatened. We received her messages, clear and explicit, and we passed them on to the other Great Powers. . . . India had plenty of critics in the Western world and we were considered very simple and naive in the art of politics to be taken in so easily by a few threats. Now the world sees that it was something more than bluff."[33]

Nehru went on to outline China's reasons for fearing the American advance, which he agreed was a threat to legitimate Chinese interests. It was China, not the United States, that had tried to avoid an extension of the Korean War; China, not the United States, that had been dealt repeated affronts to its dignity and great-power status. Though appalled by China's invasion of Tibet, he nevertheless conceded that Tibet was Chinese territory. The Chinese revolution was part of an Asian liberation from the grip of Western imperialism, an epochal event with which the United States and Britain had yet to come to terms. This was the context, he continued, in which Korea was to be viewed: "The basic fact of the situation of the Far East is the emergence of China as a strong, stable, and centralized State. . . . The whole balance of power has changed . . . because of this new China. Very gradually a realization of this is coming to the Western countries; but the process is slow. It will have to be much faster, if disaster is to be avoided."[34]

Pannikar had much the same attitude. China, he wrote, had to be understood as a great power—and treated as such: "The position of a country which commands the allegiance of 450 million people and which has authority over the largest single organized community in the world cannot be that of some secondary position to any other country."[35] No such statement about China is to be found in any of the American diplomatic records from the early 1950s.

The Propaganda War

As with policy, so with propaganda. The American ideological war against China was predicated on the image of a puppet regime selling out Chinese national interests to the Kremlin. The central objective of American propaganda, therefore, was to "stimulate Chinese nationalism and direct it against the policy of the Chinese Communist regime linking China to the USSR," to sow "fear and hatred of Soviet imperialism and of its symbols in China such as

Soviet advisors and troops," and to "stimulate attitudes among the Chinese that will remove China from the Soviet orbit." A corresponding effort sought to persuade the Chinese that they could achieve their national interests "only in association with the free world"; a strong and independent China was incompatible with an alliance with the USSR.[36]

As in the late 1940s, this psychological warfare aimed to convince the Chinese that their "growing economic hardships [were] the consequence of placing Soviet interests ahead of Chinese interests" and that Soviet policies were the "continuation of Czarist imperialist aggression against China."[37] The message was clear: the United States had

> pointed out the prodigality with which the Communist command has expended Chinese and Korean lives in carrying out Moscow's power drive; the brutal indifference of the Commie rulers to human life, and specifically to the lives of their own forces; the criminal subservience of the Peiping puppets in the sacrifice of Chinese fought on a foreign battlefield in the sole interest of Soviet imperialism. . . . We have stressed the truth that Moscow, and Moscow alone, gains from Chinese losses in Korea.[38]

The propaganda campaign painted the Chinese national character in strident primary colors. As Assistant Secretary of State for Public Affairs Edward W. Barrett put it, the Chinese "are prone to hate foreigners," and the Chinese communists had used this xenophobia against the West; now the West could "throw it back in the face of the Russians, and their Chinese spokesmen, the Chinese Communists." The Chinese fear of foreign exploitation was so intense, and past resentment toward the West and Japan so great, that even the slightest Russian arrogance could be fanned into a conflagration of Chinese anger. The wretched poverty of China was also a boon for propagandists: hardships could be blamed on the Russian-induced war effort. As the American embargo worsened conditions, antigovernment discontent would only grow; the Chinese, after all, had a "shrewd canniness" in weighing "costs and profits, to translate grandiose schemes into 'what's in it for me?' terms." They would come to see that they were suffering because of the acts of their government and then turn on its friendship with the Russians.[39]

American propaganda focused on three key groups in China: the CCP, the armed forces, and the elites. First, the United States tried to create schisms in the CCP and ultimately to force an open split with Moscow. Little in the way of concrete action was required. The policy relied on Moscow's overreaching itself and creating a reaction that could then be exploited by propaganda.[40] Second, though difficult to reach, the armed forces were most vulnerable to the charge that "in Korea Chinese are being made to fight Russia's war."[41] Third, the educated classes had been the people most closely tied in the past to the Americans and were therefore presumably the "most vulnerable to American psychological warfare." Intensely nationalistic, they sided with the Chinese communists for purely nationalistic, not ideological, reasons. If their allegiance could be broken, internal dissidence would spread, and a new leadership might emerge. Businessmen, too, were likely to become quickly dissatisfied.[42]

The impact of the psychological warfare is hard to assess. For example, the groups it targeted were often ones the Chinese communists were most concerned about: intellectuals, students, "class enemies," and wavering elements. Were both sides agreeing that these were objectively real social forces made uneasy by CCP rule? The ambiguity provided a useful double-edged psychological-warfare weapon for the United States, first shaping its propaganda for those groups, then attacking the CCP as paranoid for mobilizing its own resources against those very groups.

Psychological warfare was useful to the United States in another way as well: it deflected attention from the rational Chinese response to such American actions as the military buildup and intervention in Taiwan. According to the State Department, "The leaders of the Chinese Communist government are obsessed with the notion that forces hostile to them exist and are working positively for their destruction. . . . Foreign forces regarded as hostile and as having previously aided their internal enemies, are still situated in positions surrounding mainland China and are regarded as seeking to isolate, subvert, and perhaps attack physically Communist China."[43]

The program of appealing to Chinese nationalism and depicting the Soviets as hungry imperialists, however, faced one enormous obstacle: Jiang himself. Still, the fact that few Truman administration leaders had illusions that Jiang offered any ideological message for the Chinese people at all reinforced Washington's view that "outside propaganda and covert involvement were the most promising means."[44]

Propaganda and Policy

Washington's approach was predicated on the conviction that China's role in Korea "must be regarded as *an integral part* of the unfolding strategy of world communism, of the Kremlin-Peking attack on the free world, and definitely not as an isolated Chinese-U.S. or even a Chinese-UN affair."[45] From the highest levels of propaganda and policy making to all levels of implementation, this was the prevailing line. Policy shaped propaganda, and propaganda expressed basic policy assumptions; they were inextricably bound.

Consider, for example, a 1951 State Department effort to send a message through intermediaries to elements in the Chinese communist leadership. The cultivation of these contacts, like Acheson's "openness" toward recognition in late 1949, were part of the strategy to drive a wedge between nationalism and communism, and thus between the Chinese and the Soviets.[46] Meetings took place beginning in January 1951, with Charles Burton Marshall and John Paton Davies Jr. of the Policy Planning Staff; an unnamed "second party," who was an American; and an unnamed "third party" whom American officials believed to be connected with key members of the Chinese leadership.[47]

The Americans were both blunt and hostile. They presented their case by setting events in the broadest historical context. "Two general developments" in the previous four or five centuries had shaped the "present crisis in world relations." The first was the expansion westward out of Europe, "generally in the following sequence: discovery, exploration, conquest, colonization, development, independence, and cooperation." But everyone knew that those "imperialist phases" were now over: "In seeking liberation from western imperialism the Oriental peoples are contending against something that isn't there any more." The other great development "began roughly 350 years ago. It is the expansion from Eastern Europe. . . . The cardinal fact of the eastern expansion has been that the Russians have not developed any mode for the conduct of affairs except that of domination." The Western expansion evolved toward freedom and cooperation; the Eastern did not. When once it had been the West that was imperialistic, now "the Soviet system represents imperialism. It is out for conquest and subordination of other peoples. . . . Its ideas devour all other ideas just as its power system absorbs and subordinates other peoples. The subtle danger of the combination of Russian power and the communist idea is that it enables the Russians to penetrate conquest by dissimulation. Imperialism is carried on in the name of liberation."[48]

American documents often complained of the insistent communist tendency to lay out a worldview before getting down to details, yet here the Americans were doing it. Proceeding from this broad historical context, they defined the Soviets as America's "mortal enemy. To us that is the most important consideration in the world picture." As long as Peking remained publicly aligned with Moscow, there would be no basis for diplomatic relations, admission to the UN, or discussions about Taiwan. "The crux of the question is whether Peiping looks at things through Moscow's eyes." The Chinese had to understand that the difficulty between Washington and Beijing came down not to issues but to the situation that those "in determining positions in Peiping have put themselves in thrall to the enemies of the United States. To the degree that Peiping has come to serve others it cannot serve its own interest. Its own interests dictate peace and accommodation with the United States. The present situation serves only Moscow's interests. It cannot be eased until the Chinese make the fundamental decision to cut the cords to Moscow."[49]

The discussion next turned to various Chinese leaders and generals. Who was susceptible to an anti-Russian line? If divisions at the top led to civil war, that would hardly be a calamity for the United States. The Americans then spoke of the great restraint their country had shown in Korea.

> This restraint has not been pleasant for Americans. If we followed the dictates of our emotions, we would take naval and air action against the Chinese on the mainland. We would lay waste their cities and destroy their industries. We would let the Chinese people know the terrible potential consequences of the irresponsible actions taken by the men in power in their government. . . . If [greater] war comes, and China is still acting in Moscow's interest, China would certainly count on no immunity from our wrath.[50]

That these meetings—together with a follow-up in Hong Kong—ultimately yielded no results is less significant here than the illustration they provide of the way policy, tactics, and propaganda were bound together. The issues—Taiwan, recognition, the UN—were secondary. Only a Chinese regime hostile to the USSR could be acceptable to the United States. There was no middle ground. Even as the Korean War wore on and some officials began to see increasing signs of China as a more independent "junior partner" of Moscow, the Truman administration never altered its main ideological weapon against the PRC.[51]

Taiwan and the Isolation of China

The deployment of the Seventh Fleet into the Taiwan Strait abruptly overcame the immediate contradictions in U.S. China policy. Now there was no possibility of recognizing Beijing in the foreseeable future or agreeing to Beijing's assumption of China's UN seat.[52] Publicly, the United States justified its policy by arguing, in Truman's words, that "the occupation of Formosa by Communist forces would be a direct threat to the security of the Pacific area and to United States forces performing their lawful and necessary functions in that area." The strait was to be "neutralized": Nationalist attacks on the mainland were to be prevented and the island protected from the communists by the U.S. Navy and Air Force.[53]

American officials repeatedly emphasized their evenhandedness: the "neutralization policy" was meant to lessen the "provocation" for the Chinese communists to intervene in the Korean War, and the United States was not intervening in the Chinese civil war; Formosa was an "international issue." Although few other governments agreed, one Defense Department memo noted: "The U.S. must dissociate its action in Formosa from the concept that the occupation of Formosa by the Chinese Nationalists or the Chinese Communists is an internal affair, and, instead, propound the concept that our actions in relation to Formosa have been to maintain status quo of Formosa and to prevent armed conflict in and over this territory which does not yet belong legally to either of the contestants."[54]

Some analysts acknowledge that the Chinese communists could not, of course, have been expected to accept such an argument. "To China," writes the scholar Harry Harding, Taiwan was "an internal affair in which no foreign country had the right to interfere. To the United States, in contrast, the Taiwan question was an international matter in which Washington had legitimate interests and concerns. This fundamental difference of perception lies at the root of the dispute."[55] The latter perception was an overwhelmingly American one. Following Truman's announcement, "a majority of the countries of the United Nations were quick to disassociate themselves from the policy of the United States with regards to Formosa. As a result the United States finds itself in the position of defending the integrity of Formosa and the Chinese Nationalists without assistance of any other United Nations powers."[56]

Nonetheless, in the eyes of Washington the Korean War had circumscribed its option with respect to Taiwan. If the United States should fail in Korea, one ORI report stated in the dark days of early January 1951, as the Chinese military was rapidly pushing south, then it would be in Taiwan "that the Chinese Communist challenge, if it is to be met at all in Asia, can best be met, for here American air and sea superiority could best be employed." Although it was "unfortunate" that the United States was tied to a regime that was "a heavy political liability" and that America would probably have to act without the support of its allies, "simply stated, the situation in Korea tends to drive us to what would be in and of itself a wrong course of action."[57]

The British, the Indians, the Indonesians, and the Japanese all expressed strong opposition to both the deployment of the fleet and the alliance with Jiang, factors that, far from preventing the spread of the war, risked its immediate expansion; all saw Washington's actions as direct intervention in China's civil war. "Viewed through Asiatic eyes," U.S. Ambassador Lewis W. Douglas wrote Acheson from London, "Formosa belongs to China, quite irrespective of what sort of Government it may or may not have." Therefore, Asians would see Beijing's efforts to exercise its sovereignty over Formosa not as

> an act of aggression but merely a normal, natural, and legal measure. They could not understand why the U.S. should intervene by stationing its fleet in a certain position to prevent a lawfully established and recognized government from performing its normal functions over the Island of Formosa and its inhabitants. . . . The free Asiatic peoples . . . believe this change to

have been induced by purely strategic considerations on the part of the U.S. and by the dislike which the U.S. has for the Chinese People's Republic combined with the desire to maintain another outpost of the Western world from which the Orient could be dominated by the West.

And if China invaded Taiwan? Then, Douglas concluded, "we would find the world divided with practically all of the Asiatic countries siding with the Chinese Communists and indeed some of the Western European countries."[58] Even after Chinese intervention in the Korean War, "India, Indonesia, Burma, Ceylon, Pakistan, may be expected to criticize. . . . India wants Formosa turned over to Communist China. . . . Indonesia, which is strongly influenced by India, would probably have the same attitude. Ceylon, Burma, Pakistan would oppose U.S. support to the Nationalist Government."[59]

Charlton Ogburn of the State Department's China desk reported that the Indonesian ambassador to the United Nations, Mr. Soedjatmoko, had argued that there was a "widespread feeling in the UN that the world is being carried into a general war because of the policies of the U.S. towards Formosa and indicated that he himself is of that opinion." In response, Ogburn recounted, "I then asked if he was certain that he would recommend that we acquiesce in a turnover of Formosa to the Chinese Communists and reconcile ourselves to a settlement of Indochina between the French and Ho Chi Minh. Mr. S. replied that he was quite willing to be quoted and that this was what he recommended." Ogborn told Soedjatmoko that he had been "shocked" to hear India's ambassador in Washington, Madame Pandit, say that the Chinese Communists were "not aggressive" and that "they had been provoked by events on their borders." Soedjatmoko, too, was surprised, since his embassy's rule was that no one was to speak out on China and the Korean question; still, he added, if they did, they would all undoubtedly agree with Madame Pandit. Ogburn tried a final argument. "I said I was convinced that if we should turn over Formosa to the Chinese Communists as the price of some kind of settlement of Korea that the next thing we knew the price of reaching a settlement with the Chinese Communists would be turning over Indochina to them, then Thailand, then Burma, then Malaya." Soedjatmoko disagreed: "In that event, the Communists would not be Chinese, but Vietnamese who would have every interest in preventing China's penetration of Indochina."[60]

The Pakistani ambassador, O. A. Baig, was equally blunt. "The people of Asia," he told Dean Rusk and U. Alexis Johnson, "consider that by taking unilateral action to prevent Formosa falling to the hands of the Chinese Communists the United States took the first overt act against the Chinese and, therefore, the Chinese intervention in Korea is not entirely unjustified." It was puzzling, he noted, that whereas Korea was considered a UN matter, the United States had acted unilaterally over Taiwan. Could not the United States see that the situation was "comparable to the American Revolution and the U.S. should consider its intervention in Formosa in the light of the attitude it would have taken if a European power would have declared a *cordon sanitaire* around a portion of the United States to have prevented consolidation of the gains of the American revolution"? Rusk, in response, invoked the basic American ideological and strategic rationale: U.S. actions must be "considered in the pattern of overall Communist aggression rather than a local Korean or Asian problem"; Chinese intervention could not be viewed as "having been provoked by the U.S. policy toward Formosa, but rather as a part of the pattern of Communist aggression and, therefore, indivisible from any aggression anywhere." The issue was communism. "Whatever policy China's national interest may dictate," Rusk concluded, "the experience with Communist satellites in Europe has shown that once a country came under Communist domination, it was thereafter difficult for it to act except at the dictates of Moscow."[61]

Nehru was probably the single most forceful noncommunist Asian leader among these critics. "To associate Formosa in any way with this [war in Korea] was wrong and dangerous," he wrote to his chief ministers on September 1, 1950. "It was a challenge to the new China which, according to us and all those who have recognized this China, has a right to Formosa, if not immediately then in the near future." The fact that "the remnants of the Kuomintang regime are still in Formosa and challenge China and are given protection, is a constant irritant to the Chinese Government and people. It is more than an irritant; it fills them with fear and when people are excited and afraid, anything may happen."[62]

Acheson, however, cabled both Bevin and Nehru that it might be one thing to turn "Formosa over to REP of CHI as constituted at time of Cairo Declaration; quite another to turn it over to Peiping regime which is acting in support of Moscow conspiracy against the free nations." In separate cables he listed identical reasons that the United States would not and could not recognize Beijing. Acheson's seven reasons are a remarkable assembly of arguments:

1. Peiping has shown little indication of a genuine desire to estab normal relations with other states.
2. It has singled out Amer citizens and interests as special objects of hostility.
3. It has made no pretense of accepting and carrying out the internatl obligations of China.
4. There is still room for doubt that it exercises effective control throughout the mainland of China or is supported by the Chinese people.

5. It is lending support to Communist insurgents in the Philippines, Malaya, Burma and elsewhere, has recognized Ho Chi Minh and is actively interfering with efforts to transfer polit power in Indochina by peaceful processes.

6. It is cooperating with a degree of Sov penetration of China which can only lead to China's dismemberment.

7. Its recent defiance of the United Nations in connection with the Korean situation is, of course, a new and grave factor.[63]

Nehru saw in this list a profound American refusal to acknowledge the great changes sweeping Asia and the intensity of the nationalistic response to colonialism and imperialism. In 1952 he argued that "the big blunder committed by some countries, notably the U.S.A., in refusing the new China, has been one of the principal reasons for all that has followed. It was patent that peace in the Far East could only be established by some agreement of the major powers interested and among these were obviously China and the U.S.S.R."[64] Neither he nor the British were at all persuaded by Acheson's reasons. As far as they were concerned, the only international aspect of the Taiwan situation was U.S. involvement, which they saw as intervention in the Chinese civil war and a potential course toward war with China.

These arguments did nothing to dissuade the United States from its long-term military commitment to Taiwan. The documents show little debate over the commitment itself, only over the way to handle its consequences. O. Edmund Clubb argued that the fleet's position should be maintained in part as a response to "continuation of Chinese Communist aggression against Formosa (and why not Tibet?) [which] constituted a threat to peace in the Pacific."[65] Long before the Chinese began fighting the Americans in Korea in November 1950, this act had drawn a line. As Acheson cabled to the Indonesians, "We have emphasized that we consider conclusion inescapable that while musical strains issuing from Peiping are Chinese, [the] organist is Russian."[66] That was the ultimate justification for intervention.

Once the fleet was in, almost no one in Washington argued for pulling it out. Clubb noted to a receptive Rusk that "the logical alternative to withdrawal of the seventh fleet, whether with or without the advice of our friendly supporters, would appear to be the much closer welding of the Nationalist forces into the American defense system."[67] Discussions in the State Department suggested that the United States had only three options:

(1) Washington could announce that the Seventh Fleet would remain in place, armistice or no armistice, "for the simple reason that there is no evidence that Peiping has renounced its hostile designs and the

armistice has not in fact restored peace and security to the general area."[68]

(2) Washington could "take the wraps off Chiang Kai-shek" with "no commitment to assist him in his defense or help him other than by military aid and advisory program in any attack he may contemplate against the mainland."[69]

(3) Washington could "pull the 7th Fleet out but state that the U.S. will send it back on a defensive mission in the event that Formosa is imminently menaced from the mainland." The harsh reality, however, was that should the fleet be sent back, "we could not secure UN support for such action . . . and hence we would have to accept charges of unilateralism, imperialism, and so forth." Moreover, pulling the fleet out, even with a firm promise to return if necessary, would be a devastating blow to morale on Formosa, thus further increasing the chances of invasion.[70]

The first option won the most favor. The JCS strongly endorsed it: "Irrespective of the situation in Korea the United States [should] plan to continue the present policy of denying Formosa to communist forces" and immediately grant aid to the Nationalists.[71] Any modification of this position "would probably result in the loss of Formosa."[72] Appealing to the UN was hazardous; other nations could not be counted upon to see Beijing's "aggressive designs." Acheson wrote to Nitze in July: "I do not see how we can put out of our control—by invoking UN action, for instance—the denial of the island to the Communists so long as (1) we wish to maintain our present, or a better position, in the Pacific, and (2) as long as the Chinese and the Soviets are a militant menace there. If this is so, we ought to define positions on the subject which will give us adequate time and try to make others understand the facts of life."[73]

The United Nations presented a problem because, first, Washington feared being charged with aggression and, second, there was such limited support there for its position.[74] Publicly, Acheson could not rule out a role for the UN. In November 1950, with delegates from the PRC headed for a UN session in December, Nitze formulated Acheson's position before a congressional committee. The UN, he said, was useful because it offered the possibility of avoiding two unacceptable outcomes:

a. A commitment into the indiscernible future on a distant position, as to which we alone would be involved, since unity among allies on this issue is lacking, and perhaps unattainable.

b. Withdrawing our support and interposition altogether and thus allowing the position to go over to a hostile regime.[75]

Internal discussions after the start of the Korean War focused on the scope and character of Washington's commitment to the Nationalist regime. The officials arguing for full cooperation with Jiang were a minority during the Truman administration, though the advantages of such an approach were obvious: the GMD already maintained an armed force (though how competent was debatable); it was a functioning government; and it offered a relatively secure base. The major drawback was obvious, too: the regime was a "political dodo." Neither Clubb nor most other officials could forget Jiang's brutality and corruption, and they intensely disliked supporting him.[76] Jiang had been "so completely discredited in China" that he would obtain practically no support from any groups likely to oppose the communists: "Any opposition movement would have to hold the promise of a 'new deal' rather than a reimposition of the old discredited Kuomintang system."[77] According to a September 1950 memo, "Any critic is in dire danger of being arrested as a Communist and disappearing. There is no such thing as a system of justice."[78] The issue, then, was how to use American power to alter the deplorable political and military situation.

Some officials examined means of easing Jiang out of the picture, though cautioning that "our purposes would be best served were any changes on Formosa to occur in such a way as to permit constitutional continuity . . . thereby obviating questions of recognition and Chinese representation in the UN." American actions should be "as unobtrusive as possible"; any leader labeled "an instrument of American policy" would face an unnecessary handicap. A genuine anticommunist opposition revolt on the mainland would supply the proper context to "create a lever for exerting pressure on Jiang."[79] Or, as O. Edmund Clubb put it, "In the event that changes are achieved along a line which brings to the Nationalist leadership a man or group of men exercising much more attraction than the present hierarchy over the mainland, a strong blow would have been struck at the Peking regime which depended for much of its 1945–49 success on the popular dislike and distrust of Generalissimo Chiang Kai-shek and his immediate clique."[80] Such a development would provide the context for cultivating a third-force strategy, both in the overseas Chinese community and, ultimately, in China itself.

The debates over Jiang were intense during the early months of Washington's commitment to Taiwan. Acheson certainly did not wish the military protection of the island to be viewed as a defense of Jiang. But the pressure to create a defense relationship with the Generalissimo was strong, and he had his advocates not only in Congress but also in the Defense and State Departments. The Fox Report on the GMD military capacities led to a military assistance program in the fall of 1950, "a victory for the views of General MacArthur, Secretary Johnson, and the JCS, not over the active opposition of the State Department, but rather over its reluctance and its distrust of the Kuomintang." The report was "optimistic about Nationalist chances of successfully resisting a Communist attack provided material assistance was given."[81] State remained more pessimistic. As Livingston Merchant wrote, "I think the regime is rotten and beyond reclamation. I think the army will prove useless in combat, whatever the state of equipment and training."[82]

By the middle of 1951 the movement toward Jiang was solidifying. It was a direction in which few other Asian countries were willing to follow Washington. Many saw the GMD as "hopeless and unacceptable." Great Britain, too, was highly critical. The overseas Chinese ("apart from a few opportunists") could not stomach Jiang, and the United States knew it would be hard to mobilize others behind its policies in Southeast Asia. Moreover, Jiang had proved impossible to work with in the past, and there was little reason to believe he would countenance an effective military that would challenge his system of cronyism.[83]

The Refusal to Negotiate on Taiwan

Many Washington policy makers hoped that Jiang would ultimately either go along, however unwillingly, with reforms or be swept out. Then perhaps Taiwan could be held up as a beacon of what a noncommunist Chinese government could accomplish. The island was naturally rich; if the cost of maintaining a large military establishment could be handled, a compelling alternative to the mainland might develop.

After June 25, 1950, the United States had no intention of negotiating away its position on any issue relating to Taiwan. Though Washington had directly involved China by committing the Seventh Fleet in response to the outbreak of the Korean War, its policy thereafter was to insist that the issue of "aggression" in Korea be kept completely apart from issues relating to China; otherwise, as Acheson said, aggression would be rewarded. Truman told Atlee that negotiations over the status of Taiwan would be unpalatable domestically, but he also knew that such negotiations, in either the UN or an Asian context, could result in the virtual isolation of American policy.[84]

Some American officials initially argued against separating the issues of Korea and China, if for no other reason than to offer some encouragement to China to stay out of Korea. Philip Jessup, Washington's representative on the UN Security Council, proposed that the United States urge India to begin discussions with Beijing on several questions: was China ready to establish its diplomatic relations on the basis of "respect for international obligations and for the normal rules governing diplomatic and consular intercourse"? If the Chinese communists were seated in the United Nations, were they "prepared to cooperate in the world of all UN organs"? What guarantees could they give that they would "not, particularly through the overseas communities in Southeast Asia, seek to subvert and overthrow established governments"? Jessup also wanted India to "ascertain their views concerning the desirability of placing the Formosa question and perhaps the Indochinese question before the United Nations as part of the whole problem of re-establishing peace in the Pacific area."[85] But it was precisely such linkage that Washington came so adamantly to oppose. It clearly understood that it would find itself a minority among Asian governments if these issues were linked and that there was little support for its intransigence on Taiwan, China's role in the UN, and recognition.

Nehru was particularly vocal in his opposition to the American effort to isolate China. Not only was recognition necessary, he argued, but also an understanding of the Chinese position. The determination to exclude China from the United Nations was detrimental to both the universality of the organization and the peace of Asia. "This China representation in the Security Council has become farcical," he noted in March 1950, "because the old Nationalist Government of China has been completely driven out of continental China. . . . The whole future of the United Nations is imperiled by this question." There was no way to deal with the issue of Taiwan, he insisted in July, unless the PRC was brought into the UN at the earliest possible time.[86] In August he once again appealed to the UN to admit China.

Nehru's ambassador to China, K. M. Pannikar, had told him that Taiwan, not Korea, most concerned the Chinese:

> In my opinion what has caused greatest resentment in China is not so much the military protective measures that America has taken to safeguard her lines of communication to Korea, but the fact that American air and naval forces *are giving protection to a clique* which claims to de jure government of China and whose representatives under American patronage is [*sic*] representing China in international bodies. I would like to emphasize that Chinese government is persuaded that the ultimate objective of America is to bring down the People's Government of China. They are convinced that Chiang Kai-shek and his group are being maintained by Americans in Taiwan and upheld in the Security Council in order to give legal cover for future aggression against mainland. This may be groundless fear but she can adduce many arguments in support of it, such as alliances with Siam, intervention in Indochina, MacArthur's visit to Taiwan, America's implacable hostility to Peking Government's claim in Security Council.[87]

Nehru had instructed his ambassador to show these dispatches to the Americans. As the American ambassador in India commented to Washington after reading them, Pannikar was arguing that the Formosa issue might be defused if the United States would give China assurances on one of the following alternatives:

(A) After the Korean situation was eased, U.S. would withdraw protection KMT remnants in Formosa; or (B) if UN would accept Peking as sole rep China; or (C) if UK, India, and other powers which had recognized Peking could give assurances that they would use their influence to see that U.S. did not aim putting forward Chiang legal cover for aggression against it or at keeping KMT remnants in Formosa permanent under U.S. protection.

Ambassador Henderson's response was quite typical: "I did not believe U.S. government would be inclined to give such assurances so long as there was danger that China or Russia might directly or indirectly engage in further acts of aggression in the FE [Far East]." Rather than exploring Pannikar's points further, he closed the discussion, saying that in case of "Peking aggression . . . U.S. might be compelled to take steps to break system and industries which could be used for military purposes."[88]

The issue of Taiwan had become central; any move to expel the Nationalists was portrayed as a direct challenge to American military involvement in the Taiwan Strait. Officially, the United States argued that the questions of Communist withdrawal from South Korea must take precedence over all other issues—a position the British went along with in the Security Council.[89] At the same time, Washington wanted to make clear that it fiercely opposed any solution in Korea that would pave the way for China's entrance into the United Nations, though it was noted internally that "if the Communists propose or agree to a settlement which, as regards Korea, is satisfactory but which has as a condition the cessation of U.S. 'intervention' respecting Formosa, the U.S. would probably find itself under heavy pressure from its friends and allies to accept this condition."[90]

The American refusal to reconsider the Seventh Fleet's role or the nation's increasing commitment to the defense of the island was strikingly evident in the Atlee-Truman discussions of December 1950. The British prime minister essentially proposed that the United States consent (directly or indirectly) to discuss a cease-fire agreement that would include the issues of recognition and Taiwan. Acheson was adamant that any such consent would amount to giving "concessions," which would only encourage communist aggression, and Truman agreed: "If we surrendered Formosa, [he said], we left our flank open. Our position would then be wrecked. . . . He just could not agree to that. . . . He was not, however, in any mood for an unnecessary surrender to give in to China which is actually the Russian government." Returning Taiwan was not deemed sound militarily, and it "was not sound from a political point of view here."[91]

There was simply "no presently achievable solution for the disposition of Formosa," and "little room for negotiations at this time." The Seventh Fleet could not be withdrawn and the United States no longer wanted to say whether the island should ultimately be returned to China. As an internal report noted, "It appears that there is no PRESENTLY achievable solution for the disposition of Formosa which will satisfy United States policy objectives."[92] As Under Secretary James Webb stated, "The United States Government has no intention of modifying its objectives with regard to Formosa in return for a settlement in Korea."[93]

A cease-fire in Korea, wrote Troy Perkins of the China Desk, thus risked "embarrassments for the U.S. with respect to Formosa and [would] require difficult decisions." Negotiations over Korea would probably reveal that the American Taiwan policy is "(1) an obstacle to any general settlement with Communist China and to efforts to weaken or break the Peking-Moscow linkage, or (2) a cause of serious disunity and division in the Free world." But any shift in the American position on Taiwan might well result in its loss to the military power of the communists. And if the issue went to the UN, there was "no way of guaranteeing what the final decision of the UN would be."[94]

An October 24, 1951, memorandum to the Secretary of Defense from General Omar Bradley, chairman of the JCS, asserted that "the problem of the status and ultimate disposition of Formosa should not be submitted to an international conference for examination prior to the restoration of peace and security in the Pacific area, in any event not before the satisfactory settlement of certain international problems." Bradley's list of issues that should first be dealt with included a "political settlement of the Korean problem"; the "rearmament of Japan" sufficient to enable it to contribute "materially to its own defense"; a "settlement of the Indochinese problem"; and, last but not least, the "establishment or restoration of a regime not aligned with or dominated by the USSR on the Chinese mainland."[95] What would be left to negotiate after all this—and with whom—is unclear. As an NSC staff study concluded, the problem was that there "was no tenable basis for an over-all peace settlement," given U.S. interests in the Pacific.[96]

From one perspective, American policy had come to a dead end. A policy based on the notion that the Chinese communists were selling out the country's territorial integrity and independence to the Soviet Union had ended with the United States intervening in the Chinese civil war: using its military power to divide the country; supporting guerrilla movements in the provinces; and shoring up a loser whom most Asian governments thought deserved to lose and whose government, it was universally understood, could not survive without American support. In an increasingly nationalistic Asia, Taiwan was a new Western dependency.

Yet from another perspective American policy was highly successful in reshaping Asia. The Korean War allowed for a mobilization of American power in Asia to such a degree that Washington could significantly dictate policy to other Asian countries. However deep the resistance of various Asian governments, however effectively they sometimes opposed U.S. wishes, they now had to deal with a powerful American military, political, cultural, and economic presence as a fact of life.[97]

Concessions versus Isolation: Two Memorandums

Washington understood that its Taiwan policy constituted "an obstacle to any general settlement with Communist China and to efforts to weaken or break the Peiping-Moscow linkage."[98] And for several months in 1951 it feared that a settlement in Korea might undercut its position on Taiwan. This fear lay behind the lack of enthusiasm that greeted a March 1951 memorandum from Robert Strong of the China Desk titled "Proposal for an Offer by the United States to the Chinese Communists for a Settlement in the Far East." Strong agreed that splitting China from Russia should be our "prime objective" and reiterated the basic line regarding communism versus nationalism. But then he shifted ground, arguing in favor of a general settlement that would offer the CCP reasons to declare its independence. He proposed the following U.S. "concessions":

1. Recognition of the PRC and exchange of Ambassadors.
2. U.S. support for PRC claim to UN membership.
3. Withdrawal of U.S. political and military support from Formosa, to be followed by withdrawal of economic support at such time as Peiping demonstrates good faith.
4. Guarantee that U.S. forces will not cross the 38th parallel.
5. Include the PRC in negotiation and signing of a Japanese peace treaty.
6. Negotiation of a Sino-American treaty of friendship, commerce, navigation, and a consular convention. No special privileges to be sought in China by the U.S.
7. Present economic and financial embargo to be dropped by the U.S. when good faith shown by PRC.
8. U.S. support for the territorial and administrative integrity of China, including inclusion in any regional security pact.

In return the United States would demand:

1. Abandonment of the present PRC policy of "leaning to one side."
2. Settlement of Korea problem recognizing the security interests of China and Japan (and the Soviet Union).

3. Negotiation with regard to treaty and other obligations inherited by the PRC from the Nationalist government (including U.S. Government property).

4. Non-intervention in the affairs of border states and reference of the Indochinese struggle, and any border or other such questions involving China, to the UN.

5. Acceptance and observation by the PRC of international standards of conduct (this provision may be unnecessary and provocative).

Strong's basic point was that the United States needed to offer China *something*—even "recognition, UN membership and Formosa"—as an incentive for its distancing itself from the USSR.[99]

Little, of course, came of this proposal, which countered the efforts to isolate China that the Korean War had opened up. As a December 28, 1951, memo for the Secretary of Defense from General Bradley and the JCS put it (anticipating the prevailing view of the Eisenhower-Dulles years):

> We believe the possibility to be remote that our making of gratuitous concessions: (1) might lead to real modification of the CC attitudes in the present circumstances; or (2) would justify measures which might increase significantly either the military potential or the political prestige of CC, or which would discourage Chinese anti-communist forces. While we cannot foresee clearly the final answer to an aggressive CC closely linked to the Soviet Union, we are convinced that in present circumstances Chinese aggression must be discouraged by our establishing a posture of political and military strength, as well as through vigorous support of principles of collective security, through denying any gratuitous reward to the aggression, and through making his aggression as costly to him as possible.[100]

Isolating China: The Military Dimension

The invasion of Korea by no means resolved the difficulties confronting American strategists in Asia. The war having stretched military forces to the limit, the debate continued over the relative priority of Europe and Asia. The JCS escalated its insistence that providing military protection to Southeast Asia lay in the national interest. The communist insurgencies in the Philippines and Malaysia were seen as still strong, and Indonesia and Burma were under growing threat from Chinese diplomacy, propaganda, subversion, and, possibly, intervention. The "central problem" the United States faced in Asia was thus China: "A solution to this problem, through a change in regime in control of mainland China, would facilitate the achievement of United States objectives throughout Asia."[101] Ties between Southeast Asian nations and China threatened an opening for Communist influence and infiltration. As warnings about Chinese intervention continued, the JCS grew less opposed to military containment—a line drawn around China—and the United States now strongly supported military-assistance programs in Indochina, Thailand, and the Philippines.[102]

Isolating China: The Ideological Dimension

The intensity of the ideological war against China spread in these years far beyond nationalism versus communism. The earlier hostility toward the Chinese revolution became a full-scale attack on the very humanity of the regime. The Chinese accusation that the United States was using biological weapons in Korea generated enormous anger in Washington.[103] The charge was evidence of a "horror weapon. It is an attack not only against the United States, but against the very structure of human civilization, . . . one of the most serious crimes against humanity they have committed." As the acting director of the Psychological Strategy Board put it, "Surely, this is an opportunity which should not be missed to array on our side the moral and cultural leaders of the whole world, including the very ones who have sometimes been most easily duped by communist peace-propaganda."[104]

The highly contentious and complicated prisoner-of-war issue dragged out the armistice negotiations and became inseparable from Washington's efforts at psychological warfare. The army's chief of psychological warfare, General Robert McClure, was the "first to raise the issue of whether all prisoners of war should be repatriated, pointing to both the humanitarian and propaganda aspects involved."[105] As a consequence of their failure to defeat China's military forces decisively in battle, American officials saw China's prestige growing in Asia.[106] The POW issue became a way of salvaging what could not be attained in battle.[107] It became another way of denying China the respect deserved by a great power, of putting it down as uncivilized. Washington's argument was "that the world moral and psychological warfare position of the United States in its opposition to Communist tyranny demands that we accept no course of action which would require the United States to use force to repatriate to the Communists prisoners."[108] To give in on this point, Acheson wrote Truman, "would seriously jeopardize the psychological warfare position of the United States in its opposition to Communist tyranny."[109] (It should be noted that this position developed before the later accusations that the Chinese were "brainwashing" American troops to cooperate with their captors.)

C. B. Marshall of the Policy Planning Staff wrote that the POW issue offered propaganda possibilities unlike any other: it went "to the heart of the contention between Communism and the tradition we live by. It bears on the rights of men to make choices and to claim protection." Or, as C. H. Peake of the Far Eastern Division put it, this was a policy that rested on the "fundamental humanitarian principle of individual human rights." The West had fought the war to maintain the principle "against the totalitarian state and the assertion of the rules of such states that the individual lives only to serve the state." The POW issue thus served to "universalize the struggle in Korea."[110]

The United States fought hard for the UN resolution labeling China an "aggressor," finally succeeding on February 1, 1951. It was a highly useful resolution for both the immediate and long-term isolation of China and became a mainstay of the propaganda warfare, despite Washington's recognition that South Asians believed it to have been passed "only as a result of bludgeoning tactics."[111]

Nehru continued to argue that communist Chinese acts in Korea were not wholly unjustified and that Taiwan should be returned to Beijing. But such opposition, though troublesome, could be overridden propagandistically. The campaign over the POWs and identification of China as an "aggressor" became touchstones.

Isolating China: The Economic Dimension

No major ally of the United States, let alone any neutral nations, ever enthusiastically supported the embargo against trade with China. But four key factors emerged with utmost clarity during the Korean War. First, it would be necessary to keep the embargo in place after the war, for it helped to consolidate American policies in Asia, economically as well as politically. Washington, fearing that once an armistice was signed, U.S. allies would move to ease the embargo, declared in an October 30, 1951, Department of State position paper, "Even if there is an armistice in Korea . . . we would not wish to relax trade restrictions against Communist China so long as its troops remain in hostile and threatening posture."[112]

Second, the "China differential" quickly became enshrined in the embargo: China was to be treated more harshly than the USSR, and isolation to the extent possible—and not simply in trade—was critical. The United States knew that a total embargo was impossible; with even its allies opposed, exceptions had to be made. Barter agreements with China, for example, were difficult to stop. But open and ongoing Chinese trade relationships with other Asian countries were tenaciously monitored and, as often as not, successfully limited. For example, in 1951, Indonesia appeared to be choosing an independent foreign policy under which it might barter rubber to the Chinese "devil."[113] Washington insisted that the policy violated the UN embargo, while the

Indonesian press attacked Washington's effort to control world trade.[114] Despite the outcry, Washington made it clear by cable that it would view any such policy as a significant "move in direction USSR and satellites at expense of [Indonesia's] happy relations with U.S. and its allies."[115] The pressure was effective; the barter agreement faltered.[116]

Third, debates continued in the following years as to how effective the embargo was—and how to define "effective."[117] The war had already forced the Chinese communists onto a war footing, increased inflationary pressures, and strained economic relations between urban and rural areas.[118] Some argued that the embargo would not merely weaken China's access to military equipment and other defense-related needs but would also slow down the country's industrialization.[119]

Fourth, it was essential to cut Beijing off from the overseas Chinese communities, a potential source of both political and financial support.[120] Mail and remittances were to be interrupted as frequently as possible. Asians who visited China were tracked by the American consulate in Hong Kong, and their actions, once they returned home, were often closely followed.

The embargo was never viewed as an economic tool alone; the reasons for the imposition of this "quarantine" were political as well. Every aspect of the isolation policy was related to every other, and so to relent on one threatened them all. Moreover, whenever the possibility of relaxing economic controls on China was reexamined, it was feared that questions regarding the mission of the Seventh Fleet with respect to Formosa would also be raised.

The objective in Asia was to isolate China while creating new trade patterns that would sustain this policy economically. Cutting off China's ties with Japan and elsewhere in order to build up an Asian economy was to be key to American economic policy in the coming decades, and its success required that the American market open up more and more to "free world" trade. The prognosis was sometimes judged bleak: "There will be political and economic deterioration. . . . The free world cannot count on any more favorable eventuality than a continuation of the present basic stalemate through 1955 and . . . should be prepared for a deterioration of its position in the Far East." It was not clear how to help Asian economies most effectively—or, more specifically, how to generate both private and public capital flows in the region while avoiding the perils of inflationary financing. Any positive economic results would require a "long period of time," but drawing the line against communism and overcoming local anti-imperialist and antiforeign sentiments provided the needed context for this arduous process.[121]

If Washington's efforts to shape Asia economically were to take hold, local nationalisms would have to be cultivated, because not all brands of anticommunist nationalism were dependably pro-American. Finding the best way to influence this "intense nationalism" remained a formidable "political and propaganda task" for the United States. If neutralism was acceptable on a political level—at times—it was less so economically; closed markets were considered objectionable throughout the period.[122]

Isolating China: The Japanese Dimension

Japan was central to the policy of isolating China and reorganizing Asia economically, politically, and militarily. A "hard Cold War policy," as the historian John Dower calls it, had begun to emerge toward Japan prior to the outbreak of hostilities in Korea:

> U.S. officials had already begun to think explicitly of Japan's role in a future global conflict between the United States and the Soviet Union—and from this it was only a short step to the logical next stage in strategic planning: the notion that it was not only necessary to deny Japan to the enemy but also essential to incorporate Japan in a positive manner in the U.S. Cold War strategy. When this step was taken, it marked the end of the soft Cold War policy.[123]

Most of the key elements were in place before Korea: the "offshore island chain" line of defense; the increasing preoccupation with Southeast Asia; the call for the creation of a Japanese military; and the intense discussions, pro and con, of the peace treaty with Japan and of the way to hold Japan most effectively in the anticommunist camp. By early 1950 "the general principles (if not numbers) of long-term bases in Japan and Japanese rearmament had been agreed on." Okinawa was to become a major military installation and a key aspect of American defense strategy.[124]

The Korean War highlighted the significance of the Japanese economy. It also provided American officials with the opportunity to control Japan's future, including its trade with China. Containing China and controlling Japan became inseparable concepts.[125]

The future of Japanese-American relations was tied—"to a degree greater than in the case of other countries"—to the problem of trade. American foreign economic policy faced no greater hurdle, for any success in shaping Japanese policy required

(1) opening European markets, despite their fears of competition from low-priced Japanese goods, and obtaining the most-favored-nation agreements that Europeans had already reached with Germany but opposed with Japan;

(2) despite domestic opposition, opening the American market to Japanese goods;

(3) opening Southeast Asia to Japanese exports, notwithstanding "distinct limitations in the way of early accomplishments," and remaining vigilant against any "growing isolation from the West" (the immediate problems were the "political and psychological antipathies remaining from wartime experience");

(4) restricting Japanese trade with China, particularly trade in raw materials and the extension of credit.[126]

The weight to be placed on each of these points was widely debated. It was difficult, for example, to publicly advocate opening the American domestic market; no one had any clear sense of the outcome, and the situation seemed unstable and threatening. But there was increasing consensus on one point: the necessity of isolating the PRC from Japan, which the United States accomplished "against the wishes of most Japanese, including the conservative leadership."[127] The issue neither of Japan's trade with China, of its relationship to Southeast Asia and global trading patterns, nor even of its long-term security integration with the United States was satisfactorily resolved in the early 1950s. But the context in which these issues were discussed had decisively shifted with the war and the American campaign against the PRC.

An NSC study in June 1952 bluntly stated:

> Japan may try to take advantage of the United States–USSR struggle for power; desiring to restore Japanese influence on the continent of Asia and to regain the advantages of China trade, Japan might conclude that an accommodation with Communist-controlled areas in Asia would serve Japanese interests. The extent and nature of this "accommodation" would be conditioned by Japan's ability to satisfy its economic needs through relations with the free world.[128]

Even without such an accommodation, the Japanese might "attempt to build up a paramount position of influence in the Far East to the detriment of the independence of other free nations of the Far East and contrary to the interests of the United States." Japan's access to raw materials and to markets for its exports "will significantly affect Japan's basic orientation," and trade with China was thus pivotal.[129] Consequently, the NSC study called for ways to "prevent Japan from becoming dependent on China and other Communist-dominated areas."[130] But Washington realized that this was a long-term problem and that the China issue would be a tenacious one in Japanese politics.

Without the relentless American opposition, ties between China and Japan might well have expanded in innumerable ways.

An OIR report of April 1952 asserted that the China question "cuts across almost all the major problems confronting the Japanese in their efforts to achieve security, independence, and a viable economy." Many Japanese "of all shades of political opinion" desired "some sort of relationship with the Communist-controlled mainland that would permit trade relations and provide Japan with a greater political flexibility."[131] At the same time, they wanted greater independence from the United States, even while perceiving the benefit in the security of the military alliance. Trade with China would thus serve two purposes: first, it would assist in the development of an independent Japanese economy; second, it would permit a degree of political flexibility that might placate the Communist bloc, enhance Japan's position in Asia, increase its bargaining position with the West, and reestablish historic ties with the Chinese mainland. Such a relationship was appealing even to Japanese nationalists and conservatives, the report concluded.

Ambassador Robert Murphy, writing from Tokyo, warned against complacency: "The directors of Japanese foreign affairs evidently consider themselves better fitted on the China question to be mentors than students of the United States." There was "reason to believe . . . that Japan already has formulated in considerable detail a long-range China policy which is by no means a duplication of our own." The Japanese believed they could develop a profitable modus vivendi with Communist China "without compromising either the external or internal security of Japan." Robert Murphy reported his discussions with an official of the Ministry of Foreign Affairs, Kumao Nishimura, one of Prime Minister Yoshida Shigeni's "closest advisors on China." Nishimura warned against Washington's attempting to force a "precipitate settlement" of relations between Taipei and Tokyo "at the cost of prejudicing a possible comprehensive settlement in East Asia." Beijing, he added, was not subordinate to Moscow: "A nation of 450 million can never be dominated by a nation of 180 million." Japan regarded the communists as "firmly entrenched, militarily, politically, and economically." In eras when China was strong and united, it had had particularly close ties with Japan, and it was likely to again. Moreover, Japan was "highly qualified to play the leading role in influencing Peking in the direction of increasing coolness towards Moscow." Murphy concluded that there was "strong and varied evidence, therefore, that Japan is determined to pursue a positive policy toward Peking, with a view to establishing a relatively normal commercial and diplomatic intercourse as soon as possible. . . . The foremost condition is a Korean truce, which the Japanese expect to be coupled with cancellation or tacit lapse of the United Nations sanctions." The danger, he argued, was that "the Japanese may in dealing with Peking go farther than they realize in weakening the collective security of the free nations in the Far East."[132]

The fear was that Japan would find itself somehow beholden to the Chinese communists if trade between them became extensive.[133] Constant pressure on Japan proved necessary, and the United States did not hesitate in these years to apply it. For all the outcry American officials raised against Beijing's subordination to Moscow, it would be hard to find anything comparable in that relation with the subordination of Japan to American economic and strategic interests.[134] The United States openly sought to manipulate key global economic factors in order to control Japan in both short and long terms. American resistance to independent Asian nationalism emerged in various ways during these years but nowhere more pervasively than in its relations with Japan.

U.S. economic policy was both tinted with an ideological multilateralism and hardened by economic necessities. The United States was seeking ways to reduce its economic support of Japan while keeping Japan committed to the American alliance in Asia. That meant cutting Japan off from China and promoting offshore military procurement. As John Dower explains:

> Essentially, what took the place of an independent, autonomous foreign policy in post-Occupation Japan [after 1952] was the pursuit of what later became fairly labeled "economic nationalism." Yoshida and his successors did receive a payoff in the form of economic favors for hewing so closely to the U.S. containment policy in Asia; to compensate for the denial of the China market and simultaneously integrate Japan more tightly with other capitalist economies, Japan was allowed to pursue protectionist policies domestically and at the same time was given privileged access to U.S. technological licenses and patents.[135]

Was this all part of a long-term coherent strategy that began in the late 1940s? No. The Korean War and developments on Taiwan played highly unexpected roles in shaping the policy of containing and isolating China. Yet in critical ways it *was* a remarkably consistent policy, both ideologically and economically. Indeed, without taking into account this underlying consistency, it would be hard to make any sense of the way that, once the Korean War began, events were seized upon to justify following ideological inclinations and to resolve bitter policy debates.

5 FROM MONOLITHIC TO INTERNATIONAL COMMUNISM

The picture that emerged in the early years of Eisenhower's administration was, in some ways, almost the reverse of Truman and Acheson's. Suddenly China was no longer a Soviet satellite, a "slavic Manchuko," nor were the Chinese communists any longer strangers to nationalism, or the embodiment of a power somehow alien and external to the real China. And no longer were they leaders selling out their country to Moscow or handing over China's provinces to the Soviets.

An NSC document of October 1953 reflected this shift: "Peiping is motivated by interacting factors derived from the concurrently Chinese and Communist nature of the regime. As a nationalistic Chinese regime, Peiping wishes to reassert China's position as an Asian and world power. As a Communist regime, it assesses its enemies and friends and its objectives in terms of the objectives of world communism and the Marxist analysis of history."[1]

But that meant that Chinese nationalism no longer looked like such a positive force against communism. China was threatening both as communist *and* as nationalist. Both aspects were expansionist and contrary to American interests. Now there was "Chinese imperialism."[2] As NSC 166/1 argued:

> The nationalist and communist imperatives of the Peiping regime impel the Chinese Communists toward eventual recapture of the historically Chinese territories which the U.S. and the West now hold or protect; toward eventual expulsion of Western or Western-allied forces from adjacent mainland areas; and toward substitution of Chinese Communist influence for that of the West in the other areas of the Far East. Even if particular Far Eastern

issues were resolved to the satisfaction of Peiping, the Chinese Communists, as communists, would continue to maintain a basic hostility to the
West in general and the U.S. in particular.[3]

Nor were the Chinese about to let the Soviets influence their border provinces.[4] Port Arthur would not long remain under Soviet military influence.
However much communism served to bind China to the USSR, the two countries related "entirely on the basis of state to state negotiation, assistance and
advice. As Dulles noted in a November 1953 NSC meeting, "the Russians handle
the satellites through disciplinary control over individual Communist party
members. They appear to deal with Communist China as a close, but relatively independent ally."[5] China was not a satellite; the USSR was no longer
disputing border regions. China, Dulles concluded, was "Moscow's only voluntary and genuine ally."[6]

This shift from the views of the Truman years did not emerge out of any new
studies of Soviet-Chinese relations. No one argued that China was becoming
more independent, or that the earlier depiction of the Chinese communists as
puppets had been inaccurate, or that the nationalism-versus-communism
argument now lacked merit. Policy papers simply tended to assert the new
view as though there were nothing new about it: for example, "From the
beginning, the Chinese Communist regime escaped Satellite status both
because of the size and remoteness of China and because the regime rose to
power primarily through its own efforts."[7]

Of course, this new view had several important implications. Though ideologically linked with Moscow, China was now perceived to be acting in its own
national interests. "Communist China is more an ally than a Satellite of the
USSR," a 1954 National Intelligence Estimate concluded. "It possesses some
capability for independent action, possibly even for action which the USSR
might disapprove but which it would find difficult to repudiate."[8] As John Foster
Dulles declared on his return from the Berlin Conference of February 1954, it was
now "clear that the Soviets do not feel in a position merely to hand out orders to
Peiping. They treat the Communist Chinese regime as a partner who has to be
consulted and, in certain instances, even restrained by persuasion and by economic pressures."[9] And Ambassador Charles Bohlen telegraphed from Moscow,
"It seems increasingly obvious that Soviet Government does not have controlling
influence over Chinese actions and even degree of influence is problematical."[10]
Instead of domination by Moscow there was, as some analyses phrased it, "an
alliance bound together not only by ideological ties, but by common hostility to
the U.S., military interdependence, and the mutual advantages of concerted
diplomatic and 'revolutionary' activities."[11]

Another analyst argued that "the apparent close community of action between the Russians and the Chinese does not eliminate either the basic conflict of national interests or the underlying conflict on doctrine." Mao's nationalism, not his Communism, was his most salient political feature. No longer were splits in the leadership seen in terms of those loyal to Moscow and those "more Chinese." The idea of factions "within the Chinese Communist Party at logger-heads with each other must be discounted. . . . There is no evidence of a split between the Moscow-trained and those with purely native experience. . . . [L]atent nationalism of the Chinese Communist leaders is one of the cohesive factors."[12]

The precise character of the relationship between Chinese nationalism and communism remained an open question. Experts differed, asking "How much Chinese? How much Communist?" in the mixture that made up Beijing's policies. Sometimes the two aspects were deemed antagonistic, sometimes reinforcing: "The history of China through the centuries demonstrates that there is no basic incompatibility between rigidly orthodox, doctrinal, authoritarian government and the Chinese temperament," went one widespread interpretation.[13] Hard-liners tended to stress communism; liberals and those more inclined toward a "soft" policy generally stressed nationalism. Dulles used both, though he emphasized the deeper fanaticism of Chinese communism.

Even if the United States and China could reach an accommodation on their conflicting national interests (which Dulles argued was inadvisable), "no compromises," in the words of one NSC paper, "could in Chinese Communist eyes resolve the basic conflict between the two systems."[14] Even if Washington could reach an accord with Chinese nationalist aspirations, communist goals would remain universal and contradictory to U.S. global objectives—which is why, in the end, *dominoes* and *credibility* were almost always invoked more strongly in terms of communist than of Chinese expansionism. These were the code words for a strong globalism; it was the nature of the global order itself that was at stake when "international Communism" was proclaimed the enemy.

The Uses of Hostility

In the early Eisenhower years the NSC repeatedly discussed its desire to drive a wedge between the Chinese and the Soviets. Dulles advocated relentless hostility against China. Pushing China toward the USSR, he argued, would serve to intensify their natural divisions more effectively than enticing China away. In a December 1953 meeting with French and British leaders in Bermuda, Dulles declared that "we were justified in believing that there was strain" between China and the Soviet Union and that "there were two theories for dealing with this problem. One was that by being nice to the Communist Chinese we could wean them away from the Soviets, and the other was that pressure and strain would compel them to make more demands on the USSR which the latter would be unable to meet and the strain would consequently increase.... The United States adhered to the latter view."[15]

But the utility of such tension was not limited to the hoped-for break between China and the USSR. When, in the formation of policy, the short term is discarded in favor of an unspecifiable long term, it is useful to look at the immediate interests served by such a stance.[16] In this case, the question involves an assessment of the advantages for the pursuit of American objectives of a hostile international environment in Asia.

In the early years of the Eisenhower administration there were repeated internal discussions about the assistance of "tension" and "hostility" in shaping American policy. International tensions would help mobilize Western European allies and override their more parochial, nationalistic interests in the name of American global interests. Stressing the underlying hostility of the communist threat worked to dispel "illusions" about the fundamental character of communism; justified unpopular policies; and softened congressional resistance to foreign aid, mutual-aid funds, reduction of tariffs, and so on. Hostility would also force the Soviets and the Chinese to compromise the economic appeal of their societies: "The Soviet leaders have just realized that the Soviet economy cannot provide both guns and butter. So they have cut the butter. This tends to make trouble among the Soviet masses. This trouble will grow."[17]

All the more so for China: "External pressures hasten the destructive process," adding to "the strains which will lead to disintegration."[18] Dulles liked to argue that unrelenting hostility was the only way of getting results when dealing with the communist world in general, not just China. But China was a special case: it was more vulnerable, its economy weaker, its desperation of a higher magnitude.

Eisenhower's policies combined nuclear preparedness with the waging of political, ideological, and economic warfare on "international communism." As the historian Richard Immermann concludes, from Eisenhower's perspective "there was no contradiction between conventional prudence and restraint and unconventional risk taking and aggression. They complemented each other ... [and] that strategy depended on exacerbating Soviet insecurity."[19]

But if the advantages of tension for achieving American objectives in Europe remained considerable, it was never as central there as it was to American containment policies in Asia. In Europe, a reduction in tension, however difficult, opened up relatively attractive alternative ways of challenging Soviet domination of Eastern Europe and Soviet control at home. This approach had its costs, but they could be minimized with a two-track policy of apparent flexibility paired with unrelenting political, economic, and ideological warfare under the guise of arguing for "openness" and the "free flow of goods, people, and ideas."

Not so for China. Washington regarded a high level of tension as a critical element in its effort to draw a line across Asia. There containment and acute tension went hand in hand; any "flow of goods, ideas, and people" was inimical to American interests. Restraint on interchange between China and other Asian countries was essential. The Eisenhower administration was continually making tactical adjustments in Asian relations with China, trade, and the embargo, because the "rigor of our policy might defeat our purposes by creating economic conditions in these countries that would drive them into the arms of the Communists." But this flexibility was an exception designed to reinforce a policy of maximum isolation.[20]

Ideologically, Eisenhower and Dulles's wedge strategy provided a highly effective bureaucratic rationale for the policy of "containment without isolation" toward the Soviet Union and "containment with isolation" toward China.[21] Washington's private acknowledgment that the USSR and the PRC were indeed separate nations each with its own interests was not incompatible with Washington's public view that both nations represented the threat of "international communism," a threat to be countered with the development of an equally compelling global strategy, a key piece of which was the creation of a capitalist economic order in Asia. Fighting "international communism" was the single most useful and effective explanation for this global commitment. At the same time, it helped obfuscate the centrality of Taiwan in shaping the character of American containment policies in Asia—a crucial point, since so few of Washington's allies directly supported the U.S. stance on Taiwan.

The relentless hostility toward China reflected not just the legacy of Korean War attitudes, in other words, but fundamental strategic objectives as well. Hostility was both fueled and required by the policies the United States pursued in Asia, policies that had become inseparable from support for the Nationalists on Taiwan. If there had been no Taiwan, no rival government, things naturally would have been different. But Taiwan and a rival Chinese government did exist, profoundly shaping the character of the American tactical ability to seek certain global objectives in Asia.

In this sense, Taiwan became a microcosm of American policy. It enabled the United States to pursue its global objectives as it did in Asia, and it shaped how they were to be implemented. The occasional discussions about altering Washington's China policy never could deal with the consequences that might follow a change in the status of Taiwan. The advantages of continuing a Taiwan-based containment policy were always deemed to outweigh the costs and the risks of changing it. Eisenhower's occasional comments about trade between China and the United States never led to any action. Nor did he and Dulles ever act on the idea that the USSR and China could, or even should, be split in the short term. Why? Because an immediate split was never plausible unless the United States were willing to shift certain basic aspects of its Asian policy. And this, Washington would not do; such an objective risked too much. The effort to isolate and contain while building up an alternative, pro-America Asia was the goal, and until the nascent capitalist order in Asia was sufficiently strengthened and China had adjusted to it, there was no place for China there.[22]

The Chinese—"the special hostility of the regime"[23]—of course, were blamed for the acute tension in Asia, but its utility was manifest to Washington. It was critical for holding the line, for developing the Taiwan-based policy of containment with isolation upon which Washington's global policies in Asia came to depend. In addition, Washington always hoped that China would "face internal problems much greater than those of the USSR," that hostility and embargoes might finally prove fatally unsettling.[24]

Bipolar Globalism

As in the Truman years, "bipolarity" lay at the core of the new administration's global strategy. But the character of this bipolarity was seen as profoundly changing. Unlike Truman, Eisenhower and Dulles found themselves defending a bipolar globalism against Soviet appeals for "peaceful coexistence" and arms reductions. The character of East-West conflict was changing, though in Washington's view Soviet intentions were much the same: "There is no basis for concluding that the fundamental hostility of the Kremlin toward the West has abated, that the ultimate objectives of the Soviet rulers have changed, or that the menace of Communism to the free world has diminished," declared the State Department.[25] But Moscow was using "more flexible techniques" in foreign relations, which could "without sacrificing essential Soviet power position"— Ambassador Bohlen warned in a cable from Moscow—"be more dangerous in long run than rigid, aggressive technique of Stalin regime which had since the end of the war driven home the Soviet menace to the free world."[26]

These more flexible Soviet strategies combined with the growing dread of nuclear war (and popular fears of Soviet nuclear capabilities) to fuel stronger impulses inside the free world "toward neutralism and disengagement." A Soviet peace campaign threatened that the West "will find it increasingly difficult to keep its armaments program at the present high pitch," since any apparent lessening of tensions would cool the drive to "build up national and coalition military establishments."[27] The USSR, noted a 1955 NIE assessment, "generally showed itself under Stalin's leadership uncompromising in negotiation, abusive in propaganda, and aggressive in action. It was soon joined by Communist China."[28] Western unity, Washington officials repeatedly declared, was forged against the ruthless and inflexible character of Stalin's Russia. As UN Ambassador Henry Cabot Lodge noted, Stalin's death on March 5, 1953, "eliminates the violent sounds which helped to keep our allies together."[29] The United States had created a "defensive coalition under the impetus of an acute Soviet threat. Should this threat appear to diminish, it would be difficult to maintain the support of Western peoples for continued rearmament, close integration of national policies, and vigorous anti-Communist efforts."[30]

Skillful Kremlin propaganda could divide the allies. "Whenever the Soviet 'soft' line is dominant, our allies will be eager to explore it seriously, and will probably wish, in seeking a basis of 'coexistence,' to go to further lengths than the U.S. will find prudent," a 1955 NSC analysis observed. It would be a "major task," therefore, to maintain "the necessary unity and resolution in the free world."[31] In the long run, neutralism might spread in Europe, perhaps even leading to a "Third Force." The "selfish pursuit of separate national interests and ambitions previously submerged by a sense of common danger" appeared likely.[32] And though a lessening of Cold War tension might allow Europeans to focus more on domestic needs, the risk was just as great that "a rearmament slow-down would instead lead to unemployment of manpower and resources."[33] The challenge, then, was to placate the pressure for negotiations with the USSR and China.[34]

The NSC, then, viewed the "Soviet peace offensive" with alarm. Although the effort reflected a response to the success of American policies that had led to a rearmed Germany, a strong American nuclear force, mounting military burdens on the Soviet economy, and a variety of domestic pressures on the USSR's new collective leadership, it threatened to "create an even more serious threat to the Free World than did Stalin's aggressive policies." The loss of "obvious hostility" and perpetual crisis made it harder to develop a "cohesive" policy among allies. The "further blurring of the lines which have divided the Communist and the non-Communist worlds" was a "dangerous political trend."[35] The bipolarity that had been such a source of American strength was being challenged as never before.

Exacerbating Washington's anxiety was the concern that its allies had gone along with its policies out of a narrow concern over the danger of war rather than broader ideological convictions. Washington insisted that ideological clarity was pivotal to its global role and strategy; without it, the "full mobilization of Free World counter strength" would be impossible to achieve. The Soviets' "peace offensive," their call for summitry and general negotiations, was thus a particularly unsettling policy for the Eisenhower administration, one that could place serious strains on the Western alliance and deepen disputes over issues ranging from China to trade to nuclear policy. A thaw could "result in increasing neutralism and a trend toward a greater number of uncommitted states"; even Latin American countries might "take more independent positions."[36] How, then, could the United States effectively assert its power in an era of reduced tensions and calls for negotiations?

One of the perceived strengths of the communists was the "fixity of Communist purpose to impose Communism on the world and the unified direction of Communist action [that] give the Communists a tactical political warfare advantage in determining the nature, direction, and intensity of courses of action to be used against the non-Communist world."[37] The Eisenhower administration sought a comparable ideological and strategic fixity of purpose to counter the new flexibility of the Soviet Union. To Washington, the unbridgeable divide between the USSR and the United States—military, political, economic—was the ideological fulcrum for policy and for psychological warfare.[38] Even if Washington's allies did not wish to face global realities, "the central fact of today's life" was that "we are in a life and death struggle of ideologies."[39]

Such a bipolar stance served many purposes. It continued to make the United States and the Soviet Union the two central powers—the United States the center of the "free world" and the creator of the global strategy to oppose international communism (the ideological counterpart to bipolar globalism). Washington regarded and proclaimed its policies as genuinely international, as opposed to those of allies and neutrals who pursued more regional, national, or parochial interests. Only the United States really kept (or had to keep) the diverse global factors in mind in assessing regional and local issues.

Bipolarity, moreover, ultimately made both Washington and Moscow responsible for the global implications of their allies' and satellites' acts. The Eisenhower administration predicated its policy of "massive retaliation," for example, on a degree of direct or indirect Soviet control over China—a necessary assumption for the policy's strategic consistency, for how could one threaten the Soviet Union with nuclear retaliation for Chinese aggression if China were truly independent? This was another reason American strategists were reluctant to envision a China fully separate from the USSR. "In the event of general war," the Joint Chiefs wrote in 1954, "the enemy will include the USSR, the Soviet Satellites, and Communist China."[40]

A China truly independent from the Soviet Union would emerge only in the late 1950s and early 1960s amid a shift to the policies of "mutual assured destruction" and multipolarity, and to what were perceived as revolutionary threats to American interests. The global bipolarity of the 1950s was giving way as the use of conventional and counterinsurgency forces in a war made more and more sense to military planners.[41] Though they could envision using nuclear weapons in peripheral wars if China became involved in a land war in Asia, that was not what massive retaliation was ultimately about. Stripped of its bipolarity, it lost its full strategic rationale—which was, in part, why Eisenhower in moments of crisis in Asia repeatedly reaffirmed his belief in some ultimate tie between China and the USSR. "If the U.S. got into a disastrous nuclear war with the Soviet Union and in the course of the war simply ignored Communist China," he warned, "we would end up in a 'hell of a fix.'" The United States simply could not permit China to sit out such a war and "develop after perhaps forty years, into another Soviet Union"; the United States would have to "disarm and remove the threat of Communist China. We simply could not just ignore a Communist China which remained untouched and intact. . . . To do so would be unrealistic in the extreme."[42] Eisenhower might wonder about the possibility of a long-term split and how to bring it about, but he did nothing to do so directly, and, given his strategic doctrines, he had reason not to.

Monolithic versus International Communism

For both domestic and international ideological reasons, Eisenhower and Dulles often spoke of "monolithic communism"; in internal discussions, "monolithic" gave way to "international," but this was a distinction without a policy difference. In 1954, speechwriters planning Dulles's remarks in Caracas were not inclined to identify more than one variety of communist:

> There are no different varieties of orthodox communists, there are no degrees of militancy, no degrees of subservience to Moscow among them: there is only a single type, no matter what his national origin or apparent coloration of the moment may be, and he is invariably, inflexibly and exclusively dedicated to the furtherance of the interests of an authoritarian national state called Russia, because he believes that the surest way to attain his goal is through achievement of world domination by that national state. . . . And at no time should there have existed any doubt concerning the first allegiance of any true communist. . . . No place in the world escapes the attention of the International communist apparatus or is immune from application of the standard communist technique, no matter how remote from the Communist center of power or how seemingly secure. None of us can say: "But our communists are different."[43]

This insistence on the international character of communism lay at the heart of Washington's strategy, and the national security bureaucracy used it both domestically and internationally to justify American globalism. Dulles spoke bluntly of its utility at home: "It's a fact, unfortunate though it be, that in promoting our programs in Congress we have to make evident the international communist menace. Otherwise such programs . . . would be decimated."[44] This was especially true for programs such as economic aid and tariff reduction, but the communist threat was routinely invoked even to promote popular Cold War legislation. "International communism" was not simply an extension of Soviet or Chinese national power; it was a fundamental challenge to the American way of life and the American vision of global political and economic order.

At the same time, in debates within the national security bureaucracy, it was also quite permissible to view Beijing as independent. Doing so did not, however, require dismissing "Kremlin-directed" or "monolithic" communism, which could operate as a general ideological line while allowing for strategic distinctions between the Soviet Union and China. It depended on what the argument was about. The more it hinged on general developments in Asia, the more the fear of international communism emerged.

Dulles was a master of this language. In 1957 he was asked whether he considered communist China a satellite nation, "or do you see another relationship between Moscow and Peiping?" His answer captures the nuances the administration applied to this topic:

> I doubt that Communist China is a satellite country in the same sense, or the same degree, that the Eastern European satellites are. I would say that there is perhaps this difference: I think that both the Soviet Union and Communist China are under the domination of what might be called International Communism. I believe that the countries of Eastern Europe that we call the satellites are, you might say, in addition under the domination of the Soviet Union as a state, and in that respect there is perhaps a difference between the two.[45]

In this context, John Lewis Gaddis is persuasive in arguing that Dulles did not see "international communism as monolithic" but less so in arguing that Dulles did not believe in "international communism."[46] To determine that Dulles perceived the likelihood of a split between the USSR and China and that he had "a sophisticated long-term strategy for encouraging fragmentation within the communist world that almost certainly influenced U.S. policies" requires demonstrating that his vision included tactics and a strategy compatible with those emerging divisions.[47] In the short run, there was no such strategy. Gaddis is unconvincing in concluding that "the strategy was intended to drive Mao *toward* Moscow, not away from it, in the expectation that this course of action would *most quickly* weaken the Sino-Soviet relationship."[48] This is why NSC's Gordon Gray, while noting that Washington's official policy was to exploit differences between the Soviet Union and China, could say, "I may be less than fully informed but I believe that we are doing virtually nothing to implement this policy."[49] Dulles acted and argued as though there were no such strategy except in the long run, and this long run, moreover, was not about policies that would induce those splits so much as about ways to create an international context in which China, once split off from the USSR, would have to accept the American-backed Asian order. Even if one saw a split coming, no "soft" policy was acceptable, Dulles insisted. And in any case, a split was not expected in the near future. That was fortunate, for action "based on this assumption would enable the Chinese Communists during the intermediate period before the break to take over the entire position in Asia and the Far East."[50]

The Soviet Union versus China

Underlying the frequently invoked prediction of a likely long-term split between the two communist powers was an implicit distinction between the Soviet Union as an imperial nation-state and China as a revolutionary, anti–status quo power. The Soviets were a global power, Dulles argued, with predominant interests in Europe and the Middle East; "their motivation internationally is essentially one of preserving leadership already won." China's interests were largely regional, and its nationalistic aims ("powerfully motivated by the urge to restore China's traditional greatness"), predominantly in Taiwan and Southeast Asia, were yet to be fulfilled.[51] Dulles thus found it easy to utilize the language of international communism in public (both China and the USSR had to be dealt with in terms of extreme pressure) while acknowledging the two nations' differences in internal government discussions.

With regard to Europe, the issue was less and less about communism than about Soviet power. "Red imperialism rather than ideological Communism is the enemy and the first obstacle to progress toward U.S. policy goals; and reduction, neutralization and atomization of the Kremlin's power potential appear as prime goals at present," a Policy Planning Staff paper declared in August 1958. The natural flow of influence was no longer ideologically from Russia; now the "natural flow of influence will be from West to East and closer contacts will promote this flow."[52] U.S. policies now could rely on "the concept of evolutionary development rather than the concept of liberation" for effecting change.[53] Some officials dissented, but it is notable nonetheless how pervasive such views were becoming.

It was China, therefore, that posed the real revolutionary threat to American interests in Asia. Of course, just how to interpret the implications of their contrasting strategies remained a critical issue. As Dulles put it in November 1954, "It is true that the Russian communists have recently talked more softly. But it is equally true that the Chinese Communists have talked and acted with increasing violence. . . . Perhaps International Communism is trying by a new way to deceive the free world. They seek to be soothing in Europe. They are provocative in Asia."[54] Or, as a summary of the Quantico report, which studied the psychological aspects of U.S. strategy, put it, "Moscow has consistently demonstrated that its world policy is a unified program in which a setting of *detente* in one region is used to minimize resistance to aggression in other areas."[55]

But these positions were ideologically quite compatible with another message: that China was somehow more radical, more violent, and, ultimately, more dangerous. This message meant that Moscow might not actually be able to control Beijing. Dulles told Molotov at the Berlin conference in February 1954 that the Chinese regime was "recklessly seeking to show off its strength and extend its power," a posture that could "lead by one step after another to a chain of events which would have a result none of us wanted." He added that he hoped the Soviet Union could exert some restraint on the Chinese.[56]

As one NIE put it in November 1955, China was "still dominated by unrealized territorial claims, revolutionary fervor, and strong nationalism and anti-Westernism."[57] Where the Soviets were consummate chess players, Dulles noted, the Chinese were dangerously unpredictable. The USSR, more committed to the policies of "non-violence," was unlikely to begin another Korean-style war, whereas China was more likely to risk war—in Taiwan, Vietnam, or Korea. The USSR's interests in Europe were far more status quo, involving the consolidation of Eastern Europe. In Washington's eyes, the Soviets' interests were global in ways that China's were not. China's were intensely regional and involved a dangerous challenge to the Asian status quo. It was seeking to alter what it perceived as the "illegitimacy" of Asia's regional order; indeed, its very emergent nationalism, its desire to unify the country, was seen by the United States as demanding that outcome. Unlike those of the Soviet Union, therefore, which had to balance greater "global" interests, China's goals were intensely focused on one region. And Asia was highly vulnerable, no economic order having yet emerged that was viable for American interests. For these reasons the Soviet Union, even in the mid-1950s, could find itself contrasted with China as a more "moderate" power.

Ideologically, Dulles preferred stressing China's hostility to the international order (its "communism") to acknowledging its opposition to particular American policies—particularly regarding Taiwan. Such a stance made it easier to argue that the Chinese revolution was "more intense and prolonged" than the Russian October Revolution had been and that the Chinese communists' "greater belligerent attitude" was evident in their long record—from their conquest of the mainland to their aggression in North Korea, their conquest of Tibet, their intervention in Indochina, their threatening actions in the Taiwan Strait, and their "belligerent propaganda." They had, Dulles insisted, a "fanatical determination to eradicate any impression of good will for the United States in their part of the world."[58] They were the "most fanatical Communists in the world," concurred Walter Robertson, Assistant Secretary of State for the Far East.[59] Although Eisenhower, like Dulles, could occasionally speak more mollifyingly about China, particularly if seeking to impress a leader such as Nehru: he "would like to get our people over their currently adverse attitude toward Red China," he told Nehru in 1956.[60] Yet his communications with other Western leaders, such as Churchill, and his own diary depict the Chinese as demonic: "completely reckless, arrogant, possibly over-confident, and completely indifferent as to human losses."[61]

What was said in secret policy discussions had an emotional tone and an ideological stridency that differed little from what was said publicly.[62] In public, Dulles put forth a view of the Soviet Union as more subtle, perhaps less violent than a China "dizzy with success." In a speech to the Advertising Club of New York in March 1955, he said that the "aggressive fanaticism of the Chinese Communist leaders present[s] a certain parallel to that of Hitler." In private, he said much the same. "Both the Chinese and the Soviet Communists have, of course, the same ideological motivation," he argued, but

> the manifestations are different. . . . So far, the expansion of the Soviet Union has been accomplished by coldly calculated and deliberate steps. For the first twenty years after the October Revolution, the Bolsheviks concentrated upon consolidating their internal position. They did not risk external ventures. When they did more outwardly, it was done skillfully under the cover of alliances with other powers which could have successfully opposed them. Thus, it was under cover of an alliance with Hitler that the Soviets took their first bite out of Eastern Europe. It was under cover of alliances with Great Britain and the United States that they took their second bite after the German defeat in World War II. . . . [S]o far at least they have not taken reckless risks.

China stood in violent contrast, Dulles declared: "The temperament of the Chinese Communists is different, and while in the long run the Soviet method may prove more formidable, yet in the short run, the Chinese Communist method may prove more dangerous and provocative of war."[63]

Hostility toward China became increasingly inseparable from Washington's fear of its revolutionary potential. But as long as a split between the Soviet Union and China was seen as only a long-term possibility, this vision of a "revolutionary" China never emerged fully triumphant.[64] That would happen only in the early 1960s, when, with the breakup of the bipolar world, China was finally seen as a fully independent power pursuing revolutionary objectives.

The Soviet Union: *Containment without Isolation*

Bipolarity proved compatible with quite distinguishable policies toward the Soviet Union and China: containment without isolation for the former, containment with isolation for the latter. Slowly but in diverse ways the tensions with the Soviets declined in the 1950s. Europe was the key to the shift, for however intense the conflicts over Berlin and the emergence of even a highly tentative regional status quo, there remained a sense of what a resolution of tensions would involve, at least in the short run. The policy of containment had successfully created a line behind which capitalist integration in Western Europe was working both to incorporate Germany and to inhibit the possible rise of statist nationalism. By 1956 the U.S. balance of payments had shifted, permanently easing the flow of dollars out of Europe. That development, along with the arrival of currency convertibility, spurred a limited but meaningful movement toward intraregional trading along the lines of the multilateral vision of the 1940s. European capitalism was recovering, and economic relations with the United States were improving. Policy makers might haggle over such problems as the integration of Germany into Europe, but they nonetheless achieved a relatively successful degree of strategic and economic coordination.

Initially, Eisenhower and Dulles were critical of their allies' efforts to forge stronger links with the USSR. Whereas the British and the French seemed largely indifferent to the threat of Moscow's emerging global status, Washington was opposed to any "appearance that the West concede[s] the Soviet rulers a moral and social equality which will help the Soviets maintain their satellite rule by disheartening potential resistance." It feared that a period of relaxation might allow the Soviets to build up their strength, economically and otherwise. Where France and Britain wanted freer trade, Washington worried over what might happen if the Soviets gained strategic goods and other economic benefits. In addition, Moscow wanted a Far Eastern conference that, in the eyes of Eisenhower and Dulles, would "advance the status of Communist China as one of the great powers (and coincidentally demonstrate to Communist China that the Soviet Union is a loyal and useful ally")." While Washington stood in bitter opposition, France and Great Britain appeared to side with the USSR.[65]

The issue was clearly posed and sharply debated throughout the Eisenhower years. Some policy makers still held to the possibility that isolation might weaken Soviet control; thus it might be best to "minimize contacts of all kinds" and treat the satellite states—the "captive nations"—as "pariahs." Yet it began to look more and more as though "writing off" these nations might simply aid Soviet control. It was "reasonable to suppose," therefore, that "a policy of promoting continuing contacts of all kinds, of encouraging a flow of information, a reasonable amount of trade, tourism and normal contacts on the official level" could encourage evolutionary processes of independence and resistance in those states and, gradually, more "open societies."[66]

Over time Eisenhower did shift his position somewhat. The relative coherency of NATO, Europe's growing economic vitality, and the solidification of general ground rules for a Soviet-European status quo all worked in favor of a policy of openness, trade, and contact—of ending isolation. Such interchange could conceivably corrode Soviet dominance in the satellites and, ultimately, communism in the Soviet Union itself. Washington's policy toward China remained strikingly different, however. China was to be isolated, its links with all those areas of the world that the United States could control summarily severed. Trade, scientific exchange, communications, and visits by students, journalists, and everyone else—Washington vehemently opposed them all.

NSC leaders recognized that that the Soviets "regard the Satellite areas as areas of greatest danger to the USSR"; they had long sought American acceptance of "the permanence of Soviet domination of Eastern Europe." From his earliest months in office, Dulles had argued that "it is possible to detach satellite areas" from Soviet control.[67] That objective remained constant, though some of the tactics shifted. "Eastern Europe may well turn out to be the Achilles heel of the Soviet Union," an NSC memo suggested. "We must be alive to the opportunities to capitalize . . . on foreign trade, etc. to take the offensive and exploit Soviet bloc vulnerabilities."[68]

As a 1958 NSC document put it, "Greater U.S. activity, both private and official, in such fields as tourist travel, cultural exchange and economic relations, including exchanges of technical and commercial visitors" would ultimately work against Soviet control and domination. "Experience has shown that a U.S. policy designed to ostracize the dominated regimes has had the concurrent effect of inhibiting increased direct U.S. contacts with the people of the dominated nations." More contact would not only increase the pressures for "internal freedom and independence from Soviet control" but also "enable the United States to probe, within the party and government bureaucracy, for those individuals or groups who show signs of independent thought, nationalist aspirations, or willingness to use their influence to modify their nation's subservient relations to the Soviet Union."[69] The split between those "amenable to close Soviet control and the 'national Communists'" was growing more exploitable.[70] This forceful call for greater contact with Eastern Europe and the Soviet Union itself came, as often as not, from those linked with the CIA and its programs of ideological warfare. But it was reinforced by a general belief in the moderating effects of global trade and the liberating impact on a closed society of a wide range of contacts of all kinds.

Despite often strong congressional resistance, after several years of debate the pro-contacts side clearly won out ideologically for the remainder of the Eisenhower administration. Nowhere was its success more evident than in the willingness of Washington to promote contacts even as the Hungarian uprising of 1956 was being crushed by the Soviets. At that very juncture, Washington was looking for ways to open contacts that would encourage and support Wladyslaw Gomulka in Poland. Assisting those "nationalistic Communist leaders" who "assert their independence of Moscow" seemed advisable: nationalism was the great weakness of the Soviet system of domination in East Europe, and support for its disruptive tendencies would certainly pay dividends in time. The Titoist model was not directly applicable; the East European satellites lacked Tito's independent base and the autonomy of his rise to power. But the idea of Titoism as a powerfully corrosive influence on the Soviet empire was still attractive.[71]

True, John Foster Dulles remained cautious about opening up trade with Eastern Europe, but his reasons no longer had the same ideological focus. Instead, he often reverted to the argument that such policies would not obtain congressional support or that calling for openness with Eastern Europe might result in similar calls by the Soviets and East European countries for greater trade and contact with South America. Still, all agreed that what was really required was a complicated and perilous combination of harsh and soft methods. As one NSC analysis put it, "It may be that the U.S. will have to undertake to follow simultaneously two policies with inconsistent courses of action, representing divergent approaches to the one objective."[72]

Containment with Isolation and the Asian Economic Order

Whereas in Europe the line containing the Soviet sphere could be drawn across a region that was relatively stable in military, economic, and ideological terms, the situation in Asia was entirely different. By the mid-1950s the economic market system in Asia was weak and highly vulnerable; traditional colonial trade patterns were altering very slowly. Japan had not yet been strongly integrated into the world economic system, and though the traditional economic ties between China and East Asia were largely broken, the United States feared they might be mended with potentially devastating consequences for its Asian policies. Southeast Asia was often viewed in terms of Japan's economic future—not so much because of the inherent value of the region itself as because of how its "loss" to the communists might influence Japanese trade policies. "The situation of the Japanese is hard enough with China being commie," Dulles noted in a January 1953 meeting, "and if Southeast Asia were lost, then Japan would be thinking of how to get on the other side."[73]

Dulles believed he was holding the line to gain time—not just for animosity between the Soviet Union and China to grow but for a new Asian balance of power (military, political, and economic) to emerge to which China would then have to conform. Dulles's "pactomania" was part of his inflexibility; he regarded strengthening military establishments as a crucial factor in the success of American policy in various Asian countries. But that emphasis was hardly the whole story. Dulles often spoke of the long-term likelihood of a split; the questions were whether the West could hold out for as long as twenty-five years, and whether, even if it could, the circumstances then prevailing would allow the split to be effectively utilized.[74] To focus only on Dulles's intensification of military pressure to provoke a split is misleading. He was also buying time to transform the Asian political and economic landscape. He and many others argued that containment was inextricably bound with economic, political, and military development.

In the aftermath of the Korean War, the economic situation looked gloomy all across Asia. As Walt Rostow, an influential government advisor, put it:

> If Japan is left to wallow along from year to year in the trough of a chronic balance of payments crisis; if the Philippines fail to make good in concrete results the social and economic promise of Magsaysay's political success; if Indonesia remains indolent and distracted in the face of its growing population problem; if India fails to reproduce major results from its efforts at a democratically engineered rural revolution; if Formosa fails to develop both as a creative element in Free Asia and a political rallying point for a new China—if, in short, Free Asia does not substantially improve its performance, an indifferent outcome on mainland China could still represent an important relative achievement both to the Chinese and to the Asians generally.[75]

Washington perceived the vital necessity of shaping a new Asian economic and political regional dynamic—an objective that, in the long run at least, seemed plausible. According to Clarence Randall, the chairman of the Council on Foreign Economic Policy, the United States was properly focusing the bulk of its economic efforts on Japan as well as on Taiwan and South Korea.[76] There, in response to the communist "threat," the United States was encouraging a range of reforms, especially in land distribution, which were largely unimaginable elsewhere.

Japan remained central to American economic policy in Asia throughout the 1950s. The means for ensuring Japanese economic viability were continually debated. So, too, was the possibility of Japan's opening trade with China. Although in the late 1950s the urgency of this proposal subsided, the two issues were always inseparable. Washington noted uneasily the "strong Japanese desire to restore commercial relations with the China mainland," a stance all too attractive to those Japanese leaders who "have indicated a conviction that Japan could usefully function as a bridge between China and the West."[77]

A big part of the difficulty, and the reason for Washington's profound anxiety, did not involve the issue of trade. As a summary of Sino-Japanese relations concluded in the last months of the Eisenhower administration, the Japanese did not regard China as an enemy. They saw the Soviet Union and China very differently: the former as a traditionally hostile, barbaric Western power to be viewed with fear and suspicion; the latter as fellow Asians to whom Japan owed much of its own culture, with whom it had shared economic and other ties for many centuries, and with whom it had to live in harmony regardless of the nature of the ruling Chinese regime. Add these factors to the widespread Japanese belief that "all Japan's economic problems would be solved if only there were close trade and other relations with ChiComs," and it becomes clear that the potential for Sino-Japanese accommodation was always there.[78]

Some Washington officials—and none more caustically than Dulles—argued that the Japanese could not produce goods in enough quantity to be of interest to the United States. Some advocated Southeast Asian or Latin American markets for Japanese exports, but others stressed the age-old tie between Japan and China. Eisenhower himself sometimes did so: "The effort to dam up permanently the natural currents of trade, particularly between such areas as Japan and the neighboring mainland, will be defeated," he once observed.[79] But he often backed down, too. After one such comment from him, Dulles pointed out "the uniform Communist practice of funneling trade into the particular channels that they desire, rather than to permit it to be a means of contact between peoples." Eisenhower conceded that "of course if the Secretary of State's view on the funneling of trade by the Communists was correct, that would change the whole picture he had in mind when he referred to Japanese trade with the people of Communist China."[80]

Dulles sometimes expressed different opinions, but he usually argued that the Japanese should not depend on trade with China and that, in fact, China had never really been a major Japanese market in the past.[81] But almost everyone agreed that Japan would not adopt a position of neutrality if it remained economically viable. Dulles observed in one meeting that "if Japan were in economic difficulty and not able to trade they might as an act of desperation become neutralist but short of that there is little likelihood of that happening."[82] Trade negotiations were laying the foundation for areas in which the American market would be opened up, and "Japan was allowed to restrict severely the access of American products to its market while retaining relatively free access to the American markets."[83] Western Europe had been heavily pressured to accept commercial and financial policies consistent with a liberal international system, but the United States exerted no comparable pressure on Japan.[84]

By 1960 the American embassy in Tokyo was reporting positive results from these policies, including healthy "U.S.-Japan relationships in political and security fields" and the "substantial expansion of Japanese exports, making possible Japan's present economic prosperity."[85] Despite conflicts over the negotiations leading to the security treaty of 1960, the cancellation of Eisenhower's trip to Japan because of massive public demonstrations, and the continued efforts by some Japanese officials to secure firmer ties with China, Washington by and large assumed—as it had since the late 1940s—that Japan's economic needs would be the most significant factor determining its basic political direction. And thus it went on doing its utmost to integrate Japan more and more fully into the international global market system through the American market and to encourage Japanese involvement in regional markets.

At the same time, the United States was moving beyond bilateral economic ties with Asian countries. "That period is passing," the American embassy in Tokyo reported. "This is the time for reappraisal and for making a determined effort to provide the leadership that may serve to draw the nations of the area into closer economic relationships so that the strength of one may serve to offset the weakness of another." The greater problem, however, remained the relative dearth of private capital flowing into Asian countries.[86] Inter-Asian trade had not developed to "any considerable degree in the post World War II period."[87]

Washington's economic self-interest, one policy report concluded in 1953, "would be furthered by measures to restore a workable international economic system kept in balance through increased trade and investment rather than through massive grants of aid." A key means of dealing with "free-world economic instability" was "increased U.S. imports from non-communist areas." That also meant putting pressure on Europe to open up its market to Japan. And Asian governments had to be persuaded to take measures to protect American capital, so as to encourage trade and investment. "Extreme nationalism" remained a serious problem: various Asian nations "want to control the development of their own resources." But "even where socialism or extreme nationalism does not prevail, adequate investment laws have not been enacted, and the equity concept is slow in developing, even in Japan."[88]

If the region could be developed and trade among Asian nations expanded; if investment opportunity could grow and private capital enter; if mutual-aid programs could be put in place to encourage these tendencies, then not only would hostilities between the Soviet Union and China work their way to the surface, but the context in which China found itself would also have altered.[89] China would then have to adapt to an Asian economic system effectively controlled by the United States. Asian countries would be strong enough economically to ignore the appeal of Chinese communism and its statist methods of development. In the mid-1950s, Dulles and others did not regard a China split from Russia as necessarily a good thing, which was exactly the point Kennan had made in the Solarium study: "A Communist China, even independent of Moscow, predominant in the power equation in the Far East and attracting Asian support, is very much against our interest."[90]

Of course, in an altered future international environment, this might no longer be the case. Then even a two-China policy might be considered—as Dulles himself did on occasion.[91] When he discussed his long-range objectives with the British ambassador in February 1955, he spoke of bringing about "sufficient independence between Peiping and Moscow as to create a balance of power relationship." But he noted that the gradual return of Japanese power in an economically integrated Asia was also critical.[92] This need for time is why over the years those American officials who were thinking in more immediate geopolitical terms often expressed surprise at how little was done to induce a Sino-Soviet split.

Policy makers rarely articulated the specifics of the Asian economic order they envisioned. But their overall vision was implicit in the NSC's routinely expressed concern that expanded trade between China and the rest of Asia could encourage changes that would prevent the emergence of the multilateral economic system they so badly wanted. Unless Asia was ready, such trade would almost certainly unleash economic *and* political changes that could rapidly expand China's influence in the region. How to prevent this trade and its perilous side effects remained a central issue throughout the Eisenhower years. In negotiating an end to the Korean War, for example, how could Washington continue the containment and isolation of China when so many other nations saw the coming end of the war as an opportunity to establish trade and cultural relations with China and to support its entry into the United Nations? If their widening contacts with China risked undercutting the position of the Chinese Nationalists, they also threatened the still highly vulnerable "stabilization" of the Asian economic order: "Any such relaxation," one briefing paper argued, "would start a process which could not be stopped. . . . The psychological and political effects of such a retreat on the part of the U.S. would be out of all proportion to such limited trade advantages as might accrue to our allies.[93]

Containment with isolation, therefore, required the drawing of lines based on ideological hostility toward China. The Nationalists embodied the immediate and direct military and political aspects of containment, but they also underlay American economic strategies as well. The openness in Eastern Europe required a powerful base in the economic vitality of the United States and Western Europe. But noncommunist Asia's economic viability and attractiveness would have to be greatly built up before consideration of various strategies for contact with China could begin to emerge in the mid-1960s.

Eisenhower often commented that over time, trade would undermine all communist regimes. The Eisenhower in Stephen Ambrose's biography is a man who would have expanded trade with China if domestic opposition had not been so intense. Ambrose quotes the president's remarks to his commerce secretary that "the history of the world down to this time proved that if you try to dam up international trade, the dam ultimately bursts and the flood overwhelms you. Our trouble is that our domestic political situation compels us to adopt an absolutely rigid policy respecting our trade with Communist China and the Soviet Union." Eisenhower and Dulles were in general accord that trade and cultural exchange with Eastern Europe could weaken the Soviet hold there. "Trade is the strongest weapon of the diplomat," Eisenhower said, "and it should be used"; it "would in the end weaken the Russian hold on Eastern Europe." The "last thing you can do is to force all these [satellites] to depend on Moscow for the rest of their lives. How are you going to keep them interested in you? If you trade with them . . . you have got something pulling their interest your way."[94]

But with China, the idea that trade could undermine closed societies never jibed with the need to build up an Asian economy and to sustain a viable political balance in the region. Whereas policy makers designed their trade policy in the Soviet bloc simply to restrain the area's war potential, in China the aim was also to impede industrialization.[95]

"Opening" China did not look like the immediate way to weaken it. The fear was just the opposite: that trade and contact would expand China's influence in Asia—in Japan, Indonesia, India, Burma, Ceylon, and so on—and in the wealthy ethnic Chinese communities.[96] As one NIE in February 1957 concluded, "If tensions were reduced, closer relations between Communist China and other Asian countries would probably develop, with an eventual enlargement of Peiping's ability to influence Asia."[97] Thus "tension"—short of open hostilities in the Taiwan Strait—remained quite compatible with the American vision of the U.S. role in Asia. Neither the Japanese nor the Indians favored this approach, though Jiang, Ngo Dinh Diem of Vietnam, and Syngman Rhee of Korea did. The point, though, is that such tensions coincided with Washington's global interests. A line of containment could not be drawn without them.

And so the desire of Asian countries to trade with China had to be resisted, and resisting it required a global embargo as well: no one could be allowed to open up more than minuscule amounts of economic interchange with China. Reluctantly, under intense pressure from its allies, the United States was willing to acquiesce to some modification of trade controls, but "we much prefer to hold the line where it is," Dulles said firmly.[98] The United States was engaged in "economic warfare," he concluded.[99] Admiral Arthur Radford, chairman of the JCS, argued that any compromise would amount to "prima facie evidence that this government is retreating under Communist pressure," undermining the resolve of our allies and encouraging Asian nations to seek accommodation with China.[100] But Dulles cautioned that a modicum of flexibility was necessary; minor trading could not be stopped without excessive diplomatic costs. And if the United States became too rigid and brittle, "then the whole structure of multilateral controls might collapse. It is better to make some minor concessions than to jeopardize the multilateral system of control. We would rather write off 10% of the structure and save 90%." Dulles used this argument against both the JCS and the Nationalist government, both of whom were strident in their opposition to any apparent flexibility.[101] He was advocating not a softer approach but a harsh one malleable enough to survive criticisms from allies. Without those criticisms or opposition from other Asian governments, it is difficult to imagine Eisenhower and Dulles compromising at all. Eisenhower repeatedly approved a restrictive approach, believing there was too much at stake to proceed otherwise. The issue was never merely an embargo; it was China's role in Asia.

Opening the floodgates, moreover, was a risk that came in various forms. Any establishment of trade and diplomatic contacts between Beijing and South American nations posed a real threat to Washington's Asian policy as well, especially vis-à-vis the issue of seating Beijing in the United Nations. Without Latin America and its twenty votes, the United States would have been in the minority on this issue. By the late 1950s, only five of the twelve Asian states in the UN supported the United States, only eight of the thirteen NATO countries, and only four of the fourteen Middle Eastern countries.[102]

Controls were thus seen as a valuable way of reinforcing communist China's pariah status. The prolonged and detailed debates over the specifics of the embargo and the drawn-out discussions with the British[103] and the Japanese should not obscure what was obvious to American officials: the embargo effectively denied the American market to China, a market that was a constant factor in all of Washington's calculations about the operations of the global economic system that the United States was seeking to achieve. There were disagreements as to the embargo's actual costs to China, but few thought China wanted it to continue or would not benefit from its end.

Thailand

Though a feared neutral Japan was potentially the "biggest domino," there was continuing concern over the balance of economic power throughout Asia, which always seemed vulnerable to China's pressure for expanding trade. Declining markets for agricultural goods and minerals made some Asian nations particularly so.[104]

Thailand provides a revealing example. From the late 1940s on, regarding Thailand as a strong anticommunist and anti-Chinese base, Washington backed Prime Minister Pibul Songgram's government. But even as Thailand supported the SEATO alliance and became the recipient of more and more American aid, Washington detected strong undercurrents of "neutralism." Consequently, it carried out significant propaganda warfare from the early 1950s on, increasing it even more in the wake of the Geneva Conference on Indochina and the meeting at Bandung.[105] Washington was alarmed by reports from its officials in Bangkok that the Thai government might be "reassessing its anti-Communist outlook." Prince Wan, the foreign minister, appeared to be "sedulously spreading the impression that he has been softened personally by Communist professions of good faith and is generally assuming a weak-kneed role."[106] The government seemed to be opening trade relations with China through Hong Kong and Macao; parliamentary groups were secretly meeting with Chinese leaders, including Mao and Zhou Enlai.[107]

Though the Thai government comprised a contentious coalition of forces under Pibul, American diplomats concluded that what was happening was a manifestation of the "Thai political tradition of attempting, as a small nation, to maintain its independence by keeping in line with apparent trends in the international pattern of power." Their worst fears began coming to pass when the Thai government informed Washington on June 13, 1956, that it was removing nonstrategic goods from the list of commodities prohibited from export to China. Dulles expressed to Prime Minister Pibul his "disappointment" that the Thais had taken steps to weaken the embargo, which "might appear to constitute a weakening in free world opposition to Communist aggression."[108]

The Thais appeared unmoved. Shortly thereafter, the American embassy in Bangkok reported in alarm that both a secret parliamentary delegation and a large cultural troupe were on their way to China. Pibul argued that Thai public opinion was forcing him to take steps on trade, that it was in Thailand's interest to have a market for its rice. Washington was unsure to what extent Pibul himself was involved in the apparent policy shifts.[109] Nevertheless, throughout 1956 and 1957 the NSC closely followed this unsettling turn of events. Thailand wanted "to have an 'anchor to windward' in case Communist China should achieve greater influence in Asia and the world," but such a process of "marginal accommodation" posed a significant threat to American interests, exposing the Chinese community in Thailand to increased subversion, undercutting SEATO, and encouraging a neutralist direction in Laos. An anti-SEATO press campaign was developing without any apparent opposition from the government. Chinese communist films were being shown in Thailand, and the cultural exchange program was continuing to grow. Should China be admitted to the UN, Bangkok might very possibly recognize Beijing. It was becoming clear, moreover, that there was a "seemingly deliberate effort" to conceal the scope of Thai-Chinese relations from Washington.[110] Clearly, the Thai groups went to Beijing "with the tacit approval of Bangkok," reported one intelligence study of China sent to Dulles.[111]

What U.S. countermeasures, then, did Washington consider feasible and desirable? Thailand seemed to be developing a more flexible approach to China even as it sought to retain its friendly ties with the United States. But to Washington this flexibility was a dangerous illusion. To some extent, American officials blamed themselves. Talks with the Chinese communists at Geneva, rumors of easing of trade restrictions between China and the Western allies, and the visits of American journalists to China all made it harder for Washington to rein in the Thai government. When American journalists sought passports stamped for travel to China, Dulles complained that their action threatened to open up precisely what needed to be held shut for as long as possible: "I am convinced that our Far Eastern policies . . . could be gravely impaired if there were a general influx of Americans into Communist China at [this] time. . . . I could list here if time permitted twenty reasons which are cumulative, such as the non-recognition of the regime; so that we cannot issue a 'passport to it'; the existence of a quasi-state of war and the continued application of the Trading with the Enemy Act; the illegal jailing of Americans already in China despite promises to let them out; the effect upon free countries of Asia of what the Chicoms could plausibly claim to be a resumption of 'cultural exchanges' with the Chinese Communists; the increased prestige and influence of the Chinese Communists in the area that would be consequent to this, etc. etc."[112]

The case of Thailand illustrates Washington's fear of rewarding neutralism. If the United States aided neutrals, then why should U.S. allies such as Thailand stick too closely? How could one discourage neutralism from spreading when it offered attractive possibilities of greater trade and cultural exchange?

"Extreme Nationalism"

During the Eisenhower years the key NSC code words for the threat from the "underdeveloped world" were neither "social revolution" nor "revolutionary nationalism" but "extreme nationalism." The term covered a broad range of concerns: neutralism, controlled economies, socialist philosophies, local control over natural resources, state planning, and restrictions on the flow of private capital. "Extreme nationalism" was never reducible simply to "communism"; rather, communism was considered itself a variant, one of many global tendencies toward utilizing the state sector to withstand, shape, or control the impact of the international economic order the United States was trying to shape. Washington's prevailing lens for assessing China in the 1950s was totalitarian theory, a perspective that meshed tightly with an emphasis on the statism of extreme nationalism.[113]

Extreme nationalism threatened to push nations toward a socialist worldview deeply threatening to the long-term international role the United States was laying out for itself, though in practice Washington often compromised for immediate short-term considerations. In the view of the national security bureaucracy, extreme nationalism was shaped by profoundly distorting emotional and psychological misperceptions that arose from the weakness of capitalist development in the underdeveloped world. In this context, containment in Asia was part of a larger effort to draw a line against communist "development." Some initially saw the line as mainly military, others as mainly economic, but all saw it as a bulwark for what Truman and Acheson called "moderate nationalism" against the appeals of "anti-imperialism."

When India's Nehru spoke of Western hostility to a pan-Asian movement; when Egypt's Gamal Abdel Nasser suddenly seemed to embody an autonomous third force, a powerful "radical nationalism"; when Latin America leaders were seen espousing nationalism, statism, and social reform—in all these instances, what the United States was really dealing with on a regional level becomes clearer. The leaders of the Eisenhower administration viewed such intense nationalism, in all its sundry forms, as the most direct and powerful challenge to American economic power in the underdeveloped world. The objective, therefore, was to "moderate extreme nationalism, with a view to aiding the orderly self-development of the peoples of the free world."[114]

Various factors had led to the "sharply accelerated growth of nationalism."[115] Once the Soviet Union obtained nuclear weapons and once its foreign policy became more attuned to and supportive of nationalist movements, the non-Western world had greater leverage and flexibility. The tendency of the world after the late 1940s, Washington concluded, was not away from but very much toward nationalism. "International communism" might use it and speak for it in ideological terms, but extreme nationalism in and of itself remained a critical, immediate, and perilous global economic problem.

Radical Nationalism: The Middle East

In assessing Washington's analysis of the eruption of nationalism throughout the globe, NSC documents reveal a remarkable similarity of vocabulary and tone. What was true of the Middle East was just as true of Latin America or Asia or Africa. When the Eisenhower administration saw China as a danger because it was both communist *and* nationalistic, it did so partly because of its global preoccupations with the rising forces of nationalism.

With each passing year of the Eisenhower administration, the United States became more and more preoccupied with "radical nationalism," especially with the rise of Gamal Abdel Nasser in Egypt and then the collapse of King Faisal's pro-Western (and pro-British) Iraqi regime in 1958. Washington had hesitated to move too forcefully into the Middle East during the Truman years; with U.S. forces clearly stretched, most internal discussions had still centered on ways to cooperate there with the British, militarily and strategically. Under Eisenhower, however, the issue of a more independent American role became increasingly critical, as Arab nationalists grew more and more hostile to the British.

The Soviet Union's arms deal with Egypt in the spring of 1955 and the Suez crisis the following year (when Egypt nationalized the canal) broke traditional Western colonial power in the region. The United States was now the greatest foreign power there, and with the virtual collapse of conservative resistance to radical Arab nationalism, dealing with this revolutionary nationalism became an issue of paramount concern to Washington.

The Soviets, with their more flexible and dynamic policy in the Middle East, allowed Nasser and others greater leverage in their own maneuvering. Though some American officials regarded Nasser as little better than a communist, most saw his goal as some variant of neutralism, however blind he might be to its pro-Soviet implications. Radical nationalism was more dangerous because of the proximity of Soviet power, not because Moscow was directing it; without the Soviets in the background, Nasser would never have been the threat he was. Nasser, Eisenhower said, "embodies the emotional demands of the people of the area for independence and for 'slapping the white man down.'"[116] He "intends to avoid Soviet domination and to refrain from a firm and permanent alignment with either side in the East-West struggle."[117]

He was no "stooge of the Kremlin," agreed Richard Russell, a special assistant to Dulles. "His role is a more ambitious one. He undoubtedly sees himself as a 'third force,' able to do business on equal terms with both the West and the East. He would, however, be a 'third force' whose objectives, although of a different kind, would be as inimical to the interest of the West as those of the Kremlin." Nasser's movement was fueled by "deep and powerful hatreds" directly mainly at the West, and it threatened to "merge the emotions and resources of the entire Middle East and Africa into a single onslaught against Western civilization."[118]

For once, even the JCS, faced with Nasser's enormous popularity in the Arab world, stressed something other than communism. The great danger, they warned, was that as Nasser's influence increased, "other Arab states initially, and subsequently other nations, will use his successful act of nationalization as a justification for themselves expropriating and nationalizing U.S. and Western enterprise."[119] American bases would be threatened ("first in the Middle East, and then in domino fashion, in North Africa, then Iceland, the Philippines, Spain and the Azores"); the rebellion against the French in Algeria would strengthen; "governments throughout the region identified with the U.S. will weaken, expropriation would spread."[120] And Nasser, as a champion of Arab nationalism, might be able to play off the West against the USSR.

Some historians have argued that Washington's obsession with superpower maneuvering resulted in "much simplification and even distortion of local politics and alignments," including the failure to understand the ascendancy of the "rising forces of local nationalism" or that the difficulties in the region were "not primarily due to an ideological clash between our brand of democracy and Communism."[121] In critical ways, however, Eisenhower and Dulles did see the immediate problem as local nationalism, not communism. Even if radical nationalism could be placed on a continuum leading to communism, the one was nonetheless distinguishable from the other. Eisenhower and Dulles complained that British and French actions threatened to blur the "Western world" in the Arab mind, risking uprisings against American presence as well. In this area, it was the British, so critical of U.S.-China policy, who justified their actions by the global threat of the Soviet Union. As Eden wrote Eisenhower, "I have no doubt that the bear is using Nasser, with or without his knowledge, to further his immediate aims. These are, I think, first to dislodge the West from the Middle East, and second to get a foothold in Africa so as to dominate that continent in turn."[122]

Washington's differences with the British were over the likely effects on Arabs and Asians of a Suez invasion. British methods were thought to risk inflaming the Middle East and uniting Arabs in an enormous emotional onslaught against the West that would threaten U.S. allies and interests throughout the region. By 1956, Washington had concluded that British power in the region was coming to an end; the challenge for the United States was to find some way to ensure its long-term presence as the champion of the West— but separate from the hated legacy of the British and the French—against the enormous danger of a unified and nationalistic Arab world. The United States, Dulles argued, could not much longer continue walking a "tightrope between the effort to maintain our old and valued relations with our British and French allies on the one hand, and on the other trying to assure ourselves of the friendship and understanding of the newly independent countries who have escaped from colonialism."[123]

Extreme Nationalism: Latin America

Latin American nationalism was commonly depicted as likely to lead to an attack on foreign investment; it offered fertile ground for "Marxist economic attitudes." Such attitudes flourished, a wide range of American observers concluded, because many Latin Americans believed that their fates were being determined by a force outside their control: the global trading patterns that the United States was shaping in its own interests.

Communists were depicted as masters at distorting America's progressive economic role.[124] Control over natural resources was a key issue.[125] The United States was sharply criticized for opposing policies that developed natural resources such as oil in conjunction with state controls while supporting methods relying on foreign investments. Here the United States found itself challenged on the issue of "economic self-determination," repeatedly losing debates in the UN Social Committee. As one U.S. assessment put it:

> Paragraph 3 of article I [of draft article on self-determination in UN Social Committee] stated that the right of people to self-determination shall also include "permanent sovereignty over their natural wealth and resources" and that in no case might a people be deprived of its own means of subsistence on the basis of any rights that might be claimed by other states. The U.S. delegation opposed the paragraph in the belief that it might tend to undermine the confidence of the private investor in the security of his investments in underdeveloped areas and thus discourage the flow of capital to those areas.[126]

If the challenge in Southeast Asia was to channel nationalism between European colonialism and communism, in Latin America it was to channel resentments away from the United States, stressing the "Communist threat" so as to provide a useful weapon against the dangers of "extreme nationalism." In the Middle East there was hope that the United States might not itself be the immediate target of the hated colonial legacy, but there was little such hope in Latin America. Statism and anti-imperialism were the right and left hands of Latin American nationalism, the one providing the means by which the other could mobilize popular discontent against foreign investment. Reliance on popular forces was risky, and in the Eisenhower administration the support for the military was direct and ideologically consistent: "It is rather beside the point to seek to have Latin American governments modeled after our form of democracy." A too rapid drive toward economic development risked "further extremist tendencies" rather than "political stability." The United States supported moderate timing, direction, and character in development, such that it did not inflict excessive hardship on elite groups, did not arouse unfulfillable aspirations, and did not cause unduly abrupt social changes.[127]

The ideological challenge was thus acute and quite similar to the challenge in Asia. How could Washington provide a convincing picture of economic development through the free market and private enterprise? How counter "Communist propaganda which consistently and often effectively portrays the United States as the defender of 'so-called exploiters' in opposition to the interests of the common people?"[128] The economic dimensions of the problem were compounded by the fact that nowhere else in the world were the accusations against "outside forces" shaping nations' destinies more closely tied to American economic power. The "devotion to the concept of national sovereignty is one source of the extreme nationalism to which so many of our present problems may be ascribed," concluded one extensive analysis in October 1953.[129]

There is little doubt among historians that the Eisenhower administration "wanted all Latin Americans to understand that the Cold War was the predominant feature of international relations in the postwar world."[130] Many historians have examined the ways in which Latin American interests clashed with Washington's anti-communist ethos, pointing out how the Eisenhower administration "in fearing a Communist conspiracy in Latin America had injected global concerns into what were purely regional affairs," which distorted local developments.[131] Here, as elsewhere, Washington did "not worry about confusing regional and global issues." It did not seek to understand how "economic nationalism" might be useful to the development of an economy like Brazil's but opposed it as a manifestation of procommunist orientation and incipient neutralism.[132]

The issue in evaluating the character, consequences, and function of anticommunism involves, in the end, assessing the character of American globalism and the ways in which it was tied to anticommunism, its bipolar view, and its long-term commitment to reshaping world capitalism. In Latin America, as in China, it is easy to find American misperceptions and distortions of local "realities." But these are only one aspect of the situation, because anticommunism remained first and foremost a way for Washington to inject its global preoccupations into local situations so as to be able then to pursue its local interests. That this approach "distorted" local realities is easily documented, but it is less clear that American officials failed in assessing the most basic issues confronting them: economic nationalism, statist developmental policies, ideological warfare, models of development, private investments, and the priority of American global interests over the regional interests even of their allies—these were all inseparably tied to the *ideological* emphasis on communism in Latin America. Ideologically, it was always far more effective for the United States to speak publicly of the dangers of communism and use this threat to undercut the appeals of radical nationalism.

China and the Growing Fear of Nationalism

Most "extreme nationalists" were staunchly anticommunist in their domestic policies; often they were far more afraid of a mobilized populace than American analyses suggest. Their statism was frequently no more than a modest pragmatism: various governments hoped to offset their own weaknesses by appealing to both sides in the Cold War for support.[133]

But Washington remained tremendously fearful, constantly concerned over the fragility of the international economic order amid the underlying fear that both extreme nationalism *and* communism were obstacles to American global objectives. The "under-current of apprehension regarding China's real intentions" was to be fanned by U.S. propaganda warfare—designed to accentuate both China's "communism" and "historical Chinese expansionism." But the efforts were only modestly successful, because as Washington analysts concluded, China was in a highly advantageous position to draw on the "continuing distrust of Western intentions," "the tendency in Asia to equate capitalism and private enterprise with colonialism," and the widespread belief that American military bases increased the risk of war in Asia and endangered the independence of Asian nations.[134]

Nationalism was intensifying; Soviet power augmented it, and China suggested some of its most ominous traits. If the military threat was not always imminent, the ideological one was omnipresent.

Threatening Models of Development

China and the USSR both posed another challenge in Washington's eyes: their model of development. In the 1950s, rival models of industrialization were a matter of intensifying concern in their appeal to the underdeveloped world. Asia was desperately poor, its economies were sluggish, and, however high the hopes for the long term, the immediate future was bleak. "Many Asian leaders have an intellectual sympathy for Marxist economic concepts," one analysis noted. "Many believe also that in their underdeveloped countries there is no feasible alternative to state planning and financing of major economic development," making them more tolerant of the communist model "even when there is recognition of and opposition to its excesses."[135] Dulles spoke often after 1955 of the American failure to appreciate the "phenomenon of Russian industrialization," which "challenged the industrial and political supremacy that up until now the West could maintain over the underdeveloped nations of the world."[136]

From the early 1950s until the Great Leap Forward (1958–60), China's regional variation on the communist model appealed to neighbors seeking to make profound social and economic as well as political changes. By the mid-1950s China appeared to be finding a formula for rapid development, and the contrast with India became an issue in Washington.[137] As the NSC put it in March 1956, "The speed of industrialization and of improvement in living standards achieved respectively in India and in Communist China may come to be regarded in some Asian countries as a test of whether totalitarian or nontotalitarian methods are best suited for pursuing their own economic growth."[138] Another NSC staff report noted in 1957 that "the outcome of the competition between Communist China and India will have a profound effect through Asia and Africa."[139] Neither India nor Japan "exerts a successful counter-influence in the area," concluded still another NSC study.[140]

By 1959, an NSC memorandum was warning that "a fundamental source of danger we face in the Far East derives from Communist China's rate of economic growth which will probably continue to outstrip that of free Asian countries, with the possible exception of Japan."[141] The Chinese model of development was, of course, anathema to American ambitions in Asia. When President Sukarno of Indonesia returned home from China in October 1956, openly enthusiastic at Mao's rebuilding of the Chinese economy, U.S. leaders felt deeply "let down," and Sukarno's enthusiasm "constituted a 'watershed'" in Washington's increasing hostility toward him.[142]

China also threatened a cultural conflict with the West in ways far different from those of the Soviet Union. Dulles particularly feared the Chinese model's appeal to countries that were far more backward and had started with far less than the Russians. Russia might sometimes be depicted as barbaric, but it was still Western—and white. Underlying Eisenhower and Dulles's comments about the Chinese communists' "irrationality" and "fanaticism" and lack of respect for human life was Washington's unease with China's revolutionary appeal, its rich cultural legacy, and, not least, its ability to reach out to people of color.

Psychological Warfare

Although aspects of the Truman administration's propaganda warfare campaign had continued under Eisenhower, it was necessary to introduce new elements to address the threats of "Chinese imperialism" and of the Chinese development model. Consequently, there were vigorous efforts to mobilize Asian opinion against China's growing power.

The articulation of these propaganda objectives reflected what was basic to American policy. Although the central task was to stymie Chinese expansion and rapid economic growth, various policy studies warned that China would exert its greatest influence on Asians who were impressed by its economic growth and less concerned than Westerners with the preservation of human values amid development. Those human values and human rights had to be reasserted with renewed determination and shaped into a more effective challenge to the terms of totalitarian development.[143]

As the nationalism-versus-communism dichotomy faded, propaganda needed to focus on ways that the "methods and purposes of the Communists are in conflict with the real interests and aspirations of China." Elements remained of the vision from the Truman years of the communist as outsider, but it was far more important for propaganda to make crystal clear that the "leaning-to-one side" policy—that is, an independent nationalist government's nevertheless leaning toward Moscow—was not the product of an honest effort to meet the country's development needs.

Perhaps the most challenging task was to "generate the vision of a new China, which would move effectively towards authentic Chinese goals, by means which do not involve Communist methods and the violation of essential values in Chinese life." This was central to how "psychological warfare and covert operations in the narrower sense" could "acquire a new strength and vitality." Only by drawing on all the Chinese outside the mainland would it be possible to "formulate and project a new positive program for China's future . . . [which] promises to fulfill the real and persistent aspirations of the Chinese revolution which Communism has captured for the time being." The "instabilities and tension in Chinese Communist society" had to be exacerbated and the "vision of a realistic and attractive alternative" assertively pursued.[144]

Finally, propaganda warfare both inside and outside the country needed to focus on the remaining Soviet presence in China and the failure and injustice of Chinese communism. To create a poor image of China abroad and anxiety within, rumors should be spread about peasant resistance to collectivization, about famines and crop failures (without specifying areas, to encourage greater fear), and about Mao's bad health and his ineffectiveness.[145]

Even though the available documents make it hard to evaluate the real impact of these propaganda efforts on China, the extent to which American diplomatic reporting focused on precisely these issues is noteworthy. Whether and how that reporting itself was influenced by all this propaganda remains an open question.

From Extreme to Revolutionary Nationalism

During most of the Eisenhower administration, Washington viewed extreme nationalism and the Russian model of state planning with particular alarm. But by the late 1950s, revolution and "revolutionary nationalism"—from Cuba to Nasser's Egypt to Vietnam to Africa, where decolonialization was spreading rapidly in the late 1950s and the 1960s—was becoming a greater preoccupation for American officials. The language of "revolutionary" and "radical" national-ism, which replaced "extreme nationalism" in the 1960s, had its antecedents in the 1950s in statements by Dulles and others that China's "violent revolution" was still "undiminished"—in notable contrast to Russia's.[146]

If the JCS saw the Soviet Union as a greater military threat than China, if strategic military policy focused mainly on Moscow's capabilities and inten-tions, China was nevertheless regarded as the embodiment of an emerging mind-set that even more fully rejected the "American way." A bipolar world was a more controllable world for the two superpowers than a multipolar world with an independent China seen as supporting revolutionary alterna-tives. In the 1950s, "extreme nationalism" fit well with the vision of a bipolar worldview—with efforts to coordinate global capitalist development and also with the Soviet conception of a socialist camp and of several neutral countries such as Egypt and India, to which it might extend aid. An "extreme national-ism" that *actually* mobilized the masses in revolutionary directions remained little more than a feared undercurrent during those years. When it burst forth in the shape of revolutionary nationalism, so too was the image of a revolu-tionary China seen as pursuing far more than its own national interests. China's independent pursuit of its legitimate national interests was, therefore, repeatedly denied—for being communist and leaning toward Moscow in the 1950s, and for fostering and exporting a revolutionary ethos in the 1960s.

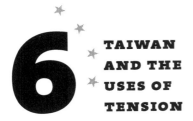

6 TAIWAN AND THE USES OF TENSION

The most prominent feature of the Eisenhower administration's policy toward China was its relentless animosity, its refusal to negotiate on any basic issues, and its adamant insistence that allied and neutral nations accept its policies. On all the fundamentals—Taiwan, trade, recognition, the United Nations, military and nuclear encirclement—American policy was bitterly hostile to the PRC. Though the United States sometimes softened its approach to deal with European and Asian criticisms of its inflexibility, it did so largely in order to continue its policy of isolating China. And in many ways the United States was remarkably successful in its efforts.

Taiwan as Linchpin

Taiwan tightly tied together global and bilateral policies. In the end, support of Taiwan was the single most useful way for the United States to hold the line in Asia. As the American government adamantly insisted that it would not, indeed could not, sacrifice Taiwan to the communists, neither the British nor the French were willing to seriously challenge this position. The Indians, among others, did challenge it, though with full awareness that Washington would not budge on Taiwan. This stance brought other issues into prominence: the embargo, the United Nations, the offshore islands. But these were (as understood by Washington) subsidiary issues that arose from global policies inextricable from U.S. bilateral relations with the Chinese Nationalists. The American commitment to Taiwan was clearly understood in Washington as the indispensable means for deflecting pressure from allies and neutrals who sought change and who, for their own reasons, were far less enthusiastic about an emerging multilateral system of trade. But it also placed restraints on any officials who hoped to draw immediate advantages from the longed-for split between the USSR and China. American officials knew, as Charles Bohlen put it in March 1953, that should this rift transmute from theory to "a real possibility," then "the question of the Chinese Nationalist Government and our relation to it will be immediately brought to the fore."[1] In other words, there was always an immediate reason not to explore any signs of a split that would endanger Taiwan.

It was clearly understood that a general Asian settlement would require a resolution of the Taiwan issue; the two were inseparable.[2] Washington's refusal to consider such a settlement was inseparable from its effort to isolate, contain, and weaken Beijing. But at the same time, Washington tried to play down the possibility that Taiwan might actually be an impediment to improved U.S.-Chinese relations. Even though the island was the linchpin of the American effort to isolate China, no other nation strongly supported Washington's position. To most Asian governments, Jiang's Nationalist regime was an unappealing relic of the civil war, and there was really no way for the United States to use it as effective propaganda against the mainland. Washington thus sought to focus attention on China's aggressiveness and hostility toward the United States, downplaying its own intervention in the Chinese civil war and highlighting "international issues" such as the nonuse of force and the peaceful development of Asia.

Unlike Truman and Acheson, Eisenhower and Dulles regarded Chinese communist nationalism as hostile to the United States and likely to remain so for some time. In public, Dulles was sympathetic to Jiang, but in private he knew that Jiang had no future on the mainland. Nor was he much concerned with achieving "one China," comprising a reunited mainland and Taiwan. Because Eisenhower and Dulles never spent much thought on how to appeal to Chinese nationalism, they were less inhibited about backing a GMD they knew had no meaningful nationalist credentials. Taiwan was never an *ideological* problem for Dulles. He never saw Chinese unity as a persuasive nationalistic stance. "The territorial integrity of China became a shibboleth," he told Hugh S. Cumming Jr. on the eve of Cumming's departure to become U.S. ambassador to Indonesia in 1953. "We finally got a territorially integrated China—for whose benefit? The Communists'."[3] Offending the Chinese communists' nationalist sensitivities was of little concern to him; he had no intention of appealing to their nationalism against their communism. He was far more concerned with mobilizing the nationalism of other Asian countries against Chinese nationalism and promoting anticommunism against Chinese communism.

A June 1953 memo setting forth principles of a settlement with communist China did not even address Taiwan as an irredentist issue. The Chinese communists would simply have to accept that "the status of the Island was to be determined by vote of the Formosan people . . . to be admitted to membership in the UN and to have all the other rights of sovereignty (among them the privilege of granting the U.S. base rights on the island)." They would also have to accept a rearmed Japan and settlements in Vietnam ("neutralization and demilitarization") and Korea, and they would have to stop assisting communist parties in Asia—in return for all of which they were to be "recognized as the lawful government of China and to be given membership in the UN." And "trade and financial control affecting Communist China" would be "reduced to the level of those applying against the Soviet Union."[4]

Washington's policy toward China, spelled out in NSC 166, was clear. As the main enemy of the United States in Asia, China was to be isolated and contained. The rival government on Taiwan was to be aided and protected and its position in the United Nations jealously guarded. And the embargo was to remain as tight as possible.

American Opposition to a General Pacific Settlement

Even the relatively limited internal discussions of a Pacific settlement never sought to do more than move toward a two-China policy involving recognition of both Taiwan and the PRC. In November 1954 debates in the NSC, Commerce Department officials submitted a proposal arguing that since the communists "had consolidated effective control over the mainland and their imminent collapse could no longer be expected," external pressure, harassing actions and air raids, embargoes on commerce, and other acts that might "reinforce efforts of opponents within the country to block or delay" the process of consolidation were "no longer tenable."[5] Yet this position remained a minority one. It collided with strong sentiment for the eventual replacement of the communist regime. In November 1953, Robert Bowie, then the director of the State Department's Policy Planning Staff, reported that the JCS wanted NSC 166 amended to state that the "ultimate objective of the U.S. is the replacement of the Chinese Communist regime by one which, at a minimum, would not be hostile to the United States." Achieving that objective, he noted to Walter Bedell Smith, was beyond American capacities; Smith replied that it was "merely a statement of the obvious. . . . We could agree to repeating it over and over just as the Romans had made a watchword of *Carthago delenda est*." Eisenhower said the idea that "the destruction of the military power of Communist China was not in accordance with the long-range interests of the United States 'scared the hell out of him.'"[6] He approved the change shortly thereafter.[7]

The 1954 Commerce Department proposal, like almost all general discussions of Asia from the late 1940s on, raised the issue of Sino-Soviet relations. If the United States sought a split between the Soviet Union and China, "even though current intelligence does not suggest the existence now of many, if any, factors tending to breed internal conflict," then why was it doing nothing to achieve it?[8] Chinese industrialization was likely to make the Soviets profoundly uneasy in the years to come. But because the controls on imports and exports had been undermined by the recent relaxation of controls on Eastern Europe, the Commerce officials argued, the current policies only made China all the more dependent on the USSR for both markets and capital goods—the opposite of the objectives of the proclaimed policy.

The opening of Western markets to Chinese goods, the proposal argued, and of Chinese markets to Western capital equipment necessary for Chinese development might "substantially increase the areas of Chinese independence of action with respect to Russia" and increase the tension between the two powers. Since American allies were clamoring for the easing of the embargo, such a course would have the added advantage of reducing friction with them.

How, in practice, could the tension between the Soviet Union and China be increased? The proposal put forward eight points:

(1) Diplomatic recognition by the U.S. of Communist China as the *de facto* if not the *de jure* government of China.
(2) Acquiescence in U.N. membership for Communist China and possibly a seat on the Security Council.
(3) Creation of an independent Republic of Formosa (Taiwan), with membership in the United Nations but not on the Security Council.
(4) An agreement on the part of Communist China to abandon all claims to Formosa as part of Communist China.
(5) The holding of free and supervised elections in a United Korea without delay and firm commitments to abide by the outcome.
(6) Some possible improvement in the Indo-China deal.
(7) An undertaking by China for whatever value it might have to refrain from providing physical or other types of support to subversive groups (Nehru states he has advocated this).
(8) The lifting of trade restrictions on sale of Chinese goods in the U.S. and elsewhere and the reduction of export controls on the part of COCOM countries, including Japan, to the COCOM level.

In addition, the United States should "refrain from assisting or encouraging offensive actions to harass Communist China or its commerce, and restrain the Chinese Nationalists from such actions," and there should be a limited opening up of Sino-Japanese economic relations, which would also ease Japan's trade problems.[9] Although the Commerce Department's proposal was meant to be "suggestive only," assuming that the pressures to recognize China intensified, or that Beijing was increasingly likely to enter the UN, or that trade barriers grew harder and harder to enforce, it offered a way of encouraging China to pursue a course independent from the Soviet Union.

In NSC debates, the foregoing proposal fell under the rubric of Alternative A, the "soft" policy of "peaceful coexistence," which resembled British proposals. It is noteworthy that this policy was viewed as soft or flexible rather than as an alternative form of waging the Cold War against China. But at no time was it ever given serious consideration by Eisenhower, Dulles, the leaders of the CIA, or the JCS. One major difficulty was what Dulles called the *immediate* context of America's interests in Asia; it was, he said, an issue of timing: "A policy not only had to be right, it had to be right at the right time. The question of gains for Communist China in the intermediate period was one of great gravity for the U.S. . . . For this reason any weakness of the Western position was fraught with danger."[10] In the long term, when the split between the Soviet Union and China finally materialized, a two-China policy might be possible, but until then the objective was to prevent the expansion of Chinese power and influence in Asia, and that made Taiwan's continued role as the government of China essential.

The real problem with Alternative A was that it undercut the ideological and strategic linchpin of American policy: the isolation that kept China in its place. Richard Nixon argued in an August 18, 1954, NSC meeting that "a soft policy would result in complete Chinese Communist domination of Asia." No one disagreed. Radford and other members of the JCS pushed for Alternative D, which called for a more militant policy "designed to confront the regime with a clear likelihood of U.S. military action against China proper unless Communist China takes public action to change its belligerent support of Communist expansion." Dulles warned that few American allies would support such a policy. Alternatives B and C, however, were hardly compromises between A and D; both were designed to isolate and reduce Chinese power and influence. As Radford noted, moreover, the differences between B, C, and D did not much matter, "since if the United States undertook to carry out the policies in Alternative B or C, the situation envisaged in Alternative D would almost certainly come to pass, whether we liked it or not."[11]

Alternatives B, C, and D were all predicated on the conviction that any lessening of hostility toward China would weaken the effort to isolate it that underlay the entire containment policy. In almost every debate on China during the Eisenhower administration some officials would argue for flexibility on specific issues—trade, the United Nations, the two-China policy—but no one, not even those seeking flexibility on particular issues, challenged the prevailing consensus that the global and Asia-wide requirements of the policy required that the line being drawn had to be sustained by ideological hostility.

In the early years of the Eisenhower administration, the pressures for a Far Eastern settlement came from allies and neutrals alike. A September 1953 CIA estimate of the probable reaction to a Chinese Nationalist invasion of Hainan with direct American air and naval participation acknowledged these pressures as strong and persistent. India and other Southeast Asian countries were "inclined to believe that a real settlement of East-West differences, at least in the Far East, is possible at the present time," and to the French such a settlement had "come increasingly to seem the best possibility for reducing their commitment in Indochina."[12]

Eisenhower and Dulles repeatedly argued that the question of a general settlement was inseparable from the morale of the Nationalists. In these discussions, "morale" was an accordion word, expanding or contracting as necessary to justify various degrees of support for the Nationalists. The issue was never just Taiwan itself; Taiwan's "morale" was tied up with the fate of South Korea, South Vietnam, the Philippines, and SEATO members such as Thailand. Eisenhower used some of his most vehement language in asserting Taiwan's centrality: "We are convinced that the psychological effect in the Far East of deserting our friends on Formosa would risk a collapse of Asiatic resistance to the Communists," he wrote Churchill in January 1955. And again in March: "We cannot fail to conclude that the time to stop any advance of Communism in Asia is here, now"; the "loss of Formosa would doom the Philippines and eventually the remainder of the region. . . . [T]he loss of Formosa would be catastrophic; the Philippines and Indonesia would rapidly be lost to us."[13]

The JCS and Eisenhower often spoke of the critical role of Taiwan in the island defense chain.[14] But though Taiwan was seen as militarily indispensable, far greater emphasis was placed on its paramount importance in the isolation of China. Taiwan was the key to UN ostracism, to the embargo, to stemming Chinese communist influence in the overseas Chinese community. It was the indispensable military and strategic linchpin for drawing a line in Asia behind which both economic and military stabilization could take place. This was the reason discussions of general settlements in Asia were so often over timing rather than over the issues themselves.

In late 1957, Robert McClintock of the Policy Planning Staff noted in "Review of U.S. China Policy: A Pacific Settlement?" that in the not too distant future the PRC might well be voted into the United Nations. With the overseas Chinese community showing increasing pride in "a strong government in

Peking dominated by no foreign influence," the "U.S. cannot prevent increasing trade with China on the part of Western Europe and Japan." Consequently, McClintock argued, the United States might do better trying to "negotiate a general settlement with Mainland China than by holding on to policies which time inevitably will change." Under such a settlement, the United States would withdraw its opposition to Beijing's UN membership, but only if Taiwan were admitted "as the Independent Republic of Taiwan, neutralized, with its territorial integrity guaranteed by the signatory powers." Tibet would also be "neutralized, its independence and territorial integrity guaranteed," as would Vietnam and Korea. The old rationale for a new policy had not changed: "The recognition of the People's Republic of China as a Pacific Power and its admission to the United Nations might start the process of schism between China and the USSR which as stated above is an objective of our policy."[15]

McClintock's proposal drew little opposition from either Eisenhower or Dulles except over timing: raising such issues in the present context would be misinterpreted, they believed. Dulles did not regard the proposal as a soft stance, but tactically it might be so interpreted, especially by Taiwan, which bitterly opposed the entire idea. Dulles and Eisenhower had both concluded that American power in Asia was now sufficient to hold the line—it was "the major factor damping down the growth of Peiping's influence"[16]—and the American military presence in Taiwan was an indispensable part of this power.[17]

Dulles argued that the United States would be able to prevent China's admission to the United Nations for some years. As McClintock noted, "So long as the U.S. supplies not only the butter, but most of the bread, to many of the members of the UN, we can count with some assurance on being able in fact to buy their vote."[18] Eisenhower's warnings that domestic popular opinion might not tolerate a continued American role in a United Nations that welcomed "Red China" also reminded both allies and neutrals of the perils of voting for admission.[19]

Containment and the Uses of Tension

The isolation of China rested on a variety of factors, none of which—except Taiwan—was vital in and of itself. But any weakening on one factor risked the appearance of weakening on all the others. The image of the floodgates was never simply a Cold War illusion. Isolating China meant quashing even steps that critics of the policy saw as only minor variations. The intensity with which Eisenhower sought to isolate China dominated his strategic, ideological, and economic policies in Asia from the very beginning. Some advantage was eventually seen in reducing tensions in Europe, but never in Asia.[20] For a country that did not wish to see tensions escalated in the Taiwan Strait, the United

States pursued a continued policy whose implementation required a startlingly high level of tension. Isolation and tension went together, and in the 1950s, containment without isolation was not yet viewed as a possibility.

Washington, of course, portrayed China itself as the source of the tensions, its policies and attitudes ultimately shaped quite apart from specific American actions. When arguing in this way with allies and neutrals, Washington tried to keep the focus away from its relations with Taiwan. American officials stressed their global concerns and China's inherent hostility to the requirements of the global order. The reasons they gave for its hostility were many: among them, it needed the "foreign devil" to justify its draconian internal policies; the regime gained support by developing a "deeper and deeper hatred of the West, particularly the United States";[21] communism was inherently aggressive; China's nationalistic, "center of civilization" mentality made it seek to dominate Asia.

The problem was that American policies seemed to many Asians and to some Europeans to be what was engendering the tensions. China's proclamations of peaceful coexistence were often judged worthy of consideration, and its economic development was widely believed to need a more peaceful Asia. But any reduction of tension was fraught with peril for American interests. A December 1957 NIE concluded, "If Communist behavior is such that tensions in the Far East are substantially reduced, most Asian countries, except Nationalist China, Korea, and Vietnam, would probably cautiously relax their present suspicions of Peiping and move gradually toward broader contacts and normal diplomatic relations with Communist China. This, in time, would enlarge Peiping's ability to influence these countries." If, on the other hand, the "Sino-Soviet Bloc dropped its general line of peace and coexistence in Asia," then the result would be greater tension: "there would probably be a clearer demarcation of Communist and non-Communist influence in Asia."[22]

Contrasting Asia with Europe, Dulles noted a "lack of 'depth' in resistance in Far Eastern countries, vulnerable to Communist pressure and to the temptations of neutralism. Any indication of softening on the part of the U.S. would have extremely serious repercussions—discouraging those who oppose Communism and encouraging those ready to make an accommodation with the Communist Chinese."[23] Beijing could then effectively "exploit growing sentiment for trade with the mainland," and would "encourage informal contacts as an entering wedge . . ."[24] Any contact or opening—cultural exchange, trade, travel, journalism—risked setting an example that other Asian countries would be sure to pursue.

But Washington could not afford to appear utterly immovable.[25] The pressure to defuse Asian tensions was strong from allies and even stronger from neutral nations in Asia. Partly in response to such pressures, Washington argued for the "nonuse of force" position in the Taiwan strait, insisting that this issue had to do with the peace of the region: Beijing, not Washington, would thus appear warlike. But in practical terms it was not easy for Washington to persuade other nations that it was not the aggressor in Taiwan. This image problem was abundantly clear at the Bandung Conference in 1955. Even as American diplomats were trying to put a positive spin on the outcome of the latest crisis in the Taiwan Strait, privately they were worried. In reporting on the meetings, one of them noted that

> Chou En-lai enjoyed a tremendous triumph. In his public appearances Chou possessed great stage presence. He was dignified, calm, affable, and subtly conveyed his feeling that he ought to be the main figure of the conference. His statements were moderate in tone and content, and he cleverly used Cicero's technique by mentioning anti-Western sentiments or pro-Communist sentiments, and then stating that for the sake of harmony and unity he would not expand upon them. He was clever also in appearing to "turn the other cheek" while actually giving up nothing of his original position. He made a tremendous impression on all the press, the delegates, and other observers. He was very successful in his personal contacts. . . . Everywhere he laid emphasis on the fact that China's only desire was to cooperate with her Asian neighbors and to live in peace. His efforts were very successful. The Embassy believes that Chou's maneuver on Taiwan favorably impressed the delegates, placing the U.S. on the defensive.[26]

Negotiating American Style

The Chinese seemed peaceful; the United States, warlike. Zhou Enlai seemed flexible, willing to negotiate; Dulles, rigid and hard-line. The issue was already evident in U.S. discussions over how to handle the negotiations at Geneva, set to begin in April 1954, on Korea and Indochina. In these circumstances the United States decided to assume the appearance, but not the reality, of flexibility. Washington had concluded that it could prevent the conferences from discussing a general settlement of Asian issues but also knew that it could not afford to take "a purely negative position."[27] A May 3 memorandum prepared in Geneva laid out the tactics the United States subsequently followed: "No agreement will be reached which is inconsistent with the basic U.S. objectives. Toward this end, the U.S. should . . . endeavor to stimulate the Communists to the adoption of harsh negotiating tactics and inflexible positions. The Working Group is preparing detailed suggestions of fruitful ways of playing on Communist and particularly Chinese Communist sensitivities."[28]

Yet this harsh position was complicated by the advent of "informal talks" between Chinese and American representatives at Geneva beginning in June 1954 over the issue of foreign nationals held in each country. Dulles concluded that he could not refuse to talk about the release of Americans held in China, but he sought in the following years to keep the issues narrowly focused—on repatriation of American citizens held in Chinese jails (the Chinese insisted they were CIA agents)[29] and on an insistence that the United States would not negotiate under the "threat of force" (i.e., regarding Taiwan). The difficulty was that Washington wanted to appear to its allies and neutral nations willing to negotiate, while in reality it was determined to ensure that negotiations with the PRC had no consequences. But by this very willingness, Washington risked being perceived as having shifted its policy.

U. Alexis Johnson, the chief U.S. negotiator in Geneva, agreed with his colleagues that the PRC was unlikely to sign a no-force agreement about Taiwan. In public, American officials spoke of such an agreement as a prerequisite for preserving international peace, but in private they understood that by accepting a "no-force position" Beijing would be accepting the right of the United States to negotiate issues that cut to the very core of the PRC's claims of sovereignty over Taiwan. Taking such a position would constitute a tacit acknowledgment of the Nationalist regime; a no-force agreement would imply acceptance of the status quo and greatly weaken Beijing's claim to be the sole government of China and the only one entitled to occupy China's seat in the United Nations. It would also weaken Beijing's claim on Taiwan and decrease its influence in the overseas Chinese community.[30]

Dulles was not only quite aware of all this; he was counting on it. As he said in an address to the U.S. Chiefs of Mission in the Far East on a visit to Manila in March 1955, "The Chinese Communists themselves have made it as clear as it is possible for any government to make it clear that their unalterable purpose is to take Taiwan and that they will not tolerate the existence of a rival Chinese government. I can see from their standpoint why they should do that."[31]

The renunciation of force would, further, leave Taiwan's outlying islands in the hands of the Nationalists. (The United States refused to negotiate this issue on the grounds that it could not negotiate anything that affected the Nationalists without their involvement.) But Alexis Johnson argued that Beijing might well see itself in the stronger position on this matter, since many Asian and neutralist countries sided with the PRC on the offshore islands question. Washington's adamancy threatened to lead only to its further isolation. And on top of everything else, a renunciation-of-force agreement would not even bind the Nationalists, whose raids were continuing unabated as the negotiations began.[32]

Still, Washington worried that Beijing might devise a way to finesse the issue and come up with a peaceful way to resolve the dispute; to keep that from happening, it insisted on an absolutely unequivocal renunciation-of-force statement from the PRC. Even so, debates over the technical language of the various drafts left Washington deeply concerned:

> We have a feeling that we may be getting into a fairly tight corner on the renunciation of force item although basically our position is unquestionably sound. . . . The Communists are attempting to seize the initiative on the renunciation of force item and masquerade as the real sponsors of the renunciation of force concept. We are getting an increasing number of queries as to where we expect to go if the Chinese Communists should unexpectedly agree to sign some form of textually acceptable renunciation of force declaration.[33]

Ambassador Johnson was unsettled to find that "whatever their motives their draft almost completely meets position I have been taking." The Chinese ambassador, Wang Pingnan, had proposed that both sides announce that "the People's Republic of China and the United States of America are determined that they should settle their disputes between their two countries through peaceful negotiations without resorting to the threat or use of force" and that "the two Ambassadors should continue their talks to seek practical and feasible means for the realization of this common desire." This position, Johnson warned Washington, was coming perilously close to the nonuse of force. Wang, he observed, "omitted usual qualification 'conditions permitting.'" He further noted that the Chinese proposal "may contain legal loopholes with respect [to] Taiwan. . . . [I]t seems to me it would be extremely difficult for Peiping [to] issue this statement and then turn around and attempt [to] justify attack in Taiwan area."[34]

Dulles replied that the statement "evades a clear cut renunciation of force both generally and specifically with respect to Taiwan" and—knowing full well that the Chinese would reject such a position—instructed Johnson to insist on a clear statement that the two parties "renounce the use of force in general, and with particular reference to the Taiwan area"; otherwise, the Chinese communists might be seen as offering a concession, which would pressure the United States to offer concessions in return. Because there remained the danger that this draft might be made public, Dulles instructed Johnson to place "primary emphasis" once again on the release of American prisoners, in order to show that communists did not live up to their promises. It was time to take an even "stronger line" on this issue from the "overall standpoint." In other words, it was time to pull back from compromise language on the use of force:

"You can point out that Washington felt so strongly on this subject [the prisoners] that your instructions were to deal exclusively with it for this meeting."[35]

Walter Robertson listed a series of ways to slow down any progress further:

If agreement is reached on an announcement and the Communists then propose discussing withdrawal of U.S. forces then we take the position that we cannot make agreements on this, but that the disposition of our forces would naturally depend on the military situation there and when the threat of use of force is removed, we would take this into consideration in our deployment of forces. If the Communists press further for discussion of the status of Taiwan and related matters we must insist on the position that these affect the interests of the Government of the Republic of China, and we cannot discuss them without the presence of this Government.[36]

Washington's tactics led Johnson to express "serious doubts about the efficacy of the course I had been asked to pursue the past two meetings" and to emphasize that it was "not at all clear as to where to go from here."[37] It was going to become obvious, he added a few days later, that "our only interest is in obtaining the release of all of the Americans and that if and when this is accomplished we will be quick to cut off any further negotiations. I feel that our future moves should take account of this probable estimate on their part."[38]

One historian assessing the talks concluded:

The more agreeable the Chinese had been during the talks, the more Dulles and his advisors had become nervous about where the talks were headed. Prior to the talks, when radical change appeared impossible, Dulles had been willing in private to speculate about China's future in the international community. But as the talks began to reflect a radical change in the PRC's approach toward the United States, unmatched by comparable political change in the United States, Dulles became increasingly less willing to show any flexibility in his opposition to the entry of the PRC into the United Nations, much less recognition by the United States.[39]

Zhou Enlai and the Chinese negotiators continued to indicate various ways in which they wished to improve relations with the United States—trade, cultural exchange, an exchange of journalists. Every such suggestion constituted a problem for Dulles, not because it was unacceptable in principle but because he wanted to reinforce a hard-line policy.

Zhou was working hard to make the American position untenable. The Pakistani prime minister wrote to Eisenhower in December 1956 that China wanted to find practical and feasible ways to improve relations with the United States and was willing to negotiate over trade, the return of prisoners, and the renunciation of force. He passed on a message from Zhou: "We would ask you to tell your American friends that we want to be friendly with them. We are prepared to negotiate and extend our hand of friendship. Please see if you cannot bring about an understanding between us." Zhou added he was prepared to travel to the United States.[40]

Eisenhower and Dulles would have none of this. Their policies were designed with precisely the opposite objective: to defuse and also deflect international pressure on them to be more flexible toward China, and to sustain the tension in Asia crucial to the continued isolation of China. To do these things, they were willing to appear flexible on specific points, but they pulled back whenever any steps threatened to suggest a significant shift in policy on Taiwan. Taiwan was a matter of great concern both to Asian powers and to Washington's European allies, because it directly raised the possibilities of war between China and the United States. But there was no way to defuse the issue successfully during the Eisenhower administration.

The Geneva talks embodied the dilemma in any step toward more normal relations with China. The very fact of discussions suggested to some that a "deal" might result, "leaving in the lurch our Asian friends." The secrecy and the duration of the talks fed rumors and gave support to those in Asia who were urging closer relations with Beijing and to those in the rest of the world who believed the PRC should assume the China seat in the United Nations. For the United States even to continue talking was a blow to American prestige, argued Walter McConaughy, the director of the State Department's Office of Chinese Affairs: "The tactical advantages we have obtained at Geneva could be preserved by the right type of break-off statement." The talks had secured the release of most imprisoned U.S. citizens, he continued, and they had not led to any "conclusive" prevention of a communist attack on Taiwan. (The Nationalist regime had been deeply opposed to the talks.) The dilemma for the United States arose from the circumstance that its policy was "to deal with them only when we must. Under these circumstances, the Communists have the initiative in the talks, being in a position to make (and to publicize at the opportune moment for them) proposal after proposal of a seemingly praiseworthy character, such as those on trade and travel and cultural exchanges which we must reject. This keeps us on the defensive and gives the Communists a great advantage."[41]

The Future of the Republic of China

Dulles admitted that many of his own tactics were not peaceful and that he was tempted to consider far harsher steps toward China, an approach he spelled out in his address to Mission Chiefs in Asia in March 1955. In his conclusion, he said that "perhaps the most important of all" his convictions was his certainty that

> this expansionist movement of Communist China will not be checked until at some point we are prepared to check it with force. . . . They are going to find out we really mean business, . . . the only question is time and place where we must confront the issue. Are we better off to confront China after we have given up important positions, after we have greatly impaired morale of the Nationalists, after we have further shaken the confidence of the non-Communist peoples of the Western Pacific in our determination? I said to Mr. Eden that what is going on here is, in my opinion, somewhat the same as what went on in the early days of Hitler. . . . This situation is similar, and someone has to decide when and where we make our intentions clear. I think we are better to decide that in this area than you are [I told Eden]. We have the responsibility, we have the treaty responsibility and I do not think you are better qualified than we to make the decision.[42]

In all the major areas of Amerian policy, this need to hold the line firmly (or the wish to go even further) without appearing utterly inflexible plagued the Eisenhower administration. But the contradiction was seen as a burden to be borne, not a strategy in need of readjustment. So it was in dealing with the Nationalists. Some of Jiang's more ardent supporters—such as Ambassador Karl Rankin and Assistant Secretary of State Walter Robertson—may have believed he had a future on the mainland. But Eisenhower and Dulles agreed that only a major upheaval there might enable Jiang to return; they considered him incapable of organizing such an uprising, and they rarely budged in their determination to prevent him from trying.[43] They worried more about Jiang's morale (and that of other Asian allies) than about his likely move on the mainland. They worried more about his weaknesses than about his strengths. His long-term prospects were dim. As his mainland supporters on Taiwan grew older, the basis for his regime became more and more vulnerable, and a post-Jiang leadership was unpredictable.

American policy in the offshore islands crises of both 1954 and 1958 reflected Washington's desire to preserve a kind of hostile coexistence with China. Eisenhower and Dulles both refused to support Admiral Radford's military approach to the Jinmin-Matsu disputes in 1954. Dulles wanted neither all-out war nor the surrender of the islands; Eisenhower took the same view, arguing that though the islands were not militarily necessary for the defense of Taiwan, they were essential to the *morale* of Taiwan and to the credibility of the United States.

Eisenhower and Dulles well knew they were holding the line not militarily but—however regrettable—with a patchwork of tactics very unlike what they were doing in Europe. Thus the challenge, on this issue as on almost all others involving American-Chinese relations, was how to defuse and contain an explosive situation while continuing to back the Nationalists.[44] Some administration officials, more narrowly focused on the specifics of the issue, argued that the islands should be let go and Jiang's troops withdrawn. But Eisenhower, while lamenting Jiang's having committed so many of his troops to the offshore islands, feared the impact on Nationalist morale should the Chinese communists, take them by force. The upshot was a policy opposed by many European and Asian allies (and neutrals) and, especially in 1958, by congressional and Democratic critics. NSC debates did not always address the overarching policy of isolating China. They might center on the complexity of holding the offshore islands (which ones, at what cost) or the extent of Jiang's troop commitments, but these tactical debates did not challenge the larger policy.

Just as Eisenhower and Dulles often expressed their desire for an eventual split between the Soviet Union and China but did nothing to hasten it, it appears quite plausible from the available records that in the long run they would have liked a two-China policy in one version or another but did nothing to achieve it in the short run. Quite the contrary: they overruled proposals in that direction and remained unwilling to budge on their Taiwan policy.[45]

In October 1958, shortly before a trip to Taiwan, Dulles discussed Assistant Secretary of State for Policy Planning Gerald Smith's proposal for a two-China policy. Smith argued that a Nationalist evacuation of the offshore islands would strengthen a two-China policy and deny the communists the ability to shake things up by attacking the islands according to their own timetable. The islands should be evacuated *and* stronger guarantees given to Taiwan.[46]

Dulles strongly disagreed, but he was deeply concerned about the long-term position of Jiang's Republic of China. As he wrote in a memo for his files, the "ROC primarily represents a civil war survival and that background makes it essentially militaristic in outlook. This may need to be changed." The ROC needed "a larger and more acceptable" mission. If it could come to represent what was best in Chinese culture, it might win greater support in the free world. But "it cannot play this role and enjoy the support of the free peoples if the image of the Republic of China which is transmitted abroad is that of a regime whose existence appears to be dependent upon a return by force to the mainland. This is an unattractive image and one which is largely regarded as unrealistic and highly dangerous to world peace." Dulles worried that in time, various pressures would succeed in "liquidating" the regime. "It is doubtful," he wrote, "whether even the U.S. can long protect the ROC under present circumstances. It is far from certain that a subsequent U.S. administration will be willing to be as staunch for the ROC as has been the Eisenhower-Dulles administration of foreign policy." He saw three basic threats: first, the overt threat of the PRC's vast military and propaganda capabilities; second, the growing dependence of the ROC on the Taiwanese population, people who had never had an interest in the continuation of the civil war ethos; and third, the desire throughout the free world for "a liquidation of the civil war, which carries with it the risk of general war."[47]

The occasion for Dulles's reflections was the 1958 crisis over the continual massive military presence on the offshore islands that remained after the August 1958 crisis eased. He wanted to find ways to persuade Jiang to withdraw some of his troops; perhaps the offshore islands might even be demilitarized if the Chinese communists would agree not to seize them. Dulles noted that "acceptance of a two-China situation by the GRC might come sometime in the future when the Army was Taiwanese," but now was not the time, and he opposed taking steps to achieve that objective.[48]

As the crisis eased, he listed seven motives for U.S. cooperation with the ROC:

(1) To keep the anti-Communist government on Taiwan strong enough to withstand any Communist assault.
(2) To prevent more Chinese from being forcefully subjected to Communist tyranny.
(3) To be ready to help the Chinese on the mainland if the opportunity presents itself as a result of organized dissatisfaction.
(4) To stimulate the possibility of revolt on the mainland by making Taiwan a model of political, economic, and social welfare.[49]
(5) To keep the overseas Chinese from becoming a tool of Peking.
(6) To preempt the seat of China in the United Nations so that it would not go to the Chinese Communists, giving them increased prestige and influence in the world.
(7) To preserve Chinese culture.[50]

Dulles then analyzed each objective in the light of force reduction on the offshore islands and the impact of a de facto armistice in the Taiwan Strait. The first two could be achieved with fewer forces on the islands, he wrote, if they appeared to be the Nationalists' own program rather than a response to American pressure and policies—which would require that the Nationalists forgo using the islands for "provocative purposes."[51] The best way to achieve the third point was a greater, not a lesser, concentration of forces on Taiwan. Troops could be deployed more easily from there than from islands that were easy to attack and subject to artillery barrage.

Point (4) called for lessening the division between those who regarded Taiwan as their home and those who hoped to return to the mainland. Taiwanese were reportedly not eager to die in defense of offshore islands in which they had "no sentimental interest." Points (5) and (6) required assuaging other nations' deep uneasiness over a situation that "involves them in a risk of world war because of the military disposition by the CHINATS [Chinese Nationalists] which, in their opinion, are unnecessarily provocative." Nationalist use of the islands, in their view, amounted to a constant threat to invade the mainland and to blockade mainland ports. For Dulles, that was only a "paper threat which in reality is non-existent"; the Nationalists would need to emphasize that they were not planning to invade the mainland before they could gain the support of these other nations.[52]

For Dulles, American global credibility had to be preserved at all costs. The United States had options, especially if the Nationalists could be talked into great flexibility. But any success by the Communists militarily or any forced surrender of the islands could damage the entire foundation on which Washington's China policy had been built. Change was preferable. Dulles wanted Jiang to "make clear that, so far as [the GRC] is concerned, and on a basis of *de facto* reciprocity, it will conduct itself as though there were an armistice along the line of present division and indeed, would be willing itself to conclude such an armistice." He wanted Jiang to renounce any "attempt forcibly to return on the Mainland unless invited by Chinese elements there that are respectable in their quantity and responsible in their quality." Commando raids would have to end; so would provocative overflights. A resolution of the offshore islands problem would come when the ROC recognized the danger of having opposing military forces in such close proximity; in other words, Dulles wanted a form of demilitarization along the lines of the Korean armistice. A reduction of the ROC military forces would also reduce the enormous financial strain on the Taiwanese economy.[53]

An apparently innocuous point was actually central to Dulles's plan. That the communists were turning against China's great cultural traditions, he reasoned, offered Taiwan a golden opportunity to speak on the culture's behalf. For the overseas Chinese community, Taiwan could at last play a more positive role. Jiang's image was still too discredited to embody the ideal of freedom. But the crass materialism of the Chinese communists, as Dulles saw it, stood in telling contrast to the richness of China's historic culture—numerous artifacts of which Jiang had taken with him when he fled the mainland in the late 1940s.

But Dulles's plan came to naught. In moments of crisis, including this one, he pulled back from long-term goals, which posed too much risk to his immediate objectives. He would ride out the crisis rather than risk creating another one by urging Taiwan to shift its policies. He leaned toward a two-China position only in the long run.

In August 1958, Dulles drafted the policy that was later quoted in Eisenhower's memoirs. It remains a particularly strong and emphatic articulation of the administration's thinking in the Jinmin-Matsu crisis. Chinese pressure on the islands seemed "designed to produce a cumulating rollback effect."[54] The fear of falling dominoes resurfaced: the loss of these tiny islands off the Chinese coast, Washington feared, would have the most serious repercussions on the Philippines, Japan, and other Southeast Asian nations. The blow to the Nationalists might lend force to subversive movements, and the loss of Taiwan would be a staggering blow to the United States. If the PRC felt confident that the United States would not intervene (and if the United States did not do so), then the odds were that it would attack the islands, and it could be expected to triumph if it was willing to suffer significant losses. Such developments would likely encourage forces on Taiwan to "bring about a government which would eventually advocate union with Communist China and the elimination of U.S. positions on the island."[55]

The Eisenhower administration never considered Taiwan secure. It was ideologically vulnerable, threatened by possible abrupt shifts in its international position at the United Nations and utterly dependent on the steadfastness of the United States. Its loss would "seriously jeopardize the anti-communist barrier consisting of the insular and peninsular positions in the Western Pacific, i.e. Japan, Republic of Korea, Republic of China, Republic of the Philippines, Thailand and Vietnam." There were the neutralist dominoes as well. Ultimately, even Japan might be lost.

Dulles's policy was approved at the working levels and the top levels of the State and Defense Departments. According to M. H. Halperin, it said "in effect that the loss of the Offshore Islands could well mean within a few years the collapse of the entire American position in the Far East." Not everyone agreed. Officials in the Bureau of Research and Intelligence did not. Regardless of how the islands were lost, they argued, U.S. prestige would suffer, neutralist sentiment would grow, and communist control would be seen as a sign of greater communist power. "These reactions would be minimized, however, if any change in the status of the Offshore Islands were to come about as the result of negotiations," the argument continued. Halperin's study, however, found an "almost total lack of influence" by that bureau during the crisis.[56]

Why? The opposite question is really more apt: Why should anyone have expected otherwise? For the pattern repeats itself in each and every particular of U.S. policy touching on China: the fear was always that the weakening of any American position could lead to cataclysmic consequences. It was just that fear that brought nuclear weapons so directly into the discussions in both 1954 and 1958. The military demanded they be available, should the United States risk war. Eisenhower and Dulles entertained the possibility precisely because they believed so much was at stake. They were not willing to force the Nationalists from the islands while providing even stronger guarantees to Taiwan. That was the direction of the two-China policy, and it was not the risky course they wanted to take.

There were times when, it is clear, Eisenhower and Dulles did wish to restrain the Nationalists. Many American officials, as Halperin's study suggests, became concerned that the Nationalists "might indeed be trying to pull the United States into a major war with the Chinese Communists."[57] Yet there is little indication that the United States ever really wanted to put a stop to a wide range of Nationalist activities on the mainland, or to separate CIA operations from those of the Nationalists, in either Taiwan, Tibet, or the Chinese community in Southeast Asia.

Washington concluded that the Chinese communists were shifting away from the soft line they had adopted in the Bandung period. Dulles never doubted that the American success in holding the line was tightly bound to U.S. support for a rival to the Beijing government. A harder line from Beijing—the espousal of the position that the "East wind is prevailing over the West wind"—might reflect Beijing's hubris and an overestimation of Soviet strength. There was the additional and growing fear that once Beijing obtained nuclear weapons, their foreign policy would become even "more truculent and militant."[58] But it was also understood by American officials as a sign that Beijing had not obtained its objectives, and an indication that the American position had held. It had to keep holding in order to buy the time needed to consolidate the American position in Asia.

Dulles's June 1957 China Speech

In his San Francisco speech of June 28, 1957, Dulles offered one of his most articulate statements on China policy. The United States, he warned, confronts a regime "bitterly hateful of the U.S." It had come to power "by violence, and so far, has lived by violence," and it did not disguise its "expansionist ambitions." The Chinese communists had fomented revolutions in the Philippines and in Malaya, had taken Tibet by force, and were supporting the war in Indochina. It was imperative that Washington abstain from any moral, political, or material act that would encourage such ruthless leaders. If the United States thought diplomatic recognition, the opening of trade, cultural exchange, or a seat in the United Nations would encourage the "passing" of the Chinese regime, Washington would support it, but in fact, any such move would only encourage Chinese aggression and contribute to Beijing's prestige. As for encouraging a split between the Soviet Union and China, "there are no doubt basic power rivalries between Russia and China in Asia," Dulles said, but they would fully emerge only with a communist victory, and then "they would quarrel over the booty—of which we would be part."[59]

Robert Bowie, in a State Department memorandum on the speech, succinctly summarized the premises of American policy:

a. Communist China is hostile to the U.S. and has acted and probably will continue to act in ways which are contrary to acceptable standards of international behavior and adverse to U.S. interests.
b. Communist China is a solid partner of the Soviet Union and an active agent of international communism.
c. U.S. moves toward accommodation to the Chinese Communist regime will not have a significant effect on the character of the regime or its relations to Russia and international communism.
d. Any move by the U.S. which appears to be in the direction of accommodation to the Chinese Communists will: (1) increase the prestige of the Chinese Communists; (2) have unsettling effects in Taiwan; (3) dispose the Asian friends of the U.S. to move toward closer and possibly dangerous relationship with the Chinese Communists.

From these premises, Bowie continued, the speech drew the following policy conclusions:

a. The U.S. should not recognize Communist China;
b. The U.S. should exert its maximum efforts: (1) to maintain the international status of Nationalist China as the only government of China; (2) to isolate the Chinese Communists economically and diplomatically, with special stress upon their continued exclusion from the UN or any of its agencies.[60]

Though Bowie wrote his memo to challenge a key aspect of Dulles's approach, what is most revealing is their shared assumptions. Bowie's concern was that the policy could not succeed for much longer, particularly on the issue of keeping China out of the United Nations. The United States had to prepare for such an eventuality instead of wasting political resources on seeking to isolate China: "I do not believe that over the long run, or even in the fairly near term, the effort to isolate Communist China as a pariah will succeed." He agreed with the premises of American policy; the challenge was to reshape it so as to extend its success. That, for Bowie, meant a two-China policy. If the Chinese got their seat in the United Nations over American objections, Bowie, like Eisenhower and Dulles, foresaw a domino effect. Chinese Communist prestige would be "greatly enhanced"; other Asian countries would "hasten to accommodate themselves to a regime which has won an important political victory over the U.S.," and the United States would lose its leverage in limiting their accommodation with the Communists. International support for an independent Taiwan would lessen; the consensus would grow that communist China was the "only China." Repercussions in Taiwan might extend even to some elements seeking "rapprochement with the mainland."[61]

Bowie's assessments of tactics and specifics differed from Dulles's, but his premises did not: the goal was a contained China forced to accept the basic status quo of a U.S.-organized Asia. Even with the guaranteed independence of Taiwan and membership in the UN, the Nationalists would still be ferociously opposed, but this was "an advantage, not a handicap. . . . The unwillingness of either 'China' to accept the other as a permanent entity will help us to buy time." Maneuvering around the issue of Taiwan would also "complicate and delay" seating China in the UN, and allow the United States far greater leverage and ability to shape the outcome. The end result would be some kind of "protective guardianship of Formosa."[62]

Dulles's disagreement did not mean he would not have liked the ultimate outcome of a permanently protected Taiwan separate from China. But to him and to Eisenhower such an outcome was, in the immediate and practical sense, not viable at all—not because it was unacceptable to Beijing but because it was unworkable for the United States. Taiwan could not be separated from American global objectives in Asia in the 1950s; the timing was not yet right, and this for the most practical of reasons. Dulles was not being moralistic or Eisenhower simply stubborn in holding to their Taiwan policy. No American official wanted to risk the consequences of a policy shift. That is why, for all the talk about a two-China policy, no practical steps were ever taken to implement it.

In his last years in office, following the September 1959 Soviet-American summit at Camp David, Eisenhower brought up the issue of China in letters to Khruschev, stressing once again the need for the Soviet Union and China to agree to the "renunciation of force" that he knew was the basis for maintaining any long-term status quo in Asia along American lines.[63] Despite the difficult situation in Indochina, he wrote, there had nonetheless been "a basic trend over the past five years toward a stabilization of the line of demarcation between Communist and non-Communist Asia."[64] But Khrushchev had not budged on the issue of Taiwan at the Camp David summit, although the Americans had hoped that the summit would provide a "suitable opportunity" to pressure him on the need to "restrain the aggressive acts of the Chinese Communists." In this context, Taiwan was the critical issue, not Indochina.[65]

In his letters, Eisenhower reminded Khruschev that they had found grounds for hope and eventual agreement on many subjects but not on China:

> You left me with the clear impression that you thought the People's Republic of China had the right to seek to take territory of the Republic of China, that is to say Taiwan, the Pescadores and other islands, by force of arms, . . . [that this was] a question of civil war, . . . [that] Chiang Kai-shek should be regarded as a rebel defying the legitimate government of the country, . . . [and that this was] a domestic question and not an international question.[66]

Khrushchev had simply reiterated the Soviet position that "Taiwan is a province of China and what goes on with respect to the island is part of the process of the Chinese revolution and the Soviet Union fully understands China's aspirations in that respect."[67] Eisenhower wanted some indication that the Soviet Union was prepared to prove more flexible on Taiwan, since "containment with isolation" was still the linchpin in his commitment to establishing a new Asian order. He did not get it. As it turned out, the weakest point would be not Taiwan but Indochina.

7 REVOLUTIONARY CHINA AND CONTAINMENT WITHOUT ISOLATION

A vision of China as a militant, revolutionary, ideologically expansionist nation dominated the Kennedy and Johnson administrations. China was dangerous not simply because it was communist or intensely nationalistic but because it was the nation that most fully embodied the forces sweeping through the discontented Third World. It combined the radical nationalism and the revolutionary fervor that Washington saw as the hallmarks of "wars of national liberation."

Interpreting China was no longer a question of communism versus nationalism (as with Truman and Acheson) or how much of each (as with Eisenhower and Dulles). During the Kennedy and Johnson administrations, Washington's China was a deeply disturbed revolutionary nation relentlessly at war against the imperatives of modernization, proclaiming a virulently expansionist nationalism that combined a commitment to anti-imperialism and guerrilla warfare with the building of revolutionary socialism. Yet this China was every bit as much an ideological construct as the Truman administration's Kremlin-dominated puppet had been. The context for both was a pervasive globalist ethos wherein policy, the key code words, and ideological concerns became inseparable. The language encoding that globalism was changing, but the fundamental process of global strategizing in the national security world, which had created these Chinas, had not changed.

The Kennedy-Johnson era was marked by energetic efforts to coordinate the policy of the core capitalist areas (creating a "new trading world") and to incorporate further and consolidate American influence in the Third World.

The problem was that more and more Third World leaders were turning toward various kinds of radical nationalism to develop their countries. The decade of the 1960s was the golden era of "modernization" in the national security bureaucracy because visionary globalism now required updated ideological weapons against radical nationalism and revolutionary alternatives of all kinds. In this new world the USSR and its relatively moderate nation-building efforts seemed less threatening than the more radical methods surfacing throughout the Third World, from Cuba to Vietnam.

Dean Acheson warned Kennedy not to let his administration "be diverted from the main battleground of Europe into sentimental crusades against colonialism and hopeless efforts to democratize the underdeveloped world."[1] But Kennedy and his leading advisors had believed other ideas. Limited wars, non-overt aggression, and revolutions were all placing the world "in a state of uncontrollable change, rushing in directions no one could foresee"; the threat to American power was even harder to make sense of than Kremlin-directed communism had been in the 1940s. Washington believed that a line had to be drawn between two ways of developing the future: modernization through further incorporation into the international capitalist system, and the revolutionary but backward and emotionally desperate efforts by poor nations to find alternative ways of development that challenged such incorporation. This was the context in which Washington saw and analyzed, in Arthur Schlesinger Jr.'s phrase, "a boiling and angry China."[2]

A long-range study produced by an interdepartmental task force observed in June 1966 that the "national interests" of the United States and China clashed on two fundamental points. First, "the United States stands for orderly, peaceful change, and China for revolutionary change leading to a Communist world." Second, although the United States was willing to accept China as "one of many components in a regional balance of Asian power," Beijing would "settle for nothing less than regional hegemony and aspire[d] to acceptance as one of the three global powers and eventually to leadership of the Communist world."[3] As a State Department memo stressed, for China to "achieve Great power status" directly or indirectly would impinge upon American interests.[4]

Just as during the Truman administration the American commitment to an orderly global process had been logically separable from but in practice interwoven with the fight against communism, so now the United States confronted a Third World in violent upheaval *and* a China fomenting those upheavals. If the USSR's role as enemy in the 1940s and 1950s had illuminated what was at stake in the American effort to develop orderly processes of global change, so in the 1960s could China's role as enemy reveal what was at stake in the efforts to modernize the Third World nonviolently. "The most likely peril to the peace of nations in Asia, Africa, and Latin America during the next decade is the whole range of militant dissidence fomented, encouraged, or supplied by Communist China," the same 1966 study predicted.[5]

The peril for the United States was a "basic one" not because of the "intrinsic attractiveness of the Chinese model" or the "substantive applicability of Chinese doctrine" but because the "weakness and frustration of many nations and groups in the underdeveloped world . . . makes them turn away from sober, unsatisfactory rationalism towards Chinese solutions for their problems." Put differently, Chinese "demagogically" urged them "to rebel against the facts of their abysmal economic situation or the actual power conditions in which they exist."[6]

Another factor made China doubly ominous: "Mainland Southeast Asia—Vietnam and Thailand in particular—has become the major testing ground of the ability of the U.S. to check Communist aggression."[7] As Kenneth Young, American ambassador to Thailand, put it, "Southeast Asia is the critical bottleneck stopping Sino-Soviet territorial and ideological expansion—territorial in Asia, ideological in the whole world. Southeast Asia is somewhat like the hub of a wheel; lose the hub and the wheel collapses."[8] The more the focus tightened on Vietnam, the larger the place China took in both regional and global assessments of radicalism in the Third World. China must not be allowed to expand, ideologically or in any other way: "The U.S. should firmly oppose ChiCom political and military domination of any territory outside its present borders," particularly Taiwan. India and Japan had to be encouraged to "withstand Chicom pressure." The Chinese model must be destroyed "by political and psychological covert as well as overt methods" and the image of the Chinese as "successful modernizers" shattered.[9]

Some American military officers warned that war with China was inevitable "if the United States was determined to take decisive action in Southeast Asia and avoid the mistakes of Vietnam."[10] Under Secretary of State Chester Bowles at times agreed: "We are going to have to fight the Chinese anyway in 2, 3, 5 or 10 years and it is just a question of where, when and how."[11] The advisability of such a war, or of a strike at Chinese nuclear facilities, was widely debated.[12] A revolutionary China, bitterly hostile to American interests and a potential military enemy, was central to the virulent imagery of the early and mid-1960s.

Counterrevolution and "Containment without Isolation"

Beginning in the early 1960s, however, the depiction of China as a revolutionary, ideologically expansive force in Asia was interwoven with what appears as a surprising shift in American policy. The Eisenhower administration had aimed for containment with isolation. Quietly at first but with growing emphasis, the Kennedy administration began to speak of containing China without isolating it. The perennial bilateral policy concerns remained: the United States was not about to recognize Beijing; it feared a significant defeat should China be voted into the United Nations; and it continued to worry over the fate of Taiwan and of Jiang's regime. China's role in Southeast Asia appeared highly threatening to broader U.S. policy objectives in Asia. Yet the June 1966 long-range study of policy toward China concluded that the United States should seek "to reassure Peking publicly, privately, and by our actions that we do not intend to work for the overthrow of the regime, nor do we consider the present hostility immutable." It advised that Washington stop speaking of the regime as unstable or "transitory," and seek to "decrease or remove irrelevant points of friction, and gradually introduce additional positive elements."[13]

After the unabashed hostility of the Eisenhower-Dulles years, in the 1960s Washington began using a new kind of language about Beijing's isolation from the "world community": now China was "understandably maladjusted," psychologically distraught, angry at the world, and projecting its hatred onto the United States.[14] In this psychologized vision the patient needed to be brought to an understanding of the real forces that had shaped its emotional state.[15] "China presents us with what is fundamentally a psychological problem," Edwin O. Reischauer, the American ambassador to Japan, cabled from Tokyo. The Chinese communists were driven by "understandable psychological compulsions and in any case not open to reason."[16] The process of dealing with such a patient would be protracted. "China is very sick but is not likely to be cured from the outside," W. W. Rostow quoted LBJ's "favorite China's watcher," Al Jenkins, in a letter to the president in 1966.[17]

In a notable ideological shift evident especially after 1963, China became responsible for its own paranoia, its self-imposed isolation, and its revolutionary adolescence, but Washington determined to change a number of policies seen as contributing to such hostility. In March 1962 Rostow spelled out the new approach.[18] The required "evolution" of the Chinese communist state, its acceptance of "peaceful coexistence," would be slow and arduous. A firm American line would contribute to change, and change without it would constitute an enormous defeat for the United States. "Until it is demonstrated that the game of 'Wars of national liberation' is not viable and that the borders of China and North Vietnam are firm, the acceptance of Communist China within the world community and in the UN would be a major disaster," Rostow argued.[19] Firmness, however, had to be based on a policy that "should make clear that there is no final bar to the entrance of Communist China into more normal relations with the U.S. if it is prepared to modify its aggressive stances and behavior and recognize de facto the existence of an independent Taiwan." The United States needed to move toward a posture that would "place the onus for continued hostility squarely on Peiping and keep open the possibility that, at some future time, Chinese communist authorities might opt for a policy of less hostility and greater relative dependence on the West."[20]

Under Eisenhower and Dulles a two-China policy had privately been regarded as a long-run possibility; under Kennedy, the possibility moved to the near future. Rostow said in 1962 that China could enter the United Nations as soon as it accepted an "independent Taiwan," and there was nothing heretical about this opinion under Kennedy, though there was no sense of how to make it happen.[21] But it still required that China change its attitudes. And no one wanted to upset the relationship with Jiang unnecessarily; as long as a two-China policy was only theoretical, Kennedy saw little point in arousing domestic opposition over a shift that appeared so unpromising. Still, Washington's belief that a two-China position was inherently moderate and rational for the not too distant future helped it to deal with the strong support for the PRC's entry into the United Nations. Quietly building a case that drew on the reluctance of allies and neutrals simply to vote for the ouster of Taiwan became a way to avoid a possible defeat in the General Assembly.[22] The real concern was that U.S. commitment to Jiang was letting time run out on a UN resolution to provide the legal basis for a Taiwan permanently separate from the mainland. A two-China policy (or an independent Taiwan developing within the shell of the Republic of China) was widely desired: "It would not be so easy for Peiping to justify striving to conquer a Republic of Taiwan which wanted only to maintain its independence and levied no claims upon the mainland," and it was "clearly unwise" to continue supporting Jiang's "dying myth" about returning to the mainland. He had become "an old man of the sea clinging to Uncle Sam's back. The problem is how to shake off the old man without upsetting the boat in the process."[23] The best outcome would be that both Jiang *and* Beijing had to accept the reality of a separate Taiwan.

No one expected an immediate response from China. It became an article of faith in the Kennedy-Johnson years that "the present Chinese Communist leadership has a vested interest in having the U.S. appear to the world at large and to its own populace as implacably hostile." Even so, the United States should avoid "unnecessary provocations" and pursue "informal negotiations with Communist China on specific matters of mutual concern." Washington needed a strategy that would make China's exclusion from the United Nations appear to come from "Peiping's unwillingness to accept reasonable conditions rather than U.S. intransigence."[24] As Harlan Cleveland, Assistant Secretary of

State for International Organization Affairs, wrote in a long assessment of Communist China and the United Nations:

> Even before the CHICOMS decide to try bargaining for a change, it will serve us well to break out of our traditional mold to demonstrate to the rest of the world—which ought to be helping, not jeering—that it is CHICOM international behavior, not considerations of American domestic politics, that is holding back a detente with Peking. . . . We should envisage a continuous *process of bargaining with Communist China, by which the CHICOMS would progressively modify their behavior in return for progressively greater opportunities to play a role in the community of nations.*[25]

By the end of the Johnson administration, this approach had become widely accepted. It proved quite compatible with the escalation of the war in Vietnam; indeed, escalation may have been among the most important factors that allowed for the shift in emphasis. Some saw the defeat of wars of national liberation as the goal that, once achieved, would require China to adapt to the new Asia that was slowly, if painfully, emerging. Others argued that this escalation was precisely what should encourage the United States toward greater "flexibility" on China and a rethinking of its long-range policy objectives. In this context, American flexibility (on rhetoric, trade, journalists, and so on) could be defended against domestic accusations of "weakness," and the onus for the existing hostility placed on China—thus easing pressures from allies who criticized the United States for its intransigence, especially on questions of Taiwan and the United Nations.

In a February 1968 memorandum to President Johnson, Secretary of State Dean Rusk stressed that for the time being the U.S. could take "only very limited steps," since any "significant concessions" would be "seriously misunderstood" both overseas and in Congress. Rusk thus opposed any change in the U.S. opposition to the PRC's entry into the United Nations, but on private contacts (passports, travel) he was more positive—though he expected the practical effect to be "nil"—and he also recommended some minimal trade steps, such as waiving certain controls over American subsidiaries abroad and granting permission to export food, fertilizers, and farm machinery to China. A longer memorandum on China policy that Rusk attached made it clear that significant changes would take a long time. The key lay in the "evolution of attitudes in mainland China," which would have to abandon its attempts to impose its system on Taiwan or its neighbors. Any sudden shift in U.S. policies would undercut the GRC, heighten fears of a U.S. withdrawal from East Asia, and undercut arms negotiations with the Soviets. Yet even if no major steps could be taken, the signal was nonetheless that the United States was ready to move toward a new relationship.[26]

Rusk had one of the more hard-line stances in the Johnson administration, yet even his tone and perspective were noticeably different from what had gone before. He was uneasy about allowing China greater influence in Asia, which might tilt the balance toward neutralism.[27] But he was also comfortable quoting Senator Mike Mansfield's goal of a "Southeast Asia . . . not cut off from China but still not overwhelmed by China." Gradually, like the Russians, he predicted, the Chinese "would come to devote more talk and less action to the violent overthrow of governments." China's isolation was a reflection of its black-and-white, either/or views, its bipolar vision of the world rooted in its revolutionary and visionary attitudes toward the world and its own internal developments. The long-term objective was to bring "China into the international world."[28]

When Richard Nixon wrote his widely noted article for *Foreign Affairs* in 1967, he noted that, "taking the long view, we simply cannot afford to leave China forever outside the family of nations, there to nurture its fantasies, cherish its hates and threaten its neighbors. There is no place on this small planet for a billion people to live in angry isolation." In so arguing, he was echoing Rusk and others in the administration, as he was in his observation that in the short run the United States needed "a policy of restraint, of reward, of a creative counter pressure designed to persuade Peking that its interests can be served only by accepting the basic rules of international civility," so that China could finally be pulled "back into the world community—but as a great and progressing nation, not as the epicenter of world revolution."[29]

By the end of the Johnson administration, containment without isolation had largely triumphed as an approach. Assistant Secretary of State for Far Eastern Affairs William Bundy summarized the prevailing public attitude in a February 1968 speech on China policy, reiterating the two pillars of U.S. policy—that the Chinese communists had a "record of self-isolation" and of "persistent hostility toward the US," and that their "aggressive posture toward outside world" was responsible for the poor state of Sino-American relations—and yet declaring that the United States was ready to "seek reconciliation with mainland China."[30] Or, as Under Secretary of State Nicholas Katzenbach said that May, the United States was trying to "find ways and means of improving our relations with the people and authorities of mainland China consistent with our commitments to other states in Asia."[31]

This view was no less ideological than what had preceded it. Again, it was shaped by U.S. global preoccupations and Asia policies.[32] A vision of modernization had come to the fore to explain Third World developments, the course of the Russian and Chinese revolutions, and the rapidly expanding and deepening role of the United States throughout the Third World. It justified détente with the Soviet Union (especially after the Cuban Missile Crisis), but not with China.[33] It encouraged far greater economic integration with both the advanced capitalist areas and the Third World.

That vision of a modernizing world was profoundly counterrevolutionary. Not only communism and nationalism but now also revolution and radical nationalism in the Third World became immediate concerns, requiring a massive American response under the rubrics of "modernization," "nation building," and "development." Though still a fragile and perilous undertaking, this response was succeeding, to a degree, in drawing a line—except in Southeast Asia. It was progress that justified greater flexibility toward China and long-term policies that would take advantage of China's waning revolutionary élan.

This ideological perspective also helped justify limited détente with the Soviet Union, now viewed as an expansionist nation-state but no longer a great revolutionary threat—in stark contrast to Beijing's revolutionary nationalism and its stake in the Third World revolutionary process that Washington so deeply feared. Thus, a "hard" approach that saw a hostile, ideologically expansionist, revolutionary China could blend with a "softer" approach toward Russia. But at the same time, that hard approach could bifurcate when China was seen gradually to shed its revolutionary ways as it confronted the realities of the "modern world." Both the Soviet Union and the PRC were subject to the same processes; they were merely at different stages.

American Policy and the Sino-Soviet Split

During the 1960 presidential campaign, George Kennan wrote Kennedy of a "serious possibility that the international situation prevailing at the time a new administration takes office may be as calamitous and menacing as was our internal situation at the time when F.D.R. assumed the reigns of government." In June 1961 he warned that the upshot of the world meeting of communist parties the previous autumn had been the "agreed calculation, between Russians and Chinese, that America's world position and influence could effectively be shattered in [the] coming period."[34] Charles Bohlen wrote similarly to Rusk of the communist conviction that "what they term the correlation of forces" is "swinging in their favor throughout the world."[35]

Two days before Kennedy's inauguration, President Eisenhower reportedly dismissed as propaganda Khrushchev's speech of January 6, 1961, calling for Soviet support for "wars of national liberation." Kennedy's response was quite different. He plowed through the 20,000-word text himself and—on the advice of the American ambassador to Moscow, Llewellyn Thompson[36]—gave copies of it to all his top aides and told them to "read, mark, learn, and inwardly digest" it. He read portions of it aloud at the first session of his

National Security Council. His new Secretary of Defense, Robert McNamara, recalled years later, "It was a significant event in our lives."[37]

The Kennedy administration issued a clarion call for a renewed mobilization of American power after the "lethargy" of the Eisenhower administration. Kennedy, first as candidate and then as president, sounded a sharp alarm: "The balance of power is slowly shifting to the Soviet–Red Chinese bloc." And shortly after taking office, he warned, "The climax of the struggle with Communism will come—soon."[38] The combination of the Soviets' growing nuclear strength and their increasing activity in the Third World alarmed him greatly. His response was a massive military arms race and a preoccupation with counterinsurgency and nation building.

Initially, the Kennedy administration saw Moscow, not Beijing, as leader of this vast effort to shatter Western influence throughout the southern part of the globe. Moscow, with its support for "wars of national liberation," appealed to revolution-minded leaders desperately seeking ways to destroy the remnants of colonialism and to modernize their economies and outmoded societies. "There is no longer any question that radical change will occur in the world, but only a question of what direction it will take," concluded a January 1961 National Intelligence Estimate. "The very future of the West will depend to a large degree upon the manner in which it mobilizes and employs its political, economic, and military resources to shape and guide the process of change."[39] Kennedy feared that the United States was falling behind; the Soviets appeared emboldened by their space success with *Sputnik* and an optimism that the "balance of forces" was now in their favor.

Yet while administration leaders saw a "new assertiveness" in Soviet policy, arising from heightened military and economic power and "the continued desire of the Communist leaders to remake the world in their own image," at the same time they noted a "certain mellowing of Soviet domestic and foreign policy. . . . This trend finds expression in a realistic appreciation of the consequences of nuclear war and of actions which could escalate into nuclear war; greater flexibility in dealing with non-Communist forces; and in sporadic movements towards detente with the United States and the West." In some ways, Khrushchev was more ideological than Stalin had been in his foreign policy, and thus more dangerous, but fundamentally he calculated his objectives according to the needs of the Russian state, not world revolution.[40]

"Stabilization" between Eastern and Western Europe did not preclude conflict. The "total penetration" approach, which aimed to corrode the power of Eastern European regimes through the "free flow of ideas, people, and goods," encouraged a growing economic interconnection, though it would prove difficult to open up the American market for a variety of reasons, including congressional opposition. The policy nevertheless reflected increasing confidence in the vitality and attractiveness of consumer capitalism.

Kennedy's briefing papers for his 1961 summit meeting with Khrushchev in Vienna delineated "two differing trends." On the one hand, the president's advisors believed, Khrushchev thought the USSR was gaining an advantage in the global "correlation of forces"; on the other, they did not think he would press that advantage for "revolutionary" objectives. Russia was now very much an imperial power, a nation-state that calculated its interests in terms of quite specific national objectives. As such, its top priority was consolidating its position in Eastern Europe and resolving the Berlin question in a way that would solve Moscow's German problem. U.S. officials thus expected Khrushchev to push for Washington's acceptance of the "permanence and legitimacy of the satellite regimes of Eastern Europe" as the sine qua non of "tranquil East-West relations" and, in addition, to insist that the USSR "should have a voice equal to that of the West in international councils." This equality was a key part of Khrushchev's policy of coexistence and of his efforts to attain respect for and acceptance of the Soviet Union's international role. Kennedy's advisors also thought the USSR was after a "paternalistic alliance (where possible) with the forces of nationalism in the underdeveloped world"; a "gradualist," less violent approach to the spread of communism; and more open and normal relations with the West, including expanding trade and cultural contacts.[41]

There were two "deeper contradictions" in Khrushchev's policy. First, he hoped that by incessant "though relatively unprovocative pressures (primarily political) he [could] expand and consolidate Soviet influence in the underdeveloped world," but he wanted to avoid seriously adverse reactions from the United States. It was unlikely that he could have it both ways: "These two trends hold profoundly different implications for Soviet relations with the Free world." Second, an "even deeper contradiction" arose from his double role as ruler of the USSR and leader of the communist world. The former made the security and political-economic concerns of the USSR primary, but these concerns were "circumscribed or nullified" by its obligations as the "center of the bloc and communist movement."[42]

These contradictions put the Soviet Union in a difficult position vis-à-vis the PRC. Beijing's "challenge from the left" required the Soviets "to prove their militancy"—putting them in "a tactically awkward situation since in controversies among exponents of revolutionary doctrines the psychological advantage always rests with those who are *more* revolutionary."[43] At the same time, the Soviets were obviously pursuing policies "directly counter to Chinese Communists' interests." Moscow's determination to keep the PRC from developing nuclear weapons was "one important reason why the Soviets have seriously entertained the idea of a supervised nuclear test ban."[44]

What emerged by the end of the Kennedy administration, then, was an increasing effort to develop better relations with the Soviets. This was evident in the Laotian crisis of the early 1960s. When Senator Richard Russell asked Rusk whether the Soviets were more interested than the Chinese in reaching an accommodation on Laos, Rusk agreed that they were, adding that perhaps one reason was their fear that "the Red Chinese would try to take over all of Southeast Asia."[45] Kennedy spoke similarly, telling the Lao king that "the Soviet Union did not want Laos to fall under the Chinese orbit."[46] Although an awareness of Sino-Soviet differences dates back to the 1940s, the sense of a strong China seeking hegemony in Southeast Asia against Soviet wishes grew stronger in the Kennedy years as they saw Moscow concerned over China's exploiting the situation in Laos, taking an "unpredictable and reckless course of action which would endanger world peace and upset the balance of power between them."[47]

Washington believed that the Soviet Union had a growing recognition of the "complexities of the world scene"; it was more sophisticated, less simplistic and dogmatic in its views than China. Beijing was violent, hostile, unreasoning—and, concomitantly, more revolutionary. The Chinese were "still possessed by much simpler, bipolar views of a black-and-white world,"[48] whereas the Soviets thought "Communism can make gains without local wars. They will back wars of 'National Liberation' provided the risks are controllable. The ChiComs think local wars are the best way to spread Communism and will accept higher risks."[49] Moreover, the Soviets had lost some of their "optimism about Third World developments": postcolonial nationalism "in most areas openly diverged from the hoped for association with Soviet policies, and the USSR has not succeeded in establishing patronage, much less control, over the new nations."[50]

Issues between the United States and the Soviets—Berlin and Germany's future, the status of Eastern Europe, nuclear armaments—were increasingly believed to belong to a relatively stable Cold War stand-off. Those between the United States and China, by contrast—Taiwan, the UN seat, recognition—were far more volatile and offered little concrete ground for discussion. The United States was anxious to block both China's nationalist objectives and its revolutionary ones. As the State Department's briefing paper for Kennedy's summit with Khrushchev put it:

We are well aware from Chinese Communist ideological pronouncements that Peiping's hostility towards us stems basically from what Khrushchev calls a "dogmatic" interpretation of Marxism-Leninism, rather than from any specific actions on our part. So long as Peiping adheres to a doctrine of "unremitting struggle" against the United States and our allies, we will have no recourse but to maintain our systems of individual and collective security arrangements, including our mutual defense treaty with the Republic of China.[51]

China appeared in these documents much as it did in American public opinion and congressional debates: militant, aggressive, more violent than the Soviets, rashly callous about the consequences of nuclear warfare.[52] Khrushchev might be on a quest for global power, but he was still more flexible and realistic than his "xenophobic" Chinese counterparts: "Historically, a strong China has always been expansionist and xenophobic."[53] Thus, "when judged against that background, the tremendous population pressures of contemporary China, combined with the fervent aspirations of her present leaders, bode ill for the future."[54] The issue for Beijing was just how far to go: "Communist China continues to face the problem of the degree of militancy it can advocate and support in promoting revolutions without risking a serious clash with the West and its allies. It also has newer problems of assuring its economic and military security in the light of its changed relations with the USSR."[55]

With Khrushchev in a difficult spot, the pre-summit briefing papers argued, the United States should push him into greater opposition to Chinese communist designs and objectives. He should urge China to "renounce the use of force," including in the Taiwan Strait. Kennedy should demand his reasons for supporting an "expansionist, militant" China: "Does the USSR really believe that the chances of avoiding a nuclear war will not be lessened after the [PRC] becomes a nuclear power? Can the USSR safely conclude that its espousal of the policies of a militant, expansionist [PRC] is fully consistent with Soviet national interests?" The president was advised to "take the initiative in projecting the subject of China policy into the years ahead" and pointing to the need for resolution of acute political problems, disarmament, nuclear disarmament—which it was hard to believe that China would support.[56]

Khrushchev could be pushed hard on these issues because he was understood to have his own reasons for pursuing détente. He "probably believes," according to the briefing papers, that it would create a political deterrent to forceful U.S. actions against Cuba and Laos. He probably hoped it would take the wind out of the expanding arms race. And no doubt he found it compatible with his own emphasis on consumer welfare and ultimate communist victory through economic competition and peaceful coexistence. He would certainly be interested in "whatever new ideas the U.S. may have concerning measures to check the spread of nuclear weapons."[57]

In Vienna, Kennedy pointed out to Khrushchev that there was now a "balance of power between Sino-Soviet forces and the forces of the United States and Western Europe" but that he was "concerned how this balance of power might be affected as China developed its military potential."[58] The ominous issue of Chinese nuclear capability was critical for both superpowers. In the mid-1950s the Eisenhower administration had acknowledged that its refusal to negotiate in any serious way with China was not the way to get it to comply with any disarmament measures. Its refusal also put pressure on the USSR, since Moscow would "have difficulty in refusing to supply Red China with nuclear weapons in future years" and "yet must have a reluctance to place such power in China and with the possibility of a future clash of interests in the Far East."[59] Nothing was done at the time, though, in part because the Eisenhower administration thought that China was at least five to ten years away from producing an atomic bomb.[60]

By the early 1960s, the issue loomed large in Washington. "The whole reason for having a test ban is related to the Chinese situation," Kennedy observed. "Otherwise it wouldn't be worth the disruption and fighting with Congress, etc."[61] One State Department memo summarized the dangers of a nuclear-armed China: "(1) The direct use of nuclear weapons against US bases or Asia countries; (2) the use of nuclear weapons as an umbrella for overt non-nuclear military operations and support for insurgency; and (3) political and propaganda exploitation of its nuclear capability to capitalize upon and to create opportunities for achieving Chinese Communist objectives."[62] Often Washington posed the issue in terms of a Soviet desire to rein in the Chinese—Soviet negotiations on the test ban treaty were "designed in part to delay or prevent" a Chinese nuclear capacity.[63] Rusk, who was among the most cautious diplomats on the issue of China, acknowledged that the nuclear questions "could contribute to what appears to be a split" between Moscow and Beijing. There were "political advantages" in the way such a split might lead to more favorable relations with Moscow.[64] Increasingly, it was argued (and hoped) that Moscow and Washington had "a common interest in insuring that China does not attain a nuclear capability." The JCS favored turning to Moscow for help: "The Soviets are in the better position to exercise the leverage on Communist China."[65] Averill Harriman's instructions for his meeting in Moscow in June 1963 told him to "indicate to the Soviets that we would not expect to make any public announcements of a joint US-USSR campaign to prevent the Chinese from acquiring a nuclear capacity but would consider that a tacit understanding that we would do so as part of the understanding between us."[66] Harriman himself saw Khrushchev aiming "to isolate the Chinese Communist regime, using . . . the test ban treaty as an instrument."[67]

An increasing contrast was made between Russia and China after the Cuban Missile Crisis. Kennedy spoke bluntly of the far greater recklessness and consequent danger of the Chinese: "We would be far worse off—the world would be if the Chinese dominated the Communist movement, because they believe in war as the means of bringing about the Communist world. . . . The Chinese Communists believe that . . . if war comes, a nuclear third world war, they can survive it anyway with 750 million people. So we are better off with the Khrushchev view than we are with the Chinese Communist view, quite obviously."[68] And in a New Year's Eve background discussion with reporters in 1962, Kennedy, while noting that there was "no evidence yet that he [Khrushchev] is going to change his basic support of international communism's drive," nonetheless detected a coming shift in Soviet attitudes:

> Looking at it from a ten year perspective, you would think that as the Soviet society has greater improvement in the standard of living and becomes more of a "have" nation, as the new generation begins to shift in power so you are getting near generations who did not grow up in the 1917 atmosphere, that there would be a lessening of the hard line, perhaps, in time, and more of an identification, perhaps, with Europe. In addition, if the Chinese Communists exploded a bomb, which we assume they will, and continue to maintain their very hard policy, I would think the chances of friction would be increased.[69]

An enormous effort went into interpreting the Sino-Soviet split during the Kennedy years. There was little rejoicing over China's acknowledged independence.[70] Nor was there much discussion about how American policies had encouraged the split or might further shape it. In fact, the Kennedy administration never fully reached a consensus about the Sino-Soviet split. Did such bitter ideological hostility, for example, preclude the two countries' "common commitment to the communist cause and especially their common enmity toward the anti-communist world"?[71] Kennedy officials were not sure; they passionately reaffirmed the existence of the "Communist threat"—by which they meant antithetical ways of development and revolutionary means of coming to power. But if the rupture between China and the USSR were real and serious, would the Soviet's nuclear umbrella still hold? Or were the Soviets so concerned about Chinese nuclear capabilities that they could tolerate an American military strike against Chinese nuclear installations? Or should Washington, as some officials (including the JCS) argued, try another approach: bring the Chinese into arms control talks before they attained a limited nuclear capability?[72]

In the end, the Kennedy administration saw détente as requiring that Moscow make a choice: "The Soviets will probably have to decide whether to incline toward competing with China in hostility to the US, or as we consider somewhat more likely, toward pursuing the logic of their 'peaceful coexistence' line and searching for new ways to demonstrate its validity." On no issue did the two superpowers share more immediate interests, concluded one CIA analysis, than that of "delaying the emergence of a nuclear-armed Communist China."[73] Indeed, Washington could—and did—defend détente as a means of controlling the spread of nuclear weapons, as well as of Chinese power. Senior officials—those long involved in America's policies toward the USSR, such as Kennan, Bohlen, and Harriman—warned against irritating the Soviets by changing policy toward China. CIA and other government studies in the early 1960s began depicting China's leadership as blind to developmental realities, the country staggering under the "economic and psychological chaos" of the Great Leap Forward.[74] But China remained a frightening and fanatic revolutionary center standing against a modernizing world that was desperately in need of nuclear restraint and nonproliferation.[75]

The China-India Border War

Washington's reaction to the October 1962 border dispute between China and India testifies to its increasing willingness to distinguish the character of the threat from Moscow and of that from Beijing. Kennedy himself had spoken of India as "the key area" in Asia and the most important neutral nation in the world.[76] Its contest with China "for the economic and political leadership of the East, for the respect of all Asia" would determine more than just Asia's future: "If China succeeds and India fails, the economic-development balance of power will shift against us."[77] When the opportunity to bring India into the Western camp seemed to have arisen, Philip Talbot of the NSC wrote, "India's new anti–Chinese Communist and pro-West (especially pro-U.S.) turn can give us a major breakthrough in Asia. . . . India can become an important asset in our confrontation with China. The problem is how the West can exploit this sudden great opportunity."[78]

Washington moved with speed and decisiveness "to secure India's alignment with the West."[79] Ambassador John Kenneth Galbraith thought that India would now be of "great political value. To put this value on a solid operational footing," he proposed persuading India that "our help to them must be part of a joint effort to contain China in South Asia. This is logical. American support on their Northern frontier will cause the Chinese to bulge out somewhere else."[80] This image of an amoebalike power oozing first toward one border, then another, testifies once again to the fear of China's revolutionary intensity and its virulent nationalism. Using India to contain China could deal with both.

President Ayub Khan of Pakistan was not convinced. He saw the conflict as a limited border affair rather than a broader Chinese military challenge that Washington initially tried to play up in order to assuage Pakistan's preoccupation with India, simultaneously encouraging Nehru to agree to some mollifying steps on the Kashmir question.[81] But that a "panicky Nehru" requested that U.S. personnel man fighter jets and radar stations[82] and that he may have feared for a few days that India's cities might come under Chinese attack does not fully explain Washington's immediate and intense efforts to obtain an American-Indian alignment with military dimensions. The risks were evident—"If we back India against the Chinese," Rusk noted, "we may drive the Paks off the deep end; if we abandon the Indians, they might move toward the USSR and China again"[83]—but so were the gains. Chester Bowles wrote that the situation offered "a major windfall for U.S. strategic interests which, if played skillfully, can lead to a close association with the second largest nation in the world, evolving into a de facto alliance and ultimately, under favorable circumstances, even into a formal alliance."[84]

The CIA did not assess Chinese strategy as simply a process of aggression, expansion, or outright conquest. Instead, it saw China as attempting "to consolidate its control over Tibet and to safeguard it against infiltration and subversion." Given American efforts (with tacit Indian consent) to aid Tibetan unrest, the Chinese did not face an easy task.[85] Yet here, as in Vietnam and numerous other "crisis situations," China's objectives were evaluated once again in terms of its "expansionist ambitions."[86] Washington knew how complex the details of the border dispute were, and it knew that in taking India's side publicly it was overlooking these complexities.[87] But the United States was aiming for an expanded role in India, and it needed Chinese expansionism as the justification; a mere border dispute would not provide it.[88]

Washington understood that India had not made its case in the Third World very effectively. The reaction of nonaligned governments was, as the reporter Neville Maxwell put it, "reserved and wary—in a word, non-aligned." Jomo Kenyatta of Kenya and other African leaders were noncommittal. Kwame Nkrumah of Ghana, whom Nehru had only recently visited, wrote to protest the sending of arms by the British. In the Middle East, one Indian correspondent wrote at the time, "Not a single expression of sympathy for India has come from any Arab Government, any political party or newspaper, or public personality even a week after the invasion," and Nehru lamented that the "so-called non-aligned countries" were "confused."[89]

Yet in the West, India won the ideological war, because it was useful for Washington to have it do so. In national security bureaucracy memos and discussions, India's actions in the border dispute were secondary; what was primary was the opportunity to bring India into closer alignment with the United States, and for this purpose an expansionist China was a crucial component.

So it was that China came to be seen in Washington as the most unaccommodating and threatening great power on the globe. In military terms it was far weaker than the Soviet Union and likely to remain so for many years, despite the dreaded imminence of its nuclear weaponry. As Secretary McNamara told Congress in 1964, "The Soviet Union has by far the greater capability to cause us injury or otherwise damage the interests of the Free World," but China was "the more reckless and belligerent of the two."[90] China appeared to be committed to destroying the system and repudiating the rules of the game—a game the Soviets now found they had reasons to play.[91]

The Third World: Developmental Containment

Kennedy's concern with the Third World—with the growing gap between rich and poor, white and nonwhite[92]—was evident in his May 25, 1961, address to a joint session of Congress on his legislative program. The revolution in the Third World was "the greatest in human history," he said. Asia, Latin America, Africa, and the Middle East—"the lands of the rising peoples"—were the "great battleground for the defense and expansion of freedom today." The adversaries of the United States had not created this revolution, but they were seeking to "ride the crest of its wave—to capture it for themselves." Where Truman and his advisors had spoken of communism's seizure of the rising nationalism in the underdeveloped world, and Eisenhower and his of the perils of extreme nationalism and of the blindness of neutralism to communism, Kennedy focused directly on the revolutionary process itself—a process that he thought the United States needed to learn how to channel effectively. Aggression, Kennedy argued, was now

> more often concealed than open. . . . Arms, agitators, are sent, propaganda waged. And the fighting is done by others—by guerrillas striking at night, by assassins striking alone . . . [killing] four thousand civil officers in the last twelve months in Vietnam alone. This is a contest of force and violence, but also of will and purpose, a battle for minds and souls as well as lives and territory. And in that contest, we cannot stand aside.[93]

From Cuba to Vietnam, the risk was growing. As the Taylor study group told Kennedy after the Bay of Pigs, "We are in a life and death struggle which we may be losing."[94]

It is revealing to contrast the crisis atmosphere of the early 1960s with the time of the NSC 68 report for Truman. If NSC 68 was a full-blown expression of the theory of global containment, the means advocated to achieve it were limited. Massive retaliation and the covert warfare of the Eisenhower years sought to implement the same goals without a full-scale Keynesian militarism. But the Kennedy administration, faced with what it sensed was a tidal change in the Third World, shifted the emphasis to counterinsurgency, nation building, military Keynesianism, and developmental strategies.

NSC 68 had been predicated on bipolarity, a worldview that encompassed both the problem and the means to deal with it. The ideological rationale at home and abroad was stark; allies were to be bludgeoned, if necessary, into accepting its many implications. But in the 1960s, American officials found themselves facing a less bipolar world, a growing split between the Soviet Union and China, and a war of ideology in the Third World that included a debate over peaceful versus revolutionary change.[95]

Some of the implications of this shift are evident in Walt Rostow's basic national security policy study of March 1962. It stressed the "revolution of modernization" that was creating a turmoil of "anti-Western sentiments, racial passions, particularist tendencies of all sorts" that communists could exploit. Third World nations needed help: nation building and counterinsurgency were two pillars of a process of developmental containment: that is, containment of communism by developing Third World countries in a capitalist direction. In language reminiscent of NSC 68, Rostow wrote, "This would be our purpose even if Marx and Lenin had never existed, but, because their heirs are now attempting to impose their version of the future on all mankind, the requisite urgency and scale of national effort is greater." As before, ideological mobilization was critical. The struggle would be long and arduous. "We must seek to indoctrinate our own people and the peoples of the free community with a deeper understanding of the issues at stake," Rostow wrote—the power of ideology would be as important as military force itself in determining the course of events.[96] Modernization was the ideological counterpoint to revolution, and "economic development" in the Third World was very much Washington's central ideological concern by the early 1960s.[97]

The policy of containment suddenly required a far more subtle, pervasive, multidimensional, and highly coordinated approach toward other nations. In the early 1960s, containment and nation building came together to shape an ethos of developmental containment which became a critical part of the global strategy to deal with communism in the Third World.[98] Rostow set forth the goals: militarily, no area in the underdeveloped world could fall under communist control; ideologically, it was imperative that the Third World "evolve in directions which will afford a congenial world environment for our own society"; economically, "the resources and markets of these areas" had to be "available to us and to the other industrialized nations of the free world."[99]

The Capitalist Core

The Kennedy administration regarded the United States as the pivot of this increasingly dynamic and vital global capitalist order: only the United States was as yet intricately involved economically in both Europe and Japan; only Washington had a global perspective. Since the "core areas" of capitalism remained critical for American power, generating some unity among them was "the first and highest priority."[100] Traditional geopolitical concerns remained. Greater Western European unity would strengthen resistance to the communist threat and pose ever greater attractions to Eastern Europe; it would provide the political and psychological framework for tying Germany more firmly to the West, weakening its "chronic temptation" to seek national unity ahead of its Western ties.

At the same time, economic rivalry among the core capitalist powers was increasing as the extreme postwar disequilibrium in the world economy came to an end. Conflicts erupted over the increasing unwillingness of Europe and Japan to subsidize American military forces, over European and Japanese trade with the Soviets, and over conflicting protectionist interests. Kennedy's efforts to deal with a growing balance-of-payments problem; issues of U.S. capital investment in Europe, the efforts to unify core central bankers in the cause of preserving Breton Woods and the rule of the dollar, the Kennedy Round of tariff negotiations—all are reflective of European recovery and Japanese economic growth.[101]

To cope with this situation, Washington continued to encourage the integration of the core areas under an American military and economic umbrella. Despite its worries over European nationalism, the United States tended to believe that the emergence of a united Europe "deliberately prepared . . . to play the United States and the USSR off against each other" was "relatively slight, so long as essential European interests are protected within the Atlantic Partnership."[102] There were dangerous sore spots: de Gaulle's independent stance and *force de frappe*, Britain's role in the Common Market, the determination to keep Germany from having nuclear weapons while still binding it to the West. (The Soviets "might try to offer the West Germans unity in return for neutrality. . . . It would be a great temptation for West Germany," Prime Minister Harold Macmillan told Kennedy.)[103] Internal memorandums from these years convey a sense of crisis and conflict within the alliance, of bitter disputes over economic issues and military troop payments. Nonetheless, American leverage remained enormous.

In the Pacific, the issue was that Japan, unlike Europe, in the 1960s had not yet developed economic strength, and it needed access to the American market. Yet there was a notable easing of immediate concerns over Japanese policy in the Kennedy-Johnson years. Not even the election of Prime Minister Hayato Ikeda, who held a more flexible position than his predecessor on trade with the PRC, set off alarms. Few NSC memorandums of the period recall the apprehension of the late 1940s to the late 1950s over the possible development of Japanese neutralism; in the aftermath of the U.S.-Japan National Security Treaty in 1960, old fears subsided. Ambassador Edwin O. Reischauer warned that Japan could not be taken for granted.[104] But by the mid-1960s the prospect of a few limited Sino-Japanese trading possibilities did not elicit much concern.[105] Perhaps trade between these two countries could even have a beneficial effect, encouraging "the exposure of the Chinese to the outside world," according to the June 1966 long-range study, which concluded, without much evident fear, that in the next decade "economic relations between Japan and mainland China will probably expand greatly and Japanese recognition of Peking is likely within the decade."[106]

Even though China was likely to remain a contentious issue between Tokyo and Washington, the odds were nonetheless "against a major split on recognition and other basic issues, partly because of the broad consensus in Japan in favor of self-determination on Taiwan." Japan was almost certain to remain "firmly anti-communist, internally less divided, more conscious of its responsibilities."[107] Washington could often be strident on China in its discussions with Tokyo, but this tone suggests an attempt to hold the general line on issues, not to put pressure on specific trade decisions. Washington retained control of the great Japanese economic levers that had been put in place at the beginning of the Cold War era.[108] A central one, however—the as yet incomplete opening of the American market—was fraught with domestic difficulties in the United States.[109] Indeed, the United States was particularly sensitive about the influence of its markets in relation to Japanese trade with China. It was a long-term worry that Japan would become as vulnerable to the Chinese market as it was becoming to the American one.

Though Japan's role in Asia was "similar to the critical role of West Germany in Europe," it still lacked a sufficiently strong domestic political base for contributing to American defense objectives. But Washington was increasingly calling upon Tokyo to become more involved throughout Asia. In time, Rostow concluded, greater coordination might be possible even with the Europeans "in the common enterprise of the north." Japan would share the costs and responsibilities for maintaining the balance of power between the communist and noncommunist world—especially in growing efforts to "help the developing nations modernize their economies and their societies while not succumbing to communist subversion."[110]

The North/South Divide

While favoring greater economic integration in Europe, U.S. policy makers in the early 1960s stressed the importance of incorporating the Third World into all economic planning. As George Ball told Kennedy, "We cannot be in a position of forming a cabal of the industrialized countries against the rest of the world."[111] And Kennedy himself said to the German economic minister, Ludwig Erhard, that "it would be most unwise to give the impression of our creating a rich white man's club."[112]

George Ball, who had chaired the Foreign Economic Policy task force in December 1960, wrote the president that Americans must come to "understand the shape and implication of the new trading world," in which a coordinated opening of the core capitalist economies would accompany the "opening [of] the markets of all industrial nations to the expanding industrial exports of developing countries." Ball warned that there would be strong domestic opposition from business interests and their congressional allies, for this policy required that the United States "accept some temporary and local injury to certain American firms, industries, and communities."[113] But he insisted that this "new trading world" was crucial to maintaining America's global economic preeminence. Thus it was necessary to promote a greater opening of the American market, particularly to "accommodate expanding exports from low wage areas such as Japan."[114]

To Ball and others, the world was becoming more economically interconnected. A growing multilateralism and an increasing flow of goods and capital would continue to strengthen the advanced capitalist world while providing means to reshape its relations with the Third World.[115] The sometimes passionate invocation of the sufferings of the two-thirds of the world's population that lived in the poor countries reflected more than humanitarian concern, however. It was part of a drive to draw these countries more fully into a diversified global economic order capable of undercutting revolutionary appeals to the discontented. "A standard canard used to be that we had to choose between bilateral and multilateral ways of acting." Harlan Cleveland observed, "This sterile argument ran out of gas after about ten years. . . . [O]ur purpose is to put the resources that go beyond our borders in the service of our national aims, if we can figure out what the resources are and what our aims are." Multilateralism, he said, was often far more effective than a bilateral approach, particularly when dealing with nationalistic opposition to American interests.[116]

Washington wanted to shape a global market system that could penetrate Third World economies far more deeply. Often the most articulate proponents of such views, such as George Ball, are seen as Eurocentric, but it is more accurate to stress their determination to restructure the global economic order by coordinating the core capitalist areas and their relationship to the South. The shift to issues of North-South relations required the "instruments of policy" to be "increasingly economic."[117] The bitter Cold War confrontations of the 1940s and the 1950s had always involved disagreements over reordering relations among the core capitalist nations in order to strengthen American power and against the Soviets; now that reordering appeared critical to stemming revolutionary tendencies in the Third World as well.

The Johnson administration pursued these objectives further. Karl Kaysen, chairman of the Task Force on Foreign Economic Policy, wrote in 1964 that the war-torn nations of Europe had been rebuilt, and the Soviet Union—slowly but surely confronting the realities of a nuclear world—was pursuing its national (and imperial) interests in a less revolutionary fashion. But global poverty, racial issues, the population explosion, and revolutionary conflict all made the Third World the "largest source of cumulating instability in the years ahead." The United States had "an immense stake in a process of change in these countries." Repeated failures of Third World nations to "climb up from poverty" would leave an explosive situation of poor and dissatisfied nations in an age of nuclear proliferation.[118]

Even given the most optimistic projections for growth, there would be a "widening absolute gap" in a world where the elimination of poverty had become "an articulate political goal everywhere." The "malcontents" and dissatisfied might mobilize against the United States and the world it represented. The old colonial systems had at least "served as the basis of order between the peoples of highly different cultures and levels of development living great distances from each other."[119] But with their collapse, with the heightened awareness of economic and political disparities among states and populations within states, and with the growing appeal of state planning and a communist model of development, the United States faced a crisis in bringing the Third World's economic incorporation into the global capitalist system.

Any change "characterized by social and political chaos, massive popular dissatisfaction, worsening living conditions, and, quite likely, tendencies toward coercive systems of government on the Communist model" were "blatantly unacceptable."[120] As Lyndon Johnson testified before the House Committee on Foreign Affairs in 1961, "You cannot, in my opinion, have one man who is affluent and has all the riches of the world and have everybody else be impoverished— and have a happy situation. They are going to take it home under their dress.

They will come and get it in the night time. They will tear the window down to get it because women are not going to see their children starve."[121]

The difficulties were staggering. The institutional changes needed for modernization had so far occurred only fitfully, and programs necessary for nation building were not penetrating deeply enough into the infrastructure of the poor nations. And unless the commitment to multilateralism could hold the line against American domestic interests and their congressional supporters, the international economic order could begin to disintegrate into the conditions that had led to the Great Depression. The enemy here was clear: "Any significant departure from the universalist system could lead to an orgy of Congressional restrictionism, and the total breakdown of any rational commercial policy whatever." Progress depended almost entirely on American trade policy, for the United States was the genuinely "universalist power among the non-Communist nations," Kaysen wrote, that sought something better than the "best deal going at the moment."[122]

To deal with the Third World, the Kennedy and Johnson administrations argued that the American market was the vehicle for shaping international economic relations with the South, and particularly for encouraging select allies—such as Japan, Taiwan, and South Korea—to develop their economic strength and thus reduce the burden they placed on the United States. If the American domestic market did not open sufficiently, American capital would not flow into the right areas overseas; it would keep going to the extractive areas instead of promoting the development of highly profitable manufacturing areas.[123]

Meanwhile, "self-sufficiency" and revolutionary models of development had to be exposed as inefficient and economically irrational. Government-to-government programs alone were not sufficient to the task; to bring the countries in the South into the global trading system would require a wide range of private and semigovernmental groups able to "penetrate widely and deeply into the instructional structures of the recipient countries." The Western business corporation, skilled in combining capital, technological knowhow, organization, and management, was the ideal institution for drawing these nations into the global economic order.[124]

Washington officials were confident in their eagerness to contrast revolutionary methods and Third World policies of "self-reliance" with rewards of participation in the global marketplace. The old restrictive economic policies had served as "a symbol of U.S. unwillingness to grant the USSR full respectability as an equal in the post-war world order, a symbol that the U.S. dares to *discriminate* against the USSR under contemporary conditions," but now the United States was in a position to "resort to 'the continuation of politics by other means.'"[125] The Soviet Union had its own agenda, of course, which included commercial terms that would not undercut its state-controlled system.[126] But Washington officials were increasingly confident that in this new way of waging the Cold War, the Soviet Union could be accepted as an equal *and* the object of a transformative economic dynamic.

Secretary of Defense Robert McNamara echoed widely shared sentiments when he argued in 1963 that "peaceful trade between the United States and the USSR would tend on the whole to mold the Soviet Union in the Western image."[127] The goal with the Soviets, as well as the Eastern Europeans, was always, in part, to "encourage tendencies toward independence and autonomy in individual countries and to turn them increasingly toward the West in their external dealings and perhaps even in their internal political systems," even if the United States had been slow to seize the opportunities.[128] The developmental containment policies emerging in the Kennedy years led to this highly influential current in the Johnson administration: on global economic interconnection, and on gradual changes that would moderate revolutionary approaches and deepen the economic penetration of capital and modern business techniques into the southern world.

In the long run, these hoped-for changes applied as fully to China as to any other nation. Kaysen argued that the question of trade with China was a political as much as an economic issue: "Besides denying ourselves markets, a policy of trade restraints seems to have little impact on the Communist regimes in these places, cuts channels of communication by which one might hope to influence policy there, and causes endless friction with our allies."[129] The opening of the domestic American market to Third World countries and selected allies had been a key Cold War strategy. Now the possibility was raised in relation to China, as William Bundy suggested in a 1966 memo to Rusk: "A chance to begin developing an export market in the U.S. would have the most attraction for the Chinese Communists, and we could expect them sooner or later to test our willingness to accept their goods."[130] As one CIA study noted in analyzing the trade embargo, ultimately the critical factor was not the cutting-off of minor trade or credits but the denial of the American market; this was the one economic offer of real interest to the Chinese communists.[131] If the United States were to remove unilateral controls, "the greatest gain to China would be in its opportunity to earn dollars by selling in the rich US market . . . [and this] could contribute substantially to Peking's ability to import grain and industrial equipment."[132]

The 1966 Long Range Study was more blunt:

No regime, and particularly the exchange-short regime in Peking, could take lightly the prospect of being admitted to the greatest market in the world, and we should view the relaxation of foreign assets control in conjunction with modifying the controls on exports as an important bargaining instrument. Once engaged in selling to profitable U.S. markets, even via third countries, Communist China would be less free to act in ways which might threaten to cut off that source of scarce foreign exchange. As a result, China might gradually acquire a practical interest in developing and maintaining a measure of detente.[133]

Roger Hilsman's "Open Door Speech"

Such views underlay the major Kennedy administration speech on China policy, which Assistant Secretary of State for Far Eastern Affairs Roger Hilsman delivered to the Commonwealth Club in San Francisco on December 13, 1963—three weeks after the president's assassination. Hilsman thought of it as the "Open Door Speech"; Kennedy, he recalled later, had believed that "the time had come to do something about China."[134]

Hilsman began by acknowledging what practically every Washington official had been saying since the mid-1940s: that the "passions of nationalism" were at "flood tide in much of Asia."[135] Since the late 1940s, "Communist aggression" (initially invoked in its most undifferentiated, generalized form) had been manipulating nationalism to its own ends. But Hilsman placed far more stress on nationalism's revolutionary aspects and on the necessary American response: nation building in the Third World. Nation building required that the United States have the capacity, the ability, and the recognized right to involve itself in a wide range of what had traditionally been viewed as internal social, economic, and political processes and to shape them into aspects of a more modern, stable nation. Its ultimate success required that national leaders "transcend parochial nationalism" and see that "regionalism" in areas such as Southeast Asia entailed the "interdependence of all peoples" and thus a toning-down of nationalist stridency.

Hilsman believed that Americans had failed to perceive the intensely nationalist aspect of the Chinese revolution and thus the tragedy of its seizure by Marxism-Leninism; he called on Americans to "be objective, and to see to it that dislike of communism does not becloud our ability to see the facts." True, the signs were not encouraging. China's "dangerously overconfident" leaders were wedded to "outdated theories," and in pointing to positive "evolutionary forces at work in mainland China," Hilsman admitted that he might be "too optimistic." Yet even as he attacked the Great Leap Forward for the "arrogant disdain" of the laws of economics that had led to economic collapse, he foresaw a second-echelon leadership that was far more aware of economic complexities. He also believed that the Chinese economy would ultimately modernize in ways that would testify to the inadequacies of state control. This "closed and stagnant" nation could be contrasted with the robust Taiwan: "Here the modernization of Chinese society has taken place outside the Communist straitjacket—and the results are extraordinarily impressive."

Hilsman observed that while the Chinese communists were waging and supporting guerrilla warfare, the USSR was "developing a modern industrial society." The Soviets also favored negotiations in limited matters—notably nuclear arms—whereas the Chinese practiced a "fundamentalist form of communism which emphasizes violent revolution even if it threatens the physical ruin of the civilized world"; unlike the Soviets, they were locked into a "paranoid view of the world." In addition, the Soviet Union's neighbors, particularly in Europe, were well-defined states with relatively settled lines of demarcation, whereas many of China's Asian neighbors, newly established states struggling to maintain their independence, offered greater opportunities for aggression and subversion than were open to the USSR. But these invidious comparisons notwithstanding, Hilsman and other Kennedy policy makers believed that the United States would be wise to appear open to improvements in its relations with China. China's isolation could not be laid at the door of the United States; the Chinese used "hatred as an engine of national policy," and the United States was "the central figure in their demonology, and the target of a sustained fury or invective." Yet Washington would keep trying. "If I may paraphrase a classic canon of our past," Hilsman declared, the United States would "pursue today towards Communist China a policy of the open door: we are determined to keep that door open to the possibility of change."

Modernization

By the early 1960s, therefore, American policy was focusing on restructuring economic relations with the other core capitalist areas amid a deepening North-South divide and a fear that communism (more than Soviet power) was a serious threat to the peaceful development of global capitalism in the Third World. In NSC documents of the Kennedy-Johnson years, "communism" no longer meant a Kremlin-dominated movement or a Sino-Soviet alliance, however contentious. "Communism" meant a process of state-driven anticapitalist development—and, in China's case, the promotion of revolutionary means of transformation both inside and outside China. Only in this context does Washington's China policy take on its fullest meaning. Ideologically, another vision of the world had led Washington to question the value of isolating China. That vision had a name: modernization, the most sophisticated counterrevolutionary explanation of global processes to emerge in the Cold War era.

Modernization came to flourish amid increasing U.S. economic commitment to multilateralism. Using the domestic American market to influence the character of development in the South, American officials envisioned a single world capitalist system that would finally bridge the economic gap between East and West, North and South. This was no more a plan or blueprint for policies than any other ideological formulation, and under its growing purview there were still bitter disputes, but its emergence testifies to a powerfully rooted internationalism in the NSC. Modernization offered a compelling internationalist vision, a bold globalism promising not only freedom but also development and well-being for the poorest nations. Fitting China into the scheme was not difficult. Officials and scholars had flirted with modernization for several decades precisely because it offered such a clear response to the revolutionary processes of the post–World War II era so powerfully present in China in the 1940s.

By the late 1940s, modernization theory was already becoming an influential way to explain the "lessons" of the "loss" of China.[136] Its analysis of China fit snugly into the global vision of the Kennedy-Johnson years. Modernization incorporated the older themes of anticommunism and freedom but dressed them—far more concretely—in the garb of universal order, development, and benevolent self-sacrifice and assistance on the part of the United States. Above all, it was an international vision: it included the entire underdeveloped world, economically, culturally, socially, and ideologically.

Modernization was trumpeted by its theoreticians as a new and progressive way to transform the poor and backward nations of the world.[137] Though the term itself was not widely used until it became publicly associated with the goals of American foreign policy in the Point Four Program of 1949, its widespread use thereafter testifies to its success in creatively explaining America's global interests in the Third World.[138] Traditional imperialism had used the language of power, conflict, and exploitation: empire was empire, conquest was conquest. (The conquered, it was often argued, were better off under the rule of the civilized than left to themselves.) Modernization theory used the vocabulary of international order, worldwide development, and foreign aid. It argued that American power—manifest after 1945 in military bases, nuclear might, and a triumphant economic system—was unique in its nonexploitiveness, pursuing as it did an international but wholly magnanimous agenda. The international organizations America had created or supported (the International Monetary Fund, the World Bank, the United Nations) were there to help overcome the chaos innate in the modernization process itself.

Those who increasingly spoke the language of development and modernization found the Eisenhower administration frustrating. Its initial policies had been shaped by military and budgetary concerns rather than any theory of history. From 1953 to 1956 it appeared to be pursuing a policy designed to limit the burdens of cost and manpower in drawing the line of containment across Asia. Bilateral and regional military alliances were far more critical to this effort than modernizing aid. Eisenhower seemed to be focusing on the threat of another Korean-like attack, when to the modernizers the "primary communist threat in the developing world after 1953 . . . was the ideological and economic attraction, of subversion and guerrilla warfare—what came to be called 'wars of national liberation.'"[139]

In truth, the administration was divided. Eisenhower himself wanted to expand foreign aid, and he encouraged various aspects of nation building, especially in the later years of his administration. But he also worried about the costs. Dulles agreed that a nation-building program was necessary, but he was more immediately concerned with tying it to psychological warfare and intensifying competition with the communists in the Third World. He would not throw his full weight behind modernizing proposals unless Eisenhower made an unambiguous policy decision.

On one side were budgetary conservatives, led by George Humphrey and Herbert Hoover Jr., who opposed developmental aid. On the other side, a less fiscally conservative group, including Nelson Rockefeller, Allen Dulles, Harold Stassen, Clarence Randall, and C. D. Jackson, argued that it was urgently needed. Only with the impact of *Sputnik* in 1957 did the tide start to turn. Soviet technological success combined with a variety of other factors to encourage a favorable atmosphere for developmental economics.[140] As a departing act, Eisenhower sent Congress a budget calling for a 30 percent increase in development aid.

In the late 1950s, modernization began to appear in NSC documents as the explanation for global processes. By then, Washington strategists were becoming preoccupied with the role of elites and intellectuals in Third World countries, for they were the individuals who would direct and manage modernization there. The challenge was communism's great appeal to Asian intellectuals, particularly in "its proven ability to carry backward countries speedily through the crisis of modernization and industrialization." Washington saw a fierce competition of "Western vs. Communist techniques" for industrializing underdeveloped countries. In the early 1960s, especially in Africa, the ability of communists to exploit the "ineptness" of leaders was another concern.[141]

So were revolutionary warfare and "indirect subversion." As Rostow later wrote, this was the phase of modernization's "activism, progress, and to a degree, disappointment." In the years of the Alliance for Progress, the World Bank Consortia, and the UN Decade of Development, developmental containment offered an ideologically persuasive way to justify counterinsurgency and nation building. Though Rostow's writings attracted controversy and contention, his underlying assumption that the forces at work in the developing world "inherently [lent] themselves to instability and violence" was widely accepted. Tension was the result of conflicts between modernizers and traditionalists among the modernizers, struggles of power, of a panoply of forces "unleashed by the intense, often xenophobic nationalism" that accompanied the end of colonial rule; of frustration at the slow pace of economic and social progress; and of the "urgent desire to assume a place of dignity and independence on a crowded and contentious world scene." The conflict between communists and noncommunists added an "extra dimension" to all this instability, but although communists sought to manipulate these conflicts, they did not cause them. Still, their interests were served by creating turmoil, which they could then use in their quest to come to power.[142]

This is what Dean Rusk argued in more simplified form in 1964 before an executive session of the Foreign Relations Committee. There were "two revolutions," he said. The first was the revolution "of modernization, economic and social development, education and all these things, the rising expectations." The other was "the Communist world revolution, . . . the dynamic force that concerns us all." Modernization, then, was inherently a bitter conflict with an alternative method of development.[143]

Models and dominoes went together.[144] Successful Chinese industrialization would threaten the West's interests in India; successful guerrilla war in Vietnam would threaten the rest of Southeast Asia. A model of revolutionary social transformation constituted a serious threat. It was not a question of numbers: "The danger of Communism derives less from the number of Communists than from the powerful attraction they exercise on dissatisfied elements."[145] Combine this attraction with the "initiation of sweeping reforms" that Castro had undertaken, and it exerted a "profound psychological impact throughout Latin America." This "indigenous Cuban example" presented a huge danger, though not militarily—"he almost certainly will refrain from efforts to export the revolution by military means"; rather, clandestine operations and propaganda would be his methods. But "if Castro succeeds in consolidating his regime, the importance of his influence and example will grow." By 1961, Washington officials were convinced that the Cuban Revolution had "introduced a new and critical phase in the struggle for power by the forces of the radical left. It has provided them with a concrete example of revolution and a basis for Cuban and increased Communist material and propaganda assistance for their own movements." The "hitherto politically inert masses" might now become mobilized and give the left a leading role in the modernizing process under way throughout Latin America.[146] Cuba, Vietnam, China—they all frightened Washington, above all as models.

And so modernization was considered quite compatible with an expanding role for the United States in training the military in developing countries "to conduct counter-insurgency, anti-subversion, and psychological warfare operations."[147] It was a shift of emphasis in military assistance to Latin America, "from hemispheric defense only to internal security, anti-submarine warfare, counter-insurgency, and civic action programs."[148] The justification was the need to develop a "counter-penetration viewpoint" to communist infiltration. The communists based their plans and actions

> on a consideration of all the internal strengths and weaknesses of a country, all the internal discontents and the groups that have been organized to alleviate these discontents, consideration of all the groups dedicated to the status quo, the uncommitted groups, and a comparison of the specific objectives, relative capabilities, and possible alignments of these groups. . . . Furthermore, they consider all the external forces acting upon any situation, country, group or individual in terms of their objectives and capabilities, and how these forces can be used or influenced to serve Communist ends.[149]

In its efforts to develop a counterstrategy, policy makers said, the United States should seek to have comparable knowledge and programs.

Even in those areas where the United States had suffered defeat, such as China, there was hope for an ultimate victory. Although revolution had triumphed in China, if Washington could hold the line, then slowly, almost imperceptibly, China would become more moderate. Modernization theorists were passionate in their argument that all revolutions, in the end, must give way to rational imperatives: development, material incentives, and the immutability of human nature.[150]

In many ways, this modernization ethos was a highly sophisticated international formulation of New Deal ideology. The essence of New Deal thinking as it gradually became codified in the post-1945 period was that liberal spending through government-created and -administered programs would preserve order and security and, thus, the fundamentals of American capitalism. New programs of aid to poor nations would be parallel to social-welfare programs within the United States, providing security to overcome chaos and nip revolution in the bud. Drawn inextricably into a revived world market system, these countries would, in the process, become more responsible—just as American labor unions had drawn in many of the poor in the 1930s and then demonstrated their responsibility during the war.

In this new world system the role of modernizing elites would be pivotal. But so was government—both the U.S. government and the reformist governments of the Third World. The latter required the full panoply of American aid on numerous levels, as well as the coordinated efforts of international organizations. The emphasis on government was critical. Modernization theory asserted the place and function of the state far more vigorously than the market-oriented ethos of the 1980s and 1990s would do. Nation building was not a process that came about simply or even largely through the incorporation of a nation into the world-market system but one that required the active involvement of the United States—in aid, in investment, and in the championship of "independence" against revolutionary movements.

8

MODIFIED
CONTAINMENT
PLUS
SUBVERSION

*Over this war—and all Asia—is
another reality: the shadow of
Communist China. The rulers in Hanoi
are urged on by Peking. This is a
regime which has destroyed freedom
in Tibet, attacked India and been
condemned by the United Nations for
aggression in Korea. It is a nation
which is helping the forces of violence
in almost every continent. The context
in Vietnam is part of a wider pattern
of aggressive purpose.*

Lyndon B. Johnson, 1965

As President Johnson rapidly escalated the Vietnam War, Washington continued to label China the paramount threat in Asia.[1] According to the June 1966 Long Range Study, China's primary objectives were "(1) the promotion of the world Communist revolution, principally through advocacy of 'wars of national liberation' against 'bourgeois' states, and (2) the restoration of China to its past position of grandeur and influence in Asia, and the extension of this influence onto a worldwide stage."[2] Both goals testified to the "Chinese desire to be recognized as the equal of the U.S. and the USSR"—a goal directly in conflict with American interests in Asia and Washington's plan for an "orderly, peaceful evolution towards an international system." The fact was that Chinese inequality was part and parcel of Washington's regional and global policy toward China.[3]

In the words of an internal State Department history of Chinese-American relations, "In 1965, Vietnam became at least in part a zone of confrontation between U.S. and Communist Chinese foreign policy objectives—a test case for Mao and [Defense Minister] Lin Biao's 'wars of national liberation' formula and the extension of Chinese Communist influence in Asia."[4] As McNamara concluded: "The trends in Asia are running in both directions—for as well as against our interests; there is no reason to be unduly pessimistic about our ability over the next decade or two . . . to keep China from achieving her objectives until her zeal wanes."[5]

McNamara's own views differed little from Johnson's public statements. The decision to bomb the Democratic Republic of Vietnam (DRV) in February 1965 and to escalate troop deployments in July "make sense only if they are in support of a long-run United States policy to contain Communist China," he wrote. The Chinese threat was multiple: "to undercut our importance and effectiveness in the world" and, more remotely but more menacingly, to "organize all of Asia against us." It was necessary to hold the line until Chinese "zeal" waned.[6]

"Zeal" was a code word for revolution, a radical process at work in the Third World, Vietnam, and China though not in the USSR. But it was more: facing a Sinocentric worldview "as strong in Peking today as it was under the emperors centuries ago," it was possible to envision the end of monolithic communism and at the same time to voice a fear of "Communist expansion" in Southeast Asia.[7] The issue, as Johnson argued both then and in his memoirs, was not simply Vietnam: Ho Chi Minh's "military campaign against South Vietnam was part of a large, much more ambitious strategy being conducted by the Communists," a "Djakarta-Hanoi-Peking-Pyongyang axis, with Cambodia probably to be brought in as a junior partner and Laos to be merely absorbed by the North Vietnamese and Chinese."[8]

Yet during the Johnson years, far more than in the Kennedy administration, Washington gradually abandoned the language of containment with isolation. China remained very much "the enemy," but Washington's confidence in the viability of the global economic order was growing, despite major problems arising from the economic costs of the Vietnam War. Now the debates were centered on developing a more sophisticated and multilayered strategy toward Beijing.[9] During the Kennedy administration the furthest the United States had been willing to go—as Roger Hilsman's "Open Door Speech" of December 1963 had suggested—was essentially to sit tight, "waiting for Peking to 'shape up.'"[10] But since Peking did not seem to be shaping up, and with the situation in Vietnam deteriorating, what was the next step?

The Johnson administration's answer lay in the aim that had been at the core of containment from the beginning: the gradual alteration of the Communist system. But isolation of China was no longer mandatory. Times were changing. "Our aim," wrote one NSC staffer, "has always been the 'domestication' of Communist China. A strategy of containment plus moral preachment has achieved little success in this regard. So why not try modified containment—plus subversion? By the latter, I simply mean the careful use of free world goods, people, and ideas—instruments which have proved their long-term corrosive value in our relations with other totalitarian societies."[11]

Containment without isolation still left unresolved the perennial issues of Taiwan, recognition, the United Nations, and trade. But the contexts in which these issues had long been debated had begun to shift. The reasons for this new approach and the way it became official policy illustrate once again how

Washington's behavior toward China reflected its understanding of its own global strategies and needs.

American Strategy in Asia

A 1966 national security memo summarized the five crucial aspects of containment without isolation: (1) traditional military containment—the deterrence of and resistance to overt and covert Chinese aggression; (2) the frustration of communist expansion; (3) a limited but critical role for the Soviet Union in containing China; (4) generous assistance to the fragile societies on the Chinese perimeter that were in the process of nation building, and the defeat of revolutionary romantics in the Third World; and (5) "systematic efforts to help erode the Chinese totalitarian state, to influence Chinese behavior, and to combat Chinese ignorance and fear of the outside world."[12]

Military Containment

The June 1966 Long Range Study of China summarized a number of military alternatives that had been debated and concluded that the "basic U.S. strategic military concept in Asia" was to continue providing "a credible deterrent to all forms of Chinese Communist aggression with emphasis on the likeliest forms." Of the three broadly defined strategies—disengagement, containment, and showdown—the only acceptable one was containment: that is, "seeking concurrently to check the spread of Chinese Communist power and influence and to induce moderation of Peking's current expansionist politics." "Moderation" was a new note, in harmony with the Johnson administration's view that holding the line in Vietnam would give other nations time to become more economically and politically viable. Even more strikingly, the study expressed some of the earliest notions on the use of soft power against China.

As often happens in policy disputes, two extremes were established only to be discounted: in this case, disengagement and showdown.[13] Yet both had their advocates, though military support for a showdown, while limited, probably surpassed diplomatic support for disengagement.

Disengagement

The Long Range Study described advocates of disengagement as seeking the gradual liquidation of American commitments to the nations on China's periphery. Essentially, this approach meant ending nation building as a containment strategy. Bases would be evacuated and American forces redeployed to Guam, Hawaii, and the continental United States; military assistance programs and even economic aid would be terminated, all in the belief that Asia was not fundamental to the security of the United States. The American military was already overextended, and it was ultimately futile to "keep China from dominating her 'natural' sphere of influence." Besides, China's "public commitments to revolutionary goals" amounted to just so much bluster, and in any case, the nations on its periphery could take care of themselves.

The Long Range Study quickly dismissed this thinking. The concept of natural spheres of influence "is out-of-date in a shrinking world," according neither with power realities nor with security requirements in the second half of the twentieth century. Were the United States to disengage, weak noncommunist states would quickly reach accommodation with Peking and Hanoi. Holdouts would face either "liberation struggles" or possibly direct attack. Even Hanoi's chances of "maintaining some degree of independence from Peking would disappear as our power receded." The rest of the dominoes would then fall—first Taiwan and South Korea, then Japan, which would be driven to reappraise its entire foreign policy (though its role in the global economy might serve as a partial restraint).[14]

In time, Japan or India or even the USSR might emerge as an effective counterweight to China; in essence, China was not really *the* great power of Asia, and so it had to be resisted. No Asian power was to be an equal of the United States, and the "domination of much of Asia by a single, hostile power would run counter to our most fundamental interests in that part of the world."[15] A regional balance was essential, and that still required an active American presence.

Showdown

A showdown, the Long Range Study argued, was no better an alternative than disengagement. Its advocates assumed that the Chinese were on a "collision course" with the United States, that "war is inevitable and it is best to get it over with before China acquires substantial numbers of nuclear-armed long-range missiles." But they were wrong: containment could work, and it was possible to attain a regional balance of power. A "more sophisticated argument" was that even if war was not inevitable, China might have to knuckle under to an American demand to cease its indirect warfare and aggression: "If she failed to respond to a threat, we could force her to submit more easily now than later." But again, though this argument deserved "more serious consideration" than it usually got (and more than disengagement deserved), a "careful weighing" of all factors showed that it was not in America's national interest. The argument here was cultural and psychological: showdown strategy denied the inordinate "pride and intransigence" of the Chinese leaders ("and indeed of the Chinese people"), which might compel a forceful response.[16] Besides, it was impossible to ascertain what demands could actually lead to the elimination of communist aggression. Could China realistically be expected to stop North Vietnamese attacks on South Vietnam? What would the United States do about violations of "good behavior"?

Furthermore, although the United States might destroy the modern sector of the Chinese economy, the regime would probably survive in the rural areas. A war with China that had "no boundaries" would be a nightmare: the United States could find itself also at war in Korea and Southeast Asia while pursuing a "possibly futile" effort to subdue the communist regime in China. Nor could Washington expect the Soviets to stay out, and they would probably support Peking, if only to weaken the West. Since the United States would appear as the aggressor, Japan might be pushed toward neutralism, and allied outrage and world opinion could deeply wound American power and prestige.

Arguments against a showdown did not rule out a limited attack for the purpose of destroying facilities for advanced weapons production and any such weapons that might be already deployed or stockpiled. Such an attack, the study argued, could be successfully conducted at the present time, setting back the Chinese nuclear program, though only by about four years. But there were risks here, too: again, the Soviets might intervene; most other governments would probably view such action as a "dangerous and irresponsible act of unprovoked aggression"; and "of greatest importance, our attack would constitute an act of war."[17] Wiping out Chinese nuclear facilities would leave major Chinese military strengths untouched, and Washington would have to confront the possibility of a "violent reaction" elsewhere, such as in Southeast Asia, where it could be harder to cope with. And even if the Chinese nuclear-weapons program were delayed, the United States would have to face serious consequences in the future for its actions.

Should war in Vietnam escalate, or should China provoke a war, then such an attack would take on a very different coloration. In that event, the "wisest choice" might combine two objectives: *setting back the regime's advanced-weapons program and economic programs directly related to military production,* and *crippling the regime's ability to project its power abroad and forcing the withdrawal of invading forces.* The reasons advanced for not undertaking such actions without provocation do not apply equally *after* hostilities have already begun between the U.S. and China."[18]

Containment Strategies

Only containment—whether close in, remote, or from the offshore island chain—remained a viable strategy. That meant deterring or defeating (1) overt aggression, which had not been seen since the Korean War; (2) indirect aggression, of which Vietnam was a "classic case"; (3) subversion and diplomatic maneuvering, with China contesting the United States for world-power status and influence. In Asia, nation building had to be pursued as essential if remote containment were ever to succeed; but in addition, Beijing had to be reassured not only that the United States did not seek to overthrow the regime but also that Washington would modify export controls, finally allow travel and cultural and educational exhibitions and exchanges, and possibly even open up the American market to Chinese goods. At the same time, extensive propaganda would be directed at Chinese elites.[19]

With the war in Vietnam in mind, the long-range study argued that "U.S. land power on the mainland of Asia is relevant to the problem of containing Chinese communist military aggression, and that the U.S. should not attempt to rely on air and sea power alone."[20] In Southeast Asia a strategy of "close containment and forward defense" had proved necessary, though it had been challenged ever since the Korean War by sizable parts of the military—with dwindling persuasiveness since the stabilization of Europe, however. In South Asia, a strategy of remote containment would be effective and, in time, might work for Southeast Asia as well. The Pacific bases and the offshore islands were the military backbone of these policies—which, even if China began to moderate its position, Washington would need to commit itself to indefinitely.

If such deterrence should fail, the study continued, "the U.S. must be able to provide timely reinforcements to indigenous and other allied forces as appropriate in such strength that the aggregate can deal adequately with the aggression."[21] The next decade would require the development of plans for a rapid conventional deployment, as well as a continued forward containment policy in Southeast Asia. The Long Range Study was based on the unduly optimistic premises that the United States would win in Vietnam, that wars of national liberation would be discredited, and that U.S. public support would continue for close-up containment. Once Washington won the war, moreover, the United States would encourage Hanoi to be independent of Beijing and should open up trade and cultural relations with North Vietnam in order to draw it into the "international economic environment."[22] "Communist internationalism," the authors believed, was a thing of the past.

The development of Chinese nuclear weapons, however, posed a perilously difficult problem. The Chinese appeared to have "a growing regional strategic capability and the beginnings of a counterdeterrent force targeted against the continental United States."[23] Although the United States might develop a sea-based antiballistic missile (ABM) system that would draw in Asian allies, to do so would raise a further dilemma: "The ABM debate would be very costly if it succeeds in magnifying the ChiCom nuclear threat in the eyes of Communist China's neighbors, and in convincing such countries that our concern about being unable to deter a nuclear attack by Communist China is so great that we need not be counted on unless we can be sure of escaping all conceivable nuclear injury to ourselves." And so it was "crucial" to "get across to allies and friends" that the Chinese were not oblivious to the dangers of nuclear war. When it suited Washington's purposes, it was willing to depict China as perfectly responsible. "At least up to this time, Communist China's military calculations have been cautious and rational, and that we have no reason to suppose they will be less rational in assessing the cost of employing nuclear weapons."[24]

Vietnam and War with China

Even though the Long Range Study carefully opposed more extreme positions, the fear that China would be provoked into intervening in Vietnam was a real one, and few civilian leaders during the Johnson administration wanted such a war or saw the Vietnam War as an opportunity to resolve the China issue once and for all.[25] Indeed, the goal of bringing China into the community of nations ideologically undercut the need for a military solution—that was the appeal of gradually inducing moderation in Beijing's policies. Generally, Johnson and his top aides believed that the war was unlikely to spread to China; some argued that the American public would not support such an expansion.[26] As long as the United States neither invaded the DRV nor threatened its existence, the Chinese would not go to war.

Johnson, Rusk, and McNamara all wanted to avoid another Korea but considered it likely that should war break out between China and the United States in Vietnam, it would quickly have to expand beyond the limits accepted in the Korean War. If China entered the war, the United States planned to attack it directly.

In July 1965, Under Secretary of State George Ball wrote a long memorandum on the dangers of war with China. He noted that American intelligence had agreed in November 1964 that if the United States struck above the 19th parallel, "Chinese Communist aircraft operating from Chinese bases would probably assist in defending North Vietnam against United States attacks." Once this happened, the pressures on Johnson to knock out those bases would be enormous—and would extend to "striking at Chinese nuclear production installations." Should the Chinese air bases be hit, there was a real possibility that China would move "massive ground forces into North Vietnam, and subsequently into Laos, South Vietnam and possibly Thailand." Then the debate in the United States over the use of nuclear weapons would rapidly escalate, even though, as Ball argued, their use would "generate probably irresistible pressures for a major Soviet involvement."[27]

The Soviet attitude toward China was widely debated. Despite the bitterness of the Sino-Soviet relationship, however, it was generally agreed that the USSR would countenance neither a total Vietnamese defeat nor the collapse of the Chinese communist regime. McNamara and Bundy's hawkish position, Ball argued, "would accept the risks of substantial escalation, including the acceptance of ground warfare with Red China." All three agreed that "even a single nuclear weapon would impose the ultimate test for the integrity of international communism. While no one can be certain, the best judgment is that the Soviet Union could not sit by and let nuclear weapons be used against China."[28]

In the papers that have so far been released, few analysts disagreed. Few believed that the actual destruction of the DRV would be acceptable to either Moscow or Beijing, but few saw any reason to limit the use of destructive weaponry in the South. Ball wrote, "We can do almost anything we like in the South, with little if any damage directly involving the big Communist powers." Both China and the Soviet Union, he argued, recognized the difference between losing a war of national liberation and the "capitulation of a sister socialist state under direct air attack by an 'imperialist' power."[29]

The Vietnam War influenced almost every immediate step in Washington's relations with China. If the long-term goal was to end China's isolation, the short-term imperatives of the war often dictated harsh American responses to any improvement in China's international stature. Witness the anger and dismay over the French diplomatic recognition of China in 1964—not because it threatened American interests in the long run but because Washington feared it would encourage Beijing (and Hanoi) in the short run.[30]

Simplification and the "Communist Enemy"

An expansionist and threatening China repeatedly turned up in national security documents, in starkly simplistic language, as an immediate and potent rationale for the Vietnam War. Yet Washington's China was both simplistic and complex—multilayered, in fact—depending on what was being argued over. Complex debates within a simplifying overview: these were the hallmarks of the national security bureaucracy's ideological faith. "Communism" or "the communist bloc" had always been a multilayered notion— geopolitical (in the interrelationship of Soviet and Chinese interests), economic (in the vision of the global order necessary to American aims), strategic (in addressing the ability of the U.S. military to meet threats to its preeminent power), nuclear (in the question of whether Washington's nuclear weapons strategy was effective if China was no longer under the Soviet nuclear umbrella), and ideological (in the drive to create a global vision compelling enough to guide Washington officials and persuade those of other nations)—a vision that always encompassed issues of credibility, of holding the line against aggression, and of keeping American commitments around the world.

Identification of the enemy as China, or communism, or the communist bloc took on its particular meaning according to the issue under discussion. Moreover, in a single document or group of documents, China could appear as the model of revolutionary nationalism, as a nation advancing interests bitterly at odds with those of the USSR, as a centuries-old enemy of the DRV, and as part of the communist alternative to the American global order. National security officials repeatedly explored the complexity of China's relations with the DRV; the implications of the Sino-Soviet dispute for Hanoi's policies in South Vietnam, the usefulness of Beijing as a revolutionary model for guerrilla warfare and national development, the Chinese military strategy (offensive or defensive) and nuclear weapons program. And yet after engaging in such detailed reviews, the very same government officials could still invoke, both in public *and in private,* the most sweeping simplifications.

In recent years, various high officials of the Kennedy and Johnson administrations have lamented that at the time they lacked a full appreciation of the antagonism between Vietnamese and Chinese nationalism, or that they failed to distinguish adequately between China's national interests and its revolutionary objectives. "If we had [had] more Asia experts around us, perhaps we would not have been so simpleminded about China and Vietnam," McNamara has written.[31]

As sincere as these claims may be, they do not really illuminate or even address the inner ideological and strategic workings of the bureaucracy. They overlook the often extremely detailed discussions on such issues in the documents. The question of how ideology works in the national security bureaucracy is really a question about the complex uses of simplification: as propaganda directed at others, as a form of self-indoctrination that allows for policy co-coordination, as a means to a cohering belief, and as a method of defining global objectives.

It is probably safe to say that the complexity of bureaucratic debate does not usually challenge the simplifications of global policy formulation. These formulations are inherently simplifying; that is part of their function, which is to provide a way of deciding upon the allocation of resources, time, and commitments within an overarching sense of national priorities. Ideologically, for example, "Communism" remained the enemy in national security documents throughout the Johnson years because it constituted the most forceful expression of a kaleidoscope of forces, tendencies, and currents that were hostile to the multilateral economic and geopolitical order the United States supported.

Communism still represented the opposite of visionary globalism, and the communist enemy could thus be continually invoked in the documents. When discussions touched on the relationship between the Vietnam War and the global order, a slighting reference to communism (or "totalitarian communist governments" or "international communism") was both a simplification and an ideologically accurate reflection of Washington's globalist commitment. When specific issues on waging war involved Washington's relations with Beijing and Moscow, then the splits within the "communist movement" could be analyzed in great depth, but globally, communism remained the overarching framework. If a debate focused on possible ways for Washington to cooperate with the USSR, the emphasis on the communist enemy might easily shift toward China and the spread of communism in Southeast Asia in ways that made the debates between the DRV and China almost irrelevant *at that level*. But when arguments broke out over the state of the relationship between China and Vietnam, the emphasis could shift back to their historical enmity— even as the Maoist model for upheaval in the Third World was being held up as a grave threat to American interests. The emphasis depended on what was being discussed. Yet precisely because these debates over particulars ultimately fit into a globalizing strategic perspective, they often concluded with another sweeping characterization of the enemy—as "Communism" or "revolutionary China." To see this process merely as simplification or misperception is to overlook the bureaucracy's pervasive ideological environment. Simplifications underlie innumerable detailed debates, and the higher up in the bureaucracy one goes, the more these simplifications meld with a fervent globalist commitment.

JCS documents were structured according to these multiple levels and their varying strategic implications. In assessing the *"basic threat* to US security," for example, they referred to the "Sino-Soviet bloc." They did not deny the antagonisms among and between America's enemies, but they made the assumption that focusing on those differences was not very useful in defining the basic threat to U.S. security. That threat arose from (a) the Soviets' growing nuclear capacities; (b) the Soviets' subversive strategies, their perception of weaknesses in the free world, and, "particularly in the neutralist and less developed societies, the taking advantage of pressure for economic and social change"; and (c) the ability of totalitarian communist governments to act ruthlessly and to repudiate agreements "without being subject to moral restraints." Both the Soviets and the Chinese threatened aggression, economic warfare, and blackmail.[32]

Splits between communist nations, whether the Soviet Union and China or Vietnam and China, did not keep the "Communist bloc" from having maintained basic unity in tactics toward Southeast Asia.[33] Here the issue was tactics, in line with the JCS's preoccupation with subversion, revolutionary processes, and the calls of Third World nationalists to sever their countries from the global economic order. Moscow, Beijing, Hanoi—they all agreed on the classic principles for subversion and extending their influence through indirection and infiltration, "the differences being a matter of degree and emphasis."[34]

The message was clear: the "breakup of monolithic and international communism" had not weakened the "Communist threat." The "techniques of revolution, of party organization, of propaganda, or public control, which the Communists invented or developed," remained available for those who wished to use them, and "Communists will be the most effective teachers of these techniques." Moreover,

> Communism, whatever its variety or international orientation, will continue to associate itself with some basic impulses common to large sectors of mankind: the urge to rapid change, the demand for social justice, opposition to vested interests of all descriptions. And even though communist countries may on occasion be as hostile to one another as the Chinese and the Soviets now are, Communists will long retain an underlying enmity toward the West, if only because their convictions are in so many respects incompatible with traditional Western concepts of political and economic life.[35]

The increasingly powerful Soviet Union, though ossified somewhat into a nonrevolutionary nation-state, still manipulated revolutions to its own ends. China, though militarily it was on the defensive, embodied a commitment to revolutionary change that offered an inspiration to revolutionaries in the underdeveloped world, especially in Southeast Asia. In other words, communism remained the larger enemy, even as the split widened.

Sometimes discussions of the communist danger involved no analysis of conflicting nationalisms at all. At other times, such distinctions were the elemental realities of intelligence.[36] Consider a rather typical 1963 memo, from Thomas Hughes, director of the State Department's Bureau of Intelligence and Research, to Rusk: "The Viet Cong insurgency appeared to be planned, controlled, and supplied from Hanoi. There is no evidence of direct Chinese Communist involvement in these areas although Peiping may be consulted on general strategy questions. . . . [W]e believe that the North Vietnamese remain wary of Chinese dominating and do not wish to become completely beholden to their northern comrades."[37] Such wariness on the part of the Vietnamese was never completely set aside in assessments of Sino-Vietnamese relations. In 1967, answering the question "Is Hanoi in Peking's Pocket?" Hughes addressed differing DRV and Chinese long-term interests:

Peking would like to establish hegemony over, if not control of, Southeast Asia, including Vietnam. Hanoi desires a reunified but independent Vietnam and may have hopes of bringing Laos and Cambodia within a Vietnamese rather than a Chinese sphere of influence. Hanoi's objectives might suggest maintaining a balance of power in the Far East, which might well require the continuing influence of the USSR and Japan. Current leaders in Peking clearly hope that the East Wind—meaning China itself—will prevail over the West, whether the latter blows from Moscow or Washington.[38]

The analysis had come a long way from the Truman years, when Chinese nationalism and Chinese communism were believed to be at war with each other and Beijing was portrayed as virtually dominated by the Kremlin.

The bureaucracy debated the implications of divisions in the DRV leadership between those who inclined toward the Soviets and those who inclined toward the Chinese; of the different ways the Soviets and the Chinese pursued their national interests and how these ways might conflict with the interests of the DRV. Unlike China in the 1940s, the DRV was seen as communist *and* nationalist; its leadership might disagree internally, but it was subordinate to no outside interests. An August 1966 intelligence memorandum firmly argued that the Chinese could not dictate DRV positions.[39] No one had argued this way about the Chinese in the late 1940s.

Yet such memos belonged to the very same milieu in which communism and the Chinese revolutionary model were still cited as the enemy. McGeorge Bundy could write, "We do recognize the advantages of detaching Hanoi from China," but it was a moot issue, given that North Vietnam's conduct in the South "seems to us to argue against a present policy of Free World friendliness to North Vietnam." No concrete policy implications flowed from Bundy's recognition that there were conflicts between China and the DRV; they were useless for dealing with fighting the war.

The Long Range Study provides another classic example of the multiple levels involved in analyzing communism and China. Though it included sweeping references to "Asian Communism," elsewhere a quite different understanding emerged: "We should take more seriously the potential advantages of differential treatment of Peking, Pyongyang, Hanoi and Ulan Bator. Signs that they see their national interests differently have increased since 1963 and have been accentuated both by the Chinese-Soviet conflict and by the war in Vietnam. We may expect such differences to intensify further." In this context, expanded trade between Japan and North Korea was viewed along the same lines as trade with Eastern Europe. Any steps that would support "internal liberalization," "national independence and polycentrism," and "broader association with the Free World" were to be encouraged.[40]

Most analysts concluded that Beijing could not control Hanoi;[41] the two differed over the progress of the war and over how it should be fought. Beijing was viewed as critical of Hanoi's eagerness to distance itself from the Maoist model, warning Hanoi not to minimize Mao's role as the originator of "people's war"—"But Hanoi has rejected Peking's rebuke, still avoids attributing the theory to Mao, and continues to assert its own originality." Sino-Vietnamese differences of all kinds had "increased to the point where Peking has been impelled publicly to deny them."[42] And all along, Hanoi was playing off the Soviets against the Chinese: "Although this is a narrow and tortuous path for the Vietnamese, it offers them the most profitable and flexible position they can obtain with relation to the war."[43] Conflicting nationalisms, conflicting interests provided the grist for this complex level of analysis, and yet the Long Range Study could still conclude with the globalizing simplification that it was imperative to defeat Chinese-backed "wars of national liberation" and the "Maoist model."

Simplification, Globalism, and National Security Arguments

In many aspects of United States China policy in the mid-1960s, therefore, globalizing simplifications played a necessary role. The higher the level of decision-making, the more likely leaders were to invoke these simplifications; simplifying and globalizing go together. They were not misperceiving when they did not base policies on conflicts between China and Vietnam; those conflicts were irrelevant to their policies.

Meetings between American officials and foreign allies could be quite revealing in this respect. In discussions with the Japanese, for example, Washington used simplification to reaffirm strongly the American global perspective, invoking the frightening threats the free world faced. An aide-mémoire to prepare Johnson for his January 12, 1965, meeting with Prime Minister Eisaku Sato argued that China "continues to proclaim and pursue a policy of militant revolution, is exerting expansionist pressures against bordering countries especially in Southeast Asia and, having recently exploded a nuclear device, refuses to agree to any limitations on nuclear testing or prevention of nuclear proliferation." Any U.S. concessions on the United Nations, Taiwan, or various other issues, Johnson could argue, "would tend to confirm the Peiping leadership in its view that current militant-subversive tactics are successful and its expansionist objectives realizable."[44]

When Rusk visited de Gaulle shortly after Johnson became president, he espoused a harsh, inflexible China line, expressing American concern over

Chinese "militancy," the Chinese attack on India in their border war, the influence on Sukarno's move to the left in Indonesia, Chinese activity in Latin America (particularly Cuba), and Zhou Enlai's troublemaking presence in Africa. Moscow might have calmed down, Rusk told de Gaulle, but Beijing "was taking on a 'trial gallop' the task of promoting revolution." Only an American line in Europe forced the Soviets to change, and a similar stance toward China was essential. Rusk reported to Johnson, "I told him I thought it would be a great mistake to let the Chinese or their Communist allies get any idea that such policies paid off."[45]

In April 1964 the French foreign minister, Maurice Couve de Murville, told Rusk that China might consider it in its own interests to reach "an accommodation with the West," even in Southeast Asia.[46] Johnson and his aides were perfectly aware of China's national interests, but they preferred to shift the discussion to the global issues. Thus the differences between Washington and Paris involved an assessment of Washington's global role and what it required—not of China's national interests per se. The following February, Couve de Murville met with Johnson and several of his aides, and this time Johnson invoked the domino theory (always a code for Washington's global preoccupations): "If we were to abandon Vietnam, we would be forced to give up Laos, Thailand, Burma, and would be going back to Hawaii and San Francisco." When the French foreign minister demurred ("there was a complete contradiction between our respective information of the thinking of the Chinese and the North Vietnamese"), George Ball (a noted skeptic in private about American policy) observed that France seemed to believe China was preoccupied with internal problems, whereas "we think that the Chinese are aggressive and land hungry." When Couve de Murville again disagreed, Charles Bohlen, ambassador to France, wondered how China could possibly retreat, now that it had "proclaimed its belief in militant support of indigenous movements." Johnson added that any Chinese successes "would be likely to increase their appetite," invoking another key word in the globalizing mind-set that justified American determination to stop "aggression." The French foreign minister countered that he thought China was already quite "impressed by the immense power of the United States," adding that the Soviets "would support North Vietnam against China."[47]

Although Washington officials discussed such questions among themselves, they were not about to debate them with the French; that would hardly have been an effective way of affirming Washington's power to set the global agenda or to wage the war on its own terms. At the most general level, Johnson and many of his aides could both believe in a voracious expansionist China and yet sound far more moderate in discussions of specific Beijing policies. This difference in tone—and in analysis—was not really contradictory. It is typical of the way the national security bureaucracy works.

Simplification and the Chinese as Revolutionaries

Just as there were debates in national security meetings about communism and conflicts between communist countries, there were also differing assessments of China as the enemy. The most sensational and popular Chinese version of "revolutionary" China was Defense Minister Lin Biao's September 1965 manifesto, *On People's War,* which quickly replaced Khrushchev's January 1961 speech on wars of national liberation as justification for American actions in Vietnam. There were debates over whether Lin's statement propounded an expansionist strategy or a more defensive program of "self-reliance," but either way, Beijing seemed determined to spread a revolutionary ethos that was anathema to everything America stood for. That such differences did not challenge the multilayered globalism in which China played the part of the enemy becomes apparent when one more closely analyzes a number of specific issues: Taiwan, nuclear war, the Chinese policy of "self-reliance," and Chinese "expansionism."

Taiwan

When Washington's focus was on China as revolutionary, it rarely touched on the issue of Taiwan; but when Taiwan became the focus, Washington tended to play down the revolutionary aspect of Chinese actions. A 1964 CIA analysis, "Peiping's Views of Revolutionary War," depicted China's support for revolution not as an abstract commitment to dogma but as conduct "sharply directed toward the goal of effecting . . . American withdrawal from the Taiwan Strait." The failure to pressure the United States into reducing its commitments to Taiwan during the Taiwan Strait crises of 1954–55 and 1958 had "compelled the Chinese Communists leaders to shift their strategy from confrontations or near-confrontations with the U.S. in the Strait to a more indirect strategy requiring pressures on U.S. positions elsewhere in the world."[48]

Khrushchev's "increasing reluctance" to support additional actions by Beijing in the Strait, the CIA analysis continued, made a policy shift even more imperative. It quoted Mao's remark to a Japanese delegation in 1961 that the "'immediate and pressing problem of Taiwan' made the difference between the Chinese and Soviet attitude toward U.S. policy": the Chinese strategy of applying pressure through "'small war' ('armed struggle') in underdeveloped areas [is] most distinctive." That had been the policy in the late 1940s and early 1950s, but it had shifted around the time of the 1955 Bandung Conference when a new, softer line of peaceful coexistence deemphasized overt incitement to violent revolution. After U.S.-China talks on Taiwan ended in an impasse at Geneva, however, the strategy of armed struggle reemerged, and by April 1960 it had expanded beyond the Far East to all emerging nations. An October 1960 discussion that Zhou Enlai held with the journalist Edgar Snow carried "the implication that the U.S. can be most effectively pressured to withdraw its commitments to Taipei and other governments by direct attacks on U.S. positions over a broad front, particularly in underdeveloped areas."[49]

This CIA analysis harked back to the arguments of the late 1940s that American intervention in the Chinese civil war would create an irredentist issue which would profoundly shape all aspects of the two countries' relations for years to come. To the degree that American policy on Taiwan (as well as recognition, embargo, and the United Nations) was viewed as critical to Beijing's nationalist aims, the regime's revolutionary character was downplayed. At these junctures, China became just a state using whatever tools it had at hand—not a world-revolutionary force.[50] Yet, a China using revolutionary tools toward nationalist ends was still the enemy of Washington.

Nuclear War

Publicly, both the United States and the Soviet Union stoked the popular opinion that China was playing fast and loose with the dangers of nuclear war, but in internal assessments, Washington could and did argue differently. A CIA memorandum of December 1964, for example, challenged Soviet claims of Chinese violence, fanaticism, and irresponsibility on the issues of nuclear disarmament and nuclear war. The Chinese, it argued, clearly distinguished between small "just" wars and "world war"; for "polemical reasons," the Soviets were blurring this distinction. They had made use of a quotation from a November 1957 speech of Mao's: "In China, we are engaged in construction; we want peace. But, *if* the imperialists nevertheless impose a war, we shall have to clench our teeth, postpone construction, and resume it after the war." The Soviets ignored the conditional "if," failing to point out that Mao "did not want a *world* (i.e., major) war with the U.S. unless it is absolutely unavoidable— that is, if it is 'forced' on Peiping—in which case, the Chinese would have no alternative but to resist."[51]

The Chinese believed, the analysis concluded, that they could support revolutionary wars without provoking an American nuclear attack. Against an oft-cited view that Eisenhower had effectively ended the Korean War by threatening the Chinese with nuclear weapons, the analysis argued quite otherwise: "Their *de facto* reading of the non-use of nuclear weapons during the Korean War seems to have increased their confidence that non-use will continue to be a US policy."[52] This interpretation contained two key points. First, the Chinese were quite aware of the risks and terror of nuclear war.[53] Second, an awareness of nuclear peril lay at the heart of Mao's "paper tiger" metaphor for the United States—a ferocious beast in the immediate context but not a paralyzing long-range threat. Such a stance sought to avoid an appearance of intimidation and to project boldness, part of a deliberate effort to convince the United States that the Chinese would run the risk of major war if they must. (Dulles, according to the CIA analysis, "was mistaken . . . in thinking that by merely threatening to use atomic weapons in 1954, the US would succeed . . . in intimidating the people of the world in general and those of Indochina in particular.")[54] This interpretation of the Chinese view of nuclear weapons pervades studies of China during the mid-1960s.

Another CIA assessment, "Chinese Communist Military Doctrine," concluded that China's public debunking of the threat of nuclear weapons "might reflect an inadequate knowledge of their true effects, but it was more likely a recognition that a power without these weapons must ignore or derogate them if it is to continue to insist that it is a great power." Stressing their destructive might "could only have a detrimental effect in China, frightening the people and undermining their morale and their will to fight." Their statements were not much different from the kind of things the Soviets had said before the USSR became a major nuclear power. China's leaders well understand that "nuclear weapons can cause immense destruction," but their emphasis on men over weapons, their crash program to develop nuclear weaponry, and their support for wars of national liberation were all ways of coping with nuclear inferiority, not an indication of a failure to understand the immense threat of that weaponry.[55]

Despite alarming warnings by Johnson administration leaders of a billion Chinese armed with nuclear weapons, the administration hardly panicked over the first Chinese nuclear explosion. An interdepartmental group had been studying the implications of such a test for more than a year. As an April 1964 memo to Johnson stated, the "great disproportion" between Chinese and American nuclear power made it highly unlikely that the Chinese would be tempted to any first use. They would no doubt seek to obtain all the psychological benefits they could from nearby Asian countries, but their actual ability to translate their weapon into practical military and strategic policies would be very limited.[56]

Moreover, it was unlikely that China could "produce large numbers of whatever advanced weapons are eventually deployed. For some years to come, the Chinese will probably assess the value of an advanced weaponry in terms more of its political and psychological effect than of its practical military significance." The "inevitable rise in costs associated with the production phase of even a modest effort probably has forced (or will force) the Chinese Communists to channel their efforts into the development, at any one period of time, of only a very limited range of delivery vehicles."[57] Perhaps the most notable division in the administration was over whether the Chinese believed that the United States might launch a surprise attack with nuclear weapons.[58]

If China often was such a serious enemy, why could the leaders of the Johnson administration countenance its development of nuclear weapons with such moderation? The reasons are revealing. China was the enemy above all because it was the model of a radical nationalist and revolutionary way of developing a nation's economy, and the expansion of such a model, particularly in Asia, constituted a direct threat to visionary globalism. But even with nuclear weapons, China was not much of a military threat. Indeed, if Johnson and his advisors had really thought it was, they would probably have joined forces with those in the JCS who wanted to use the Vietnam War as an opportunity for decisive military action against China.[59] But Johnson opposed such an irreversible step. The issue was not that China was an enemy. It was the kind of danger it represented.

Self-Reliance

Few national security documents from the Cold War years deny that China would have liked to open trade with the Western powers and Japan. Beijing's "insistence on the need for military, as well as economic, self-reliance is more a justification than a policy," the CIA argued. Until 1959 the Chinese were willing to accept Soviet assistance in developing their armed forces and their economy. It was their refusal to accept an unequal relationship that shook the alliance and precipitated the Soviet decision to halt economic and military assistance "in an effort to curb Chinese independence. Because there was no simple alternative open to the Chinese short of surrendering this independence, they adopted a policy of self-reliance."[60] The more China was viewed apart from a global context and Sino-Soviet polemics, the less "offensive" and "aggressive" did the documents depict its "independence." Occasionally, China's methods to seek and preserve its independence in a "hostile" milieu were portrayed as plausible (though misguided) compensations for weakness.

Expansionsim

Though Kennedy and Johnson administration officials regularly characterized China as a militant and aggressively expansionist power, once again one finds ambivalence in more specific studies. China's actions rarely matched its rhetoric; during the Kennedy years its military approach was considered cautious and "defensive." An unprovoked movement by the Chinese communists into Southeast Asia was judged in May 1961 to be "highly unlikely, either now or in the foreseeable future." An "overt invasion" would have been "out of character both with Communist China's preoccupation to date with internal problems, and with the foreign and military policies it has pursued. The Chinese intervened in Korea only in the last instance, in a situation in which, from their point of view, strong U.S. forces threatened their border. They have exercised caution in their offshore island problems, and have backed off from face-to-face encounters with U.S. forces. Their course has been cautious in Laos." Except for "aggressive" attitudes toward India and Indonesia in 1959, they had shown a "considerable concern for 'correct' relations with their neighbors to the south." Overt aggression would have shattered Beijing's determination to appear "reasonable" in Southeast Asia.[61]

A distinction between Chinese support for wars of national liberation and China's conservative military stance was widely noted; CIA studies often concluded that "the Chinese Communists' military doctrine is and will continue to be basically defensive."[62] As the Long Range Study concluded in June 1966: "The intelligence community is split on a number of important issues and puzzled by a number of questions which do not seem definitely answerable in our present state of knowledge." Among these is "the question of whether or not the Chinese are 'expansionist,' as they are often called, or defensively minded." It seems "clear from repeated military encounters that the Chinese, although highly aggressive in their talk, are extremely cautious in action. Most intelligence estimates agree that the primary purpose of the Chinese military effort is national defense."[63]

Simplification and the Sino-Soviet Split

As the split between the Soviet Union and China increasingly preoccupied Washington, officials saw an increasingly violent, fanatical, and revolutionary China—particularly when the topic was the possibility of U.S.-Soviet détente. Almost to the very end of the Johnson years, they regarded the Sino-Soviet split as irreparable: "The split with the Soviet Union will probably persist and even widen over the coming decade." If the communist regime were challenged in China, though, the Long Range Study observed, "the Soviets would probably feel compelled to grant increasing assistance to the Chinese, both to preserve their credentials within the international communist movement and to guard against destruction of Communist rule in China." It was more than a question of immediate defense; they "might also see aid to Peking as a means of prolonging war between its two major rivals.[64] This remained the dominant assessment until the Soviet invasion of Czechoslovakia in August 1968.

Following their notion of Chinese "hostility" and "aggressive attitudes," Washington analysts regarded the Soviet military buildup along the Chinese border as a measure "to improve its defenses along various sectors of the common border." After all, Soviet planners had to "prepare for the worst, including the possibility that the Chinese leaders or some aspiring Chinese leader might seek to provoke a military emergency, including a clash with the Soviet Union, to divert public attention from troubles at home and create an artificial rationale for the imposition of authority."[65] In other words, the Soviets were being defensive—even though their military buildup was greater. Washington contrasted a Soviet desire for coexistence with Chinese hostility, particularly as the latter became manifested in the Cultural Revolution in 1966 and 1967, and Washington believed that in the future, Sino-Soviet hostility might grow ("paralleled if not exceeded in some respects" by Sino-American hostility).[66]

These views fit nicely with a degree of détente between the United States and the Soviet Union. Relaxation of tensions in Europe gave every sign of proceeding as the drive toward an "open curtain" gained force. Trends in Asia were just the opposite: "toward increasing tensions with Communist China, toward the possibility of military emergencies provoked by China, and toward the possibility of a broader war arising out of the Vietnam conflict."[67]

Although the Soviets were engaging in a significant military buildup in the wake of Khrushchev's fall in October 1964, Washington had decided that Moscow was "approaching maturity" on nuclear issues.[68] It could therefore be expected to "act more like other great powers and less like the standard-bearer of world revolution." In fact, the Soviets had shown "a good understanding of the dangers inherent in each U.S.-USSR confrontation and have been careful to avoid exceeding those limits." Given the intensity of the rivalry between the Soviets and the Chinese, however, and the Soviet uneasiness with accusations of selling out, it was important that American propaganda and official statements avoid "crowing . . . about every small departure of Soviet practice from classic revolutionary Communism, internally toward economic rationality or externally toward more normal expression of great power national interest."[69]

Some Soviet interests continued to conflict with American ones in certain areas of Asia.[70] But others "correspond with or parallel ours."[71] The context had changed, however, with glimmers of the triangular relationship among the three powers that was to become increasingly prominent during the Nixon administration. It remained relatively primitive at this point because the Chinese were not yet really viewed as players—by either the Soviets or the Americans. China was still too much the revolutionary embodiment of a threat to American power.

In the "Basic triangle," according to the Long Range Study, China was the "weakest part in a shifting, dynamic three-cornered relationship." It could influence Soviet-American relationships but it could not control them. Moreover, there was little room for any of the parties to maneuver. Soviet-American détente was of paramount importance, and China's "revolutionary convictions" worked against its relations with both sides. Soviet power, even though it was increasing, did not appear to be a serious threat in Asia, particularly economically; in fact, Soviet economic aid "to appropriate Asian countries" might even prove useful, as a "benefit to the countries concerned and a means of gradually drawing the USSR into our attempts to increase the economic viability of the backward areas of Asia."[72] Cooperation was conceivable—there might even be "joint projects," as in Burma—though the war in Vietnam probably ruled that out for the near future. But it was a direction to consider, particularly in arms negotiations and in stabilizing Asia.[73]

Stabilizing the status quo was the heart of Washington's Asia policy, and administration officials hoped to work together with the USSR toward that end. The call for reducing tension with China did not imply an American withdrawal from Asia, even if China became more moderate:

> The inherent disparity in power between Communist China and the countries on the fringes of the Chinese land mass is such that no conceivable combination of military aid and development programs could produce a regional non-Communist power structure capable of establishing a balance of power within the next decade. This imbalance, coupled with substantial withdrawal of European powers leave the United States the only major non-Communist stabilizing power in the region.[74]

The Long Range Study was one of the national security bureaucracy's strongest statements in support of limited Soviet-American cooperation in Asia. Other studies put forward the possibilities that the "insurrectionary-subversionary element" in Peking's policy might be "gradually de-emphasized" and that the "Chinese could move to lessen tensions with the U.S. We should certainly seek within the context of our other Asian interests, to make this alternative as attractive as possible to Peking."[75] But that could happen only after Washington had held the line in Vietnam and the stabilization of Asia had proceeded further.

Concern grew rapidly after 1966 that the Soviets might become responsible for destabilizing Asia—particularly China, where Moscow might be tempted to intervene in any chaotic aftershocks of the Cultural Revolution. As Alfred Jenkins of the NSC wrote to Rostow, "China's apostasy has been the most horrendous of developments in the Communist world from the Soviet standpoint, and the Soviet Union would risk a great deal to be rid of it." A civil war in China might find the Soviets lending aid to the side that seemed more favorably disposed toward them. And, of course, the idea of a non-Communist China was something that "the Soviets could not tolerate."[76]

The Defeat of the "Revolutionary Romantics"

For the Johnson administration, significant changes in the global order meant that China need no longer be isolated, at least in the long term. The increasingly powerful global capitalist dynamic, the Sino-Soviet dispute, the consolidation of Europe, war-induced prosperity in Japan and other East Asian countries, and the development of détente—all these factors led Washington to argue that the Chinese revolution was losing its appeal as a model for the Third World. This argument took on more power with the crushing of the Indonesian Communist Party in October 1965, and considerably more with the outbreak of the Cultural Revolution.[77]

The shift was relatively subtle, though Kennedy administration officials had stressed the Third World, nation building, counterinsurgency, and problems in the underdeveloped areas of the South.[78] In contrast, Johnson administration officials slowly deemphasized Third Worldism, speaking more of ad hoc and bilateral relations and regional diversity, and deemphasizing counterinsurgency doctrine. As the Long Range Study noted, "The successful structuring of forces and their employment is best done on a pragmatic country-by-country basis."[79] Moreover, the Third World concept appeared to be feeding into the revolutionary ethos of the international left—and China. It provided a rubric for appeals in the South that underplayed the diversity of conflicts, encouraging simplistic rhetoric about the gap between rich and poor, racial issues, and "Western imperialism."

As the United States escalated the Vietnam War between 1965 and 1968, Washington's China remained the enemy constantly invoked as standing in the background. Yet during these years the fear of China's sway in the Third World eased significantly, owing to a number of factors. The Peking-Djakarta axis collapsed.[80] The Indo-Pakistani War revealed limits to the need to shape the politics of that region.[81] The second Bandung Conference of African and Asian nations in 1965 failed to develop an effective anti-American voice.[82] And after the summer of 1966 the Cultural Revolution appeared more and more irrational.

In fact, an increasing number of memorandums on the Third World and communism indicate a gradually building confidence in Washington that developing nations were turning away from revolutionary approaches. There was less urgency, less anxiety that the tide of history was quickly turning against the United States. Washington's preoccupation with revolution in Latin America remained strong, but its fear was easing.[83] In Africa it was much the same. As the State Department's Thomas Hughes wrote to Rusk, a communist takeover was "a false danger" there: "Both Moscow and Peiping seem prepared to work with established regimes." The most ominous situation was the South African government's policy of apartheid and widespread African criticism of Washington's implicit support of it. [84]

Further, a generation of anti-American "romantic revolutionaries" was going down to an ignominious end in various coups, defeats, and debacles of misguided development. Indonesia's Sukarno, Egypt's Nasser, Algeria's Ben Bella, Ghana's Nkrumah, Cuba's Castro, and China's Mao were often lumped together as autarkic radical nationalists who opposed everything in the global order that the United States sought to build. The "desperate ventures" of these figures were "peaking" by 1967; the tide was turning against the irrationality of revolutionary zeal and toward the more mundane labor of social and economic modernization. The result would still be a bitterly torn world but one no longer prey to revolutionary fanaticism.[85]

Some American officials attributed this change to the resolve with which the United States had held the line in Vietnam. "One is entitled to ask," wrote Edward Rice from Hong Kong, "whether the atmosphere which would have followed a clear US reversal [in Vietnam] would have been one in which surviving Indonesia generals would have reacted so stoutly and confidently."[86] Johnson summed up this view: "A number of Asian statesmen who had good reason for this opinion told me that the Indonesia turnaround would probably never have occurred if the situation to the north, in Southeast Asia, had been different—that is, if the United States and others had not taken a stand in Vietnam."[87] Walt Rostow reported that Lee Kuan Yew of Singapore believed that the war had given time for stabilization in Southeast Asia, breaking the "hypnotic spell" of communism and bringing economic development and an influx of funds.[88]

The Long Range Study repeatedly invoked the dangers of the Maoist model, which justified the war in Vietnam and necessitated the containment of China. But in dissecting the model of a "unique nation in a unique situation," it did not really find much to fear: the "doctrinaire Maoist approach has little to offer the great bulk of developing nations."[89] China, with its "able, disciplined, endlessly moldable masses who will under direction make incredible sacrifices to achieve the state's announced purposes," stood in contrast to the undisciplined, highly emotional, ideologically prone masses of the Third World, who (ironically) got the same message from the Chinese as from the West, that "only by purpose, work, and self-reliance can they achieve what they want."

So, although NSC and CIA analyses went on expressing concerns about the Chinese model, after 1965 the emphasis was different: "Seeking the broadest common denominator, Peking has thus far put little emphasis on formal Communism and instead stresses grievances Peking shares or can be said to share with the underdeveloped nations: anti-imperialism, national liberation, anti-'neo-colonialism.'"[90]

In 1965 Dean Rusk had approved guidelines for public statements about China, explaining, "We don't want to make the Chinese Communists seem ten feet tall by attributing to them capabilities they don't possess to promote revolution in Africa, Latin America, and all over the world." Too much emphasis on China's role would give it greater leverage, possibly even adding weight to the arguments favoring China's admission to the United Nations.[91]

This stand complemented policies designed to support greater U.S.-guided regionalism in Asia: pressuring South Korea to settle its long-standing conflicts with Japan, for example, and supporting General Suharto in Indonesia and seeking a resolution to the Indonesia-Malaysia confrontation.[92]

Modified Containment plus Subversion

For years it had been impossible to pursue a strategy of modified containment plus subversion. But now the situation was changing. Its advocates acknowledged that the bitterness of the Korean War years, the loss of China, and the Democratic Party's fear of a political debacle combined to prevent flexible initiatives on China; Taiwan always "acted as a brake" against them. The policies of the Chinese communists, particularly following the Great Leap Forward of 1958–60 were also to blame. But although such initiatives were likely to falter in the short run, the arguments against a flexible approach had actually diminished, these advocates declared. They based their advocacy "not on expectation of a favorable Chinese response but rather on several near-term and longer-term objectives." The major near-term objective was simply to demonstrate that the United States was not "eternally and implacably hostile" and that Americans were not "obsessive and irrational on the subject of Communist China"; the onus "for Peking's belligerence and isolation" should be shifted to China, "where it rightly belongs." The major long-term objective was to "help break down China's acutely distorted view of the outside world that plots her encirclement and destruction"[93]—a goal that required "a continued offering to China of alternative paths of behavior."[94]

These "instruments of erosion" came to the fore as the Cultural Revolution broke out. The 1960s vision of a global village, with the spread of modern communications and technology, computers, and the information revolution all making their way into modernization theory, suggested a more malleable, transformative ethos in both closed and traditional societies.[95] This "modern world" appeared to be the very essence of what Mao meant by "revisionism." Thus, while bringing China out of isolation might in the short run pose a greater danger for the free world than for China, the reverse was true over the long term. "Revisionism will grow, and contact with the outside world where people are living a different sort of life may provide a catalyst for change," Edward Rice, the American consul general, cabled from Hong Kong.[96]

Director Leonard Marks of the United States Information Agency (USIA), in recommending the establishment of a Radio Free China, agreed, urging a programming policy designed to persuade the Chinese of the advantage of "participation in the outside world" and to "induce a liberal attitude and outlook which in China today would be classified as bourgeois and revisionist."[97] Or, as the NSC's Alfred Jenkins said, more colorfully, although a "semi-demented, Mao-Communist China is perhaps the world's touchiest and most urgent problem," time was on Washington's side if it took steps to defuse tensions and encourage the forces of rationality in China.[98] Not much would happen immediately: "The likelihood of a change in Peking's policies toward the United States is . . . probably nil while Mao is alive."[99] In fact, the State Department argued, "a clear-cut victory of Mao's faction [in the Cultural Revolution] would involve a continuance of hard-line external policies, affected by Mao's tendencies towards impatience and megalomania."[100]

The committed old revolutionary, however, was facing the classic problem of all first-generation revolutionaries:

> Mao is worried about his revolution for it is clearly failing. If there is, medically, a disease definable as political paranoia, it has settled on the sometime resident of the small but not unlovely quarters overlooking Nan Hai, Peking's most exquisite lake. "Who knows whither the golden crane went, leaving but a shrine for pilgrims?" If there is any answer for the old man, it is also found in Chinese poetry—"a cup of wine under the trees; I drink alone for no friend is near."[101]

Mao's fundamental failing, wrote Jenkins, was "faith in a communist system which simply will not work and which, wherever it has survived as a system, has prospered only as it has indeed turned to the revisionism which Mao so greatly fears. He is wedded to an anachronistic 'unworkability.'" The more China followed his policies, the further it would distance itself from dignity, stability, and strength.[102]

The language of modernization included a psychologizing of events that reinforced a notion of China as "disturbingly psychotic."[103] This language was already in vogue before the outbreak of the Cultural Revolution, but after the spring of 1966 it fit all the more snugly. It appealed to many China watchers, since it suggested that in time China would have to return to more rational, bureaucratic ways of dealing with the world. Certainly changes might be expected after Mao's death. And it was with this end in mind that the United States should proceed.

American China watchers observed with astonishment and even disbelief Mao's "fanatical (and very possibly 'suicidal') attempt to bring his nation back to the revolutionary zeal, ideological purity and even simplistic methods of the era centering around 1949 'liberation'"—a course that seemed to indicate an "almost unbelievable loss of touch with reality." This was a "phony revolution," a "writhing enactment of a regime's failure" and a staggering blow to communism over which the Soviet Union was understandably in "anguish."[104] For a brief moment, as Mao appeared poised to support the most radical elements in the Cultural Revolution when they proclaimed the Shanghai Commune in early 1967, utter chaos seemed to threaten China. To have adopted "such an incredibly anachronistic attempt to run a modernizing country" would have represented a "new pinnacle of naivete even for him."[105]

The intelligence world all but spewed out analyses of the cause and course of the Cultural Revolution. Most experts saw a combination of several processes: Mao's attempt to shatter the old Party bureaucracy, in order to stymie Soviet-style revisionism, and to inspire the younger generation; a power struggle over the succession; and the eruption of deep and long-standing domestic and foreign policy disagreements among the leadership.[106]

But another factor may also have had a large part in kindling the Cultural Revolution: American policies. Modernization suggested ways in which the global environment could shape the innermost workings of a country, which meant ways in which American policies might be a part of the process. Because this level of analysis was so general and often so necessarily indirect, it was seldom pursued at length. Still, an internal Department of State examination of China policy observed that although domestic issues "have traditionally been central to Chinese upheavals," there was "little doubt . . . that the U.S. build-up in Vietnam in 1965 served as a catalyst to exacerbate old and deep divisions within the leadership, thereby helping to trigger the Cultural Revolution." Internal divisions were the cause, then, but American policy was the trigger. American officials had "never consciously intended their policy to *cause* change in Communist China," but there were "grounds for believing that U.S. policy helped spur the greatest era of change in recent Chinese mainland history."[107]

In 1965, confronted with its failures to mobilize international support against the United States, China was seen to face urgent internal and external policy questions: "What strategy should be adopted for the defense of China? How should economic planning be adjusted to support this strategy? What adjustments in Chinese relations with the Soviet Union would be required? What lines and methods of political indoctrination would most suit the strategy adopted?"[108] Though analyses like this placed the emphasis largely on foreign policy concerns, they suggested a dynamic between internal and external that almost all the assessments of earlier years had ignored.[109] Such analyses would blossom with the more complex calculations of the triangular relationship of the Soviet Union, China, and the United States during the Nixon administration.

Once the triangular relationship began to break ideological bipolarity asunder, Washington's picture of China shifted to that of a nation much shaped by the global order—susceptible to manipulation through indirect means and methods on the one hand, and constrained by that order's dynamic and "logic" on the other. Such views began to enter China analysis in the later years of the Johnson administration, though their full implications would become clear only later. Modernization theory suggested a global context that could, in time, change China, penetrating into its innermost workings and gradually shifting the very core of its ideological beliefs and its patterns of development. As the NSC's James Thomson Jr. wrote: "It strikes me that the present commotion on the China Mainland makes more desirable than ever U.S. 'intervention' in the Chinese political process through further development of a multiple strategy. We serve Peking's interests best when we live up to Peking's stereotyped image of us; when we don't, we cause confusion, at the least—and in the long run perhaps more than that."[110] This was not the language of the Dulles years, when it had been argued that there was little the United States could do. In the 1960s, Washington began to believe that all countries, including China, would have to become more responsive to the "global environment." Only in the Nixon years, however, would this notion merge with a geopolitical vision of conflicting national interests that allowed such ideas free play.

Several astute observers at the time noted other factors, sometimes global, that were "distorting" Washington's understanding of China. For Thomson, they included "the distortion bred by our own China experience (the 'loss of China', the Korean war, public and Congressional opinion, etc.); the Southeast Asian distortion (a narrowly Saigon or Bangkok perspective on China); and finally the Soviet distortion (a Kremlinological view of China that may be shaped both by the demands of our 'detente' with the USSR and by Moscow's own distorted view of Peking)." Spread these distortions out over fifteen years' worth of a "considerable number and variety of intelligence-type mechanisms that have been set in motion . . . on China's frontiers and are now compounded by our Vietnam-related activities," and it would be hard to imagine how Peking could accurately make out the meaning of American "signals" toward China.

Furthermore, Thomson noted, "there is no one in Government at a senior policy level who has within his daily ken the full sweep of our China activities from Tibet through Southeast Asia, North Vietnam, the Taiwan Straits, and Korea—not to mention matters of travel and trade."[111]

As the Long Range Study pointed out, if American policy genuinely wanted to change, it needed to coordinate its signals, set up a bureaucratic context to do that, and begin a more ambitious long-range effort to shape Peking's policies. Washington had to "reduce ambiguities in our posture . . . decrease or remove irrelevant positions of friction, and gradually introduce additional positive elements." Statements about the transitory nature of the regime had to cease, and pressure had to be brought to bear on Taiwan to halt its "probing" operations. In addition, Washington needed to reexamine its naval operations in the Taiwan Strait, to see if such information could be obtained in other ways.[112]

After the American victory in Vietnam that Washington policy in the mid-1960s still envisioned, not only would the need for containment remain, it would also require "enlargement of our substantial political, economic, sociological support and assistance."[113] Containment and nation building, in other words, were not merely temporary expedients to restrain an expansive China. They were the techniques with which Washington would shape Southeast Asian societies (among others) and "bring them into" the global system of "economic development"—the very "international community" into which the containment policy ultimately aimed to draw China. Surrounding China with a ring of modernizing states able to withstand "Communist appeals" was never, in and of itself, the goal of containment in the Johnson years; the goal was drawing in China itself.

This line of thought encouraged further efforts to pose alternatives to American policies. Some analysts urged against placing too much emphasis on matters of travel, limited trade, and a new UN approach. Others urged focusing on the future balance of power in Asia—especially the roles of Taiwan, Japan, and the Soviet Union—and considering ways that Chinese influence on Asian regional ventures might be contained.[114] These questions all grew out of the belief that Mao would fail and the corollary conviction that the Cultural Revolution itself "raised the possibility that pragmatic leaders willing to reappraise China's relationship with the United States might assume power much sooner than originally supposed."[115]

The policy of modified containment plus subversion explains the spirit of some of the public denunciations of China and wars of national liberation during the Johnson years. The two branches of the policy, containment and subversion, were not incompatible and often appeared in statements by the same individual. Thus President Johnson, espousing a more conciliatory-sounding position in a July 1966 speech, expressed the desire for eventual "reconciliation between nations that now call themselves enemies," but he also recognized the "free flow of ideas and people and goods" as the "greatest force for opening closed minds and closed societies."[116] Internal White House documents give an idea of the struggle over finding the right phrases.[117] Thus was the ideological prism slowly transformed. In September 1966 the U.S. ambassador at the Warsaw talks between the United States and the PRC dropped references to the aggressive designs of the Chinese communists in Vietnam and the rest of Asia and shifted his emphasis to "positive attempts to improve relations between the United States and the mainland regime." That same month, the State Department authorized its chiefs of missions to "establish informal social contacts with the Chinese Communists."[118]

Jenkins, as Rostow's China man, urged Rostow toward more rapid change in practical preparation for the future. Part of the reason was obvious. "I FEAR VIETNAM IS FOR FORESEEABLE FUTURE UNSOLVABLE UNLESS IT IS FIRST SORT OF WALKED AWAY FROM," reads one of his memos, in upper-case letters. Before this could happen, it continues, it might be necessary to do something "new and in a way bigger than Vietnam to give reason to the '*DEFLECTION PROMENADE*.'" The way that he was proposing to shift attention from Vietnam—"deflection"—was the new stance toward China.[119]

Thus the United States needed to acknowledge that the isolation of China was too dangerous to continue. (Even at the height of the Cultural Revolution, the preliminary working paper for the 1967 Chiefs of Mission Conference on Communist China argued, in was necessary to use this "period of instability and uncertainty" to work toward "clearing the way . . . for the possibility of an eventual normalization of relations with Peking.")[120] Washington needed to let it be known, therefore, Jenkins continued, that it favored at "any given conference the presence of any power whose agreement is necessary to the solution of the problem." Whether Peking chose, in fact, to attend was not the immediate issue, though that was of course the goal. Further, Washington needed to come down on the side of "universality in 'universal' organs," including the United Nations. ("I know it's impossible," Jenkins admitted, "but so is the road we're on.") Washington also needed to favor the "widest communication in the arts, sciences, and humanities" with China, encouraging all private contacts. Even more, Washington should favor "unrestricted commerce" except in active military situations. As a practical aside, the talks would be shifted out of Warsaw so that they could become truly private—away from the eavesdropping Soviets.[121]

The Long Range Study summed up this approach, examining possible lines of action under three headings: "inducing a Chinese Communist reappraisal of

U.S. intentions; increasing Peking's interest in a more constructive relationship with the U.S.; and exposing elite groups on the mainland to a wider range of information." The global revolution in economics and communications encouraged all these developments. The trouble was that "our near non-policy doesn't even make clear we're greatly interested in round two," which would arrive when the "lunatics in power" had to give way to their less revolutionary successors.[122]

The rationale for isolating China was coming to an end, but a dilemma remained: the policies to which the United States had committed itself by the early 1950s—support for a separate Taiwan, nonrecognition, and opposition to China's assuming its seat in the United Nations—could not be changed without a major shift on the issue of Taiwan.

The Perennial Issues

A current was developing toward flexibility on China—despite Rusk's opposition. Alfred Jenkins wrote in an August 1966 memo to Walt Rostow: "Entre nous: While I believe the Secretary to be one of the greatest in our history, on the one issue of China his style scares me. He is so orderly and judicial and a sheaf of other virtues, that he wants all the returns in before he moves. On China we are not going to get as many returns as we want; and *inaction* is an act watched by mainlanders, especially, I should think, the ChiCom moderates."[123]

The United Nations was close to admitting the PRC in the years immediately before the outbreak of the Cultural Revolution. "In 66 after you had the tie vote in 65 at the United Nations session," William Bundy noted, "it looked as though we *had* to find some way of adjusting, because the vote was going to go against us."[124] But on the issue of Taiwan there was still no resolution.[125] Nor were the United States allies solid: de Gaulle told Rusk in December 1963 "that Formosa would have to be sacrificed by the West (by implication in any agreement with the Chicoms)."[126]

The preoccupation with China and the United Nations intensified in 1964 and 1965. Peking's UN admission, reads one DOS memo, was "estimated to be a 'virtual certainty' in the foreseeable future."[127] As Robert Komer, the president's Deputy Assistant on National Security Affairs, wrote to McGeorge Bundy, there was wide agreement in the national security bureaucracy that the issue was really not substance but tactics: "Even the general nature of this tack is not really at issue—we want to retreat gracefully from an increasingly isolated position toward a stance which puts the onus for continued friction more on Peiping and less on us." So the question was not "whether to disengage from the more rigid aspects of our China policy but how and when." To confess that Washington's policies had been mistaken "isn't good domestic politics, and great nations don't win kudos abroad by admitting mistakes and saying *mea culpa*." Rather, the solution was to say that "we haven't changed our views" but "reluctantly" accept the verdict of the international community that China "should be admitted to the club."[128]

Disarmament was another critical issue. Instead of sounding the alarm at China's nuclear test, Komer argued, Washington could use the occasion to begin a dialogue on arms control. The bomb "destroys what's left of the Gimo's thesis that the civil war is still on (he knows it, too, poor man). Even *Time* has read this lesson." The Sino-Soviet dispute provided further justification for the new policy. Still, "there is no blinking the fact" that a *shift in our policy will look like a defeat*—whenever it occurs. This is the price we have to pay for having successfully maintained a fixed position for so long. Peiping is wholly unlikely to change its spots sufficiently to justify our shift on these grounds."[129]

To Rusk's argument that in the context of Vietnam any softening of the American position would "make us appear to 'falter' in the Pacific at just the wrong time," Komer responded, in what was to become an increasingly loud refrain, that given a tougher stand on Vietnam and "widespread fear abroad of U.S. escalation," U.S. policy shifts "can hardly be taken as a sign of undue weakness." On the contrary, a shift on the issue of Chinese representation in the United Nations could be used as a justification for Vietnam policy: "It would demonstrate that while we were determined to resist Communist aggression, we were simultaneously prepared to deal with the Chicoms wherever there was some peaceful purpose to be served." Washington would be "escalating to negotiate."[130]

Debates over possible ways to deal with China and thus Taiwan in the United Nations were complicated and intense in the mid-1960s. Those in favor of change advocated tying it directly to the "opening" that Washington's commitment in Vietnam offered, "mov[ing] onto a negotiating track even while we are turning up the military temperature."[131] But how to hold the line after any shift on China? Would a policy shift be seen as a defeat? The policy Washington had pursued at the United Nations for a decade-and-a-half was being "eaten away at its very foundations." Major allies did not support Washington, and minor allies were "hanging on only for fear of what it would do to their relationship with us if they were to let go." Most studies recommended going slowly—so slowly that the problem would appear to be a more general UN issue than one involving the United States and China directly. Meanwhile, Washington continued trumpeting its flexibility, while accusing the Chinese of aggressiveness.[132]

In one version, China was the "shrew" that needed to be "tamed." China had to prove itself civilized enough to join the "community of nations." Reaching accommodation on Laos and the nuclear-test-ban treaty, for example, might suggest that it was willing "to be in fact a part of the world community." Changes in behavior were the sine qua non for its entrance, and once it gave this indication, then the United States could indicate *its* "willingness to join in setting up a 'study committee'" on Chinese representation.[133]

Ultimately, no steps were taken, Jenkins noted, because of Chinese Nationalist sensibilities and associated self-interests. But should the Peking regime moderate, should it emerge with new policies and become saner, it would be not "impossible for the Taipei Chinese themselves to make a peaceful deal. In the face of a 'reasonably reasonable' mainland the ChiNats would become quickly *in extremis* internationally, and I think they would then deal."[134] In neither this memo nor others did Jenkins go any further in exploring the issue of Taiwan. Another memo concluded that when it came to basic questions, "there is nothing that can presently be done directly to resolve the problem of Taiwan. We are committed to its defense but for all practical purposes deal with Peking and Taipei as if they were separate states. This is a direction toward which our policies have been taking us for 15 years and it is probably in our interests to work gradually toward at least a tacit acknowledgement of this reality by both."[135]

Edward Rice, the Hong Kong consul general, was one of those who warned that once the policy on China's UN membership was swept aside, it would be too late for Washington to persuade the world to accept a one-China *and* one-Taiwan position. The upshot would be a single China in the UN, and that China would be communist.[136]

During the Johnson years, the most revisionist positions went no further than arguing either for a one-Taiwan-one-China policy,[137] or for a Taiwan that no longer held China's UN seat, or for it to be recognized internationally *as* China—or else sidestepping the Taiwan issue altogether.[138] The dilemma was clear, however: modified containment plus subversion required some flexibility on Taiwan and also a long-term way to deal with Taiwan, for a more moderate PRC would attract far greater international support for Beijing's being seated in the United Nations and Taiwan's being ousted—a scenario that was judged incompatible with American national interests.

Increasingly, Taiwan's claim to be the true China weighed on U.S. policy makers. Shortly before leaving his post in Tokyo, Ambassador Edwin Reischauer argued that Taiwan's leaders had to be persuaded to accept "reality." American support for the pretense that the Republic of China spoke for China encouraged "dangerous tendencies among our committed allies, such as the Koreans" and worked against planning for "regional solidarity in Southeast Asia." Most important, it stands in the way of the development of Japan, in Europe, and throughout the world of the sort of broad international concern for peace and stability in Asia that is needed to replace the one-man policeman role we are performing today. . . . We lose face by pretending to believe things that most people in the world . . . realize are not true. We lose face by letting our basic policies seem to be determined by the peculiar sensitivities of a small country like Taiwan. . . . We should not allow the peculiarities of one small country to continue to determine the position of the world's greatest power year after year.[139]

(Unlike Jenkins, Reischauer spoke of self-determination for Taiwan, a policy he believed would ensure both its continued independence and its place in the United Nations.)

Taiwan remained the critical issue hindering a shift in long-term China policy—far more so than the Vietnam War. Was there any significant flexibility? Essentially, no. During Johnson's tenure, though a few officials argued for change, they stopped short of urging major policy shifts—despite their sharp awareness that this might well be the central issue in Beijing's view.

In the Johnson years, therefore, there was ultimately no satisfactory way to reconcile modified containment plus subversion with Washington's commitment to Taiwan. On the one hand, the "calculation that policy shifts on some issues would damage our relations with our allies [e.g., Taiwan] more than they would benefit U.S.-China relations, resulted in the postponement of initiatives in several fields, most notably trade and recognition of Outer Mongolia"; wide-ranging proposals for relaxation of the embargo circulated every year after 1964, but most were never approved.[140] Even on passport control, the limited steps taken[141] were more than superseded by a sweeping court decision denying the authority of the State Department to refuse American citizens the right to travel in restricted areas.[142]

The problem of Taiwan's "morale" surfaced every time after the mid-1950s that suggestions were made for taking any steps toward Beijing.[143] In the wake of any such steps, the Long Range Study noted, American relations with Taipei "would suffer possible irreparable damage, and political stability on the island might be badly shaken." By 1966, Nationalist officials appeared to be "more dejected over the trend of events in the Far East than any time since their defeat on the mainland in 1949."[144] China's growing power was leading Jiang into a deep "depression." He had been pleased in February 1965 when the United States began bombing North Vietnam, believing that "war between the United States and Communist China was certain." By 1966, less sure, he was dejected and increasingly at a loss as to how such a war might come about.[145]

As long as Jiang was alive, he would almost certainly react to any scheme of dual representation by walking out of the United Nations, leaving the PRC in sole possession of the China seat.[146] American officials, however, felt that time was running out. The American shift in emphasis from flat-out opposition to a seat for the PRC to the milder argument that Taiwan should not be expelled had not been well received in Taipei, and the possible change in American tactics in 1966 and 1967 had reportedly left Taipei even more unnerved.[147] In response, Jiang once again went about setting up "a committee of Kuomintang officials to direct a propaganda campaign in the United States to discredit critics of a militant anti-Peking policy and champion support for the Nationalists."[148]

Essentially, there was no way to bridge the gap between supporting Taiwan and seeking to bring China into the world community. For Beijing to take the China seat in the United Nations would be "the worst possible outcome"—which is why some sort of double representation or alteration of the Security Council was frequently studied as a possible alternative—but almost all these efforts were understood to be "highly offensive to both Taipei and Peking." American efforts "to keep Taiwan out of Communist hands would be greatly complicated if, as a consequence of the GRC's loss of its U.N. seat, international opinion came to view our commitment to defend Taiwan as somehow 'illegal,' and if an isolated Taiwan drifted into a condition of psychological malaise and economic stagnation."[149]

Nonetheless, these perennial issues were no longer debated in quite the old way. The contexts had changed, both in the shifting position of American power in Asia *and* ideologically. Taiwan was no longer the linchpin it had been for the earlier attempts to isolate China, though it remained as a critical aspect of seeking to contain mainland China. And despite military defeats in Vietnam, the ideology of containment plus subversion that had emerged in these years had not been discredited. Quite the opposite: Washington, its ideological fervor undiminished, was not without hope for changing China, for bringing a modernized China into a global system in a way that, in time, would accomplish what other means had failed to achieve.

NOTES

Introduction

1. George F. Kennan, "A Fresh Look at Our China Policy," *New York Times Magazine* November 22, 1964, 27.

2. Dwight D. Eisenhower, *White House Years*, 2 vols. (Garden City, N.Y.: Doubleday, 1963–65), 2:369.

3. "Memorandum of Discussion of the 237th Meeting of the National Security Council," February 17, 1955, *FRUS,* China, 1955–57, 2:285.

4. Dean Rusk, "Chinese-American Friendship: Peiping Regime Not Chinese," May 18, 1951, *Vital Speeches of the Day* 17 (June 15, 1951): 515.

5. "Communist China: Long Range Study on Economic Trends and Prospects in Communist China," June 1966, Annex VII-2, *DDC,* 1990, 3185 (hereafter referred to as "Long Range Study"). See also *DDC,* 1991, vol. 1, 2517, and 3:2518.

6. Jack Belden, *China Shakes the World* (New York: Harper and Brothers, 1949).

7. Henry Kissinger, *White House Years* (Boston: Little, Brown, 1979), 698–99.

8. NSC 166/1, "United States Policy Toward Communist China," November 6, 1953, *DDC.*

9. Robert L. Suettinger, Introduction to *Selected China NIEs, 1948–1976* (Arlington, Va.: CIA, 2004) available online at www.foia.cia.gov/.

1. Visionary Globalism and the National Security Community

1. Several books were particularly useful in thinking about the New Deal, World War II, and the emergence of the NSW. The most valuable are Richard J. Barnet, *Roots of War: The Men and Institutions behind U.S. Foreign Policy* (Baltimore: Penguin, 1972); Noam Chomsky, *World Orders: Old and New* (New York: Columbia University Press, 1994); Bruce Cumings, *The Origins of the Korean War*, 2 vols. (Princeton:

Princeton University Press, 1981–90); David Halberstam, *The Best and the Brightest* (New York: Random House, 1969); Franz Schurmann, *The Logic of World Power: An Inquiry into the Origins, Currents, and Contradictions of World Politics* (New York: Pantheon Books, 1974); Michael S. Sherry, *In the Shadow of War: The United States since the 1930s* (New Haven: Yale University Press, 1995); Laurence H. Shoup, *Imperial Brain Trust: The Council on Foreign Relations and United States Foreign Policy* (New York: Monthly Review Press, 1977). In addition, for a more detailed discussion of modernization, the New Deal, and the ideological needs of United States foreign policy after 1945, see my "Revolution versus Modernization and Revisionism," in *China's Uninterrupted Revolution*, ed. Victor Nee and James Peck (New York: Pantheon, 1975).

2. Dean Acheson, *Present at the Creation: My Years in the State Department* (New York: Norton, 1969).

3. This was really the core of Whitaker Chambers's argument that it was treason in Washington which ultimately did in Jiang. By pointing the finger in this way, he stressed not only the influence of the few in determining history, but of the few in Washington in preparing the way for the victory of the Chinese communists. See Chambers, *Witness* (New York: Random House, 1952), 331.

4. Amy B. Zegart, *Flawed by Design: The Evolution of the CIA, JCS, and NSC* (Stanford, Calif.: Stanford University Press, 1999), 8.

5. Dean Acheson, quoted in Henry M. Jackson, ed., *The National Security Council: Jackson Subcommittee Papers on Policy-Making at the Presidential Level* (New York: Praeger, 1965), 45.

6. Barnet, *Roots of War.*

7. As President Truman later wrote, "The creation of the National Security Council added a badly needed new facility to the government. This was now the place in the government where military, diplomatic, and resource problems could be studied and continually appraised. This new organization gave us a running balance and a perpetual inventory of where we stood and where we were going on all strategic questions affecting the national security." Truman, *Years of Trial and Hope,* vol. 2 of *Memoirs* (Garden City, N.Y.: Doubleday, 1956), 77.

8. There is a useful summary of the NSC and its tasks in the DOS *Handbook on National Security Council Functions and Procedures* (Washington, D.C.: Department of State, May 1, 1952). A formerly classified handbook for use by departmental officers working with the NSC, it answered questions about the nature and organization of the NSC; discussed the format for policy statements, dealt with NSC drafts emanating from other agencies, described the role of NSC staff meetings, and described the role of progress reports and their character, timing, and form. *DDC,* 1992, 2048. See also Gordon Gray's account of the operations of the NSC in the Eisenhower years, *DDC,* 1982, 1247.

9. "History of the National Security Council, 1947–1997," National Security Council, the White House, http://www.whitehouse.gov/nsc/history.html.

10. Zegart, *Flawed by Design,* 84–87 (quot., 84).

11. See Anna K. Nelson, "The Importance of Foreign Policy Process: Eisenhower and the National Security Council," in *Eisenhower: A Centenary Assessment,* ed. Gunter Bischof and Stephen Ambrose (Baton Rouge: Louisiana State University Press, 1995), 111.

12. Forrest Sherman to Robert Cutler, in *Confidential U.S. State Department Central Files: China, Foreign Affairs, 1950–1954.* (Frederick, Md.: University Publications of America, microform, 1986).

13. Ibid., 13.

14. NSC 7, "The Position of the U.S. with Respect to Soviet-Directed World Communism," March 30, 1948, *DDC.*

15. Acheson, *Present at the Creation,* 374–75.

16. Jackson, *National Security Council,* 3.

17. Brookings Institution, "The National Security Council Project: The Nixon Administration and the National Security Council," Oral History, by Ivo H. Daalder and I. M. Destlee, December 8, 1998. http://www.brookings.edu/fp/research/projects/nsc/transcripts/19991025.htm.

18. Robert Gates, *From the Shadows: The Ultimate Insider's Story of Five Presidents and How They Won the Cold War* (New York: Simon & Schuster, 1996), 459.

19. See, for example, NSC 4, "Coordination of Foreign Information Measures," December 9, 1947; NSC 10/1, "Office of Special Projects," June 15, 1948; NSC 20/3, "U.S. Objectives with Respect to the U.S.S.R. to Counter Soviet Threats to U.S. Security," November 2, 1948; NSC 43, "Planning for Wartime Conduct of Overt Psychological Warfare," March 9, 1949; NSC 43/1, "General Principles Governing the Conduct of Overt Psychological Warfare in the Stages of War or Emergency," August 2, 1949, all in Paul Kesaris, *Documents of the National Security Council* (Frederick, Md.: University Publications of America, microform, 1983).

20. George F. Kennan, *Measures Short of War: The George F. Kennan Lectures at the National War College, 1946–47,* ed. Giles Harlow and George C. Maerz (Washington, D.C.: National Defense University Press, 1991), 302.

21. As NSC 20/4 put it, U.S. security is threatened by "the persuasive appeal of a pseudo-scientific ideology promising panaceas and brought to other peoples by the intensive efforts of a modern totalitarian propaganda machine." November 23, 1948, *DDC.*

22. C. D. Jackson, "Psychological Warfare," n.d. [1953], ddc, 1995, 2950.

23. The Jackson Committee was set up in the first week of Eisenhower's presidency to

look "into this whole business of psychological warfare. What was it? What was the problem? What were the targets? What was wrong? How could it be done right?" Jackson, "Psychological Warfare," 7. The OCB consisted of the under secretary of state, the deputy secretary of defense, the director of the CIA, the director of the Foreign Operations Administration, and a White House special assistant to the president.

24. As NSC 17, "The Internal Security of the United States," June 28, 1948, puts it, Communists have "models and guides, and their principles [are] living, vibrant norms of current procedure which are to be followed without question or deviation." In Kesaris, *Documents of the NSC.*

25. For example, see NSC 7, "The Position of the U.S."; NSC 20/1, "U.S. Objectives with Respect to Russia," August 18, 1948; and NSC 20/3, all in Kesaris, *Documents of the NSC.* As NSC 17 put it, "First the ideas and then the act. The former 'softens up' the people for the latter. . . . With ideas they spread their poisonous germs in every phase of American life either openly or by subtleties and indirection. These ideas seep into American politics, American economics, American educational institutions, American neighborhoods and American homes." "The Internal Security of the United States," June 28, 1948, in Kesaris, *Documents of the NSC.*

26. Ibid.

27. NSC 20/4, "U.S. Objectives with Respect to the U.S.S.R. to Counter Soviet Threats to U.S. Security," November 23, 1948, in Kesaris, *Documents of the NSC.*

28. NSC 20/1, "Report to the NSC on U.S. Objectives with Respect to Russia," August 18, 1948, *ddc.*

29. See the comments on cynicism in NSC 34, "U.S. Policy toward China," October 13, 1948, in Kesaris, *Documents of the NSC.*

30. The classic statement of "dirty hands" is the Doolittle Report for President Eisenhower,

(September 30, 1954, *ddc*, 1978, 139), but NSC documents are imbued with very much the same set of assumptions from the beginning. NSC 68 "United States Objectives and Programs for National Security," April 14, 1950, had said much the same four years earlier: "The integrity of our system will not be jeopardized by any measures, covert or overt, violent or non-violent, which serve the purposes of frustrating the Kremlin design, nor does the necessity for conducting ourselves so as to affirm our values in actions as well as words forbid such measures" (in Kesaris, *Documents of the NSC*).

31. For example, see "Principal Elements of a Cold War Strategy Plan," Memorandum for the Director, PSB, October 12, 1951, *ddc*, 1991, 3396.

32. H. W. Brands, *The Devil We Knew: Americans and the Cold War* (New York: Oxford University Press, 1993), 33.

33. John Lewis Gaddis, *Strategies of Containment: A Critical Appraisal of Postwar American National Security Policy* (New York: Oxford University Press, 1982), 107.

34. Acheson, *Present at the Creation*, 374–75.

35. Gaddis, *Strategies of Containment*, 59.

36. The following comments, designed to suggest ways to see the NSC as partially a world of faith and ideology, are based on the microfilmed records of the NSC from 1947 to the end of the Eisenhower administration in early 1961. See Paul Kesaris, *A Guide to Documents of the National Security Council* (Washington, D.C.: University Publications of America, 1985).

37. NSC 5602/1, "Basic National Security Policy," *DDC*. The bipolar, Manichaean dynamic of two competing powers embodying good and evil pervades the NSC documents. The early contrast of Russia and the United States is spelled out in NSC 7 in language that overlaps with NSC 68, as does the depiction of communism in NSC 58/2.

38. PPS/51, George Kennan, "US Policy toward Southeast Asia," March 29, 1949, 3:43. Unless otherwise stated, all PPS references are

in U.S. Department of State, Policy Planning Staff, *The State Department Policy Planning Staff Papers, 1947–1949*, 3 vols. (New York: Garland Publishing, 1983).

39. NSC 135/2, "CIA and National Operations," *ddc*, 1992, 2413, 1.

40. Annex to NSC 124, staff study, "U.S. Objectives and Courses of Action with Respect to Communist Aggression in Southeast Asia," February 13, 1953, in Kesaris, *Documents of the NSC*.

41. The very strengths and qualities of the United States are part of what the USSR cannot tolerate. "The Soviet leaders are convinced that their own system will not stand comparison with the civilization of the West and that it will never be secure until the example of a prosperous and powerful Western civilization has been physically obliterated and its memory discredited." NSC 20/1, "U.S. Objectives with Respect to Russia."

42. PPS/51, Kennan, "U.S. Policy toward Southeast Asia," 3:41.

43. A theme of "militant liberty" emerged in the early 1950s as part of the psychological warfare program. It became part of the response to the issue of brainwashing and the POWs in Korea. Admiral Arthur Radford, chairman of the Joint Chiefs of Staff, wrote in a memo to the CIA director that "militant liberty's" principles might "enable POW's to withstand brainwashing." See JCS Radford to CIA, November 28, 1978, *ddc*, 1981, 69A.

44. NSC 34, "U.S. Policy toward China."

45. As NSC 138/1 put it, "We shall be arguing the case for freedom and dignity of the individual and freedom of enterprise, and we shall claim the virtues of our system in providing well-being and economic growth." "National Security Problems concerning Free World Petroleum Demands and Potential Supplies," January 6, 1953, *DDC*.

46. Max Weber, *Economy and Society* (Berkeley: University of California Press, 1978).

47. This ideological dilemma very much haunted the early years of the Kennedy administration as it discussed the Alliance for Progress and the sweep of revolutionary movements in the Third World. Military action alone could not stop communism, a task force on Latin America reported to Kennedy in early 1961. "Democracy was weak in Latin America in part because the U.S. 'has stated no clear philosophy of its own, and has no effective machinery to disseminate such a philosophy.' A first task of the new administration must be to formulate a positive democratic philosophy." Arthur M. Schlesinger Jr., *A Thousand Days: John F. Kennedy in the White House* (New York: Random House, 1965), 185.

48. Great care went into classifying those who might become subject to communism's influence. One paper distinguished seven categories: (1) the open Communist Party member; (2) the convinced communist who does not join the Party and denies he is a communist because he can thus more effectively work to spread the doctrine; (3) the "fellow traveler"; (4) the "sympathizer" who has "kindly feelings" for the communists, though he may disagree with some of their positions; (5) the "opportunist" who will "play ball" with the communists to further certain selfish interests; (6) the "confused liberal" who still believes it is possible to cooperate with communism on specific issues while disagreeing with communism in general; (7) the "well meaning, socially minded, charitable people who are deceived by Communist slogans." NSC 17, "The Internal Security of the United States."

49. PPS/38, George Kennan, "United States Objectives with Respect to Russia," August 18, 1948, 2:349.

50. The concern with "Communist infiltration" and the belief that the United States did not have adequate "over-all internal security coordination" is pervasive in documents of the NSC from its inception in 1947. See, for example, NSC 17, "Internal Security of the United States."

51. NSC 20/1, "U.S. Objectives with Respect to Russia," *DDC*. NSC 17 adopted quite similar language: "From the very beginning of organ-

ized living, of society, there have existed negative elements which would tear down and destroy the established order by force and violence. Orderly change by the majority is acceptable and desirable but not the force and violence of a minority."

52. NSC 7, "Position of the U.S. with Respect to Soviet-Directed World Communism."

53. The ideological and psychological underpinnings of U.S. policy versus Soviet policy formed the subject of two sets of hearings by the Senate Foreign Relations Committee, in May 1966 and June 1969. J. William Fulbright, the committee chair, described them as "the most important and thus most ignored hearings I ever held." Senate Committee on Foreign Relations, *Psychological Aspects of International Relations: Hearing before the Committee on Foreign Relations,* 89th Cong., 2nd sess., May 25, 1966; and *Psychological Aspects of Foreign Policy: Hearings before the Committee on Foreign Relations,* 91st Cong., 1st sess., June 5, 19, and 20, 1969.

54. J. W. Fulbright, *The Crippled Giant: American Foreign Policy and Its Domestic Consequences* (New York: Random House, 1972), 153.

55. Barnet, *Roots of War,* 72.

56. Acheson testimony, Senate Committee on Armed Forces and Foreign Relations, *Hearings on the Military Situation in the Far East,* 82nd Cong., 1st sess., June 4, 1951, p. 2299.

57. Quoted in Barnet, *Roots of War,* 60

58. George Kennan caught the mood in PPS/23, "Review of Current Trends U.S. Foreign Policy," February 24, 1948: "For a truly stable world order can proceed, within our lifetime, only from the older, mellower and more advanced nations of the world—nations for which the concept of order, as opposed to power, has value and meaning" (2:126).

59. Michael Lutzker writes of the "illusion of moderation" during the Quemoy-Matsu Crisis when "Eisenhower, Dulles, and their colleagues believed that they were steering a moderate course between two extremes. They rejected a preemptive attack on the mainland as called for

by Chiang. On the other hand, they refused to risk the charge of appeasement by leaving Nationalists to fend for themselves on the islands. Thus, U.S. leaders could see their action in each crisis as the middle course." This "illusion of moderation" in courses falling between steps likely to lead to war and those dismissible as appeasement pervades NSC documents and discussions throughout these years. See Lutzker, "The Precarious Peace: China, the United States, and the Quemoy-Matsu Crisis, 1954–1955, 1958," in *Arms at Rest: Peacemaking and Peacekeeping in American History,* ed. Robert Beisner and Joan Challinor (New York: Greenwood Press, 1986), 179.

60. NSC 5906/1, "Basic National Security Policy," August 5, 1959, in Marc Trachtenberg, ed., *The Development of American Strategic Thought* (New York: Garland Publishers, 1987).

61. NSC 20/1, "Position of the United States with Respect to Providing Military Assistance," 14.

62. Ideologically, Washington should "seek to . . . project an image of the United States which reflects the fundamental peaceful intent of U.S. policies, while making clear our determination to resist aggression." NSC 5707/8, "Basic National Security," June 3, 1957, *DDC.*

63. NSC 141, "Reexamination of U.S. Programs for National Security," January 19, 1953, *DDC.*

64. China was seen as having to lean to one side or the other; so was Japan. As John Paton Davies Jr. noted to George Kennan, Japan could not be expected "to possess an independent identity," but could function "only as an American or Soviet satellite." Quoted in Michael Schaller, "The Occupation of Japan," in *The Occupation of Japan: The International Context,* ed. Thomas W. Burkman (Norfolk, Va.: MacArthur Memorial Foundation, 1982), 164.

65. One scholarly example suggests the emergence of an increasingly influential analysis of China in these years. In the concluding

paragraph of the first edition of *The United States and China* (Cambridge: Harvard University Press, 1948), John Fairbank wrote: "If we consider the United States and the Soviet Union as competing centers of a new world order, it is plain that the disintegration of the old order in China leaves that country open to reorganization under the dominant influence of one or the other of these two competing world powers. It is fundamentally a social issue in the broad sense, a question of the formation and sustenance of new patterns of life, the use of new skills and knowledge, the creation of a new social structure and new sources of political authority among the Chinese people. The outside power which can contribute most to this process can thereby gain the greatest influence in China. Our task is therefore how to contribute to solving China's problems more effectively than the Russians can contribute."

66. Stalin focused more on the likelihood of a new "general crisis of capitalism" than on bipolarity. "Stalin seemed not to understand the nature of the epoch in which he was living, especially its major characteristic—bipolarity," Vladislav Zubok and Constantine Pleshakov write in "The Soviet Union," in *The Origins of the Cold War in Europe*, ed. David Reynolds (New Haven: Yale University Press, 1994), 62.

67. See, for example, the argument of R. F. Holland, "The Imperial Factor in British Strategies from Attlee to Macmillan, 1945–63," in *Perspectives on Imperialism and Decolonialization,* ed. David Goldsworthy (London: HMSO, 1994), 173. That the British sought to avoid becoming locked into the ideological and tactical confines of U.S. bipolarity is implicit in almost all of London's efforts to resolve the conflicts between its imperial strategy and its dependency on U.S. global power after 1945. Anthony Eden was a particular target of American criticism because he embodied that effort to "prise open some cracks in the ideological mold" (ibid.), and China was one area where this British effort was evident.

68. John Lamberton Harper writes that Acheson "was convinced that a relaxation of tension in Europe would undermine all he had labored to create," in *American Visions of Europe* (Cambridge: Cambridge University Press, 1994), 329. In multiple ways, this conviction formed a leitmotif in assessments of American global policy in the late 1940s and in assessments of policy in the underdeveloped world throughout the 1950s.

69. Quoted in Frank Ninkovich, *Modernity and Power: A History of the Domino Theory in the Twentieth Century* (Chicago: University of Chicago Press, 1994), 223.

70. Quoted in ibid.

71. Sometimes they criticized those who had put forth the theory earlier—such as Dulles on Southeast Asia—only to insist that it had subsequently taken on new value. Thus Arthur Schlesinger Jr. argued, "Whether the domino theory was valid in 1954, it had acquired validity seven years later, after neighboring governments had staked their own security on the ability of the United States to live up to its pledges to Saigon. Kennedy . . . had no choice now but to work within the situation he had inherited." Schlesinger, *Thousand Days*, 497.

72. Kennan, *Measures Short of War*, 166.

73. Ibid., 166–67.

74. NSC 1/1, "The Position of the U.S. with Respect to Italy," November 14, 1947, in *Kesaris Documents of the NSC.*

75. Ninkovich, *Modernity and Power*, 222.

76. The emergence of this belief is a theme of Harper's, *American Visions of Europe.* The sense of Europe's slipping away and fragmenting, and of not fitting into U.S. global concerns was pervasive in 1950. As Harper writes, the "fear animating American policy was not so much that the Soviet Union would attack Western Europe directly; rather, it was that European doubts about the United States— by late 1950 the United States had suffered a full-scale disaster in the Far East—would translate into neutralism or worse" (298). In

this sense, Europe itself could be the biggest domino.

77. Truman's well-known account of his return to Washington in the first days of the Korean war illustrate this thinking. "I recalled some earlier instances: Manchuria, Ethiopia, Austria. I remembered how each time that the democracies failed to act it had encouraged the aggressors to keep going ahead. Communism was acting in Korea just as Hitler, Mussolini, and the Japanese had acted ten, fifteen, and twenty years earlier. I felt certain that if South Korea was allowed to fall Communist leaders would be emboldened to override nations closer to our own shores." See Truman, *Years of Trial and Hope, 1946–1952*, 378–79.

78. As John Lewis Gaddis writes, "The blatant nature of the North Korean attack made resistance necessary, in the eyes of administration officials, not because South Korea was important in and of itself, but because any demonstration of aggression left unopposed would only encourage further aggression elsewhere." Gaddis, "The Strategic Perspective: The Rise and Fall of the 'Defensive Perimeter' Concept, 1947–1951," in *Uncertain Years: Chinese-American Relations, 1947–1950*, ed. Dorothy Borg and Walter Heinrichs (New York: Columbia University Press, 1980), 103, 108 (quot.).

79. NSC 144, "U.S. Objectives and Courses of Action with Respect to Latin America," March 4, 1953, Kesaris in *Documents of the NSC*.

80. NSC 5719, "U.S. Policy toward Africa South of the Sahara prior to Calendar Year 1960," July 31, 1957, *DDC*.

81. "The United States is concerned that Africa south of the Sahara develop in an orderly manner towards self-government and independence in cooperation with the European powers now in control of large areas of the continent. We hope that this transition will take place in a manner which will preserve the essential ties which bind Europe and Africa—which are fundamentally complementary

areas. Africa depends on Europe not only as a source of the normal imports of underdeveloped countries but also as the major supplier of investment, both public and private. Europe in turn needs the African market as well as Africa's minerals and agricultural products." NSC 5719, "U.S. Policy toward Africa," *DDC*.

82. NSC 166/1 put this bluntly (and typically): "It seems evident that the potential difficulties of the Sino-Soviet connection will stem primarily from the internal workings of the partnership and only secondarily from the nature of external pressures or inducements. . . . In the last analysis a fracture of the alliance, if it comes, will stem primarily from the internal relationships of the partners and only secondarily from either the pressures or inducements of the West." "U.S. Policy toward Communist China," October 19, 1953. Kesaris, *Documents of the NSC.*

83. NSC 7, "Position of the U.S. with Respect to Soviet-Directed World Communism."

84. In *A History of Thought on Economic Integration* (New York: Columbia University Press, 1977), Fritz Machlup clearly and concisely traces the emergence of the term "economic integration," its use, and its relationship to aspects of U.S. economic foreign policy.

85. Not that the ultimate economic objectives were not continually invoked. The goal, throughout the years, was to "foster a high level of international trade and investment within the Free World by: (1) continuing to press strongly for a general reduction of trade barriers within the Free World; (2) maintaining a liberal import policy, and seeking to reduce further its own tariffs and trade restrictions over the next few years on a reciprocal basis in accordance with established trade agreement principles having due regard for foreign policy objectives, national security and total national advantage; (3) taking into account the impact on our foreign policy objectives (especially the collective security effort) of any proposed actions which would adversely affect imports

from friendly countries; (4) discouraging the further extension of discriminatory trade and currency restrictions; (5) encouraging the expansion of private enterprise and investment for Free World development, especially in less developed nations; and (6) promoting both governmental and private international economic cooperation." NSC 5906/1, "Basic National Security," *DDC*.

86. "A Report to the National Security Council by Task Force 'A' of Project Solarium," July 16, 1953, 106, *DDC*.

87. "There is no reasonable likelihood, however, that even with that substantial reduction of U.S. trade barriers which is desirable, the free world's normal supply of U.S. dollars will grow sufficiently to make possible a multilateral trading system based, to the extent that we would like, on convertible currencies and non-discriminatory trade practices. The expansion of private investment abroad, although such an expansion is obviously also desirable, is not likely to occur on a scale large enough to fill the world's dollar needs. In other words, the classical remedies should be utilized as fully as possible, but it should be recognized that extraordinary measures will also be necessary." NSC 144, "U.S. Objectives and Courses of Action with Respect to Latin America," 22.

88. NSC 141, "Reexamination of U.S. Programs for National Security," *DDC*.

89. "Report to the National Security Council," 104.

90. Ibid., 70.

91. Anti-communism and the future of German economic integration with Europe were often closely linked. See NSC 141 "Reexamination of U.S. Programs for National Security," and NSC 5433/l, "Immediate U.S. Policy toward Europe," September 25, 1954, *DDC*.

92. Task Force "A" of Project Solarium argues against continuing efforts by U.S. domestic interests to establish quotas or increase tariffs.

93. NSC 144, "U.S. Objectives and Courses of Action with Respect to Latin America," 69, 19.

94. "Report to the National Security Council," 74.

95. "It has been expected that private investors would provide a major share of the necessary capital in the industrial field, but up to the present time these investors have held back, especially those in the United States." NSC 98, "The Position of the U.S. with Respect to South Asia," January 5, 1951, in Kesaris, *Documents of the NSC*. This lament is frequent in NSC staff reports beginning in the late 1940s; it increases throughout the Eisenhower years.

96. During the early years of the Cold War, Japan's problems are repeatedly analyzed by the NSC. The basic concern is twofold: opening up world markets to Japanese goods, particularly in Southeast Asia, and implementing General Agreement on Tariffs and Trade (GATT) proposals so that Japan itself will open up to foreign capital investment and become fully incorporated in the world market system. These policies remain notably consistent. See, for example, NSC 6008, "U.S. Policy toward Japan," May 20, 1960, *DDC*.

97. Thus it is frequently noted that the absence of sufficient external capital encourages nations to "obtain the capital required to expand production [through] recourse either to chronic inflationary financing (as in recent years in Chile and Brazil) or to autarky and forced domestic savings (as in Argentina)." NSC 141, "Reexamination of U.S. Programs for National Security," *DDC*.

98. NSC 5902, "Statement of U.S. Policy toward Latin America," Annex B, January 30, 1959, in Kesaris, *Documents of the NSC*.

99. NSC 141. "Reexamination of U.S. Programs for National Security," *DDC*. NSC documents offer innumerable restatements of the idea that private capital will open the path along which poor countries can develop: "(1) to make the maximum contribution to their own economic development; (2) to eliminate

barriers to trade and investment; (3) to take measures capable of attracting maximum amounts of external private capital; and (4) to look essentially to . . . the free world international financial institutions and to private investment to meet their needs for external capital so long as this is consistent with U.S. security interests." NSC 6005/1, "U.S. Policy toward West Africa," April 9, 1960, *DDC*.

100. This fear is evident in the detailed studies of where those resources are available, who controls them, which European nations have invested most heavily in which of them, and so forth. See, for example, OCB's report on NSC 163/1, "The Security of Strategically Important Industrial Operations in Foreign Countries," December 11, 1959, and OCB's "Semiannual Appraisal of Policy on Security of Strategically Important Industrial Operations in Foreign Countries," June 3, 1960, *DDC*.

101. NSC 5429/5, "Current U.S. Policy toward Far East," January 31, 1955, *DDC*, 1976.

102. NSC 7, "Position of the U.S. with Respect to Soviet-Directed World Communism."

103. NSC 5432/1, "U.S. Objectives and Courses of Action with Respect to Latin America," September 3, 1954, in Kesaris, *Documents of the NSC*.

104. "Report to the National Security Council," 72, 17.

105. NSC, "Memo on Political Implications of Afro-Asian Military Takeovers," April 2, 1959, Mill Paper 206, in Kesaris, *Documents of the NSC*.

106. John Lewis Gaddis comments that the Eisenhower years had not focused on revolution, a lapse he saw the Kennedy administration as facing up to. See *Strategies of Containment*, 202–5.

2. China as Puppet

1. See, for example, these useful collections of essays: Andrew Gordon, ed., *Postwar Japan as History* (Berkeley: University of California Press, 1993), and John W. Dower, *Japan in War*

and Peace: Selected Essays (New York: New Press, 1993).

2. The line down the continent did to a degree isolate Eastern and Western Europe, disrupting traditional trading patterns, and in this sense, isolation did become a critical aspect of economic revitalization. But it was clear and highly enforceable, as it was not in Asia.

3. CIA, *Review of the World Situation*, January 19, 1949, *ddc*, 1977, 181E.

4. To many American officials, the struggle for control of Germany's industrial power "underlay all the tactics, strategy, and tensions of US-USSR relations in Europe" (April 20, 1949, *ddc*, 1977, 281B). The American decision to set up "a separate German government" led to a Soviet "reaction" that "took the form of an action—the blockade of Berlin—aimed at weakening this firm decision." The Western decision to divide Germany, the resulting severity of the division of Eastern and Western Europe, and the impact of Tito further reinforced Stalin's determination to ensure the security of Eastern Europe via Communist Party purges on both sides of the dividing line. CIA, *Review of the World Situation*, August 16, 1948, *ddc*, 1977, 179D.

5. CIA, *Review of the World Situation*, January 18, 1950, *ddc*, 1977, 283A, 1.

6. Ibid.

7. Dean Acheson, July 18, 1949, quoted in McGeorge Bundy, *The Pattern of Responsibility*, (Boston: Houghton Mifflin, 1952), 180.

8. Dean Acheson, "New Era in Asia," March 15, 1950, in *Vital Speeches of the Day* 16 (April 1, 1950): 355.

9. NSC 34, "U.S. Policy toward China," October 13, 1948, in Kesaris, *Documents of the NSC*, 15.

10. Acheson to Truman, *Letter of Transmittal*, July 30, 1949, in *The China White Paper* (Washington, D.C.: Government Printing Office, 1949), xvi.

11. NSC 34, "U.S. Policy toward China"; George Kennan quoted in Leonard A. Kusnitz,

Public Opinion and Foreign Policy: America's China Policy, 1949–1979 (Westport, Conn.: Greenwood Press, 1984), 25.

12. CIA, Intelligence Memorandum No. 309, "Vulnerabilities of Communist Movements in the Far East," September 30, 1949, *DDC*, 1975, 12E.

13. Ambassador Stuart to Secretary of State, July 17, 1948, *FRUS*, 1948, 7:366.

14. Dean Acheson, *Present at the Creation: My Years at the State Department* (New York: Norton, 1969), 356.

15. Marshall from Paris, May 13, 1947, in *Pentagon Papers* (Washington, D.C.: Government Printing Office, 1971), 10:101.

16. Acheson to U.S. Mission at the United Nations, August 9, 1950, *FRUS*, 1950, 7:550.

17. Dean Acheson quoted in Robert J. Donovan, *Tumultuous Years: The Presidency of Harry S Truman, 1949–1953*, (New York: Norton, 1982), 145.

18. George Kennan, PPS/51, "U.S. Policy toward Southeast Asia," March 29, 1949, 3:49.

19. Ibid., 40, 44.

20. "Appraisal of Communist Efforts in Southeast Asia: 1948," OIR Report No. 4778, October 12, 1948, *ddc*, 1976, 112C, p. 13. Acknowledging that "available information" provided no clear evidence that the "current disturbances" in Southeast Asia were "directed as a conspiracy from Moscow," the report nonetheless suggests that the "limited success" of the communists might actually represent a "calculated risk in the hope of precipitating a strong 'imperialist' reaction from the U.S., which in turn would force moderate nationalists into the Communist sphere of influence. Such calculations would be consistent with the Soviet sphere of influence."

21. In so arguing, Butterworth was echoing Acheson's dispatch of May 20, 1949, concerning Ho: "with achievement natl aims (i.e. independence), their objective necessarily becomes subordinate state to Commie purposes and ruthless extermination not only opposition

groups but all elements suspected of even slightest deviation." Acheson considered Ho an "outright Commie so long as (1) he fails unequivocally repudiate Moscow connections and Commie doctrine and (2) remains personally singled out for praise by international Commie press and receives its support." In *FRUS*, 1949, 7(1):29.

22. Memorandum by the Assistant Secretary of State for Far Eastern Affairs (Butterworth) to the Secretary of State, October 20, 1949, *FRUS*, 1949, 7(1):93.

23. Memorandum of Conversation by Cloyce K. Huston, Counselor of Mission, January 8, 1949, *FRUS*, 1949, 8:24.

24. Counsel General at Shanghai (Cabot) to the Secretary of State, July 16, 1949, *FRUS*, 1949, 8:436.

25. "The Likelihood and Possibilities of Overt Aggression by China," August 1950, British aide-mémoire, in *Confidential U.S. State Department Central Files* (hereafter DOSC): *China, Foreign Affairs, 1950–1954* (Frederick, Md.: University Publications of America, 1984), microform.

26. David Goldsworthy, ed., *The Conservative Government and the End of Empire, 1951–1957* (London: HMSO, 1994).

27. Ibid., 2.

28. For example, see NSC 17, "The Internal Security of the U.S.," June 28, 1948, in Kesaris, *Documents of the NSC*.

29. Dean Acheson, quoted in Bundy, *Pattern of Responsibility*, 183–84.

30. NSC 34,"U.S. Policy toward China," 9.

31. DOS, "Establishment of Joint Soviet-Chinese Companies for Economic Exploitation of Sinkiang," April 1, 1950, Office of Eastern European Affairs, in Kesaris, *Documents of the NSC*; DOSC, *China, Foreign Affairs, 1950–1954*. See also CIA, "Possible Political Developments of Strategic Significance between 1951 and 1954," February 28, 1950: "a situation in which the USSR would have established effective control over

Manchuria, Sinkiang, and possibly Inner Mongolia, while continuing to enjoy predominant influence, without absolute control, over the rest of China."

32. Dean Rusk, "Chinese-American Friendship: Peiping Regime Not Chinese," May 18, 1951, *Vital Speeches of the Day* 17 (June 15, 1951): 515.

33. Kennan to the Secretary of State, January 10, 1946, *FRUS*, 1946, 9:116.

34. CIA, ORE 29-49, "Prospects for Soviet Control of a Communist China," April 15, 1949, www.foia.cia.gov/.

35. CIA, ORE 77-48, "Chinese Communist Capabilities for Control of All China," December 10, 1948, www.foia.cia.gov/.

36. Kennan later wrote that communism was seen at the time as "a monolithic structure, reaching through a network of highly disciplined Communist parties into practically every country of the world. In these circumstances, any success of a local Communist party, anywhere, had to be regarded as an extension in reality of the political orbit, or at least the dominant influence, of the Kremlin. Precisely because Stalin maintained so jealous, so humiliating a control over foreign Communists, all of the latter had, at that time, to be regarded as the vehicle of his will, not their own. He was the only center of authority in the Communist World; and it was a vigilant, exacting and imperious headquarters, prepared to brook no opposition." George F. Kennan, *Memoirs, 1925–1950* (Boston: Little, Brown, 1972), 365.

37. Stalin's policies were commonly seen as a kind of inverted American globalism—European interests might have priority, but the global vision was the shaping force. Although there is much debate over what Stalin's objectives were, most notable in these years is the kind of debate that seldom occurred—for example, the conclusions of historians Vladislav Zubok and Constantine Pleshakov, which were rarely raised much after 1948:

"Stalin, as well as most other Soviet leaders, was Eurocentric and, more precisely, German-oriented. His major ambitions and challenges lay westward. In part, this was because his psychological archetypes of glory and national interest were linked with Europe (the Middle East was one notable exception). Just like the Russian empire before, he had not regarded his vast provinces in Siberia and in the Far East as of extraordinary value. The geopolitical utility of the Far East seemed to Stalin of minor importance." Zubok and Pleshakov, in David Reynolds, *The Origins of the Cold War in Europe: International Perspectives* (New Haven: Yale University Press, 1994), 61.

38. CIA, "Possible Developments in China," November 3, 1948, *ddc*, 1977, 261C.

39. CIA, *Review of the World Situation*, March 10, 1950, *ddc*, 1977, 283A, p. 3.

40. Ibid., June 9, 1950, *ddc*, 1977, 283D, pp. 1, 6.

41. Vice Consul at Changchun (Siebens) to Secretary of State, January 8, 1948, *FRUS*, 1948, 7:15.

42. NSC 58/2, "U.S. Policy toward the Soviet Satellite States in Eastern Europe," December 8, 1949, *DDC*.

43. The Consul General at Shanghai (Cabot) to the Ambassador in China (Stuart), January 20, 1949, *FRUS*, 1949, 8:63.

44. Kennan to the Secretary of State, January 10, 1946, *FRUS*, 1946, 9:118–19.

45. Quoted in Wilson D. Miscamble, *George F. Kennan and the Making of American Foreign Policy, 1947–1950* (Princeton: Princeton University Press, 1992), 217.

46. Cabot to Stuart, 8:63.

47. Much recent scholarship treats Stalin in terms of realpolitik, suggesting that he sought to influence Chinese Communist policies and options but not to dominate them. As Sergei N. Goncharow, John W. Lewis, and Xue Litai argue in *Uncertain Partners: Stalin, Mao, and the Korean War* (Stanford, Calif.: Stanford Univer-

sity Press, 1993), 25: "By all evidence, then, it seems fair to conclude that by the year 1948, Stalin had decided China would be his partner, rarely, if ever, his pawn."

48. George Kennan, PPS/13, "Resumé of World Situation," November 6, 1947, *FRUS*, 1947, 1:774.

49. PPS/39, "United States Policy toward China," September 7, 1948, *FRUS*, 1948, 8:148–49.

50. Memorandum prepared in the Embassy in China for the Minister Counselor (Butterworth), July 5, 1947, *FRUS*, 1947, 7:223.

51. Stuart to the Secretary of State, January 29, 1947, *FRUS*, 1947, 7:30.

52. Ambassador Stuart to the Secretary of State, March 22, 1949, *FRUS*, 1949, 8:193.

53. Cabot to the Director of the Office of Far Eastern Affairs (Butterworth), December 30, 1948, *FRUS*, 1948, 7:711.

54. Ibid.

55. Vice Consul at Changchun (Siebens) to the Secretary of State, *FRUS*, 1948, 7:15.

56. PPS, February 2, 1950, quoted in Kusnitz, *Public Opinion and Foreign Policy*, 26.

57. Cabot to Butterworth, 7:714.

58. CIA, Intelligence Memorandum No. 209, "Vulnerabilities of Communist Movements in the Far East," September 20, 1949, *DDC*, p. 11.

59. Cabot to Butterworth, 7:714.

60. Acheson to Am Consul, Peiping, January 5, 1950, in DOSC, *China, Foreign Affairs: 1950–1954*, reel 3.

61. Report by the NSC on United States Policy toward China, November 2, 1948, *DDC*.

62. For a detailed comparative study of defectors throughout the Communist world, see "Communist Defectors and Dissensions in the Postwar Period," OIR Report No. 5483, June 22, 1951. DDC, 1979, 287A. Here a possibly independent Chinese policy towards Moscow is formed entirely in the language of a "defection en bloc"—an interpretation quite compatible with the prevailing ideological attitudes.

63. John Lewis Gaddis, *The Long Peace: Inquiries into the History of the Cold War* (New York: Oxford University Press, 1987), 161.

64. Ibid., 163, quoting NSC 34/2, "U.S. Policy toward China," February 28, 1949, *FRUS*, 1949, 9:494–95.

65. Memorandum of Conversation by the Director of the Office of Far Eastern Affairs, September 25, 1948, *FRUS*, 1948, 6:366.

66. Cabot to Butterworth, 7:712.

67. Clubb to the Secretary of State, June 2, 1949, *FRUS*, 1949, 8:363.

68. Hillenkoetter to Truman, quoted by Yuan Ming, "The Failure of Perception: America's China Policy," in Harry Harding and Yuan Ming, *Sino-American Relations, 1945–1955* (Wilmington, Del.: SR Books, 1989), 152.

69. NSC 58/2, "U.S. Policy toward the Soviet Satellite States."

70. Kennan, PPS/59, "United States Policy toward Soviet Satellite States in Eastern Europe," August 25, 1949, 3:133.

71. From Kennan's talk at the Council on Foreign Relations, "Long Term Questions of U.S. Foreign Policy," February 16, 1949, Archives of the Council on Foreign Relations, quoted in Miscamble, *George F. Kennan*, 195–96.

72. Acheson, *Present at the Creation*, 344.

73. Quoted in Miscamble, *George F. Kennan*, 189.

74. Robert M. Blum, "Surprised by Tito: The Anatomy of an Intelligence Failure," *Diplomatic History* 12, no. 1, (Winter 1988), 39–57.

75. That the Russians might have been restraining the Yugoslavs from a highly risky and assertive foreign policy in the Balkans rarely emerges in the immediate analysis of the Yugoslav situation. See Beatrice Heuser, *Western 'Containment' Policies in the Cold War: The Yugoslav Case, 1948–53* (London: Routledge, 1989).

76. PPS/38, "United States Objectives with Respect to Russia," August 18, 1948, 2:375.

77. For example, see the Memorandum of Conversation by Walter Stuart of the Division of Chinese Affairs with the First Secretary of the Australian Embassy, June 10, 1949, *FRUS*, 1949, 9:36.

78. NSC 58/2, "U.S. Policy toward the Soviet Satellite States," 24. "The key to Tito's successful rejection of Kremlin control lies in the fact that (a) the Yugoslav Communist Party was largely his personal creation; (b) the Soviet Army did not occupy Yugoslavia; (c) he had been able from the outset to prevent effective Stalinist penetration of his party and governmental apparatus." There is no mention of his nationalistic base or of his representing Yugoslavian nationalism—an element that was useful to emphasize in public pronouncements but rarely emerged as an argument in NSC documents.

79. The phrase is in NSC 18/2, "Progress Report on Economic Relations between the U.S. and Yugoslavia," November 9, 1949, in Kesaris, *Documents of the NSC*.

80. NSC 58/2, "U.S. Policy toward the Soviet Satellite States," was quite direct on this point: "The problem is to facilitate the development of heretical communism without at the same time seriously impairing our chances for ultimately replacing this intermediate totalitarianism with tolerant regimes congenial to the Western world."

81. As the head of the Russia Committee of the British Foreign Office wrote, "Even should Tito be able to establish a neo-Communism in Eastern Europe . . . I can at present see no reason why such a process need necessarily be to our advantage. Indeed, the existence of a brand of Communism which took more account of individual national feelings might be better calculated to increase the sway of Communism than the reverse." Or as another analyst wrote: "Tito is anti-Kremlin but he remains a Communist and his example may do considerable harm to the West." See Heuser, *Western "Containment" Policies in the Cold War*, 59.

82. Harry S. Truman, *Years of Trial and Hope*, vol. 2 of *Memoirs* (Garden City, N.Y.: Doubleday, 1956), 149.

83. Acheson, *Present at the Creation*, 332–33.

84. On January 6, 1950, for example, Consul General Walter McConaughy wrote from Shanghai to warn that continued nonrecognition by the Western powers along with indirect U.S. support of Jiang's blockade of coastal areas, "is tantamount to forcing China into hands of Russia and is obviously what Russia is praying for." He offered a devastating indictment of the Guomindang: "Seldom, if ever, has a government demonstrated itself more useless and degenerate than Nationalist Government of China whose leaders have surpassed anything which even China has ever experienced of selfishness and inefficiency. Never can that government retain control of the country and sooner it is discarded better for China and world." DOSC, *China: Internal Affairs, 1950–1954* (Frederick, Md.: University Publications of America, 1984), reel 22.

85. For example, see the Memorandum by the Deputy Special Assistant for Intelligence (Howe) to W. Park Armstrong, Special Assistant to the Secretary of State for Intelligence and Research, May 31, 1950, *FRUS*, 1950, 6:349.

86. Merchant to Dean Rusk, "Comments on OIR Report Entitled 'Soviet Preferences and the China Policy of the U.S.,'" March 8, 1950, in DOSC, *China, Foreign Affairs, 1950–1954*, reel 3.

87. Memorandum prepared in the Embassy in China for the Minister Counselor (Butterworth), July 5, 1947, *FRUS*, 1947, 7:224.

88. Ibid., 7:225.

89. Ambassador Stuart to Secretary of State, October 22, 1948, *ddc*, 1976, 85D.

90. McConaughy, January 6, 1950, DOSC, *China: Internal Affairs*, reel 3.

91. Cabot to Butterworth, February 6, 1948, *FRUS*, 1948, 8:468.

92. Stuart to Secretary of State, October 27, 1948, *FRUS*, 1948, 7:523.

93. Ward to Secretary of State, October 2, 1947, *FRUS*, 1947, 7:302.

94. NSC 34, "U.S. Policy toward China," 12–13.

95. Dean Acheson, remarks to the National Press Club, January 12, 1950, in Bundy, *Pattern of Responsibility*, 185.

96. Cabot to Butterworth, December 30, 1948, *FRUS*, 1948, 7:717.

97. Ibid., 709.

98. Ibid.

99. Ibid., 717–18.

100. Gordon Chang, *Friends and Enemies: The United States, China, and the Soviet Union, 1948–1972* (Stanford, Calif.: Stanford University Press, 1990), 14.

101. Annex to NSC 48/3, April 26, 1951, in Kesaris, *Documents of the NSC*, 5.

102. Memorandum of talks between Mr. Dening and Mr. Butterworth, September 8–12 and 28, 1949, *FRUS*, 1949, 7:84.

103. John Paton Davies Jr., "East and Southeast Asia," June 6, 1950, quoted in Michael Schaller, "Consul General O. Edmund Clubb, John P. Davies, and the 'Inevitability' of Conflict between the United States and China, 1949–60: A Comment and New Documentation," *Diplomatic History* 19, no. 1 (Winter 1995): 152.

104. "The need in these areas is to develop the institutional framework within which a productive and dynamic economy can be built, to enlarge or develop classes of trained technicians and managers, to expand the production of raw materials and foodstuffs, and as appropriate of industrial products, and, in some cases, to facilitate changes in the distribution of income and the ownership of wealth in ways essential for stability and progress." NSC, 141, "Reexamination of U.S. Programs for National Security," January 19, 1953, in Kesaris, *Documents of the NSC*, 19.

105. Director of the Office of Foreign Agricultural Relations (Andrews) to Dean Rusk, September 25, 1950, [enclosure] "Statement on the Proposed United States Policy with Respect to Land Reform in Asia," April 17, 1950, *FRUS*, 1950, 6:143–46.

106. Davies, quoted in Schaller, "The 'Inevitability' of Conflict," 158–60.

107. George Kennan, round table discussion, *ddc*, 1977, 316B, p. 32.

108. Kennan, PPS/23, "Review of Current Trends," February 24, 1948, PPP, 2:122.

109. Ibid.

110. Ibid., 121.

111. Kennan to Rusk, "Position of the U.S. with Respect to Asia" (NSC 48), November 2, 1949, *ddc*, 1968, 3-H-43. Here and later, Kennan dismissed the centrality of economic development to U.S. objectives.

112. Kennan, PPS/23, "Review of Current Trends," 2:122.

113. These views stood outside an emerging ideological consensus in the national security community about propaganda warfare. Kennan's balance of power was never predicated on a global multilateral economic order shaped by the United States. He was not averse to counterbalancing American power with European and Japanese regionalism, noting the value of differing cultures as against a global society in which American values would be enshrined, reflected, and reinforced. His globalism was intertwined with a vision of a global yet limited Soviet threat, limited in that no single power, not even the Soviets in Eastern Europe, could dominate other nations over the long haul. In this sense, he, too, favored inciting nationalism against Soviet communism.

114. CIA, Intelligence Memorandum No. 209, "Vulnerabilities of Communist Movements in the Far East," September 20, 1949, *ddc*, 1975, 12E, p. 12.

115. Warren Cohen writes of Acheson's "insistence on scolding . . . them for subservience to the Russians as a means of provoking them to behave more like nationalists." In "Acheson and China," in *Uncertain Years:*

Chinese-American Relations, 1947–1950, ed. Dorothy Borg and Waldo Heinrichs (New York: Columbia University Press, 1980), 21. Acheson's approach suggests how analysis and propaganda combined with the prevailing arrogance toward the Chinese; it also suggests the relentlessness of the ideological warfare, and the extent to which Acheson knew he was employing language deeply offensive to the Chinese communists. Cohen's claim that "Acheson seized upon references to strong nationalist currents, to the determination of men like Mao and Chou to preserve China's independence and territorial integrity" (49) is less persuasive. It removes Acheson's comments from the context of countless diplomatic dispatches preoccupied with the insolence of the Chinese Communists. Ambassador Stuart's language was not all that different. Stuart to Secretary of State, April 23, 1949, *FRUS*, 1949, 9:12–13.

116. NSC 48/1, "The Position of the United States with Respect to Asia," December 23, 1949, in Kesaris, *Documents of the NSC*.

117. David McLean makes this point in "American Nationalism, the China Myth, and the Truman Doctrine: The Question of Accommodation with Peking, 1949–50," *Diplomatic History* 10, no. 1 (Winter 1986): 36. He writes: "The belief that the Chinese Communists, as ideological allies of the USSR, were fundamentally at odds with Chinese nationalism not only made it difficult to take seriously the prospect of driving a wedge between the PRC and the Soviet Union, but also helped raise the hope that such a diplomatic strategy might prove unnecessary."

118. Gaddis, *The Long Peace*, 164.

119. Although I focus here on the diplomatic writings of John S. Service, he was only one of a group that included General Joseph Stilwell, Theodore White, John Paton Davies Jr., Edgar Snow, Owen Lattimore, Jack Belden, Sol Adler, Graham Peck, and Harrison Forman. See James Peck, "The World War II Dispatches of John S.

Service," *Holy Cross Quarterly* 7 (1975): 119–30. For more on the insights of these individuals, see Peck, "America and the Chinese Revolution, 1942–1946: An Interpretation," in *American–East Asian Relations: A Survey* Ernest R. May and James C. Thomson Jr. (Cambridge: Harvard University Press, 1972).

120. Even those who sympathized made Service's writings seem naive and simplistic. The George Kennan who hails his work on the jacket of John S. Service, *Lost Chance in China: The World War II Despatches of John S. Service*, ed. Joseph W. Esherick (New York: Random House, 1974), as "an absolutely outstanding job of reporting," is not the Kennan of the late 1940s, who, analyzing Service's writings for the State Department Loyalty Board, noted a "certain naivete" in Service's understanding of the inherent totalitarianism in the "Communist system," the ruthlessness of the Leninist party, and the "forces already at work, though not on the surface, within the International Communist movement and within the Chinese Communist movement in particular." Perhaps "only an individual who had lived in Russia," Kennan argued—as Service had not—could have an understanding of how "that system works, of the jealousy of central power, of its intolerance, and its insistence on an implicit obedience by everyone who is under its sphere." Without such knowledge, the communists in China could not be understood. State Department Employee Loyalty Investigation. Hearings before a subcommittee of the Committee on Foreign Relations, 81st Cong., 2nd sess., March 8–June 28, 1950, p. 2118.

121. Edgar Snow, *Red Star over China* (New York: Random House, 1937).

122. "China faces economic collapse," Service wrote. The army was disintegrating. Both the army and the government were "permeated and demoralized from top to bottom by corruption, unprecedented in scale and openness." The intellectual and salaried classes "are in danger of liquidation." Peasant unrest was at the

exploding point. "The Kuomintang is not only proving itself incapable of averting a debacle by its own initiative; on the contrary, its policies are precipitating the crises." Service, *Lost Chance*, 140.

123. Tang Tsou, *America's Failure in China, 1941–1950* (Chicago: University of Chicago Press, 1963).

124. Service, Memorandum to General Stilwell, October 10, 1944, in *Lost Chance*, 163.

125. Service, "The Present Strength and Future Importance of the Chinese Communists," October 9, 1944, in *Lost Chance*, 249.

126. Service, "The Need for Greater Realism in Our Relations with Chiang Kai-shek," October 10, 1944, in *Lost Chance*, 163.

127. A variant of the subordination thesis was that China would so need the trade of the West that the United States would be able to use the appeal of its marketplace to great advantage. Trade was a bargaining chip. "The more the Communists develop in China, the more necessary it is for them to look toward the United States for economic goods," wrote O. Edmund Clubb in October 1947. (The Counsel General at Peiping [Clubb] to the Ambassador in China [Stuart], October 25, 1947, *FRUS*, 1947, 7:336). But their clear interest in such trade—and their bitter opposition to the embargo—was very different from a willingness to be dependent at too great a price.

128. John F. Melby, *The Mandate of Heaven: Record of a Civil War; China, 1945–1949* (Toronto: University of Toronto Press, 1968), 44.

129. Ibid., 46–47, 265–68, 205–6.

130. Ibid., 120.

131. Ibid., 266, 205.

132. Ibid., 298.

133. This theme occasionally resurfaces in State Department documents after 1949. See, for example, Chiang Mon-lin, Chairman of the Joint Commission on Rural Reconstruction, to Rusk, memorandum of the second conversation of forty-seven, April 26, 1950, in DOSC, *China, Internal Affairs, 1950–1954*.

134. Melby, *Mandate of Heaven*, 265.

135. Author interview with Lillian Hellman and John F. Melby, April 28, 1971, San Francisco.

136. As quoted in Ronald Steel, *Walter Lippmann and the American Century* (New York: Random House, 1981), 466.

137. Edgar Snow, "Will China Become a Russian Satellite?" *Saturday Evening Post*, April 9, 1949, 30.

138. Edgar Snow, "Will Tito's Heretics Halt Russia?" *Saturday Evening Post*, December 18, 1948, 23, 110.

139. Ibid., 31.

140. Snow, "Will China Become a Russian Satellite," 147.

141. This and following quotations are from ibid., 149–50.

3. Containing China before Korea

1. Stephen M. Goldstein, "Sino-American Relations, 1949–1950: Lost Chance or No Chance?" in *Sino-American Relations, 1945–1955: A Joint Reassessment of a Critical Decade*, ed. Harry Harding and Yuan Ming (Wilmington, Del.: Scholarly Resources, 1989).

2. Nancy Bernkopf Tucker, *Patterns in the Dust: Chinese American Relations and the Recognition Controversy* (New York: Columbia University Press, 1983), 3.

3. Harding and Ming, *Sino-American Relations*, 325.

4. See Acheson's statement to Senators Knowland and Smith, Memorandum of Conversation, January 5, 1950, *FRUS*, 1950, 6:258–63.

5. In *FRUS*, Truman's statement is summarized rather differently: "He indicated that the United States had no desire to establish military bases on Formosa at the present time." Editorial Note, January 5, 1950, *FRUS*, 1950, 6:264.

6. Robert Lovett's January 14, 1949, memo to Truman is a succinct statement of U.S. policy in these years: "The Department of State fully recognizes that it may be necessary at some stage for the United States to take military action if Formosa is to be denied to the communists. It

strongly believes that for political reasons, internally in Formosa and internationally, the U.S. should go to great lengths to avoid crude unilateral intervention. But that time is not yet upon us. The U.S. has not exhausted all of the political possibilities. It may still be able to foster a Chinese non-Communist local government which will itself successfully deny Formosa to the Communists. Meanwhile, the U.S. should, as it is now doing, prepare for the failure of the above contingency and put itself in a position to intervene with force if necessary. Such intervention should be publicly based not on obvious American strategic interest but on principles which are likely to have support in the international community, mainly the principle of self-determination of the Formosa people." *FRUS*, 1949, 9:266.

7. Allen Griffin, the acting chief of the Economic Cooperation Administration's China Mission, was a rare exception, stating, "We should stay out of Formosa so far as any long term operation is concerned. . . . It is my opinion that we should leave it alone." April 14, 1949, *FRUS*, 1949, 9:319.

8. Statement by Secretary of State at 35th NSC meeting on the Formosan problem, March 3, 1949, *FRUS*, 1949, 9:295–96, and Memorandum of Conversation by the Secretary of State, December 29, 1949, *FRUS*, 1949, 9:466.

9. Memorandum of Meeting, January 5, 1950, *FRUS*, 1950, 6:262.

10. NSC meeting, March 1, 1949, *FRUS*, 1949,9:295–96.

11. Capt. Wilbur W. Hoare Jr., "The Knotty Problem of Formosa," August 1953, *ddc*, 1977, 187C, p. 2.

12. Recounted in Lanxin Xiang, *Recasting the Imperial Far East: Britain and America in China, 1945–1950* (Armonk, N.Y.: M. E. Sharpe, 1995), 193. At this time Kennan was also supporting financial assistance for General Claire Chennault's Civil Air Transport (CAT) so that the airline could "facilitate CIA secret operations" in China, including the airlifting of supplies for remnant forces still fighting the communists.

William M. Leary, *Perilous Mission: Civil Air Transport and CIA Covert Operations in Asia* (Tuscaloosa: University of Alabama Press, 1984), 82. See also John Prados, *Presidents' Secret Wars: CIA and Pentagon Covert Operations from World War II through Iranscam* (New York: Morrow, 1986), 62–67.

13. Memorandum of Conversation (Sprouse) with J. F. Ford (First Secretary of the British Embassy), March 23, 1949, *FRUS*, 1949, 9:302.

14. Butterworth to Secretary of State, December 28, 1949, *FRUS*, 1949, 9:463.

15. Memorandum of Conversation, December 29, 1949, *FRUS*, 1949, 9:466.

16. CIA, *Review of the World Situation*, January 18, 1950, *ddc*, 1997, 283A.

17. Decisions Reached by Consensus at the Meetings with the Secretary and the Consultants on the Far East, November 2, 1949, *FRUS*, 1949, 9:161.

18. As Ronald McGlothlen writes, "A proliferation of words like 'decent,' 'honorable,' 'integrity,' and 'principle' obfuscated the plain truth—that only a lack of military muscle had precluded a full commitment on Taiwan and that U.S. policy still called for separating Taiwan from the mainland by diplomatic and economic means." McGlothlen, *Controlling the Waves: Dean Acheson and U.S. Foreign Policy in Asia* (New York: Norton, 1993), 109.

19. Memorandum of Conversation, December 29, 1949, *FRUS*, 1949, 9:464.

20. Ibid., 465.

21. Dean Acheson, *Present at the Creation: My Years at the State Department* (New York: Norton, 1969), 351.

22. Despite U.S. wavering, the Nationalists repeatedly and in the strongest terms warned Washington not to shift its position on the Cairo Declaration. Minutes of the 40th Meeting of the U.S. Delegation to the United Nations General Assembly, November 15, 1950, *FRUS*, 1950, 6:570.

23. Nitze quoted in McGlothlen, *Controlling the Waves,* 112.

24. Livingston Merchant to Dean Acheson, March 6, 1950, in DOSC, *China: Internal Affairs, 1950–1954*, reel 2.

25. "By 'taking over' certain expenditures on Taiwan, Rusk explained later, the United States helped the Nationalists to 'sustain their very heavy military budget.'" In effect, Acheson in April replaced the military aid he had pre-cluded in January. At a special meeting on May 25, the State Department also urged the JCS to expedite Nationalist arms shipments and explore ideas for the "augmentation and inten-sification" of "covert action in support of resist-ance on Formosa." Quoted in McGlothlen, *Controlling the Waves*, 119.

26. The United States Delegation at the Tri-partite Preparatory Meetings to the Secretary of State, May 4, 1950, *FRUS*, 1950, 3:995.

27. "Minutes on Meeting on MacArthur Tes-timony," May 18, 1951, *DDC*.

28. O. Edmund Clubb to Livingston Mer-chant, May 30, 1950, DOSC, *China: Internal Affairs, 1950–1954*, reel 25.

29. O. Edmund Clubb to Dean Rusk, June 16, 1950, in ibid., reel 23.

30. See McGlothlen, *Controlling the Waves*, 113.

31. Memorandum by the Deputy Special Assistant for Intelligence (Howe) to Mr. W. Park Armstrong, Special Assistant to the Secretary of State for Intelligence and Research, May 31, 1950, *FRUS*, 1950, 6:347–51.

32. Rusk to Acheson, "U.S. Policy toward Formosa," May 30, 1950, quoted in McGlothlen, *Controlling the Waves*, 123–24.

33. Sprouse to Merchant, Comments Respecting Proposal to Formosan Plebiscite, February 15, 1951, DOSC, *China: Internal Affairs, 1950–1954*, reel 5.

34. Rusk argued that if the United States did not draw the line in Taiwan, "then we can expect an accelerated deterioration of our influ-ence in the Mediterranean, Near East, Asia, and the Pacific. The situation in Japan may become untenable and possibly that in the Philippines.

Indonesia, with its vast natural resources may be lost and the oil of the Middle East will be in jeopardy. None of these places provide good 'holding' grounds once the people feel that Communism is the wave of the future and that even we are retreating before it." Extract from a draft memorandum, Rusk to the Secretary of State, May 30, 1950, *FRUS*, 1950, 6:350, 351.

35. Tucker, *Patterns in the Dust*, 58.

36. CIA, *Review of the World Situation*, Octo-ber 19, 1949, *ddc*, 1977, 284E, p. 6.

37. Memorandum of Conversation with British Ambassador Oliver Frank and the Secre-tary of State, December 8, 1949, *FRUS*, 1949, 9:220.

38. Ambassador Kirk to Secretary of State, November 8, 1949, *FRUS*, 1949, 9:184.

39. Memorandum from Ruth Bacon, UN Advisor of the Bureau of Far Eastern Affairs, to Livingston Merchant, December 30, 1949, *FRUS*, 9:258–60.

40. Harry Harding, "The Legacy of the Decade for Later Years: An American Perspec-tive," in Harding and Ming, *Sino-American Rela-tions*, 315.

41. Acheson to Ambassador Stuart, May 13, 1949, *FRUS*, 1949, 9:22.

42. Memorandum Prepared in British For-eign Office, August 15, 1949, *FRUS*, 1949, 9:61.

43. Agreed Anglo-American Report Summa-rizing Discussion held at the Foreign Office, May 2, 3, 1950, in DOSC, *China: Foreign Affairs, 1950–1954*, reel 5.

44. United States Delegation at the Tripar-tite Preparatory Meetings to the Secretary of State, 3:995.

45. Harding, "Legacy," 315.

46. Memorandum of Conversation by Direc-tor of the Office of Chinese Affairs (Sprouse), December 27, 1949, *FRUS*, 1949, 9:245.

47. Bacon (Nanking) to Secretary of State, January 6, 1950, in DOSC, *China: Internal Affairs, 1950–1954*, reel 18, 1–2. Bacon favored the recog-nition of Beijing, arguing that "to insist as prereq-uisite recognition they demonstrate willingness

abide by practice international law protect private property individual freedoms and diplomatic immunities is probably practical impossibility; and to declare such demonstration essential is act of self-deception equivalent saying, 'We will recognize this duck as fowl only if it stops looking and behaving like duck.' To stand on this ground means spending another fifteen-year period without diplomatic relations."

48. Ambassador Robert Murphy, May 18, 1952, in DOSC, *China: Foreign Affairs, 1950–1954,* reel 2.

49. Acheson to Djakarta Embassy, December 9, 1950, in ibid., reel 3.

50. McConaughy (Shanghai), January 6, 1950, in ibid., *China: Internal Affairs, 1950–1954,* reel 2.

51. Memorandum by Troy L. Perkins, Recognition of the Chinese Communist Regime, November 5, 1949, *FRUS,* 1949, 9:170.

52. Acheson, *Present at the Creation,* 340. Acheson does not bother to argue whether Americans' actions were actually in conformity with international law, nor does he cite those who thought Washington itself was violating international law by its actions and continued support of the Nationalists. Part of the problem with various historical accounts of this period (including that of the Ward case) is that they take Acheson's language about international law at face value instead of determining whether his claims have any merit and why, if they do, they were both privately challenged by some American diplomats and widely discounted by the leaders of other countries.

53. Rusk quoted in McGlothlen, *Controlling the Waves,* 152.

54. Memorandum of Conversation by the Secretary of State, December 8, 1949, *FRUS,* 1949, 9:219.

55. There would, Davies conceded, be "unavoidable damage . . . done to the civilian population," but the United States could warn civilians of coming attacks and "could tailor our reprisal to the provocation." Perhaps a beginning

could be made by "concentrating punitive operations . . . on installations in Manchuria rather than China proper. . . . [W]e can most profitably direct our attention to those arsenals and factories which are of the greatest importance to Soviet as well as Chinese military and economic power. And along with this we would secretly approach the Chinese Communists and tell them:

"a. We consider that we have put up with enough misbehavior on their part;

"b. We do not feel that their interests or ours will be served by their laboring under any misapprehensions regarding means at our disposal for bringing our displeasure home to them;

"c. They are, therefore, advised of a graduated scale of punitive air action which we can take against their military and industrial bases in China;

"d. We will not hesitate to take these punitive measures in accordance with the degree of provocation given to us; and

"e. We will feel free to resort to these measures so long as their regime is not recognized by us, which will be so long as their international behavior is that of bandits and blackmailers." Memorandum by John P. Davies Jr., August 24, 1949, *FRUS,* 1949, 9:536–40.

56. Ibid., 536.

57. Quoted in Wilson D. Miscamble, *George F. Kennan and the Making of American Foreign Policy, 1947–1950* (Princeton: Princeton University Press, 1992), 237.

58. O. Edmund Clubb, letter to George Kennan, April 25, 1950, in Michael Schaller, "Consul General O. Edmund Clubb, John P. Davies, and the 'Inevitability' of Conflict between the United States and China, 1949–60: A Comment and New Documentation," *Diplomatic History* 19, no. 1 (Winter 1995): 154.

59. The Second Secretary in China (Bacon) to the Secretary of State, November 8, 1949, *FRUS,* 1949, 9:181.

60. Memorandum of Troy Perkins, of the Office of Chinese Affairs, November 5, 1949, *FRUS,* 1949, 9:168–69.

61. Memorandum of Conversation by the Secretary of State, December 8, 1949, *FRUS*, 1949, 9:219.

62. Memorandum of Conversation, by Chinese Affairs (Sprouse) with Second Secretary of the Canadian Embassy, November 14, 1949, *FRUS*, 1949, 9:192.

63. The Chargé in India (Donovan) to the Secretary of State, November 7, 1949, *FRUS*, 1949, 9:177–79.

64. The Chargé in India (Donovan) to the Secretary of State, November 7, 1949, *FRUS*, 1949, 9:178.

65. Memorandum of Conversation, November 30, 1949, *FRUS*, 1949, 9:205–6.

66. Memorandum of Conversation with Madame Pandit, November 22, 1949, *FRUS*, 1949, 9:196.

67. McConaughy (Shanghai), January 3, 1950, in DOSC, *China: Internal Affairs, 1950–1954*, reel 1.

68. One China desk official in Washington said, "It might be possible for some action to be taken to discourage the present apparently somewhat indiscriminate bombing by the Chinese Air Force of Chinese cities but that no serious consideration had been given to this question." Sprouse discussion with British Consul Graves, February 2, 1950, in DOSC, *China: Foreign Affairs, 1950–1954*, reel 1.

69. "The Nationalists are operating American aircraft and are presumably using American bombs and armaments. Their action cannot affect the outcome of the civil war, . . . and the disregard of human life is deserving of the strongest possible condemnation." British consul (Graves) discussion, Department of State Memo of Conversation, February 20, 1950, in DOSC, *China: Internal Affairs, 1950–1954*, reel 1.

70. United States Delegation at the Tripartite Preparatory Meetings to the Secretary of State, 3:993.

71. Sprouse discussion with British Consul Graves, February 2, 1950.

72. Memorandum for Mr. Jessup, by Charles Yost, September 1, 1949: "Policy towards the Chinese Communists Concrete Measures," *DDC*, 1975, F359, pp. 2–3.

73. Quoted in McGlothlen, *Controlling the Waves*, 155.

74. From this, can one conclude that, as Stephen M. Goldstein suggests, the Chinese, like the Americans, had "preconceptions" and "images" that "prompted deep suspicion of Washington's motives, hardened their own position, and contributed to a situation where agreement was virtually impossible"? The answer is undoubtedly yes in general, but not necessarily in regard to recognition. There is no indication that the Chinese communists found both recognition and continued hostility incompatible, as the United States did. Goldstein writes that "from 1948 to 1950 the fundamental contradiction in New China's foreign policy was between the realization of the national revolution and the negotiation of some relationship with the United States. The nature of the Party's view of the world and the political pressures upon it made it virtually impossible to reconcile these two conflicting goals." This is an odd argument: the first sentence has the United States standing in the way of the revolution; the second suggests that "some relationship with the United States" required that the revolution be left incomplete. Goldstein argues that the Chinese would have had to compromise in order to open meaningful relations with Washington, "dropping their objections to American support of the KMT, acceding to standards of international law that they thought contradicted the country's nationalist aspirations, mollifying foreign opinion at considerable domestic political cost, and alienating the Soviet Union." But it is hard to imagine any government's tolerating prolonged support of a defeated rival government. Was "alienating" the USSR really required for recognition? What ideological conclusions can plausibly be drawn about the Chinese communists if they were

really expected to meet these "conditions"? This is not a question of Chinese pragmatism per se; it is the quite specific question of recognition. The Chinese did set conditions, as the British found out: that is, severing ties with the GMD and supporting both a PRC seat in the United Nations and the expulsion of the GMD from that body. These conditions proved difficult for the British only because of U.S. pressure, not because the British found them outrageous requests. Given the U.S. position on recognition, it is hard to see grounds for making any sweeping conclusions about the Chinese communists' ideological attitudes; they had a quite unideological view of recognition, as did most other nations. The United States was an exception. See Goldstein, "Sino-American Relations, 1949–1950," 138. A variant of this argument is made by Chen Jian, "The Myth of America's 'Lost Chance' in China," *Diplomatic History* 21, no. 1 (1997): 77–86. Chen argues that the CCP's confrontation with the United States "originated in the Party's need to enhance the inner dynamics of the Chinese Revolution" and that from a Chinese perspective "no chance existed for Communist China and the United States to reach an accommodation in 1949–50." Yet Chen argues that the two conditions the CCP laid down (cutting off connections with the GMD and treating the Chinese as equals) prevented American diplomatic recognition (and UN membership) and "accommodation." Cutting off relations with the GMD was an obvious prerequisite for diplomatic ties, which Washington refused to take. China could hardly be expected to accept recognition based on such an American position. Other nations found ways to deal with the issues of "equality" precisely because the issue for them was not accommodation or approval but recognition. The same arguments are relevant to the matter of the PRC assuming a UN seat, and here it was the United States, not China, that was often seen as flouting international law. Nor is it surprising to find that Chinese leaders were discussing policy on the assumption that the United

States was not about to budge on its views in the near future.

75. The CIA had no doubt that the Chinese communists wanted to be recognized as the national government of China "as soon as it is formed and proclaimed." See CIA, ORE 45–49, "Probable Developments in China," June 16, 1949, 33, available on CIA CD-ROM. The issue was what to do "when confronted with the Communist regime's request for recognition."

76. One figure floated at a UN conference on economic development was $13 billion. See Comments by S.C. Brown, Transcript of Round Table Discussion on American Policy toward China, Department of State, October 6–8, 1949, *DDC*, 1977, p. 301.

77. See NSC 61, "U.S. Economic Aid to Far Eastern Areas," January 27, 1950, in Kesaris, *Documents of the NSC*.

78. Ibid.

79. S. C. Brown, Round Table Discussion, 316B.

80. Cora Dubois, ibid., A-9.

81. The CIA often noted the dependency of China's urban areas on foreign trade and the highly disruptive impact an embargo would have on China's development pattern; in this context an embargo would "retard the rehabilitation of China and increase the economic difficulties that will confront the CCP." See CIA, ORE 45–49, "Probable Developments in China," 5. See also, CIA, NIE-10, "Communist China," January 17, 1951, 8. (Both on CIA CD.)

82. Memorandum of the Deputy Assistant Secretary of State (Merchant) to Acheson, November 16, 1949, *FRUS*, 1949, 9:997.

83. Jawaharlal Nehru, *Letters to Chief Ministers, 1947–1964* (New Delhi: Oxford University Press, 1985–89), November 17, 1950, 2:268.

84. See Roger W. Buckley, "Competitor and Ally: British Perceptions of Occupied Japan," in *The Occupation of Japan: The International Context*, ed. Thomas W. Burkman (Norfolk, Va.: MacArthur Memorial Foundation, 1982).

85. Annex: Draft Report by the NSC on United States Policy regarding Trade with China, February 28, 1949, *FRUS*, 1949, 9:828.

86. S. C. Brown, Round Table Discussion, 307.

87. CIA, ORE 43-48, "Strategic Importance of Japan," May 24, 1948, *ddc*, H23, 1988. The argument, in short, was that if Japan were cut off from Northeast Asia, it would have to export far more to Western markets, where it faced stiff competition, or to Southeast Asian markets, where, "in addition to U.S. and European competition, the development or expansion of indigenous industries may limit the market for Japanese goods still further."

88. NSC 48/1, "The Position of the U.S. with Respect to Asia," December 23, 1949, in Kesaris, *Documents of the NSC*, 27.

89. George Kennan, quoted in Round Table Discussion, 316B, pp. 26–28.

90. George Marshall, ibid., 392–96.

91. Barnett, ibid., 320–24.

92. NSC 41, "U.S. Policy regarding Trade with China," March 3, 1949, in Kesaris, *Documents of the NSC*, 3.

93. Japanese Reactions towards Sino-Japanese Trade Problem, OIR report, October 21, 1949, *DDC*, 1988, 4D, pp. 1–10.

94. NSC 48/1, "Position of the U.S.," 6.

95. See William S. Borden, *The Pacific Alliance: United States Foreign Economic Policy and Japanese Trade Recovery, 1947–1955* (Madison: University of Wisconsin Press, 1984), for the roots of military Keynesianism and NSC 68 as it relates to Asia and Japan. For a sharply focused plea for such military Keynesianism in early 1950, see Bernard Brodie, "National Security Policy and Economic Stability," in Yale Institute of International Studies, Memorandum No. 33, January 2, 1950 (New Haven: Yale Institute of International Studies, 1950).

96. See Alan P. Dobson, *The Politics of the Anglo-American Economic Relationship, 1940–1987* (Sussex, U.K.: Wheatsheaf Books, 1988), 112–13.

97. British Overseas Obligations: Cabinet Memorandum by Mr. Eden, June 18, 1952, in *British Imperial Policy and Decolonialization, 1938–1964* (London, Macmillan Press, 1989), 2:165.

98. As Anthony Eden put it in discussing the defense of Southeast Asia and the Middle East, "Our aim should be to persuade the United States to assume the real burdens in such organizations, while retaining for ourselves as much political control—and hence prestige and world influence—as we can" (ibid., 173). John Kent, *British Imperial Strategy and the Origins of the Cold War, 1944–1949* (London: Leicester University Press, 1993), argues that by 1949 the British no longer sought to pursue a third course somewhat apart from the United States. His analysis of the links between Cold War issues and imperial strategy suggests a shift from 1945, when the British were feeling uneasy about Russian-American cooperation as they sought to reconstitute their sterling system, and late 1949, when dependence on the United States had become acceptable. For U.S. views, see NSC report on British Military Commitment, July 10, 1950, *DDC*, 1993, 1621; and JCS, "British/U.S. Ties," December 4, 1950, *DDC*, 1975, 19D.

99. "Britain's colonial possessions provided her with the basis for an alternative strategy—as they had in the early 1930s. Nevertheless, it was widely recognized that the U.S. economy had expanded too greatly during the war to turn its back on foreign markets again. The most common fear, then, was that the Americans would sustain their drive towards multilateral trading arrangements, but would do so in ways which paid minimal heed to the adjustment needs of other industrial nations. Thus the gains of postwar recovery would be overwhelmingly appropriated by U.S. producers, leaving other western economies in a state of permanent subordination. One way out of this looming dependency was to enforce industrial efficiency at home; but under conditions of troop demobilization this

approach had severe limitations. It was in this context that British business opinion became deeply attracted to the thesis of colonial development, since the boosting of purchasing power in those underdeveloped areas where the UK enjoyed trade preferences and political control could make a vital contribution to the maintenance of the British market-share in international trade." R. F. Holland, "The Imperial Factor in British Strategies from Attlee to Macmillan, 1945–63," in *Perspectives on Imperialism and Decolonialization*, ed. David Goldsworthy (London: HMSO, 1994), 166–67.

100. See David Reynolds, "Great Britain," in his *The Origins of the Cold War in Europe: International Perspectives* (New Haven: Yale University Press, 1994).

101. Introduction to David Goldsworthy, *The Conservative Government and the End of Empire, 1951–1957* (London: HMSO, 1995), xxxvi.

102. Dobson, *Politics of the Anglo-American Economic Special Relationship*, 129–30. As Dobson points out, besides trying to protect Hong Kong and their investments in China, the British were also reluctant "to stop trade, mainly of rubber between Malaya and China, because of the economic repercussions this would have on the former." Also, see DOS, "Integration in Europe and Britain: Sterling Area, and the Commonwealth Arrangement," March 8, 1950, *ddc*, 374B, 1980.

103. Howard Schonberger looks at the British concern with the potential invasion of its sterling markets in Asia by a Japan that could no longer trade with China, observing that Dulles "regarded British opposition to his handling of China, in regard to the Japanese peace treaty, as politically misguided and based on narrow economic self-interest." Schonberger, "Peacemaking in Asia: The United States, Great Britain, and the Japanese Decision to Recognize Nationalist China, 1951–52," *Diplomatic History* 1, no. 1 (Winter 1986): 73.

104. The British were also quick to point out that while the Americans were demanding the abolition of Imperial Preference, "they were establishing a preferential trading relationship themselves with the newly independent Philippines. These, and other matters such as American discriminatory use of shipping, restrictions on agricultural imports, and tied loans, prompted the British Foreign Office to compare the beam in America's eye with the mote in Britain's." Dobson, *Politics of the Anglo-American Economic Special Relationship*, 102.

105. Goldsworthy, *Conservative Government*, 1:186–88.

106. See "The Problem of Nationalism: Letter from Sir W. Strang to Sir T. Lloyd, June 21, 1952," in Goldsworthy, *Conservative Government*, 1:17.

107. Ibid., 14.

108. Anthony Eden, "British Overseas Obligations," June 18, 1952, in ibid., 5.

109. Ringwalt (London), August 22, 1951, to Acheson, in DOSC, *China: Internal Affairs, 1950–1954*, reel 4.

110. William Turner (Bangkok) to Acheson, in ibid., reel 13.

111. Ibid.

112. Ibid.

113. Kennan to Marshall, February 10, 1948, quoted in Miscamble, *George F. Kennan*, 221.

114. PPS/23, Kennan, "Review of Current Trends," February 24, 1948, 2:123.

115. PPS/39, Kennan, "U.S. Policy toward China," September 7, 1948, 2:413.

116. Kennan to Rusk, November 2, 1949, *ddc* 1068, 3-H-43, p. 1.

117. Kennan, Round Table Discussion, pp. 25–26.

118. Consul General McConaughy at the Inter-Departmental Meeting on the Far East, June 2, 1950, *FRUS*, 1950, 6:353.

119. Strategic Assessment of Southeast Asia, Memorandum for the Secretary of Defense, April 10, 1950, PPS, 312.

120. George Marshall, Round Table Discussion.

121. For one of the very few warnings that an American troop withdrawal would likely lead to a North Korean invasion of South Korea in 1950, see CIA, "Consequences of U.S. Troop Withdrawal for Korea in Spring 1949," February 18, 1949, ddc, 1978, 16A. The conclusion was stark: "Withdrawal of U.S. forces from Korea in the spring of 1949 would probably in time be followed by an invasion, timed to coincide with Communist-led South Korean revolts by the North Korean People's Army possibly assisted by small battle-trained units from Communist Manchuria. . . . Assuming that Korean Communists would make aggressive use of the opportunity presented them, U.S. troop withdrawal would probably result in a collapse of the U.S.-supported Republic of Korea, an event which would seriously diminish U.S. prestige and adversely affect U.S. security interests in the Far East."

4. Isolating China

1. For more on the split with allies such as Britain and neutrals such as India, see "Extracts of a Memorandum of Conversations by Harriman and MacArthur," August 6 and 8, 1950, *FRUS*, 1950, 6:427–30.

2. Department of State Memorandum, November 21, 1951, *FRUS*, 1951, 7:2050.

3. The Secretary of State to the Embassy in the United Kingdom, August 13, 1950, *FRUS*, 1950, 6:433.

4. CIA, "Review of the World Situation as It Relates to the Security of the United States," July 14, 1950, *DDC*, 1977, 284G, p. 1.

5. Secretary of State to the Embassy in United Kingdom, June 27, 1950, *FRUS*, 1950, 7:186. The proxy-war notion is in CIA World Reports, September 15, 1950, *DDC*, 1977, 284D.

6. Intelligence Estimate ORI, Korea, June 25, 1950, *FRUS*, 1950, 7:150.

7. Truman endorsed this view without qualification—*Years of Trial and Hope*, vol. 2 of *Memoirs* (Garden City, N.Y.: Doubleday, 1956), 440–41—as did Acheson.

8. MacArthur stressed "Chinese imperialistic aspirations," and after the Chinese intervened, he remained "convinced that Communist China undertook the North Korean operation, the Tibetan invasion, and assistance to Ho Chi Minh on its own responsibility, and that Soviet Russia, despite its satisfaction derived from action parallel to its own objectives, [had] remained in the background." Memorandum of Conversation by the Political Advisor in Japan (Sebald) with MacArthur, November 14, 1950, FRUS, 1950, 7:1149.

9. "Chinese Communist Overt Operations," report by the Joint Strategic Survey Committee to the JCS, September 6, 1950, in *Records of the Joint Chiefs of Staff, Part II, 1946–1953* (microform), ed. Paul Kesaris (Washington, D.C.: University Publications of America, 1979), reel 3, 568–72, 579, 581 (hereafter cited as *JCS Records*).

10. "Study on Implications of Large-Scale Chinese Communist Military Operations," JCS 1924/31, in ibid., 573.

11. Ibid., 153.

12. CIA, "Review of the World Situation," 4.

13. A variant of the wedge strategy taken under consideration once China did enter the war was the idea of placing so much pressure on the Chinese Communists that they might panic and make untenable demands of the Soviets. See Guy Hope, "Further Economic Pressure on Communist China," August 27, 1952, Memo CA, in DOSC, *China, Foreign Affairs, 1950–1954*.

14. Draft Memorandum in the Department of Defense for National Security Council Staff Consideration Only," U.S. Courses of Action in Korea," August 7, 1950, FRUS, 1950, 7:532.

15. The dismembering of China extended to arguments that "Formosa would be handed over to the Soviet Union by way of a Chinese satellite regime." See Annex to NSC 48/3, April 26, 1951, in Kesaris, *Documents of the NSC*, 22.

16. The Annex to NSC 48/3 put it in both the most common and the strongest terms: "While it seems apparent that the present Peiping Gov-

ernment is controlled by Stalinists whose alliance to Moscow is complete, it is reasonable to suppose that individuals or groups may exist within the Chinese Communist party who are aware of and reluctant to accept the implications for the future historic role of China of an unswerving adherence to a policy of abject subservience to Moscow" (ibid., 11).

17. *Department of State Bulletin*, September 18, 1950, 463. See also Annex to NSC 48/3, 11.

18. Truman, *Years of Trial and Hope*, 440–41, cites the reasons Acheson gave for not openly accusing the Soviets of aggression: it would demolish the United Nations, and because we could take no direct action, it would only weaken our world position. Another reason (not cited by Truman) to focus the charge of aggression on China was the advantage for U.S. Asia policy in isolating China. See Notes on NSC Meeting, November 28, 1950, FRUS, 1950, 7:1242–49.

19. Minutes, Truman-Attlee Conversations, First Meeting, December 4, 1950, FRUS, 1950, 3:1712, 1714. When Acheson told Churchill early in 1952 that a split had once been a "real possibility" but that "Chinese intervention had made this hope seem very distant and impossible of attainment at the present," he was reiterating a position he had been espousing for several years. These themes continued into the last months of the Truman administration; see, for example, CIA, "Relations between the Chinese Communist Regime and the USSR: Their Present Character and Probable Future Courses," August 10, 1952, DDC.

20. Minutes, Truman-Attlee Conversations, 1728–29.

21. All it could do was try to show how Moscow was seeking to dominate China. U.S. information programs were instructed to depict Sino-Soviet relations with this objective in mind. As an October 30, 1952, status report put it, great efforts were being made to portray "the Sino-Soviet meetings in Moscow in a light calculated to raise doubts in the minds of Chinese

on the mainland as to the motives of the Peiping regime in their dealings with the USSR." The Foreign Information Program, *ddc*, 1992, 1722, p. 6.

22. CIA Memorandum: Threat of Full Chinese Communist Intervention in Korea, October 12, 1950, FRUS, 1950, 7:934.

23. Ibid., 933–34.

24. "Study on Implications of Large-Scale Chinese Communist Military Operations," 577.

25. Capt. Wilber W. Haore Jr., *The Korean Conflict: The Week of Decision*, chap. 2, *ddc*, March 4, 1977, 187A, p. 12.

26. Memorandum by the Political Advisor in Japan (Sibilate), "General MacArthur's Concept of the Korean Campaign," November 14, 1950, FRUS, 1950, 3:1149.

27. Draft memo by John P. Davies of the PPS, "Chinese Communist Intervention in Korea," November 7, 1950, FRUS, 1950, 7:1078–85.

28. Quoted in Leonard A. Kusnitz, *Public Opinion and Foreign Policy: America's China Policy, 1949–1979* (Westport, Conn.: Greenwood Press, 1984), 51.

29. Dean Acheson, *Present at the Creation: My Years at the State Department* (New York: Norton, 1969), 452.

30. Copies of Pannikar's dispatches were passed on to the Americans, usually through the British. For example, see the dispatches in DOSC, *China, Foreign Affairs, 1950–1954*, reel 3.

31. Truman repeated this charge in *Years of Trial and Hope*, 412; others claimed he was "anti-Western" or "despises American ideas" or was "too much the schemer" or too "emotional." See Bangkok despatch, "Attitude of Former Indian Ambassador to China, K. M. Pannikar," August 29, 1952, in ibid.

32. The State Department requested the view of various governments on Zhou's message. Their responses are revealing. Asian governments (Burma, India, Taipei) took it very seriously, as did several European embassies in Beijing (Norway, Sweden, the Netherlands). In London, the British were divided, but H. A.

Graves of the British Embassy in Washington wrote the State Department that the Chinese "would prefer to achieve the survival of a North Korean buffer state by diplomatic means, but if this fails, the possibility of open Chinese intervention exists as a real danger. If there is intervention in North Korea Chinese forces are more likely to move in than Russian forces." The American Embassy in Moscow, however, thought Zhou's warning a probable bluff to scare the Indians. And in Hong Kong the consulate stressed that the "USSR could [not] afford to risk the political dangers involved in pushing its most important satellite into a devastating war unless it were prepared to back it with the Red Army, particularly in view of the Sino-Soviet treaty." Memorandum, Diplomatic Roundup of Chinese Communist Intentions, October 1950, *ddc*, 1978, 262B.

33. Jawaharlal Nehru, *Letters to Chief Ministers, 1947–1964,* 5 vols. (New Delhi: Oxford University Press, 1985–89), November 17, 1950, 2:267.

34. Ibid., December 3, 1950, 2:278; December 31, 1950, 2:301.

35. Pannikar, November 23, 1951, Canadian Broadcasting Company transcript, in DOSC, *China, Foreign Affairs, 1950–1954,* reel 3.

36. DOS, Propaganda Plan for Communist China, January 3, 1951, in ibid., reel 6, 5.

37. Ibid., 7–9.

38. United States Information Agency answers to Senator Pat McCarran, as cited in Edward W. Barrett, *Truth Is Our Weapon* (New York: Funk & Wagnalls, 1953), 326–27.

39. See Barrett's *Truth Is Our Weapon* for his account of his years as head of the State Department's propaganda and information programs, quot. 328, 329.

40. "A Chinese-language leaflet shows two hairy reaching down hands from the north to tear Manchuria and Outer Mongolia away from China. 'Protect your country and family?' it asks. 'If so, why don't you do it at home? . . . From the so-called Sino-Korean friendship,

you get nothing but abundance of cold water. From the so-called Sino-Russian friendship, death is your only fate." Quoted in Barrett, *Truth Is Our Weapon,* 328–29.

41. In one area, the armed forces were accessible. In January 1951, U.S. propaganda warfare proposals called for indoctrinating Chinese prisoners in Korea and then releasing them to "cause doubts in the minds of Communist commanders concerning the loyalty of certain of their units" and "to undermine the campaign of hate against the U.S." This early argument for using POWs was to intensify quickly in the following months. See Assistant Secretary of State for Public Affairs, "Propaganda Plan for Communist China," January 13, 1951, in DOSC, *China: Foreign Affairs, 1950–1954,* reel 6; and White House Report, "Notes on Meeting Regarding U.S. Policies from the Psychological Strategy Standpoint, Governing the Exchange of Prisoners of War and Repatriation of North Korean and Chinese Nationals," October 2, 1952, *DDC,* 1995, 1750.

42. DOS, "Propaganda Plan for Communist China."

43. Ibid.

44. "Communist Defections and Dissensions in the Postwar Period," OIR Report No. 5483, June 22, 1951, *DDC,* 1979, 287A, p. 43.

45. Ibid.

46. John Lewis Gaddis, for example, argues that "the administration believed strongly enough in the possibility of exploiting eventual Sino-Soviet differences that in early 1951 it took the extreme risk—given the domestic political climate that existed at the time—of authorizing highly secret State Department contacts with Chinese believed to represent the views of at least some elements within the government in Beijing." Gaddis, *The Long Peace, Inquiries into the History of the Cold War* (New York: Oxford University Press, 1987), 170.

47. Memorandum of Meeting, January 6 and 7, 12 and 13, *FRUS,* 1951, 7:1467–1501.

48. Ibid.

49. Ibid.

50. Ibid. These discussions took place as the United States was still formulating the propaganda campaign with which it intended to sow division among the Chinese communist leaders. See DOS, "Propaganda Plan for Communist China," reel 22.

51. A good example is "Communist Defections and Dissensions in the Postwar Period."

52. By August the State Department was more confident about preventing China from entering the United Nations, given the "new and compelling reason for postponing a change-over" that the Korean War promised. The pressures, however, remained. Some states thought seating Beijing would "encourage Chinese Titoism, pave the way for an East-West settlement, or advance particular national interests relating to China." For the American position, see "Chinese Representation in the United Nations," paper prepared in the Bureau of United Nations Affairs, August 24, 1950, *FRUS*, 1950, 3:1121–26.

53. Statement of President Truman, June 27, 1950, *FRUS*, 1950, 7:202–3.

54. Memorandum for the Secretary of Defense, "Policy in Taiwan," August 1950, in DOSC, *China: Internal Affairs, 1950–1954*, reel 3.

55. Harry Harding, "The Legacy of the Decade for Later Years: An American Perspective," in *Sino-American Relations, 1945–1955: A Joint Reassessment of a Critical Decade*, ed. Harry Harding and Yuan Ming (Wilmington, Del.: Scholarly Resources, 1989), 326.

56. "Memorandum—Formosa, ORE Report, January n.d. 1951, in DOSC, *Formosa Files, 1950–1954*.

57. Ibid.

58. Ambassador in the United Kingdom to Secretary of State, July 14, 1950, *FRUS*, 1950, 7:380–85.

59. See DOS, Report on the Effect within China and Other Eastern Countries of United States Backing of Chiang Kai-shek, February 9, 1951, *FRUS*, 1951, 7:1574–78.

60. Charlton Ogborn Jr., DOS Memorandum of Discussion, January 4, 1951, in DOSC, *China: Foreign Affairs, 1950–1954*, reel 3.

61. Memorandum of Conversation, by the Director of the Office of Northeast Asian Affairs, with Minister O. A. Baig of Pakistan, February 1, 1951, *FRUS*, 1951, 7:1543.

62. Nehru, *Letters to Chief Ministers*, September 1, 1950, 2:183–84.

63. Secretary of State to the Embassy in India, July 25, 1950, *FRUS*, 1950, 7:466–68.

64. Nehru, *Letters to Chief Ministers*, December 4, 1952, 2:184.

65. Clubb to Dean Rusk, July 14, 1950, in DOSC, *China: Internal Affairs, 1950–1954*, reel 10.

66. Acheson to Embassy in Djakarta, September 19, 1950, in ibid., reel 7.

67. Clubb to Dean Rusk, July 24, 1950, in ibid.

68. Once again the wedge was invoked. Retaining control of the island became "a long-term bargaining weapon to achieve our overriding purpose of separating Peiping from Moscow and reversing its expansionist policy." Merchant and Perkins to Dean Rusk, July 9, 1951, in DOSC, *China: Foreign Affairs, 1950–1954*, reel 6.

69. Merchant to Rusk, July 5, 1951, ibid., reel 4.

70. Ibid.

71. Memorandum by the Joint Chiefs of Staff to Secretary of Defense, July 27, 1950, *FRUS*, 1950, 6:391. The JCS were "nervous" about the State Department's apparent willingness to place the Taiwan issue in the hands of the UN: "They asserted that the United States 'should not agree to any United Nations solution for Formosa which might enhance the military position of the USSR in the Far East.'" Memo from Bradley to Johnson, "Formosa," 8 September 1950, sec. 6, in Hoare, *Week of Decision*, August 1953, 4(5): 25, *ddc*, 1977, 187A.

72. Merchant to Rusk, July 9, 1951, in DOSC, *China: Foreign Affairs, 1950–1954*, reel 4.

73. Dean Acheson to Nitze, July 12, 1950, *DDC*, 1979, 437B, p. 2.

74. Cavendish W. Cannon (PPS) to Jessup, August 28, 1950, in DOSC, *China Internal Affairs, 1950–1954,* reel 3.

75. In November 1950, Nitze and Acheson favored finding a way of dealing with Taiwan in a UN context; shortly afterward, however, Washington shifted toward a go-it-alone stance, convinced that it could obtain at least the needed acquiescence from its allies. Briefing paper for Congressional appearance, November 27, 1950, Nitze draft, *DDC* 3-H-45, p. 14.

76. Meanwhile, discussions about a possible coup against Jiang continued. In a memorandum by Robert Strong, April 12, 1951, a lengthy analysis of a coup d'état "following preliminary measures to assure suitable conditions" enumerated the advantages: "a stronger and more suitable base from which to carry on operations; creation of more receptive conditions for United States aid and participation, and making a revolutionary move which could not but appeal to mainland and overseas Chinese." Strong concluded that to "advocate this course is to advocate the abandonment of a long lived United States policy of avoiding intervention in the internal affairs of states. However, with the right propaganda line, the job could be done with the minimum of repercussions." Nevertheless, it was slowly, if reluctantly, concluded that Jiang would probably have to stay, and the military foundations of Washington's relationship with him were laid in the Truman years. "Working Paper on Support of China Mainland Resistance and the Use of Nationalist Forces on Formosa," April 12, 1951, in DOSC, *China: Foreign Affairs, 1950–1954,* reel 5, 5–6.

77. U.S. officials had few illusions about Jiang. They reserved their harshest language for him: "The Generalissimo is emulating the control of the Communists over their subjects in order to preserve his personal power. . . . The result is a reign of terror, more silken than in other countries or in other times, but neverthe-

less in progress." Strong to Clubb, September 16, 1950, "Summary of Views on Formosa of Late August 1950," in DOSC, *Formosa Files, 1950–1954,* reel 1.

78. Strong to O. Edmund Clubb, September 6, 1950, DOSC, *China: Internal Affairs, 1950–1954,* reel 1, 1.

79. Department of State Memorandum: What to do about Chiang Kai-shek, January 18, 1951, in ibid., 1–2.

80. O. Edmund Clubb to Merchant, "Chinese Communist Aggression: Counter-moves," May 7, 1951, in ibid.

81. Capt. Wilber W. Hoare Jr., "The Knotty Problem of Formosa," August 1953, in *The Joint Chiefs of Staff and National Policy, DDC,* 1977, pp. 18, 17.

82. "Estimate of a Princeton Graduate Interested in the Far East." July 18, 1951, Livingston Merchant Papers, box 1, Mudd Library, Princeton University.

83. Strong to Clubb, January 20, 1951, in DOSC, *China: Foreign Affairs, 1950–1954,* reel 5.

84. Minutes, Truman-Attlee Conversations, First Meeting, December 4, 1950, *FRUS,* 1950, 3:1712.

85. Philip Jessup, Memorandum for Mr. Rusk, "Relations with Chinese Communists," July 11, 1950, in DOSC, *China: Internal Affairs, 1950–1954,* reel 3.

86. Nehru, *Letters to Chief Ministers*, March 1, 1950, 2:43–44; July 15, 1950, 2:145.

87. Pannikar memo to Nehru, in DOSC, *China, Foreign Affairs, 1950–1954,* reel 4.

88. Ambassador Henderson to Acheson, August 25, 1950, in ibid., reel 6. Pannikar's dispatch is included in Henderson's response to Washington.

89. Various historical accounts point to the difficulties the British had in developing full diplomatic ties with China. The PRC had been quite clear that recognition entailed acknowledgment of its full rights in the United Nations; the British initially refused to vote for the removal of the Nationalists, and then, in July

1950 voted to postpone consideration of the issue. Nehru lamented that "the U.K. Government and Norway, although they have recognized the new China, had stood in the way of its admission to the U.N." (*Letters to Chief Ministers*, August 3, 1950, 2:157).

90. Perkins to Rusk, July 9, 1951, "Effects of a Korean Cease-Fire on the Formosa Problem," in DOSC, *China: Foreign Affairs, 1950–1951*, reel 3.

91. Minutes, Truman-Attlee Conversations, First Meeting, *FRUS*, 1950, 3:1711, 1768, 1770.

92. Formosa, Position Paper Prepared in the Department of State, November 21, 1951, *FRUS*, 1951, 7:1861. The report continued: "Our negotiating position on the Formosa problem is most difficult. We cannot agree to withdraw the 7th fleet under existing circumstances in view of the danger that the CC would take over the island. We are equally unable to indicate that we agree that Formosa should ultimately become part of China since we do not know what Government will control China nor are we in position to support other proposals for the disposition of the island. Our military strength, particularly in the Far East, is still limited. Thus, our position leaves very little room for negotiation at this time."

93. Webb to Lawton, April 17, 1951, *FRUS*, 1951, 7:1632.

94. Perkins to Rusk, July 9, 1951, "Effects of a Korean Cease-Fire on the Formosa Problem," reels 2, 3.

95. Omar Bradley, Memorandum for the Secretary of Defense, "U.S Position with Respect to Formosa," October 24, 1951, in DOSC, *China: Internal Affairs, 1950–1954*, reel 6.

96. NSC Staff Study, "United States Tactics Immediately Following an Armistice in Korea," June 15, 1953, *FRUS*, 1952–54, 15:1176.

97. Along with the effort to isolate China came another objective: until the mid-1960s it was U.S. policy to advocate the overthrow of its government. The historian who tries to adduce what this really meant in terms of covert warfare and propaganda faces an inherently diffi-

cult task, since the operational aspects are impossible to evaluate accurately; references are invariably censored. But the following can be said on the basis of the available documents: before the Korean War, Washington had been casting about for ways to challenge, weaken, and undercut the Chinese communists; Taiwan is only the most obvious example. Contacts with guerrilla groups in China were undertaken before June 25, and the United States was exploring possible participation in arming the Tibetans. Arms sales to the GMD, the blockade, and bombings were more overt acts against the communists; so were the campaigns against diplomatic recognition and for the exclusion of China from the United Nations.

These efforts intensified with the beginning of the Korean War and quickly escalated after China entered it. Long lists of guerrillas operating on the mainland were drawn up, though few reports were optimistic: "They are acting in response to personal motives rather than nationalism or an idea," wrote Clubb to Merchant on May 7, 1951 (in DOSC, *China: Internal Affairs, 1950–1954*, reel 36). But the desire was there to begin small-scale attacks with limited objectives: "A central operations group should be set up immediately to inaugurate at an early date a program to utilize existing resistance groups on the mainland and augment them," wrote Strong to Clubb on January 14, 1951 (in ibid., reel 23). Countless studies of guerrilla forces came from Hong Kong. Exactly how they were used is unclear, though there are suggestions that some supplies went to these forces through Hong Kong, possibly over official British objections. Nor is it clear from the records what the relationship of the GMD was to such activities; the documents suggest a link with American intelligence but are too censored to reveal much, making it hard either to dismiss the seriousness of U.S. operations, as some historians have done, or to credit them with any effectiveness.

Efforts to create a third force, drawing on those in Hong Kong and in the overseas Chinese community who were hostile to the GMD apparently faltered but not for lack of trying (Clubb to Merchant, "Chinese Communist Aggression: Counter-Moves," May 7, 1951, in DOSC, *China: Internal Affairs, 1950–1954*, reel 4). Conflicts with the GMD were sharp, and by 1951, American officials stationed in Taiwan strongly opposed the entire effort as inimical to the strengthening of the Nationalist government.

Within a few days of the Chinese entrance into Korea in November 1950, one memo argued that since Jiang was such a poor alternative to the communists (though "under certain circumstances we might encourage him"), and since the British effort to exploit the "historic conflicts between Russia and China" had not yet born fruit, the United States should "seek to destroy China as a useful ally of Russia by concentrating our efforts on fragmentation. There are powerful traditional and current centrifugal forces at work in China." This course "holds by far the greatest promise of success. . . . The difficulties are great. Not least of them is the fact that this policy would require heavy reliance on covert measures, in the execution of which we are still inexperienced and inept" (Merchant to Rusk, November 17, 1950, in DOSC, *China: Foreign Affairs, 1950–1954*, reel 3).

This theme continued through 1954, with special attention to Xinjiang province, Mongolia and other central Asian areas, and, of course, Tibet. The documents show the intent to act and few, if any, objections to the ideas for doing so (Clubb to Merchant, "Chinese Communist Aggression"). A State Department memorandum spelled out the implications: "The United States desires the overthrow of the Chinese Communist regime; The United States is relatively unconcerned whether the overthrow of the Communist regime creates a state of chaos on the mainland; The U.S. does not wish to take the initiative in creating new, permanent leadership" (Strong to Clubb, January 24, 1951, DOSC, *China: Foreign Relations, 1950–1954*, reel 3).

Though few officials thought much of Jiang, they did think his raids on the mainland might at some point prove useful. But the other choices were painfully few and unpromising. What emerges in the confidential documents is a policy that is coherent at least in its advocacy of practically any method to disrupt and harass. Unifying such efforts or seeking to find a new leadership was not part of the policy—which is why the United States could so bluntly wash its hands of the consequences of possible chaos in China. All these activities originated before the Chinese entrance into Korea but were more widely embraced during the war and throughout much of the decade of the 1950s. Attempting to evaluate the impact on China of any particular one can yield misleading results—but the scattershot approach itself suggests the intensity and the ferocity of the American position.

98. Merchant and Perkins to Dean Rusk, July 9, 1951.

99. Strong memorandum, March 21, 1951, in DOSC, *China: Internal Affairs, 1950–1954*, reel 3.

100. Annex, NSC 48/3, April 26, 1951, in Kesaris, *Documents of the NSC*, 18.

101. Ibid., 3.

102. JCS 1924/49, February 5, 1951, Report by the Joint Intelligence Committee, "Estimate of the Scale and Nature of the Immediate Communist Threat to Security of the United States," in Kesaris, *Records of the Joint Chiefs of Staff*, pt. 2, 1946–53, reel 6.

103. A summary of the issue in Korea and the difficulties of verifying biological warfare is in SIPRI, *The Problem of Chemical and Biological Warfare*, vol. 5 of *The Prevention of Chemical and Biological Warfare* (Stockholm: SIPRI, 1971), 238–58: sect. 3, "Allegations of Biological Warfare in China and Korea, 1952–1953."

104. George A. Morgan, Psychological Strategy Board, Memorandum, July 25, 1952. The fear that this campaign might well prove effective in Asia emerges in "Staff Study—Preliminary Analysis of the Communist BW Propaganda Campaign, with Recommenda-

tions," August 7, 1952, PSB D-25b, *DDC*, 1986, pp. 1–8. See also, "Evaluation of Kremlin's 'hate-America' campaign with particular attention to germ warfare charges," *DDC*, May 13, 1952, 1990.

105. Rosemary Foot, *A Substitute for Victory: The Politics of Peacemaking at the Korean Armistice Talks* (Ithaca: Cornell University Press, 1990), 87.

106. The JCS was deeply worried: "The effect of this prestige has not stopped with the Chinese Communist Armed Forces but extends down to the rank and file of party workers in all the countries of Southeast Asia and strengthens any means used to intimidate those who have remained aloof from political issues. Continued communist propaganda attacks and political pressures to gain their ends have increased in tempo in consonance with their military victories in the North." JCS 1924/49, April 2, 1951, "Soviet Capabilities and Intention in the Far East," Memorandum by the Chief of Staff (Army) for the JCS, April 2, 1951, in Kesaris, *Records of the JCS,* 843.

107. As the draft memo from Acheson and Marshall put it to Truman (February 4, 1952): "It now appears likely that the question of voluntary repatriation of prisoners of war will shortly become the sole remaining fundamental issue in the Korea armistice negotiations. . . . any position on this question entirely unacceptable to the Communists will jeopardize the lives of the prisoners held by the Communists and forestall the possibility of attaining an armistice." Draft Memorandum by the Secretary of State and the Secretary of Defense for the President, "Final US Government Position on Voluntary Repatriation of Prisoners of War in Korea," February 4, 1952, *FRUS*, 1952–54, 15(1): 35.

108. "Final US Government Position on Voluntary Repatriation," 36.

109. Memorandum by the Secretary of State to the President, February 8, 1952, *FRUS*, 1952–54, 15(1): 44. For Acheson's initial opposition to using the POW issue for psychological

warfare purposes and his uneasiness with contravening the Geneva Convention on this point, see Foot, *Substitute for Victory*, 88–95. For an account of the conditions in the POW camps, the psychological warfare and intimidation carried on by Nationalist personnel against those seeking to return to communist China, and the U.S. awareness of the terror against pro-PRC soldiers, see William C. Bradbury, *Mass Behavior in Battle and Captivity: The Communist Soldier in the Korean War* ed. Samuel Meyers and A. D. Biderman (Chicago: University of Chicago Press, 1968), 245–327. Bradbury concluded that the Communist leaders "actually did regard their actions as very largely defensive and to some extent even as legally appropriate. First, as it happened, they were in this instance defending traditional practice with respect to the disposition of prisoners of war. Second, the Marxist-Leninist principles which guided their thinking led inescapably to the judgment that the U.N. personnel had instigated the POW's to act as anti-Communists and that those who opposed repatriation had been forced to become anti-Communists. And third, the Communist organization at this time controlled fewer than a third of the compounds; in most of the others a suspected Communist was not physically safe" (301). Further, Bradbury described the indoctrination techniques used by Nationalist officers, the military discipline and drilling: "Prisoners who exhibited any deviation from the established norms were punished or expelled from the compounds"(323).

110. Quoted in Rosemary Foot, *The Wrong War: American Policy and the Dimensions of the Korean Conflict, 1950–1953* (Ithaca: Cornell University Press, 1985), 108–9.

111. Annex, NSC 48/3, April 26, 1951, in Kesaris, *Documents of the NSC*, 7.

112. DOS, "Additional Economic Measures against Communist China and North Korea," October 31, 1951, *FRUS*, 1951, 7:2032.

113. Memorandum by the Assistant Secretary of State for Far Eastern Affairs (Rusk) to

Secretary of State, "Possible Sale of Rubber from Indonesia to Communist China," May 14, 1951, *FRUS*, 1951, 6:651.

114. Ambassador Cochran to Secretary of State, Djakarta, June 1, 1951, *FRUS*, 1951, 6:670.

115. Secretary of State to the Embassy in Indonesia, May 14, 1951, *FRUS*, 1951, 6:653.

116. The issue was evidently not without exception. If the Indonesians offered to sell needed Chinese tungsten to the United States, the ambassador was to reiterate his opposition but was told in a private aside, *"For your information only*, we have reason to believe that we are going to get the Chinese tungsten by other and more devious means." May 14, 1951, *FRUS*, 1951, 6:652.

117. Many analysts argued that the embargo was depriving China of various needed trade items; others were not so sure. NIE-32, "Effects of Operations in Korea on Internal Situation in Communist China," July 10, 1951, *FRUS*, 7:1737–1741.

118. NIE-32, Effects of Operations in Korea on the Internal Situation in Communist China, July 10, 1951, *ddc*, 1982, p. 9.

119. For example, "FE believes that the losses resulting from a reduction in exports would be important to the Communist regime, not for what they represent in terms of tax revenue, but rather in terms of capital accumulations which the regime could not compensate by levies on cash or domestic agricultural production. It would be important, in short, for its slowing down of the industrialization program of China." Matthews from Rusk, February 8, 1951, in DOSC, *China: Internal Affairs, 1950–1954.*

120. There are innumerable reports on the attitudes of the overseas Chinese communities in countries throughout Southeast Asia. NSC 48/3 continued the calls for cutting their ties with Beijing as an essential step in weakening both China's political influence and possible sources of economic assistance and capital. Annex, NSC 48/3, in Kesaris, *Documents of the NSC*, 25.

121. NSC 141, January 19, 1953, "Reexamination of United States Programs for National Security," in Kesaris, *Documents of the NSC*, 53.

122. Annex to NSC 48/3, Staff Study, 7.

123. John Dower, "Occupied Japan and the Cold War in Asia," in Dower, *Japan in War and Peace: Selected Essays* (New York: New Press, 1993), 179.

124. Ibid., 182.

125. U.S. officials differed as to how quickly and fully Japanese rearmament was necessary, but by 1951 the centrality of the policy was clear: "A durable balance of power cannot be achieved in the Far East until Japan has emerged once more as a military power of the first rank. Its weakness today is as destructive of stability in that area as was its overdeveloped military strength fifteen years ago. The retention of a rearmed, prosperous Japan as a reliable ally should be the foundation of our long-term Far Eastern policy." Merchant, "Estimate of a Princeton Graduate."

126. Draft Report, M. Gay, Far East, November 24, 1952, *DDC*, 1979, 194B.

127. The drafting of the peace treaty with Japan, Prime Minister Yoshida's letter in which he stated that Japan had no intention of establishing diplomatic relations with China, and U.S. nonrecognition policy and backing of Jiang's regime were key factors in how this isolation was accomplished. See Dower, "Occupied Japan." Yoshida himself argued that though the Americans sought in the Yoshida letter to dampen any prospects for trade after 1952, the proposed bilateral treaty with the Nationalists was itself "only a limited one which would not foreclose trade and other ties with the mainland." See Howard Schonberger, "Peacemaking in Asia: The United States, Great Britain, and the Japanese Decision to Recognize Nationalist China, 1951–1952," *Diplomatic History* 10, no. 1 (Winter 1986): 69.

128. State-Defense Draft, "United States Objectives and Courses of Action with Respect to Japan," June 27, 1952, *DDC*, 1995, 1068, p. 3.

129. Ibid., 3, 6.

130. "Interim Policy with Respect to NSC 125," July 18, 1952, *DDC*, 1977, 2480.

131. "The China Debate in Japan," April 2, 1952, in *The Occupation of Japan*, part 2, *U.S. and Allied Policy, 1945–1952*, ed. Makoto Iokibe (Bethesda, Md.: Congressional Information Service, 1991), 4-D-116, 1.

132. Robert Murphy, "The China Policy of an Independent Japan," May 13, 1952, in DOSC, *China: Foreign Affairs, 1950–1954*, reel 4.

133. DOS, Memorandum of Conversation, "Japanese Recognition of China," October 8, 1951, and with "Mr. Stuart (CA) and Mr. Sherman (NA), in DOSC, *China: Internal Affairs, 1950–1954*.

134. As John Dower writes, "Japan did not simply adhere to the lists of embargoed items that the other nations agreed upon; it actually was forced to agree to much more extensive restrictions on trade with China than any of America's other allies" ("Occupied Japan," 192).

135. John Dower, "Yoshida in the Scales of History," in *Japan in War and Peace,* 236–37. The trade-off with Japan also allowed for a focus on economic development instead of military expenditures. This was true of Australia and New Zealand as well.

5. From Monolithic to International Communism

1. NSC 166/1, U.S. Policy toward Communist China, October 19, 1953, in Kesaris, *Documents of the NSC*.

2. NSC 5429/5, Current U.S. Policy in the Far East, December 22, 1954, in Kesaris, *Documents of the NSC*.

3. NSC 166/1, U.S. Policy toward Communist China, November 6, 1953, in Kesaris, *Documents of the NSC*.

4. As one analyst noted in the early months of the Eisenhower administration, "The Chinese Communists never hesitated to press their sovereignty over these areas, even though this necessitated a Russian withdrawal in the case of Manchuria, and the Russian abandonment of already pro-Soviet regimes in Sinkiang and Inner Mongolia." J. L. Barnard to Paul Nitze, April 3, 1953, "Vulnerabilities of the Sino-Soviet Entente," ddc, 1993, 727, pp. 4–5.

5. Ibid., p. 23. Solarium's Task Force "A" simply dismissed the idea that the CCP was "so subject to Moscow's dictation that peripheral aggression or support of internal communist disruption by the Chinese can always be interpreted as supported, or even encouraged, by Moscow." "A Report to the National Security Council by Task Force 'A' of Project Solarium," July 16, 1953, *DDC*, 1984, p. 25.

6. This new perspective on Soviet penetration of the provinces came very quickly in the early days of the Eisenhower administration. In the 169th meeting of the NSC, on November 5, 1953, Dulles went on to point out that "the Soviet Union no longer seemed to be disputing Peiping's authority in such border regions as Manchuria, Sinkiang, and the like." Memorandum of Discussion at 169th session of NSC, November 5, 1953, *FRUS*, 1952–54, 14:266.

7. NIE 13-56, "Chinese Communist Capabilities and Probable Causes of Action through 1960," January 5, 1956, *FRUS*, 1955–57, 3:246.

8. NIE, "Soviet Capabilities and Probable Courses of Action through Mid-1959," September 14, 1954, *FRUS*, 1952–54, 8:1249. See also NIE 13-54, "Communist China's Power Potential through 1957," June 3, 1954, http://www.CIA.gov/nic/foia_china_content.html.

9. NSC Discussion, February 26, 1954, *FRUS*, 1952–54, 7(1):1227.

10. Telegram from the Ambassador in the Soviet Union to DOS, January 27, 1955, *FRUS*, 1955–57, 2:148.

11. NIE 13-56, "Chinese Communist Capabilities," 3:232.

12. Barnard to Nitze, April 3, 1953, "Vulnerabililties."

13. Ibid.

14. NSC 166/1, in Kesaris, *Documents of the NSC*.

15. Memorandum of Restricted Meeting of Chiefs of Delegation, December 7, 1953, *ddc*, 1978, 328D, p. 2.

16. NSC studies suggest in various ways that the calls for fomenting a policy to split China and the USSR were never set in immediate tactical contexts. In January 1954 a special committee was set up to study the exploitation of Soviet vulnerabilities. It found no "strategic concept" that could adequately offer operational guidance for such exploitation. There was too little "clarity and necessary definitive development to be particularly meaningful for planning and conduct of operations." It is hard to find in NSC documents during these years any discussion of practical, tactical, operational methods to hasten the split. See, for example, the extensive "Report on U.S. Policy for the Exploitation of Soviet Vulnerabilities," prepared by special committee under the OCB, June 8, 1954, *ddc* 1995, 2981.

17. Memorandum of a Conversation, Dulles, George Yeh, et al., February 10, 1955, *FRUS*, 1955–57, 2:258.

18. Ibid., 258, 257.

19. Richard H. Immerman, "Confessions of an Eisenhower Revisionist: An Agonizing Reappraisal," *Diplomatic History* 14 (Summer 1990): 341.

20. Memorandum of Restricted Meeting of Chiefs of Delegations, December 7, 1953, *ddc*, 1978, 328D, p. 3.

21. Dulles's hostility, particularly toward negotiations, was hardly limited to China; intense pressure, a standard weapon in his policy arsenal, complemented his similar hostility to negotiations with the Soviets. When the Austrian State Treaty was signed, an effort largely acquiesced in by the United States because of Austrian government initiatives, Dulles called it "just one of those breaks that come, if you keep on steadily, keeping the pressure on." Far more often than not, relentless hostility was his public stance toward the USSR, China, and others—a view shared by the JCS, who saw negotiation as a sign of weakness—at least in the eyes of wavering allies and neutrals ("it will be not only fruitless but hazardous for the United States to continue its efforts to arrive at solutions to world problems through the normal processes of negotiation with the USSR"). See Gunter Bischof, "Eisenhower, the Summit, and the Austrian Treaty, 1953–1955," in *Eisenhower: A Centenary Assessment*, ed. Gunter Bischof and Stephen E. Ambrose (Baton Rouge: Louisiana University Press, 1995), 157–58.

22. As Rosemary Foot writes, "Eisenhower and Dulles were well aware that any easing of international tension could backfire if it undermined the unity of the anti-communist bloc and the set of policies the United States had been developing since the start of the cold war." "Anglo-American Relations and China Policy," in *The Great Powers in East Asia: 1953–1960*, ed. Warren I. Cohen and Akira Iriye (New York: Columbia University Press, 1990), 144.

23. NSC 5906/1, Basic National Security Policy, 25, August 5, 1959, *DDC*, 1983.

24. NSC 5501, Basic National Security Policy, January 7, 1955, *DDC*.

25. Current Communist Tactics, April 12, 1953, *FRUS*, 1952–54, 8:1162.

26. Bohlen to DOS, July 9, 1953, *FRUS*, 1952–54, 8:1205–6.

27. See the intelligence analysis of March 1953, "The Communist Peace Offensive," *DDC*, 1995, 2722, p. 1.

28. NIE 100-7-55, "World Situations and Trends," November 1, 1955, *FRUS*, 1955–57, 19:131.

29. Lodge to Eisenhower, March 5, 1956, *FRUS*, 1955–57, 10:68.

30. Special Estimate 46, "Probable Long Term Development of the Soviet Bloc and Western Power Positions," *FRUS*, 1952–54, 8:1203.

31. NSC 5501, January 7, 1955, *DDC*.

32. DOS Comments on NSC 5501, October 3, 1955, *FRUS*, 1955–57, 19:124.

33. Ibid., 123.

34. DOS Comments on NSC 5501, 123. The Joint Chiefs' frequent warnings of the perils of negotiating with the Russians were mild compared with its warnings about China. See Memorandum of Discussion, 178th meeting of the NSC, March 1, 1956, *FRUS*, 1955–57, 19:222.

35. NIE 100-7-55, "World Situations and Trends," 19:141.

36. Ibid.

37. NIE-65, "Soviet Bloc Capabilities through 1957," June 16, 1953, *FRUS*, 1952–54, 8:1188.

38. Eisenhower repeatedly invoked this dichotomy both publicly and in his private correspondence and discussions, insisting, for example, that "underlying the whole" is the "most important fact of today's life": the "irreconcilable conflict between the theories of the Communist dictatorship and the basic principles of free world existence." Eisenhower to General Gruenther, February 1, 1955, *FRUS*, 1955–57, 2:190.

39. President Eisenhower to Lewis W. Douglas, March 29, 1955, *FRUS*, 1955–57, 2:422.

40. NSC 5414, March 17, 1954, *DDC*, 1995, 2343.

41. As Robert Wampler notes, this debate took place within the military as well. "The battleground was the Joint Strategic Objectives Plan for 1960. On one side stood JCS chairman Admiral Arthur Radford, who, with the air force and navy chiefs, held that by basing all planning on the use of nuclear weapons and providing for the worst case—all-out war with the Soviets—the United States would also be ready to meet lesser threats. On the other side stood Maxwell Taylor, army chief of staff, who argued that the growth in U.S. and Soviet nuclear stockpiles would result in a situation of mutual deterrence making all-out war very unlikely, but limited wars much more likely." Wampler, "Eisenhower, NATO, and Nuclear Weapons," in Bischof and Ambrose, *Eisenhower*, 174. See also the antecedents of this debate in David A. Rosenberg, "The Origins of Overkill: Nuclear Weapons and American

Strategy, 1945–1960," *International Security*, 7 (Spring 1983): 3–71.

42. In the event of war, it was essential to leave both the Soviet Union and China "incapable of further harming the U.S. after the end of hostilities." Summary of the 398th meeting of the NSC, March 5, 1959, quoted in Gordon Chang, "Eisenhower and Mao's China," in Bischof and Ambrose, *Eisenhower*, 196–97.

43. A. M. Bickel to Mr. O'Connor, February 26, 1954, "Quoted text for Secretary Dulles Speech in Caracas," in box 68, Dulles Papers, Mudd Library, Princeton University.

44. Dulles quoted in John Lewis Gaddis, *Strategies of Containment: A Critical Appraisal of Postwar American National Security Policy* (New York: Oxford University Press, 1982), 145.

45. John Foster Dulles, News Conference No. 237, April 23, 1957, Box 114, Dulles Papers.

46. John Lewis Gaddis, "The Unexpected John Foster Dulles: Nuclear Weapons, Communism, and the Russians," in *John Foster Dulles and the Diplomacy of the Cold War*, ed. Richard N. Immerman (Princeton: Princeton University Press, 1990), 67.

47. Ibid.

48. Ibid., 76.

49. Gordon Gray, Memo to Under Secretary of State, January 14, 1959, *DDC*, 1986, 1065.

50. Eden Talks Memorandum, February 7, 1956, *DDC*, 1997, 6772.

51. "The Sino-Soviet Relation and Its Potential Sources of Difference," background paper prepared in the Department of State for the U.S. delegation to the Geneva conference, April 6, 1954, *FRUS*, 1952–54, 14.

52. Paper Prepared by Spencer Barnes, PPS, "Policy toward the Communist States of Eastern Europe, Exclusive of the USSR," August 26, 1958, *FRUS*, 1958–60, 10:48.

53. NSC 5811/1, "Operations Coordinating Board Report on Soviet-Dominated Nations in Eastern Europe," July 15, 1959, *FRUS*, 1958–60, 10:95–96. See also NIE 100-3-60, "Sino-Soviet Relations," August 9, 1960, 4,

www.foia.cia.gov/. China's "revolutionary mood" is contrasted with the "relatively mature and affluent Soviet Union" that has "reached the stage where it is giving greater attention to the working conditions and living standards of its people."

54. John Foster Dulles, Address at the 33rd National 4-H Club Congress, Chicago, November 29, 1954, box 79, PRC file, Dulles Papers.

55. Quantico Report, Asia Policy, Report of the Quantico Vulnerabilities Panel (Rostow), June 10, 1955, *DDC*, 1982, 0337.

56. The effect of the American refusal to recognize China was unclear. "It is entirely possible that the Chinese Communists will continue to run amuck until we recognize them and deal with them directly rather than through the Soviet Union as an intermediary. On the other hand, there can be no assurance that if we do recognize them, they will not continue to misbehave." Secretary of State to the President, February 16, 1954, *DDC*, 1993, 2205.

57. NIE 100-7-55, "World Situations and Trends," 19:137.

58. Memorandum of a Conversation between Secretary Dulles and Mr. Krishna Menon, March 24, 1955, *FRUS*, 1955–57, 2:393.

59. Memorandum of a Conversation, September 9, 1955, *FRUS*, 1955–57, 3:83.

60. Memorandum of a Conversation between President Eisenhower and Prime Minister Nehru, December 19, 1956, *FRUS*, 1955–57, 8:337.

61. Diary Entry by the President, March 26, 1955, *FRUS*, 1955–57, 2:405.

62. Historians have noted this similarity of tone and approach between public and private in other areas as well: e.g., "In regard to Latin America the private discussions and classified policy statements of administration officials differed little from their public positions." Stephen G. Rabe, "Dulles, Latin America, and Cold War Anticommunism," in Immerman, *John Foster Dulles*, 161.

63. John Foster Dulles, Remarks to the Advertising Club of New York, March 21, 1955, box 90, PRC file, Dulles Papers.

64. NIE 100-3-60, "Sino-Soviet Relations," 1–5.

65. "Soviet Goals at Geneva," box 90, Dulles Papers.

66. Draft Paper of PPS (N. Spencer Barnes), June 27, 1958, *FRUS*, 1958–60, 10(1): 43.

67. John Foster Dulles, DOS Press Conference, July 28, 1953, box 68, PRC File, Dulles Papers.

68. NSC, Memorandum at the 362nd Meeting of the NSC, April 14, 1958, *ddc*, 1995, 1096.

69. NSC 5811/1, Statement of U.S. Policy toward the Soviet-Dominated Nationals in Eastern Europe, May 24, 1958, *FRUS*, 1958–60, part 1, 10:21–22.

70. Annex, NSC 5608, July 6, 1956, *FRUS*, 1955–57, 25:202.

71. Ibid., 25:205.

72. Progress Report Submitted by the Operations Coordinating Board to the National Security Council, February 29, 1956, *FRUS*, 1955–57, 25:126.

73. Record of meeting, January 28, 1953; Memorandum of conversation by Dulles, March 24, 1953, *FRUS*, 1952–54, 13:361–62, 419–20.

74. Memo on NSC's 211th Meeting, August 18, 1954, *FRUS*, 1952–54, 14:526–40.

75. Walt W. Rostow, *The Prospects for Communist China* (New York: Wiley & Sons, 1954), 310.

76. For example, see "Report on Foreign Economic Policy Discussions between United States Officials in the Far East and Clarence B. Randall and Associates," September 1956, *ddc*, 1991, 429B.

77. NSC 166/1, U.S. Policy toward Communist China, in Kesaris, *Documents of the NSC*, 30.

78. Telegram from the Embassy in Japan to DOS, December 16, 1960, *FRUS*, 1958–60, 18:420.

79. Eisenhower Diary entry, March 30, 1955, *FRUS*, 1955–57, 19:276.

80. Memorandum of Discussion at the 244th Meeting of the NSC, April 7, 1955, *DDC*, 1997, 2258.

81. "Japan needs solid dependable foreign trade, not kind found on China mainland which never was really major Japanese market." "Circular telegram from DOS to Certain Diplomatic Missions," October 11, 1957, *FRUS*, 1955–57, 21:399.

82. Minutes of ANZUS Meeting, October 4, 1957, *FRUS*, 1955–57, 21:382.

83. The complex ways in which the United States worked to assist Japanese exports in the 1950s and 1960s are less significant here than the anticommunist rationale that was invoked to open up the market. During the 1950s the balance-of-payments problems had not yet fully surfaced, but the tenacity of domestic interests opposing the opening of the American market was intense, as was repeated invocation of the communist threat to justify the creation of a certain kind of international market system. On the primacy of such "political economic needs" over domestic economic interests, see Alfred E. Eckes Jr., *Opening America's Market: U.S. Foreign Trade Policy since 1776* (Chapel Hill: University of North Carolina Press, 1995). Eckes's examination suffers from the sharp line he draws between political and economic interests, as though key economic groups did not profit from the opening of the American market to Japanese imports and, in time, those of other "underdeveloped areas." He points to profits by key financial and banking interests but does not fully carry his argument through, implying that the economy as a whole suffered from such policies without examining who benefited.

84. Gary Saxonhouse, "Economic Relations with the United States, 1945–73," in *Kodansha Encyclopedia of Japan* (Tokyo: Kodansha, 1983), 8:161. Indeed, the British chafed at American pressure to bow to Japanese economic needs: "Washington was intent on what British offi-cials felt was the imposition of a preferential series of financial and commercial arrangements for Japan." Roger Buckley, "Anglo-Japanese Relations, 1952–1960," in Cohen and Iriye, *Great Powers in East Asia*, 176.

85. Telegram from the Embassy in Japan to DOS, June 24, 1960, *FRUS*, 1958–60, 18:378.

86. Report by Chairman of Council of Foreign Ecomomic Policy, *FRUS*, 1955–1957, 9:38.

87. Ibid., 35.

88. Staff Report on American Economic Foreign Policy, "Tentative Conclusions Based on Re-examination of American Economic Foreign Policy," October 7, 1953, *ddc*, 1992, 836, pp. 7, 37.

89. Burton I. Kaufman writes: "By the end of Eisenhower's second year in office . . . the administration had responded to what it perceived as a critical situation in East Asia by designing a foreign economic policy intended to keep Communist China economically isolated, promote the region's economic growth along integrated lines, and tie that growth to Japan's own economic development." He then argues that the program was a failure: the embargo was not successfully maintained; cuts were made in aid to East Asia; Japan's trading problem remained unsolved; it became more competitive with its trading rivals, and so forth. But his argument does not satisfactorily separate the intended consequences of economic policy from the unintended ones. Administration officials saw the economic situation in Asia slowly improving. They debated the embargoes and trade issues, yet their policy successfully prevented China from extending its trade in East Asia. If it also led to increased Japanese competition with trade rivals, this development came nonetheless in the context of an emerging economic system in Asia that suited long-term U.S. objectives. Whether it was compatible with other American objectives and interests remains an open question. See Kaufman, "Eisenhower's Foreign Economic Policy with Respect to East Asia," in Cohen and Iriye, *Great Powers in East Asia*, 107–8.

90. Quoted in Gordon Chang, *Friends and Enemies: The United States, China, and the Soviet Union, 1948–1972* (Stanford, Calif.: Stanford University Press, 1990), 90.

91. As Chang notes, in the short term this two-China stance was also compatible with Dulles's "overall approach toward China, consistent with aggressive efforts to isolate the Chinese Communists" (ibid., 149). But even here, Dulles's approach is best viewed in the context of his sense of the time those efforts might take, and some of the altered contexts that over the course of time might develop.

92. Dulles conversation with Sir Roger Makins, February 7, 1955, *FRUS*, 1955–57, 2:236. Gaddis quotes this discussion but slights the emphasis on the changing Asia that Dulles always saw as critical to future political and economic balance-of-power considerations and thus some of the reasons why Dulles did not move quickly, given signs of Chinese and Russians disagreements. See Gaddis, "Unexpected John Foster Dulles," 63.

93. Briefing Paper, Far Eastern Division, December 13, 1954, "Communist China—Policy and Problems," in DOSC, *China: Foreign Affairs, 1950–1954*, reel 12.

94. Stephen E. Ambrose, *Eisenhower: The President* (New York: Simon and Schuster, 1984), 284, 202, 39.

95. NSC, Progress Report on United States Policy on Economic Defense, Secretary of State and the Director, Foreign Operations Administration, August 30, 1954, *DDC*, 2000.

96. The large Chinese communities in Southeast Asia, it was feared, could provide "the Chinese Communists with a significant potential channel of subversion," especially among youth. But the split in allegiance induced by Taiwan, along with the political apathy of many overseas Chinese, were invaluable for restraining the influence of the PRC—and limiting the economic ties that consequently developed with Beijing. See the analysis in NIE 10-7-54, "Communist Courses of Action in Asia through 1957," November 23, 1954, *DDC*, 1977, 3A.

97. NIE 13-2-57, "Communist China's Role in Non-Communist Asia," December 3, 1957, *ddc*, 1977, 6A, p. 2.

98. Memorandum of a Conversation, Dulles and Nationalist Foreign Minister Yeh, October 4, 1955, *FRUS*, 1955–57, 3:108.

99. Memorandum from Deputy Assistant Secretary of State for Far Eastern Economic Affairs (Jones) to Special Assistant to the President (Randall), November 20, 1956, *FRUS*, 1955–57, 10:134.

100. Memorandum from Chairman of the Joint Chiefs (Radford) to Secretary of Defense (Wilson), December 12, 1955, *FRUS*, 1955–57, 10:281.

101. Memorandum of Dulles and Yeh conversation.

102. A. Doak Barnett, *Communist China and Asia: Challenge to American Policy* (New York: Harper, 1960), 451–52.

103. The pressure on the British regarding trade finally gave way in late 1956 and early 1957: "After Suez they saw less reason than ever to keep in step with US policy, and in addition Suez had highlighted the need to strengthen Britain's economy for political and strategic reasons as well as for economic ones. As a result the British decided to try to abolish the China differential." Alan P. Dobson, *The Politics of the Anglo-American Economic Special Relationship, 1940–1987* (Sussex, U.K.: Wheatsheaf Books, 1988), 178.

104. NSC 166/1, in Kesaris, *Documents of the NSC*, 28.

105. For example, see Progress Report on PSB-D-23, "US Psychological Strategy Report on Thailand," January 27, 1954, *DDC*, 1995, 2965.

106. Letter from Acting Officer in Charge of Thai and Malayan Affairs (Foster) to Ambassador in Thailand (Peurifoy), June 22, 1955, *FRUS*, 1955–57, 22:825.

107. These contacts were closely followed and discussed in NSC meetings. American offi-

cials had extensive reports as to which Thai officials were undertaking contacts with Beijing, though the existing records are unclear as to whether they knew the full scope of the developing ties: the secret friendship agreement signed by the Chinese ambassador and Prime Minister Pibul in Rangoon in 1956, or the decision of Pibul's closest confidant and foreign security advisor to have two of his children secretly sent to China to be raised under Premier Zhou Enlai's auspices. For this aspect of Thai-Chinese-American relations, see Sirin Phanthanothai and James Peck, *The Dragon's Pearl* (New York: Simon and Schuster, 1994).

108. Telegram from DOS to Embassy in Thailand, June 23, 1956. *FRUS*, 1955–57, 22:892–93.

109. "In spite our patient educational efforts only Pibul has consistently demonstrated that he understands nature and danger of international communism," wrote Ambassador Max Bishop from Bangkok in May 1957, *FRUS*, 1955–57, 22:918.

110. Telegram from DOS to Embassy in Thailand, May 9, 1957, *FRUS*, 1955–57, 22:916.

111. Memorandum: Situation in China, June 14, 1957, box 114, PRC file, Dulles Papers.

112. John Foster Dulles to Arthur Sulzberger, April 30, 1957, box 114, Dulles Papers.

113. See Harry Harding, "The Evolution of American Scholarship on Contemporary China," in *American Studies of Contemporary China*, ed. David Shambaugh (Armonk, N.Y.: M. E. Sharpe, 1993), 18.

114. NSC 153/1, "Restatement of Basic National Security Policy," June 10, 1953, in Tractenberg, *Development of American Strategic Thought*.

115. NSC 5707, "Review of Basic National Security Policy: Basic Problems for U.S. Security Arising out of Changes in the World Situation," February 19, 1957, in Kesaris, *Documents of the NSC*.

116. Conference at the White House, July 31, 1956, *FRUS*, 1955–57, 26:64.

117. SNIE 30-3-56, "Nasser and the Middle East Situation," July 31, 1956, *FRUS*, 1955–57, 16:80.

118. Paper by Secretary of State's Special Assistant (Russell), August 4, 1956, *FRUS*, 1955–57, 16:141–42.

119. Memorandum from JCS to Secretary of Defense, August 3, 1956, *FRUS*, 1955–57, 16:155.

120. Memorandum from the Acting Executive Secretary of the NSC (Boggs) to the NSC, August 22, 1956, *FRUS*, 1955–57, 16:265, 154.

121. Fawaz A. Gerges, *The Superpowers and the Middle East: Regional and International Politics, 1955–1967* (Boulder, Colo.: Westview Press, 1994), 37, 53. Gerges is here quoting the protests of a "lone" American diplomat, Ambassador Henry A. Byroade in Egypt, against the distortive prism of anticommunism. This distorted perception led to the internationalization of regional conflicts. The Syrian crisis was a case in point: Eisenhower and Dulles saw "what was essentially a local power struggle in cold war terms" (Gerges, 89). American actions were thus portrayed as "handicapped by a Cold War ideology that divided Third World states into enemies or clients. Global interpretations were imposed on local disputes and produced results contrary to those intended" (95). Thus Dulles would often see Nasser as Moscow's man rather than his own.

122. Eden to Eisenhower, November 5, 1956, *DDC*, 1995, 2631.

123. Memorandum of Discussion at 302d meeting of the NSC, November 1, 1956, *FRUS*, 1955–57, 16:906.

124. U.S. diplomats in Chile wrote of the effective "Communist" campaigns that portrayed the copper companies in Chile as imperialistic: "They take copper out of Chile and leave nothing but a hole in the ground. . . . [T]he United States buys Chile's raw materials cheap and sells Chile manufactured goods at high prices." All this compounds the problems that arise from "influential segments of Latin American opinion" which "equate the attainment of

an economy less dependent on the U.S. market and on the operation of large U.S. companies with the achievement of full sovereignty." Ambassador in Chile to DOS, February 2, 1955, *FRUS*, 7:376.

125. The United States consistently opposed the subsidies for state-sector development, particularly in crucial industries—an act that Washington knew was highly unpopular but believed critical in the long run in Latin America to the evolution of a market system compatible with U.S. interests. The risk of autarky remained in statist approaches, a step seen as nothing but "outweighing [rational] economic calculation." NSC, Study of U.S. Problems and Policy toward Latin America, October 14, 1953, *DDC*, 1982. Also see Gerald K. Haines, *The Americanization of Brazil: A Study of U.S. Cold War Diplomacy in the Third World, 1945–1954* (Wilmington, Del.: Scholarly Resources, 1989), ix.

126. "Current Economic Development: Economic Questions at UN General Assembly," December 20, 1955, *FRUS*, 1957–59, 9:361.

127. Progress Report on NSC 5432/1, January 19, 1955, in Kesaris, *Documents of the NSC*.

128. Ibid.

129. "Latin America, a Study of US Problems and Policy," October 14, 1953, *DDC*, 1982, 255, p. 6.

130. Haines, *Americanization of Brazil*, 32.

131. Stephen G. Rabe, *Eisenhower and Latin America: The Foreign Policy of Anticommunism* (Chapel Hill: University of North Carolina Press, 1988), 40.

132. Haines, *Americanization of Brazil*, 63–64.

133. Samir Amin, *Maldevelopment: Anatomy of a Global Failure* (London: Zed Books, 1990).

134. NIE 13-57, "Communist China through 1961," March 19, 1957, *FRUS*, 1955–57, 3:506–7.

135. NIE 13-2-57, "Communist China's Role in Non-Communist Asia," December 3, 1957, *FRUS*, 1955–57, 3:649–50.

136. Memorandum of Discussion at the 273rd Meeting of the NSC, January 18, 1956, *FRUS*, 1955–57, 10:64.

137. India was a concern from the earliest days of the Eisenhower administration. The Congress Party appeared to be failing to counter the appeal of Beijing's model, and Chinese propaganda was finding a highly favorable environment in India. Visitors to China returned impressed. See, for example, "Chinese Communist Prestige in India," T. Eliot Weil (Counselor of Embassy) to DOS, August 17, 1953, in DOSC, *China: Internal Affairs*, reel 25.

138. Annex, NSC 5602/1, "Basic National Security Policy," March 15, 1956, in Trachtenberg, *Development of American Strategic Thought*, 27.

139. NSC 5701, U.S. Policy toward South Asia, January 10, 1957, *FRUS*, 1955–57, 8:29–43.

140. The 314th NSC meeting, February 28, 1957, *FRUS*, 1955–57, 3:491.

141. Memorandum for NSC Planning Board, "Current Policy in the Far East," June 29, 1959, draft revision of NSC 5429/5, in *The Pentagon Papers* (Washington, D.C.: Government Printing Office, 1971), 10:1198.

142. Audrey R. Kahin and George McT. Kahin, *Subversion as Foreign Policy: The Secret Eisenhower and Dulles Debacle in Indonesia* (New York: New Press, 1995), 81–82.

143. See W. W. Rostow's study on the Gossard China questions, January 8, 1954, *DDC*, 1979, 99A, p. 33.

144. The Genis China project began in 1953 to reevaluate and reinterpret psychological warfare methods against China; see ibid., 33, 35.

145. Ibid., 6.

146. Dulles made this point strongly to Eden in their talks from January 30 to February 1, 1956. "Eden Talks, Memorandum," February 7, 1956, *DDC*, 1997, 5108, p. 18.

6. Taiwan and the Uses of Tension

1. "Policy Implications of Stalin's Death," March 10, 1953, *FRUS*, 1952–54, 8:1110.

2. John Foster Dulles was adamant about this connection throughout his term as Secre-

tary of State. "The course of action which would most certainly undermine the Chinese Nationalist Government on Taiwan and lose the island to the Communists," he said in February 1957, "would be a general settlement, between the United States and Communist China. The President said he agreed with this statement of Secretary Dulles." Memorandum of Discussion at 314th Meeting of the NSC, February 29, 1957, *FRUS*, 1955–57, 19:438.

3. Box 68, Dulles Papers.

4. Ogburn to Robertson, Bureau of Far Eastern Affairs, "Principles of a Settlement with Communist China," June 12, 1953, in DOSC, *China: Internal Affaris, 1950–1954*, reel 9.

5. Annex B, NSC 5429/3, "Current U.S. Policy in the Far East," in transmittal note to NSC, December 10, 1954, *DDC*.

6. Memorandum of Discussion at 211th Meeting of the NSC August 18, 1954, *FRUS*, 1952–54, 14:752.

7. Bevin Alexander, *The Strange Connection: U.S. Intervention in China, 1944–1972* (New York: Greenwood Press, 1992), 143. Also see *FRUS*, 1952–54, 12:262–63, 270, 397–99, 545–47, 827–39.

8. This and following quotations from "Current U.S. Policy in the Far East," December 10, 1954, *DDC*, 1981, 490A.

9. Ibid. The history and extent of these operations is one of the less well-recorded aspects of American-Chinese relations, involving, as it does, links between the covert operations of the Guomindang and Washington. Their scope is indicated only by the time taken up in discussing how to acquire more control over Nationalist operations. There are many expressions of concern at the escalation of hostilities as a result of Nationalist activities but few proposals for putting an end to them. The JCS as often as not found such raids useful. Others, though knowing that Jiang could not easily be controlled, sought to stop them. Major U.S. allies in Europe and major Asian countries (India, Indonesia, Japan) opposed them, though without believing that their opposition made much difference.

10. Memorandum of a Conversation with British Secretary Lloyd, January 31, 1956, *FRUS*, 1955–57, 3:292.

11. Memo on 211th Meeting of the NSC, August 18, 1954, *FRUS*, 1952–54, 14:526–40.

12. CIA Special Estimate, "Probable Reaction to a Chinese Nationalist Retaking of Hainan with Direct U.S. Air and Naval Participation," September 9, 1953, *DDC*, 1995, 2407.

13. President Eisenhower to British Prime Minister Churchill, January 25 and March 29, 1955, *FRUS*, 1955–57, 2:129, 419, 421.

14. Eisenhower to Gruenther, February 1, 1955, *FRUS*, 1955–57, 2:189; Eisenhower to Churchill, February 10, 1955, *FRUS*, 1955–57, 2:260.

15. Robert McClintock, "Review of U.S. China Policy: A Pacific Settlement?" December 31, 1955, *FRUS*, 1955–57, 3:660–73, 668–69, 672

16. NIE 13-2-57, "Communist China's Role in Non-Communist Asia," December 3, 1957, *FRUS*, 1955–57, 3:652.

17. Ambassador U. Alexis Johnson to the Director of the Office of Chinese Affairs, November 1, 1955, *FRUS*, 1955–57, 3:151.

18. Paper Prepared by Robert McClintock of the Policy Planning Staff, December 31, 1957, *FRUS*, 1955–57, 3:667.

19. Memorandum of Conversation with British Foreign Secretary Lloyd, January 31, 1956, *FRUS*, 1955–57, 3:290.

20. Stephen Ambrose argues that neither Eisenhower nor Dulles believed reduction of tensions to be truly viable with implacable enemies: "At bottom, Eisenhower agreed with [Dulles's] assessment: he often said that there could be no genuine peace until the Soviet system was fundamentally changed internally. But he did want propaganda victories, which was the motive for his search for new ideas." Nonetheless, it was essential not to be outmaneuvered on the issue of reducing tensions and increasing contacts, and in the last years of the

Eisenhower administration, these contacts assumed greater significance. Ambrose, *Eisenhower: Soldier and President* (New York: Simon and Schuster, 1990), 445.

21. Eisenhower to Gruenther, February 1, 1955, *FRUS*, 1955–57, 2:190.

22. NIE 13-2-57, "Communist China's Role in Non-Communist Asia," 3:653.

23. Memorandum of Conversation, "Policy concerning Travel of Americans to Communist China," February 18, 1957, *FRUS*, 1955–57, 3:482.

24. NIE 13-57, "Communist China through 1961," March 19, 1957, *FRUS*, 1955–57, 3:509.

25. A willingness to negotiate at Geneva was argued to be necessary to hold the line on trade. "Only [the] fact that we are negotiating with Chinese Communists at Geneva enabled us to forestall probably successful action to this end [pressure to reduce trade restrictions from CHINCOM level] at forthcoming CG meeting in December." Hoover to American embassy, Republic of China, November 25, 1955, *FRUS*, 1955–57, 3:186.

26. Djakarta Embassy Dispatch, "Evaluation of the Bandung Conference," n.d., *DDC*, 1995, 1280, p. 2.

27. Papers for Geneva, Paper IV, "Estimates of Prospects of the Soviet Union Achieving Its Goals," box 90, PRC file, Dulles Papers.

28. *FRUS*, 1952–54, 16:674–75, quoted in Leonard A. Kusnitz, *Public Opinion and Foreign Policy: America's China Policy, 1949–1979* (Westport, Conn.: Greenwood Press, 1984), 67.

29. The issue of American prisoners was highly complicated. In public, the United States denied Chinese claims that they included CIA personnel; in private, it acknowledged that some were. State Department documents conceded that "Peiping probably feels that it has a convincing case against the US prisoners, or at least against certain of them" (NIE 100-6-54, "World Reactions to Certain Possible US Courses of Action against Communist China," November 28, 1954, *FRUS*, 1952–54, 14:951–56). But this could not be

debated in public, so U.S. government denials emphasized the inhumane treatment of prisoners and lack of Red Cross access, avoiding the issues of CIA, spying, and Nationalist/U.S. covert activities.

30. Ambassador U. Alexis Johnson to Director of the Office of Chinese Affairs (McConaughy), October 21, 1955, *FRUS*, 1955–57, 3:136–38.

31. John Foster Dulles, Presentation to U.S. Chiefs of Mission, Far East, in Manila, March 2, 1955, box 98, Dulles Papers.

32. Ambassador Johnson to McConaughy, 3:137.

33. Telegram from DOS to Ambassador Johnson, November 19, 1955, *FRUS*, 1955–57, 3:178, 7 n.

34. Telegrams from Johnson to DOS, December 1–2, 1955, *FRUS*, 1955–57, 3:194 and 4 n, 200.

35. Secretary of State to Johnson, December 6 and 7, 1955, *FRUS*, 1955–57, 3:206, 208.

36. Robertson (Assistant Secretary of State for the Far East) to Dulles, December 12, 1955, *FRUS*, 1955–57, 3:221.

37. Johnson to DOS, December 15, 1955, and Johnson letter No. 19 to McConaughy, December 16, *FRUS*, 1955–57, 3:223–24, and 223 n.

38. Johnson to DOS, December 22, 1955, *FRUS*, 1955–57, 3:230 n.

39. Alfred D. Wilhelm Jr., *The Chinese at the Negotiating Table* (Washington, D.C.: National Defense University Press, 1994), 193–94.

40. Prime Minister to Eisenhower, December 12, 1956, *FRUS*, 1955–57, 3:449.

41. McConaughy to Robertson, October 1, 1956, *FRUS*, 1955–57, 3:433–34.

42. Dulles, "Presentation to U.S. Chiefs of Mission, Far East."

43. Memorandum of Conversation, Secretary Dulles and Ambassador Koo, February 10, 1955, *FRUS*, 1955–57, 2:251–59.

44. Gordon Chang, *Friends and Enemies: The United States, China, and the Soviet Union, 1948–1972* (Stanford, Calif.: Stanford University Press, 1990), 120–21.

45. See SNIE 100-9-58, "Probable developments in the Taiwan Strait," August 26, 1958; and SNIE 100-11-58, "Probable Chinese Communist and Soviet Intention in the Taiwan Strait Area," September 16, 1958, www. foia.cia.gov/.

46. M. H. Halperin, "*The 1958 Taiwan Straits Crisis: A Documented History*," Memorandum RM-4900-ISA, *DDC*, 1979, 3210.

47. John Foster Dulles, "Review and Reappraisal: ROC role needs adequate role or faces liquidation," October 28, 1958, box 127, Dulles Papers.

48. Halperin, "*1958 Taiwan Straits Crisis*," 506.

49. This idea of Taiwan as a model came up repeatedly after the beginning of the Korean War, but it was hard to promote. Jiang was one reason; the antipathy of allies and neutrals was another. A January 1951 ORI report had made a case that continued to hold for some years and that paralleled Dulles's own later thoughts: "The natural resources on Formosa, if properly exploited, should permit the development of an economy relatively prosperous by Asian standards which, if accompanied by reasonable good government, might make of Formosa a dramatic demonstration for Asia of what can be done with Asian resources under non-communist administration. The contrast between conditions on Formosa and in China proper might become in time a powerful argument against communism as the solution for Asian problems. Formosa might be today the economic show window of Asia, were it not for its military overload." ORI report, Memorandum—Formosa," in DOSC, *China: Internal Affairs, 1950–1954,* reel 4.

50. John Foster Dulles, "Review and Reappraisal: ROC Needs Adequate Role or Faces Liquidation," October 28, 1958, box 127, Dulles Papers.

51. Ibid., quoted in Halperin, *1958 Taiwan Straits Crisis*, 514.

52. Ibid.

53. Ibid.

54. Eisenhower quoted in Halperin, *1958 Taiwan Straits Crisis*, 272.

55. Ambassador Johnson to Director of the Office of Chinese Affairs, October 21, 1955, *FRUS*, 1955–57, 3:136–38.

56. Halperin, *1958 Taiwan Straits Crisis*, 138.

57. Ibid., ix. As Halperin argues, "The Nationalists' maneuver to secure a U.S. backing for defense of Quemoy [Jinmin] can be seen, as it probably was, as part of the effort to involve the United States in what was expected to be the oncoming military move against Quemoy or Matsu, or perhaps one of the smaller Offshore Islands. The Chinese Nationalists were probably not interested in deterring a Chinese Communist move by a U.S. declaration, but rather enhancing the probability of a U.S. involvement by securing a public U.S. commitment prior to the outbreak of the crisis."

58. NIE-13-60, "Communist China," December 6, 1960, 20, www.foia.cia.gov/.

59. John Foster Dulles, "Our Policies toward Communism in China," June 28, 1957, *FRUS*, 1955–57, 3:558–66.

60. Memorandum from Assistant Secretary of State for Policy Planning (Bowie) to Secretary of State, Comments on San Francisco Speech, June 19, 1957, *FRUS*, 1955–57, 3:545–46.

61. Ibid., 548.

62. Ibid.

63. Washington was well aware that the renunciation-of-force issue was fundamentally about Taiwan. In the latter years of the Eisenhower administration it was repeatedly noted that Beijing worried that a policy of "peaceful existence" meant an accommodation done at the expense of their interests in Taiwan. See NIE 13-58, "Communist China," May 13, 1958, and NIE 13-60, "Communist China," December 6, 1960, www.foia.cia.gov/.

64. NSC 5913/1, "U.S. Policy in the Far East," September 25, 1959, *DDC*.

65. Background Paper, "Khrushchev Objectives and Tactics while in the US," September 4, 1959, *ddc*, 1992, 3590.

66. Eisenhower to Khrushchev, September 29, 1959 (sent through Moscow embassy), *ddc*, 1992, 3591.

67. See Memorandum of Conversation, September 26–27, 1959, *ddc*, 1982, 1090, pp. 1–6.

7. Revolutionary China and Containment without Isolation

1. Quoted in Arthur Schlesinger Jr., *A Thousand Days: John F. Kennedy in the White House* (Boston: Little, Brown, 1965), 280.

2. Ibid., 324, 176.

3. "Communist China: Long Range Study on Economic Trends and Prospects in Communist China," June 1966, Annex VII-2, *DDC*, 1990, 3185 (hereafter cited as "Long Range Study").

4. DOS memorandum, "Paper regarding measures which the U.S. and the USSR could apply to China to persuade that country to accept the terms of a nuclear test ban," n.d., *DDC*, 1997, 1481.

5. "Long Range Study," app. V-2.

6. Ibid.

7. Ibid., 31.

8. Ambassador Young to President's Military Representative (Taylor), "Defensibility of Southeast Asia and United States Commitments," October 27, 1961, *FRUS*, 1961–63, 23:28.

9. DOS (unsigned), "Premises and Programs Basic to a China Policy for the U.S.," *DDC*, 1995, 1917.

10. Comments by Air Force Chief of Staff Thomas D. White, May 2, 1961, *FRUS*, 1961–63, 24:170.

11. Memorandum of Conversation, "Laos," April 29, 1961, *FRUS*, 1961–63, 24:154.

12. For an evaulation of the pros and cons of cooperation with the USSR that entailed Moscow's acquiescence to both nonnuclear and nuclear attacks on China's nuclear installations, see DOS memo, "Paper regarding measures which the U.S. and the USSR could apply to China." Also see Anatoly Dobrynin, *In Confidence: Moscow's Ambassador to America's Six Cold War Presidents* (New York: Times Books, 1995), 136–39.

13. "Long Range Study," 216, VI-8, IV-8.

14. The usual way of putting it was that the "blind dogmatism of the Peking leaders and their tragic ignorance of the outside world" were "fundamentally an expression of frustration on the part of the Chinese people, whose traditional pride and sense of superiority to all other nations have been gravely injured by a century of continuing humiliation." Ambassador Edwin O. Reischauer on leaving Japan, August 13, 1966, *DDC*, 1978, 69C.

15. Counterinsurgency and containment fit easily with this psychologized language. The challenge of national wars of liberation, one Pentagon report noted in July 1962, required "an action program designed to defeat the Communists without recourse to the hazard or the terror of nuclear war; one designed to defeat subversion where it had already erupted, and, even more important, to prevent its taking initial root. Put otherwise— it was a strategy of both therapy and of prophylaxis." Quoted in John Lewis Gaddis, *Strategies of Containment: A Critical Appraisal of Postwar American National Security Policy* (New York: Oxford University Press, 1982), 217. Containment itself had an increasingly nonmilitary aspect, befitting Rostow's notion of immunizing poor countries from the disease of communism.

16. Ambassador Reischauer on leaving Japan, August 13, 1966, *ddc*, 1978, 69C, pp. 6, 2.

17. W. W. Rostow to President Johnson, November 9, 1966, *ddc*, 1991, 1566.

18. Rostow's 284-page draft of "Basic National Security Policy," notes Gaddis, was "comparable in purpose to, but much broader in scope than, the studies Eisenhower's National Security Council had regularly produced. Kennedy never formally approved Rostow's 'BSNP' draft, partly because of unresolved questions relating to the use of tactical nuclear weapons, partly for fear that an official

endorsement might tie the President's hands. The document was widely circulated within the government, though, and in retrospect stands, along with Kennedy's public pronouncements, as the most comprehensive guide to what the administration thought it was trying to do in world affairs." Gaddis, *Strategies of Containment*, 200.

19. Dean Rusk from Rostow, "Southeast Asia and China," January 10, 1964, *DDC*.

20. Walt Rostow, Policy NSC Memo, March 1962, *ddc*, 1977, 338A, p. 193.

21. See, for example, "Suggested Talking Paper for Discussion with Mr. Luce on Chinese Representation Question," 0188, n.d., in *Asia and the Pacific: National Security Files, 1961–1963*, John F. Kennedy National Security Files, ed. George Herring (Bethesda, Md.: University Publications of America, 1992), 0188. Schlesinger recounts a meeting with Adlai Stevenson, Dean Rusk, and Kennedy in which "Rusk asked the President whether Stevenson could be authorized to inform other delegations discreetly that the United States did not exclude the possibility that a study committee might recommend for the consideration of the General Assembly in 1962 an essentially 'two China' solution based on the successor state approach— the theory that, if an original UN member broke up into two separate states, each new state would be entitled to a seat in the General Assembly. Kennedy said that Stevenson could proceed along these lines." Arthur M. Schlesinger Jr., *A Thousand Days: John F. Kennedy in the White House* (Boston: Little, Brown, 1965), 446.

22. The Republic of China was increasingly concerned about the developing two-China policy under Kennedy, as NIE 4361, June 20, 1961, pointed out. The CIA analyzed the ROC's growing problems: the increasing likelihood that the United Nations would shift its position on the entrance of communist China and the growing fear in Taipei of a two-China policy. See *DDC*, June 20, 1961, 1995, 3017, "Prospects for the

Government of the ROC." The ROC's worries increased in the years that followed, as shown in NIE-4364, March 11, 1964, *DDC*, 1995, 3018.

23. Summary of the Policies of China, July 25, 1961, *DDC*, 1992, 2561.

24. Rostow, Policy NSC Memo, 194–95.

25. Harlan Cleveland, "Communist China and the United Nations" (original emphasis), October 31, 1964, in *The United Nations: National Security Files, 1963–1969*, Lyndon B. Johnson National Security Files, ed., George C. Herring (Bethesda, Md.: University Publications of America, 1993), 3-0920, 4, 10 (hereafter LBJ, *UN*). Also see *DDC*, 1977, 218C.

26. Secretary Dean Rusk to President Johnson, "Authorization for a New Approach to Trade with Communist China," n.d., *DDC*, 1992, 3204; "Dean Rusk, Memorandum for the President," "Policy toward Communist China," February 22, 1968, *DDC*, 1993, 1335.

27. Rusk and others repeatedly invoked this concern in their diplomatic dealings with other governments concerning Vietnam. Any diplomatic efforts with Peking (or Hanoi) on South Vietnam "would threaten the collapse of the existing resistance in South Vietnam." George Ball opposed de Gaulle's support for an international conference on Vietnam: "If we began, or attempted to begin, negotiations of the type General de Gaulle was speaking about, the result might be a general failure of the will to resist." Telegram from Ball to DOS, June 6, 1964, *FRUS*, 1964–68, 1:464–70.

28. Rusk to Johnson, "Vietnam," January 8, 1964, *FRUS*, 1964–68, 1:10.

29. Quoted from *Foreign Affairs* in Richard Nixon, *The Real War* (New York: Warner Books, 1980), 137.

30. William Bundy, Text of Speech, from Bundy to US Ambassador in Taiwan, February 25, 1968, *DDC*, 1994, 670.

31. Undersecretary of State Nicholas Katzenbach, cable to U.S. Ambassador, Taiwan, May 21, 1968, *DDC*, 1994, 672.

32. "We should try to draw China into activities on the broader world scene where, through exposure to outside reality and successful assumption of international responsibility, she might gain a degree of status and respect which could substitute in part for the unattainable goals of regional domination and super-power status." "Long Range Study," Annex IV.

33. This was a point that the Russians clearly understood, whatever their assessment of how they should act upon such awareness. See Dobryin, *In Confidence*, 135–36.

34. Kennan quoted in Frank Ninkovich, *Modernity and Power: A History of the Domino Theory in the Twentieth Century* (Chicago: University of Chicago Press, 1994), 247, 245.

35. Bohlen, March 23, 1961, quoted in ibid., 245.

36. From Moscow, Thompson himself described Khruschev's speech as amounting to a "declaration of Cold War and determination to bring about [the] downfall [of the] American system." To Secretary of State, January 19, 1961, *DDC*, 1975, 72C.

37. McNamara quoted in Peter W. Rodman, *More Precious than Peace: The Cold War and the Struggle for the Third World* (New York: Scribner, 1994), 95.

38. Kennedy quoted in Ninkovich, *Modernity and Power*, 247.

39. NIE, "Estimate of the World Situation," January 17, 1961, 3. www.foia.cia.gov/.

40. Rostow, Policy NSC Memo.

41. President's meeting with Khrushchev, Vienna, June 3–4, 1961: Background Paper, "Soviet Aims and Expectations," May 25, 1961, *ddc*, 1992, 3591, p. 3.

42. Ibid.

43. CIA, "Sino-Soviet Dispute and Its Significance," April 1, 1961, *ddc*, 1977, 161B, p. 18.

44. President's meeting with Khrushchev, Background Paper, 5.

45. Memorandum of Conference with President Kennedy, February 21, 1962, *FRUS*, 1961–63, 24:630.

46. Memorandum of Conversation, February 27, 1963, *FRUS*, 1961–63, 24:944.

47. Report Prepared by the Inter-Agency Task Force on Laos, January 23, 1961, *FRUS*, 1961–63, 24:29.

48. CIA, Sino-Soviet Task Force, April 1, 1961, *DDC*, 1977, 161B, p. 65.

49. Memo from Deputy Director of the Vietnam Task Force (Wood) to Harriman, "The Communists and South Viet Nam," May 11, 1962, *FRUS*, 1961–63, 2:387.

50. NIE 11-63, "Main Trends in Soviet Policy," May 22, 1963, www.foia.cia.gov/ and CIA CD-ROM. "In our view, the attempt to deploy strategic missiles in Cuba was in considerable part due to Soviet recognition of this trend [the failing momentum of their offensive]." The failure of the Cuban missile venture confronted the Soviet Union with a choice of going more with the Chinese or with the West, and the likelihood was that it would find more in common with Washington than with Beijing.

51. President's meeting with Khrushchev.

52. In the Kennedy years, American views of China were particularly virulent and frightened. A Samuel Lubell poll in the fall of 1963 described "striking changes" in public perceptions of the Russians and the Chinese: 60 percent of those polled then saw China as a greater threat than Russia, up from 40 percent two years earlier; even among those who selected Russia as the bigger threat, 30 percent would regard China as the main threat "once she obtains nuclear weapons." In 1961, hardly anyone polled had considered China a racial threat; in 1963, 20 percent saw the conflict with China as a profound clash of Western and Oriental civilizations. The Sino-Soviet break had deepened the perception of a growing East-West split: a third of the electorate now envisioned some "eventual alliance of the U.S. with Russia against Red China." Further, "China is pictured as being driven towards war by over-population and starvation and by 'irrational' Oriental leaders," whereas Russia suddenly seemed to

possess "all the virtues of western civilization." And the poll concluded: "An overwhelming majority of the public fears any move that will strengthen China, while many persons look towards Russia as a counterbalancing ally against the Chinese threat. . . . Deep in their minds lies the dread that Red China is moving inexorably towards a nuclear, racial war and that so far we do not know what to do to change this drift of events." James C. Thomson Jr., "Survey of American Opinion on Communist China," August 21, 1964, *ddc*, 1978, 55C.

53. "The documented exchanges of the October–November sessions reveal the extent of Chinese xenophobia," a typical assessment of these years reads. CIA, Sino-Soviet Task Force, April 1, 1961, 15.

54. President's Meeting with Khrushchev, Vienna briefing papers.

55. Kennedy-MacMillian Nassau Meeting, Briefing Book, December 19–20, 1962, in Box 154, George Ball Papers, Mudd Library, Princeton University.

56. President's Meeting with Khrushchev, Vienna briefing papers, 3.

57. Ibid.

58. "Memorandum of Conversation between the President and Chairman Khrushchev," June 3, 1961, *FRUS*, 1961–63, 24:228.

59. Progress Report Prepared by the President's Special Assistant (Stassen), "Special Staff Study for the President—NSC Action No. 1328," May 26, 1955, *FRUS*, 1955–57, 20:105.

60. Informal notes of a meeting of the NSC Council Planning Board, December 21, 1955, *FRUS*, 1955–57, 20:245–50.

61. Editorial note, Kennedy meeting on U.S. test ban treaty, February 8, 1963, *FRUS*, 1961–63, 7:646.

62. DOS memo, "Paper regarding measures which the U.S. and the USSR could apply to China."

63. NIE 4-2-61, "Attitudes of Key World Pow-ers on Disarmament Issues," April 6, 1961, *FRUS*, 1961–63, 7:37.

64. Meeting with JCS on Test Ban, August 13, 1963, *FRUS*, 1961–63, 7:879.

65. Memorandum from JCS to Secretary of Defense McNamara, April 29, 1963, "Study of Chinese Communist Vulnerability." *FRUS*, 1961–63, 7:689, 690.

66. "Points to Be Covered in Preparation of Forthcoming July 15 Mission of Governor Harriman to Moscow," June 20, 1963, *FRUS*, 1961–63, 7:732.

67. NSC Meeting, July 31, 1963, *DDC*, 1991, 3324.

68. Kennedy press conference, December 17, 1962, *Public Papers of the Presidents of the United States: John F. Kennedy, 1961–1963* (Washington, D.C.: Government Printing Office, 1962–64), 3:900.

69. President Kennedy Background Press, December 31, 1962, box 154, Ball Papers.

70. The absence of discussions of a "Titoist" model is not surprising, though it serves as a reminder of what the debate in the late 1940s was actually about. An independent Beijing *not* leaning toward the United States was anathema. The Titoist model assumed that China had to lean to one side or the other. A profoundly nationalistic, independent China defied that very model.

71. SNIE 13-3-61, "Chinese Communist Capabilities and Intentions in the Far East," November 30, 1961, available on CIA CD-ROM.

72. JCS, "Study of Chinese Communist Vulnerability," April 29, 1963, *FRUS*, 1961–63, 7:689.

73. CIA, "Implications of the Sino-Soviet Rupture for the United States," July 18, 1963, *DDC*, 1985.

74. Noam Kochavi, *A Conflict Perpetuated: China Policy during the Kennedy Years* (Westport, Conn.: Praeger, 2002), 197–98.

75. NIE 13-63, "Problems and Prospects in Communist China," May 1, 1963, 3.

76. Kennedy quoted in Robert J. McMahon, *The Cold War on the Periphery: The United States, India, and Pakistan* (New York: Columbia University Press, 1994), 273.

77. Kennedy quoted in Arthur Schlesinger, *A Thousand Days*, 482.

78. Philip Talbot, Recommendation of NSC Subcommittee on South Asia for Nassau Talks, Sino-India Talking Papers, December 17, 1962, Kennedy-Macmillan Nassau Meeting Briefing Book, box 154, Ball Papers.

79. McMahon, *Cold War on the Periphery*, 287.

80. John Kenneth Galbraith, Memo to NSC Executive Committee: India, December 12, 1962, Kennedy-Macmillan Nassau Meeting Briefing Book, box 154, Ball Papers. Robert Kumer, Memorandum for Phillips Talbot, October 24, 1962, *DDC*, 1989, 2213.

81. McMahon, *Cold War on the Periphery*, 290.

82. Ibid., 292; see also Neville Maxwell, *India's China War* (New York: Pantheon, 1970).

83. Rusk quoted in McMahon, *Cold War on the Periphery*, 297.

84. Bowles quoted in ibid., May 18, 1963, 299.

85. CIA analysis quoted in ibid., 288.

86. Ibid.

87. CIA Memorandum, "Historical Sketch of the Sino-Indian Dispute," December 18, 1962, *ddc*, 1999, 0018. Also see Maxwell, *India's China War*, 364.

88. The issue, then, differs somewhat from the way Robert McMahon has posed it. His argument relies more on American perceptions than on American interests; thus, "Kennedy's fixation with India's importance to the United States flowed largely from his belief that India could help contain an expansionist China," rather than from his desire to secure closer ties between India (or other nations) and the United States. In this view, Washington saw neutralism as a middle but not a truly valid stance which, when given an opportunity

would reveal its limitations. Kennedy could both play up the Chinese threat to India *and* seek to compromise Indian neutralism, aiding in the Cold War struggle and reinforcing notions as to who was the true friend of neutrals when the chips were down. See Robert J. McMahon, "Toward Disillusionment and Disengagement in South Asia," in *Lyndon Johnson Confronts the World: American Foreign Policy, 1963–1968,* ed. Warren I. Cohen and Nancy Bernkopf Tucker (Cambridge: Cambridge University Press, 1994), 147.

89. Maxwell, *India's China War*, 364–65.

90. McNamara quoted in William W. Kaufman, *The McNamara Strategy* (New York: Harper and Row, 1964), 88.

91. Underlying these broadly etched contrasts was another dimension: the conflicting national interests of, as an April 1961 CIA assessment phrased it, "two wholly different Communist Nation-states, each considering itself the arbiter of truth." Khrushchev's 1959 Camp David meeting had set the split in motion. China viewed the United States as the "power which had prevented it from acquiring Taiwan and thus completing the civil war, and the chief obstacle to Peiping's efforts to gain universal international recognition." The Soviets, therefore, in seeking détente with China's enemy, were pursuing their interests at the expense of their ally. Détente meant accepting the status quo on Taiwan and limiting China's Asian and international role—a price, according to this analysis, that the Soviets were clearly willing to pay. See *DDC*, 1977, 161B.

92. In 1959, after talking about the missile gap, Kennedy had addressed another gap which, he said, "constitutes an equally clear and present danger to our security—the economic gap": that is, "the gap in living standards and income and hope for the future . . . between the stable, industrialized nations of the north, whether they are friends or foes, and the over-populated, under-invested nations of the south, whether they are friends or neutrals. It is this

gap which presents us with our most critical challenge today. It is this gap which is altering the face of the globe, our strategy, our security, and our alliances, more than any current military challenge. And it is this economic challenge to which we have responded most sporadically, most timidly, and most inadequately." Quoted in Schlesinger, *A Thousand Days*, 544.

93. Quoted in Rodman, *More Precious than Peace*, 96.

94. Quoted in Thomas G. Paterson, "Fixation with Cuba: The Bay of Pigs, Missile Crisis, and Covert War Against Castro," in *Kennedy's Quest for Victory: American Foreign Policy, 1961–1963*, ed. Paterson (New York: Oxford University Press, 1994), 137.

95. Assessments of Castro's Cuba sometimes resembled those of China. "The threat posed by the Castro regime . . . stems ultimately from its inherent appeal to the forces of social unrest and anti-Americanism at a time when most of the area is in the throes of a fundamental economic, social, and political transformation, while popular grievances and aspirations are rising and impatience with the old order and with the slow pace of progress and reform is growing." The Cuban model of "social revolution," like the Chinese, brought together Communist and left-nationalist forces, with potentially catastrophic results for American interests in the Third World. Memorandum for the National Security Council, "U.S. Policy toward Cuba," May 4, 1961, *DDC*, 1995, 3520.

96. Rostow, Policy NSC Memo, 176–77.

97. "The Charles River approach," as Schlesinger called it, "gave our economic policy toward the Third World a rational design and a coherent purpose. . . . It may have fallen short of the ferocities of the situation. But given the nature of our institutions and values, it was probably the best we could do." This approach "required the modernizing of entire social structures and ways of thought and life—and for this capital was not enough. . . . [T]hey brought in structural change, land reform, the roles of the public sector and of private entrepreneurship, political development, and other social and cultural adjustments [that were] required, as Millikan put it, 'to reduce the explosiveness of the modernization process.'" Schlesinger, *A Thousand Days*, 540–42.

98. "Nation building" was a term with sweeping connotations throughout the Kennedy and Johnson administrations. The "Long Range Study" provided one of the best and most concise explanations of what it meant in Asia. American objectives would set in motion processes of "modernization" that would "cause stress and disturbance." In this context, nation building entailed five actions: (1) "To develop a nation-building program which suits the ethos of the nation": the United States had little knowledge of this area; scholars of Asia were still few; Washington needed advisors with "direct knowledge and regard for the mentality and the level of acceptance of the Asian partner"; (2) "To provide prompt and selective aid which is appropriate and adequate, but not excessive"; we had to be able to see problems "from the peasant's viewpoint"; rural programs needed to be augmented and redesigned, the gap between urban and rural bridged, the training of governmental cadres, information programs, and so on, broadened; (3) "To win confidence and support for the nation-building program from the implementing elites, disaffected groupings, and passive masses"; the resistance of a national elite to land reform had to be dealt with, bureaucratic jealousies handled, and the hostility to building up counterinsurgency forces overcome; (4) "To reorient potentially dissident elements so that they work toward amelioration of their grievances through acceptable channels": the grievances that could be exploited by Communists had to be reduced and new channels of communication opened to defuse protest; (5) "To wage counterinsurgency to defeat any subversive insurgency that arises and to do so with mini-

mal damage to nation-building processes." "Long Range Study," V-30–35.

99. Rostow, Policy NSC Memo, 85.

100. Ibid., 121.

101. See William S. Borden, "Defending Hegemony: American Foreign Economic Policy," in Paterson, *Kennedy's Quest for Victory*.

102. Rostow, Policy NSC Memo, 124.

103. Memorandum of Conversation, President's meeting with Prime Minister Macmillan, April 6, 1961, *FRUS*, 1961–63, 14:42.

104. William P. Bundy to Secretary Rusk, March 14, 1966, *Asia and the Pacific: National Security Files, 1963–1969*, Lyndon B. Johnson National Security Files, ed. George C. Herring (Frederick, Md.: University Publications of America), 4-0659, 7 (hereafter LBJ, *Asia*).

105. See the major study of Japan's economic and foreign policy in DOS policy paper "The Future of Japan," June 26, 1964, *ddc*, 1995, 3262.

106. "Long Range Study," 292–93, 11.

107. DOS, Policy on the Future of Japan, June 26, 1964, June 26, 1964, *ddc*, 1994, 3262, p. 1.

108. In NSC documents, the economic dimension is more widely discussed with regard to Japan than to any other nation: "Japan's internal policies, foreign policies and security alignment all depend in the last analysis on the orientation of the nation's economic relationships, or more simply, on where it can make a living. Throughout the post war period this has been overwhelmingly with the Free World, principally the U.S." The opening of the American market was judged by 1964 the single most important factor in Japan's economic success and its long-term relationship with the United States: "Perhaps the greatest single direct contribution of the United States to Japan's success has been the granting to Japan of sufficient access to United States markets to assure the availability of rewards for their hard work." It is a "contribution from which we ourselves have benefited. While the satisfaction of national pride will be an increasingly impor-

tant factor in mobilizing Japanese energies, it is hardly likely to displace or even rival the factor of material incentives." DOS policy paper, "The Future of Japan," June 26, 1964, *DDC*, 1995, 3262, pp. 76–77.

109. "It is difficult to see how Japan's minimum economic goals can be attained unless Japan is afforded opportunity to expand its sale in the U.S. market at least in proportion with the growth of the U.S. GNP. . . . This will require firm Executive Branch resistance of American industry demands for curtailment of Japanese imports." DOS, Policy on the Future of Japan, June 26, 1964, *DDC*.

110. Rostow, Policy NSC Memo, 141.

111. Ball to Kennedy, Memorandum from the Under Secretary of State for Economic Affairs, August 23, 1961, *FRUS*, 1961–63, 13:37–38.

112. Memorandum of Conversation, Meeting at the White House between President Kennedy and Professor Erhard, German Minister for Economic Affairs, January 8, 1962, *FRUS*, 1962, 13:60.

113. Ibid., 13:32. As Ball wrote to Kennedy, "We shall have to give up item-by-item tariff negotiations approach of the past and shall have to negotiate for a major across-the-board reduction on our import restrictions and those of the European Economic Community, aimed at opening both economies further to one another's exporters. At the same time, we must find a coordinated way of opening the markets of all industrial nations to the expanding industrial exports of developing countries. We shall have to develop an assistance program for a limited number of domestic industries which may have difficulty in absorbing the adjustment impact. And we shall have to negotiate explicit international trading arrangements in a number of key agricultural products. . . . The American people . . . will see and, I hope, begin to understand the shape and implication of the new trading world." Memorandum from Undersecretary of State for Economic Affairs (Ball) to President Kennedy, October 23, 1961, *FRUS*, 1961–63, 9:494.

114. Report to the Honorable J. F. Kennedy from Task Force on Foreign Economic policy, December 31, 1960, box 166, Ball Papers.

115. The problems of international monetary policy—such as ending the growing deficiency in the U.S. balance of payments; managing the large accumulations of short-term claims on the United States held unenthusiastically by European central banks; designing suitable international monetary arrangements to meet the needs of the world economy as the volume of international trade and payments grew—were aspects of the global economic context that included these developing attitudes and policies toward the Third World. But the focus is on those that most directly affected the Third World and China.

116. Summary Minutes of Meeting of the Interdepartmental Committee of Under Secretaries on Foreign Economic Policy, January 24, 1962, *FRUS*, 1961–63, 9:426.

117. Carl Kaysen, Report of the President's Task Force on Foreign Economic Policy," November 25, 1964, *DDC*, 1993, 1769, p. 1.

118. Ibid., 1–4, 7.

119. Memorandum of Conversation, May 26, 1961 (participants include Secretary Rusk, Dean Acheson, Charles Marshall, Roswell Gilpatric), *FRUS*, 1961–63, 9:248.

120. Kaysen, Report of the President's Task Force on Foreign Economic Policy, A-3.

121. Lyndon B. Johnson, Briefing by the Vice President to the House Committee on Foreign Affairs, March 1, 1961, *DDC*, 1995, 1111, p. 4.

122. Kaysen, Report of the President's Task Force on Foreign Economic Policy, 18, T-5.

123. "Direct investment in extractive industries," Kaysen noted, "accounted for over two-thirds of the total and supplies credits for 20%. Direct investment in manufactures was only 10%." Ibid., A-15.

124. Ibid., A-23, A-27.

125. "U.S. Policy on Trade with the European Soviet Bloc," July 26, 1963, *FRUS*, 1961–63, 9:721, 722.

126. Summary Minutes of Meeting of the Interdepartmental Committee of Under Secretaries on Foreign Economic Policy, January 10, 1962, 9:664.

127. "Minutes of the Meeting of the Export Control Review Board," August 15, 1963, *FRUS*, 1961–63, 9:731.

128. Kaysen, Report of the President's Task Force on Foreign Economic Policy, T-22.

129. Ibid., T-24.

130. William Bundy and Anthony Solomon to Rusk, "A New Approach to our Trade and Transaction Controls against Communist China—ACTION MEMORANDUM," forwarded to Rostow by James C. Thomson Jr., August 4, 1966, LBJ, *Asia*, 4-0983, p. 2.

131. Rusk acknowledged this leverage in more than one context. "He feels that a great deal can be done with the Chinese based on the fact that their trend in trade relationships has shifted over the past few years from the Red Bloc to the West in great measure." Trade could moderate; it could also be a pressure point. Memorandum of Conversation, Saigon, April 19, 1964, *FRUS*, 1964–68, Vietnam, 1964, 252.

132. CIA, "Economic Benefits to Communist China of a Removal of US Trade Controls," June 1966, 84a.

133. "Long Range Study," 218.

134. Roger Hilsman, Oral History project, in *Oral Histories of the Johnson Administration*, ed. Robert Lester (Bethesda, Md.: University Publications of America, 1988), May 15, 1969, reel 10, p. 37. "If Kennedy had been alive, I had on my desk recommendations to lift travel bans on Americans, reexamine the question of trade restrictions, invite them to the disarmament talks, and recognize Mongolia. Those would have been the first moves. But I never forwarded those to the White House, because you see, my feeling would be that you don't want any grand initiatives in foreign policy in the period when the new President has got to get his hands on the reins. The time to do that would have been after the 1964 elections, you see" (38).

135. Quotations from this speech are taken from Roger Hilsman, DOS Press Release, December 12, 1963: address at the Commonwealth Club, San Francisco, December 13, 1963, 1–2, 3–12. (Press release in author's collection.)

136. The critical factor that "focused high-level thought on the economical as well as military and political aspects of containment" was the "rise to power of the Chinese Communists in October 1949 and Mao's leaning-to-one side," Walt Rostow later wrote. In November, a special committee headed by Gordon Gray urged the dispensation of development assistance outside the framework of military alliances (a position similar to Nelson Rockefeller's in his March 1951 report on Latin America). The Korean War diverted potential development funds to security, but "paradoxically it was in this distorted setting that the most creative phase of thought about development and development policy began." Rostow, *Theorists of Economic Growth from David Hume to the Present* (New York: Oxford University Press, 1990), 376.

137. How a conception of modernization came to permeate the development of modern Chinese studies in the United States is analyzed in James Peck, "The Roots of Rhetoric: The Professional Ideology of America's China Experts," in *America's Asia*, ed. Edward Friedman and Mark Selden (New York: Pantheon, 1971); and Peck, "Revolution versus Modernization and Revisionism," in *China's Uninterrupted Revolution: From 1940 to the Present*, ed. Victor Nee and James Peck (New York: Pantheon, 1975).

138. Developmental economics became slowly established in the United States after World War II. The immediate focus was on the recovery of Europe. Developmental concerns were evident, however, in the use of the world "development" in the Breton Woods Accord, in the concept and the very name of the World Bank, and in formulations of policy by the various international trade organizations and regional economic commissions for Asia and the Far East and Latin America. Truman's Point Four program became the first major ideological initiative to support development, though its actual programs were very limited. Rostow, *Theorists of Economic Growth*, 375–76.

139. W. W. Rostow, *The Diffusion of Power: An Essay in Recent History* (New York: Macmillan, 1972), 87.

140. These factors included a growing concern with Soviet economic diplomacy in the Third World; the Middle East crisis of the summer of 1958, when radical Arab nationalism threatened the entire conservative phalanx of American support; the Indian foreign-exchange problem, which boded a series of economic headaches at a time when the Chinese and Soviet models were looking increasingly attractive to Third World countries; the corrosive effects of the fall of basic commodity prices since 1951; and, finally, the powerful drive to counter revolutionary currents in Latin America. Ibid., 88–89.

141. Mill Paper 205, April 2, 1959, in Kesaris, *Documents of the NSC*, 16, 11.

142. Rostow, *Theorists of Economic Growth*, 378, 436.

143. Dean Rusk, U.S. Senate, Foreign Relations Committee, *Executive Sessions of the Senate Foreign Relations Committee*, as cited in Lloyd C. Gardner, *Pay Any Price: Lyndon Johnson and the Wars for Vietnam* (Chicago: Ivan R. Dee, 1995), 111.

144. Thus had Rostow long implicitly argued, writing to Robert Cutler in 1954 that "if we can deny Communism its claim to possessing a uniquely appropriate formula for quick economic growth in the underdeveloped areas, its appeal there will largely be dissipated. And if its appeal in underdeveloped areas goes, one big chunk of our security problem will be solved." W. W. Rostow to Robert Cutler, Special Assistant to the President, August 16, 1954, *DDC*, 1992, p. 993.

145. NIE 80/90-61, "Latin American Reactions to Developments in and with Respect to Cuba," July 18, 1961, *DDC*, 1993, p. 604.

146. Ibid., 2, 3, 7.

147. Stephen G. Rabe, "Controlling Revolutions: Latin America, the Alliance for Progress, and Cold War Anti-Communism," in Paterson, *Kennedy's Quest for Victory*, 117. This was evident in Kennedy's ordering his subordinates "to develop new courses in riot control, psychological warfare, and counter guerrilla operations at military schools in the United States and Panama, to establish an inter-American police academy to train Latin Americans in mob control and counterinsurgency, and to fund 'civic action' programs in which Latin American military units would contribute to the economic infrastructure by building roads and bridges."

148. Department of Defense, "Military Actions for Latin America," app. A, "Recommendations with Statement of the Problem and Need for Action," November 30, 1961, *DDC*, 1981, 6a.

149. Ibid., 29–30.

150. "No responsible Chinese leadership can escape the task of social, political and economic modernization. . . . Material incentives as a means of stimulating economic performance may become an imperative necessity." "Long Range Study," 22.

8. Modified Containment plus Subversion

1. NIE 13-9-65, "Communist China's Foreign Policy," May 5, 1966, p. 2 (www.foia.cia.gov/), concluded that China "has chosen the underdeveloped, ex-colonial world as it most advantageous arena of conflict. In this 'Third World,' the Chinese not only aim to erode US strength but to displace Soviet influence."

2. Despite varying assessments under Johnson, China's policy was regarded as essentially "unchanged during the five years of the Johnson Administration." DOS, "Communist China," in *Internal History of Bilateral Relations with the United States*, chap. 7, pt. C, 1968, *DDC*, 1986.

3. "Long Range Study," 22–23, 67.

4. DOS, "Communist China," n.p.

5. Robert S. McNamara, *In Retrospect: The Tragedy and Lessons of Vietnam* (New York: Times Books, 1995).

6. Ibid., 218.

7. CIA, "China's Growing Isolation in the Communist Movement," LBJ, *Asia*, 4-043, August 5, 1966. NIE 13-9-65, "Communist China's Foreign Policy," May 5, 1965, 4 (www.foia.cia.gov/ and CIA CD-ROM), describes how this Sinocentric belief "generates an arrogant and patronizing attitude toward other nations and peoples," making the Chinese "highly sensitive to any real or fancied slights or disrespect."

8. Lyndon B. Johnson, *The Vantage Point: Perspectives of the Presidency, 1963–1969* (New York: Holt, Rinehart and Winston, 1971), 135–36. Walt Rostow made the same argument in *The Diffusion of Power: An Essay in Recent History* (New York: Macmillan, 1972), 428–29.

9. See DOS, "Communist China," n.p.

10. James C. Thomson, "The U.S. and Communist China in the Months Ahead," LBJ, *Asia*, 3-0115.

11. James C. Thomson Jr., Memorandum for Mr. Bundy, "The U.S. and Communist China in the Months Ahead," October 28, 1964, *FRUS*, 1964–68, 30:118.

12. James C. Thomson Jr., Memorandum for Mr. Valenti, "Some Propositions on a China Strategy," March 1, 1966, *FRUS*, 1964–68, 30:262.

13. Ranging from extreme to extreme, "five strategies were considered: 1. Seeking an early showdown with the Chinese communists. 2. Close-in containment and forward defense, including maintaining a significant military presence on the mainland of Asia. 3. Containment and defense primarily from the offshore island chain. 4. Remote containment and mid-Pacific defense behind buffer zones. 5. Disengagement and mid-Pacific defense." "Long Range Study," 180.

14. Ibid., 182–83.

15. Ibid., 184–85.

16. Ibid., 185.

17. Ibid., 188.

18. Ibid., 242–43.

19. Ibid., 18–21.

20. Ibid., 197.

21. Ibid., Annex III, 1.

22. Ibid., 246.

23. Ibid., 6.

24. "ABM's, Alliances and Arms Control," May 25, 1967, *DDC*, 1993, 3121: draft, pp. 42–43.

25. An example of the debates in the intelligence community over likely Chinese reactions to U.S. troop and aerial escalation is in SNIE 10-9-65, "Communist and Free World Reactions to a Possible US Courses of Action," July 23, 1965, *DDC*, 1995, 3046. The majority view was that the Chinese were not unduly alarmed by the escalation of U.S. troop commitments and of aerial strikes against Hanoi and Haiphong, being confident in an ultimate Vietnamese victory. The air strikes did risk a Chinese response from bases in South China: "We do not believe, however, that this would lead to greatly increased Chinese Communist participation in the conflict." The heads of the Defense Intelligence Agency and of naval, air force, and army intelligence believed that "the Chinese would be reluctant to engage the US in an air war or to risk US retaliation against Chinese military installations." The State Department's Director of Intelligence and Research disagreed. "The chances are *better* than even that Chinese aircraft would deliberately engage the U.S. under these circumstances.... [That would entail] extremely dangerous repercussions and if they were deliberate they could not fail to lead to a wider war." For a similar analysis, see CIA, "Communist Reactions to Non-Nuclear Air Strikes by U.S. against China," April 13, 1965, *DDC*, 1994, 11; and CIA, SNIE 10-5-65: "Estimate of Soviet and Chinese Reactions to Non-Nuclear Air Strikes by the U.S. against China," April 28, 1965, *DDC*, 1994, 12.

26. Vice President Humphrey wrote Johnson on February 15, 1965, "If a war with China was ruled out by the Truman and Eisenhower administration alike in 1952–53, at a time when we alone had nuclear weapons, people will find it hard to contemplate such a war with China now. No one really believes that the Soviet Union would allow us to destroy Communist China with nuclear weapons." Hubert Humphrey Memo to President Johnson, in *The Johnson Years: A Vietnam Round Table*, ed. Ted Gittinger (Austin: University of Texas Press, 1993), 157.

27. George Ball, "Memo to the President: Vietnam," box 163, 5, Ball Papers.

28. George Ball, to Rusk, McNamara, and Bundy, "How Valid Are the Assumptions Underlying Our Vietnam Policies," October 5, 1964, box 153, 34, Ball Papers.

29. George Ball, Memorandum to the President: "The Resumption of Bombing Poses Grave Danger of Precipitation of a War with China," January 25, 1966, box 166, Ball Papers. The JCS offered various military strategies to deal with a Chinese entry into the Vietnam War. In November 1966 the NSC proposed three possible responses in the event of overt Chinese intervention in Southeast Asia: (1) Operation Alpha, "Air and naval offensive against Communist China—holding operation in SE Asia"; (2) Operation Bravo, "Air, land, and sea offensive against South China—holding operation in SE Asia;" (3) Operation Charlie—"Air and sea offensive against South China; and a land, sea, air offensive against North Vietnam." A consensus remained that an aggressive, violent China had to be dealt with harshly, but as long as its actions were contained and its ideology undermined, it could go on existing. NSC, "China: Evaluation of All Strategies for Conduct of Limited Offensive Operations against Communist China in Response to Overt Intervention in SE Asia by Significant Communist China Forces in 1967," NSC, November 2, 1966, *DDC*, 1990, 3434. For a detailed evaluation of each of the proposed strategies, see "Alternative U.S. Strategies for Communist China, Vol. 1, Short title—LOSAC," prepared by Chairman, JCS Special Studies Group, October 14, 1966, *DDC*, 1991, 2441.

30. Though Averell Harriman, acting as Johnson's ambassador-at-large, was often flexible on China issues, on Vietnam, China, and the question of recognition he was no more flexible than Rusk. De Gaulle's act, he wrote, risked not just opening French trade with China but also bringing "French technical assistance or long term credits." The setbacks to Chinese industrial production had been such that even minor technical assistance in key industries "might well improve their industrial production or even speed up their nuclear program." And others, like the Japanese, might act in concert with the French. "I think de Gaulle should be confronted with our views in this matter." March 18, 1964, *DDC*, 1975, 104a.

31. McNamara, *In Retrospect*, 117.

32. Memo from JCS to McNamara, March 23, 1961, *FRUS*, 1961–63, 7:22–23.

33. NIE 10-61, "Authority and Control in the Communist Movement," August 8, 1961, *DDC*, 1981, 392.

34. SNIE 14-3-63, "The Impact of the Sino-Soviet Dispute on North Vietnam and Its Policies," June 26, 1963, *FRUS*, 1961–63, 3:421.

35. NIE 10-2-64, "Prospects for the International Communist Movement, June 10, 1964, *DDC*, 1992, 2413, p. 17.

36. For example, in an ongoing debate over disagreements between Beijing and Hanoi on the proper way to wage a "people's war" and the resulting implications for their relationship, differences and contrasts became the basic stuff of intelligence analysis. See, for example, SNIE 13-66, "Chinese Communist Intentions in Vietnam," July 29, 1966, in LBJ, *Asia*, 4-0005; CIA, Intelligence Memorandum, "The Chinese Position in North Vietnam," August 5, 1966, in LBJ, *Asia*, 4-0369; CIA, "Peiping-Hanoi Differences over Doctrine and Strategy for the Viet Cong," April 2, 1965, in LBJ, *Asia*, 3-0337.

37. Thomas L. Hughes, "Possibility of Greater Chinese Communist Militancy," August 12, 1963, *DDC*, 1995, 1339, p. 10.

38. Thomas L. Hughes to Rusk, "Is Hanoi in Peking's Pocket?" January 24, 1967, *DDC*, 1995, 1033, pp. 1–2.

39. "Although there are important pro-Chinese elements active in the North Vietnamese politburo, all the Hanoi leaders, whether pro-Chinese or pro-Soviet are primarily nationalistic in their outlook. Those sympathetic with Chinese ideas on continuing violent revolution are not subservient to Peking. They, like the entire leadership, are demonstrably leery of too much reliance on China or the Soviet Union." CIA, "Chinese Position in North Vietnam," 2.

40. "Long Range Study," 215, 245, 244.

41. For a typical example, see CIA, "Peking-Hanoi Differences on 'People's War,'" October 7, 1965, *DDC*.

42. Ibid., 1.

43. CIA, "The Chinese Position in North Vietnam, 6.

44. Aide-Mémoire, Prime Minister Sato Discussions, January 1965, *DDC*, 1993, 3229, pp. 1, 3. Some Asian leaders could also simplify their views to accommodate to the United States. As James C. Thomson Jr., an Asian policy analyst for the NSC, recounted, "Lee Kuan Yew, in Singapore, was an arch critic of our Vietnam involvement; but once it was made clear that that's what we were going to do, he had other fish to fry, and he became one of the people the administration kept pulling out of their pockets to support the war. . . . The Japanese similarly were appalled at what we were doing from the earliest days of escalation in Vietnam. The government, however, had to accommodate itself to us; and found it could deal with its own opposition. And once it achieved that kind of stability, having gone out on a limb in defense of our actions in Vietnam, [it] became, to some degree, more of a supporter than any right-thinking Japanese official actually is." James C. Thomson, Oral History, I-7, in *Oral Histories of the Johnson Administration, 1963–1969*, ed. Robert Lester (Bethesda, Md.: University Publications of America, 1988), 53–54.

45. Rusk to Johnson, "Eyes Only for the President," on meeting with de Gaulle, December 16, 1963, *DDC*, 1978, 274B, pp. 2–3.

46. Memorandum of Conversation, April 12, 1964, *FRUS*, 1964–68, 1:235.

47. Memorandum of Conversation, the President et al. and Couve de Murville, February 19, 1965, *DDC*, 1978, 274B.

48. CIA, "Peiping's Views on 'Revolutionary War,'" (No. 2059/64), passed on as Memorandum from Ray Cline to McGeorge Bundy, December 14, 1964, *ddc*, 1977, 6F, p. 2.

49. Ibid., 2, 3.

50. A more cautionary note appeared in some Kennedy administration assessments. Some officials even interpreted heightened tensions in the Taiwan Strait in 1962 as a response by the Chinese communists to the escalation of Nationalist raids, planned drops on the mainland; and renewed calls for liberation of the mainland; the communists might seek to exploit the situation, but their motivation was not aggression per se. Nor was it believed that the Chinese would pressure the United States by threatening to use military force elsewhere in Asia. Indeed, a seizure of the offshore islands might well damage their stand against a two-China policy, since it would increase "the likelihood of a de facto 'Two-Chinas.'" Should American backing for Jiang seem to falter, the communists might well attack his military; thus continued vigilance was essential. But fundamentally, "deterrence underlies much of Peiping's military moves. A strong element of caution, epitomized by Mao's oft-repeated injunction to 'strategically despise, tactically respect the enemy,' could result in over insurance against an anticipated GRC attack supported by US forces." See "Communist Chinese Troop Movements," January 18, 1962, *ddc*, 1977, 316C.

51. CIA, "Peiping's Views on 'Revolutionary War,'" 6.

52. Chinese officials stated that Washington believed "the mere threat to use atom bombs would scare the peoples of Korea and China. . . .

But they continued to stand upright in the face of the nuclear blackmail. . . . The only way of thwarting the nuclear bluff of the US is to have no fear of it." Ibid., quoting *Red Flag*, January 1, 1962.

53. The analysis quoted Zhou Enlai's tv interview of March 1964: "We are perfectly clear that a nuclear world war would cause enormous havoc to mankind. . . . It is claimed that China is willing to lose half her population in a war. China will never provoke a war. *But* should U.S. imperialism impose war on us, we would have no alternative but to resist firmly, and, whatever the cost, we would never surrender" (ibid., 6). Or, as Walt Rostow argued, "Historically, the ChiComs have consistently followed Mao's well-known dictum to 'strategically despise but tactically respect' the enemy; have been very sensitive to the possibility of attack upon the mainland; and have sought to avoid actions which might provoke major military confrontation and thus increase the likelihood of such attack." Rostow, "Implication of a Chinese Communist Nuclear Capability," April 17, 1964, *DDC*, 1977, 218B, p. 5.

54. Dulles quoted in CIA, "Peiping's Views on 'Revolutionary War,'" 10. Much the same point is made in an additional quotation, from *People's Daily March* 4 (1964): 10, on the escalating war in Vietnam: "US clamors to extend the war to the North can only frighten those who have lost their nerve."

55. CIA, "Chinese Communist Military Doctrine," January 17, 1964, *DDC*, 1977, 6B, pp. 3–4, 8–9.

56. Memorandum for the President, "The Implications of a Chinese Communist Nuclear Capability," April 17, 1964, *DDC*, 1977, 218B, p. 1.

57. "Long Range Study," Annex II-17, 19–29.

58. CIA, "Chinese Communist Military Doctrine," credits this potential as a possible Chinese belief; the CIA assessments that focus on Taiwan downplay it.

59. Walt Rostow argued that a strike against the nuclear installations would probably not

effectively stop the Chinese program. Rostow to McGeorge Bundy, "The Bases for Direct Action against Chinese Communist Nuclear Facilities," April 22, 1964, *DDC*.

60. CIA, "Chinese Communist Military Doctrine," 6.

61. "Suggested U.S. Responses to Likely Chinese Communist Interventions," July 31, 1963, *DDC*, 1977, 49D. As an April 1961 assessment put it, "Actual Chinese Communist foreign policies during the past two years have not been as 'leftist' as their arguments against Soviet world policies. Peiping has quieted down on the Sino-Indian border issue, has moved to compose differences with Burma (the border problem) and Indonesia (Chinese minorities), and has exerted only slight pressures in the Taiwan straits. Except in its relations with the U.S., Peiping has once more assumed the Bandung pose of 'reasonableness.'" CIA, "The Sino-Soviet Dispute and Its Significance," April 1, 1961, *DDC*, 1977, 161B.

62. CIA, "Chinese Communist Military Doctrine," 8.

63. "Long Range Study," Annex II-1.

64. "Long Range Study," 63, 187.

65. CIA Intelligence Memorandum, "Soviet Military Policy in 1967: The Challenges and the Issues," June 1967, *DDC*, 1980, 349B, p. 8.

66. "Long Range Study," 62–63.

67. CIA, "Soviet Military Policy in 1967," 7.

68. Ibid., 1.

69. "Long Range Study," Annex VI-6, 253, 252.

70. Depending on the particular location and the issues preoccupying a diplomat, opinions on this point could vary widely. Some saw the threat lessening; others still saw it as paramount. Ambassador Bowles wrote to Dean Rusk from New Delhi on September 10, 1966, "While the primary overall objectives of U.S. policy should be ultimately to reach a detente with the Soviet Union, it is equally important that we recognize the fundamental fact that right now the Soviet Union in Asia has embarked on a pol-

icy which, while seeking to avoid major wars, aims at steadily expanding the areas it controls at the expense of the U.S." *DDC*, 1995, 915, p. 8.

71. Examples included limiting the expansion of Chinese power; avoiding situations that risked nuclear war; possibly cooperating "in our efforts to increase national independence, stability and progress in Asia." As for the conflicts, "We should expect the USSR to continue its attempts to damage American interests and oppose American influence to the best of its ability, at the same time opposing Chinese expansion and Chinese influence in the Communist movement. The most likely Sino-Soviet scenario [is] continued hostility, possibly escalating to armed conflict." "Long Range Study," Appendix VI.

72. Ibid., 56, VI-20, 21, 23.

73. See "Parallels in U.S./USSR Policies in Asia," January 9, 1969, *DDC*, 1984, 2695.

74. "Long Range Study," 110.

75. "Situation in Communist China and United States Policy Alternatives," 1967, *DDC*, 1992, 3206, p. 4.

76. Alfred Jenkins to Walt Rostow, "Chinese Civil War and the Soviet Union," September 14, 1967, *DDC*, 1995, 2887.

77. CIA, "China's Growing Isolation in the Communist Movement," August 5, 1966, LBJ, *Asia*, 4-0439. This CIA memorandum assessing China's influence in Korea, Japan, Latin America, and wide parts of continental Asia is one example among many of studies pointing up the declining appeal of China and its revolutionary methods. Another is CIA "Peking's Setbacks in Indonesia," April 1, 1966, LBJ, *Asia*, 4-0626.

78. "There was a tendency, in concept and language, for [Kennedy's] administration to think of the developing world as something like a group of nations and peoples with common problems. In the notion of *le tiers monde* the French contributed a parallel and widely accepted concept. There was a similar tendency in communist thought and policy to group the

developing continents under a broad rubric as the 'anti-imperialist' crusade was conducted" Rostow, *Diffusion of Power*, 426.

79. "It is increasingly clear, for example, that the insurgency in Malaya was not that which the Philippines confronted, nor that in South Vietnam, and so on. This does not suggest that the search for patterns or for lessons should be slackened. What it does suggest is that there may be a low limit to the degree of doctrine derived from one insurgency experience that is applicable to another." "Long Range Study," V-29.

80. CIA, "Peking Setbacks in Indonesia," April 1, 1966, *DDC*, 1975, 16B. See also DOS, "A Contingency Plan for Rescue Stabilization and Rehabilitation of the Indonesian Economy," March 25, 1966, *DDC*, 1976, 281F.

81. China's role in this war was assessed largely in terms of regional issues and its tilt toward Pakistan, but the CIA analyses concluded that China had no wish to share nuclear technology with Pakistan and would remain very cautious on this issue. See, for example, CIA, "Sino-Pakistani Cooperation in the Kashmir War," October 14, 1965, LBJ, *Asia*, 4-0006; and the assessment of the nuclear questions by Thomas Hughes in a memo to Rusk, August 12, 1966, LBJ, *Asia*, 4-0395, which weighs factors affecting China's position against Chinese aid to Pakistan's nuclear development.

82. The lessening concern over the Afro-Asian movement is evident in a comparison of two CIA reports: "On Non-aligned Nations Conferences," August 3, 1961, *DDC*, 1979, 14A; and "Second Afro-Asian Conferences: A Status Report," May 10, 1965, *DDC*, 1976, 1B.

83. See the long NIE 80-90-69, "The Potential for Revolution in Latin America," March 28, 1968, *DDC*, 1992, and also the lengthy CIA analysis "Castro and Communism: The Cuban Revolution in Perspective," May 9, 1966, *ddc*, 1993, 608.

84. DOS, Thomas L. Hughes to Rusk, "An Outline Guide to Communist Activities in Africa," May 15, 1964, *DDC*, 1976, p. 9: "The East is viewed, not so much as an ally in the achievement of mutual objectives, but as an instrument (often acknowledged as one to be handled with care) to achieve some domestic, even parochial, interest. The interest may be that of demonstrating to radical elements at home one's independence of the West; or it may be quite simply to receive assistance unavailable in the West; or as frequently is the case, it may be, not the retrenchment of relations with the West, but the encouragement of greater Western support by demonstrating that alternatives to Western assistance do indeed exist."

85. Walt Rostow, Ray Cline, et al., in Gittinger, *Johnson Years*.

86. Rice, airgram A-431, "Communist China—US Policy Assessment," in DOS, "Communist China, History of Relations," December 31, 1965, *DDC*, 1986, 2925.

87. Johnson, *Vantage Point*, 357.

88. For such arguments, see Rostow, Ray Cline, and others in Gittinger, *Johnson Years*, 128. For the argument that Vietnam and Indonesia had no connection whatsoever, see "Indonesian Crises and U.S. Determination in Vietnam," May 13, 1966, *DDC*, 1977, 90B.

89. "Long Range Study," V-12. See also CIA, "Little Chance of Communist China Regaining Economic Momentum," April 1964, *DDC*, 1976, 6c.

90. "Long Range Study," V-12, 13.

91. "U.S. Posture toward Communist China: Guidelines for Public Statements," 1965, *DDC*, 1988, 2032, pp. 4–5.

92. Memorandum for Rostow, June 24, 1966, in William Jorden, "Elements of Progress in Asia," in Gittinger, *Johnson Years*, 168–71.

93. Thomson, Memo for Mr. Valenti, "Some Propositions on China Strategy," 2. For nonmilitary ways of influencing the Chinese Communists, see "Long Range Study," IV-1–19, which outlines proposals to break down China's self-imposed isolation: trade, humanitarian aid, propaganda, cultural exchange, and so on.

94. James C. Thomson Jr., Memorandum for Mr. Bundy, "Some New Year's Reflection on U.S.-China Policy," *FRUS*, 1964–68, 30:262.

95. "As the electronics-communications explosion will increasingly riddle curtains . . . so will the coming world stock market (faster and cheaper travel), and truly futuristic *personalized* global communication made possible by laser's gift of *'infinite' radio frequencies*. . . . Pressure for global cooperation should prove immense. . . . Accelerating ecumenicism and even secularization trends of the planet should in time also affect the communist faiths where they play fancy with fact." Alfred Jenkins, "Mainland Developments Demand a Clearer U.S. Policy," August 3, 1966, *DDC*, 1996.

96. Edward Rice, "Communist China and Recommendations for United States Policy," November 6, 1964, *DDC*, 1977, 117A, p. 7.

97. Leonard Marks, USIA director, to Walt Rostow, June 30, 1966, *DDC*, 1986, 534.

98. Jenkins, "Mainland Developments Demand a Clearer U.S. Policy."

99. "Situation in Communist China and United States Policy Alternatives," 4.

100. DOS, Hong Kong, "1967 Chiefs of Mission Conference—Country Papers on Communist China and on Hong Kong and Macao," January 27, 1967, LBJ, *Asia*, 7–8, 5-0134.

101. CIA cable, James C. Thomson Jr. to Walt Rostow, "Mao's Opposition," July 25, 1966, LBJ, *Asia*, 4-0419.

102. Jenkins, Memo to Rostow, "Mao's Mangy Majority," April 10, 1967, *DDC*, 1986, 56, p. 2.

103. James C. Thomson Jr. later commented on this "psychiatric approach" in which China was viewed "as psychotic—or at least as a very disorderly neurotic. 'China has gone mad'—one heard the words quite frequently (hardly surprising when even such a veteran observer as Theodore White regrettably entitled his great documentary film 'China: The Roots of Madness'). The diagnosis of insanity produces at least two prescriptions for treatment: try forms of therapy, say the dovish psychiatrists; no, tighten the straitjacket of containment, say their hawkish opponents." Thomson, "The Missing Ambassador," in *Inside the System: A Washington Monthly Reader*, ed. Charles Peters (New York: Praeger, 1970).

104. Al Jenkins, Memo for Rostow, January 20, 1967, 1, 2, LBJ, *Asia*, 5-0244.

105. Alfred Jenkins, "Attempted Turnabout," February 28, 1967, *DDC*, 1986, 89, p. 1.

106. DOS, "Communist China: A History of Relations," 1968, *DDC*, 1986, 2925.

107. Ibid.

108. Ibid.

109. Typical of these new assessments were Edward Rice's dispatches from Hong Kong. One example is his November 18, 1966, "Mainland China—Policy Disputes, Power Struggle and Cultural Revolution": "Should China go it alone in support of Viet-nam or cooperate with the rest of the Communist world? If it adopted policies of jointly supporting Viet-nam, it might expect to benefit from joint efforts on behalf of China should the war be carried to the Chinese Mainland—but that would involve a truce in Mao's struggle with the Soviets for a leadership of the world Communist movement. Should China be defended if war came by an 'active' defense (i.e. primary emphasis on defense of cities by conventional forces) such as Chief of Staff Lo Jui-ching had advocated as recently as May 1965, or by a guerrilla-style 'people's war' (as advocated by Lin Piao in his September 2, 1965 article)? Those who have built China's new industrial centers would want these centers protected in an active defense. The military professionals (like Lo Jui-ching) who would see China's armed forces as needing the output of these centers would share their view. But Mao . . . would want to convert China into one vast Viet-Nam, relying on China's strengths of manpower, space and patience. He would argue that reliance on a conventional defense would make China's industrial centers vital to its sur-

vival, whereas China should present no vital centers to a technically superior foe. Mao would want to defend China by a strategy of dispersal, believing he could over time bleed any invader white." Quoted in DOS, "Communist China: A History of Relations."

110. James C. Thomson Jr., Memorandum for Mr. Jenkins, "China Strategy," July 25, 1966, LBJ, *Asia*, 4-0469, 1.

111. James C. Thomson Jr., Memorandum for Bundy, "Seventh-Floor Assignment for Ambassador Reischauer?" February 4, 1966, LBJ, *Asia*, 4-0595, 2.

112. "Long Range Study," IV-8.

113. Ibid., 265.

114. Al Jenkins, Memo to Rostow, "Highlights of China Panel Meetings," February 1–3, 1967, LBJ, *Asia*, 5-0230, 5.

115. DOS, "Communist China: A History of Relations."

116. Address of Johnson to the American Alumni Council, "The Essentials for Peace in Asia," July 12, 1966, in ibid.

117. See James C. Thomson Jr., Memorandum for Mr. Moyers, "Press Conference Queries on China," July 20, 1966, LBJ, *Asia*, 4-0469, 132a, 1–2. The memo lists key phrases to hit. For example, Thomson wanted a nod to trade (on which Rusk was dragging his feet), and so he suggested "We exclude no instrument of national policy—including trade—in our pursuit of peace."

118. DOS, "Communist China: A History of Relations."

119. Jenkins, "Mainland Developments Demand a Clearer U.S. Policy."

120. DOS, Hong Kong, "1967 Chiefs of Mission Conference,"15.

121. Jenkins, "Mainland Developments Demand a Clearer U.S. Policy."

122. "Long Range Study," IV-8.

123. Jenkins, "Mainland Developments Demand a Clearer U.S. Policy," 2.

124. William P. Bundy, in Lester, *Oral Histories of the Johnson Administration*, reel 5.

125. The State Department commissioned several studies to assess the problem. The proposed solutions varied, and each study was able to show (often in great detail) why the approaches the others suggested would not work, but its own was usually no more resistant to criticism. For example, the analysis "Chinese Representation in the United Nations" by Thomas Hovet Jr. (July 14, 1966, DDC) concluded, after an exhaustive examination of the deteriorating American position, that we should not object to the seating of the PRC, even though it would mean ousting the GRC from the United Nations; but we should agree only after the UN had declared Taiwan and the Pescadores a "neutralized zone for a period of at least ten years." Proposals like this were greeted with very little serious response.

126. Rusk to Johnson, on meeting with President de Gaulle, December 16, 1963, *DDC*, 1978, 274B.

127. DOS, "Communist China: A History of Relations," quoting from a memorandum for Bundy, "The U.S. and Communist China in the Months Ahead," October 28, 1964.

128. Robert Komer, November 23, 1964, *DDC*, 1991, 58A.

129. Ibid., 2.

130. Ibid.

131. Harland Cleveland, Memorandum to Undersecretary of State, "The Taming of the Shrew: Communist China and the United Nations," October 31, 1964, in LBJ, *UN*, 3-0920.

132. William Bundy recalled, "I remember saying to the President, 'Mr. President, I think you've got to take this girl out, but it's not because she's beautiful. She has got stringy hair and wears glasses, but she's all you've got.' And he bought the course of action. . . . Now in the end the Cultural Revolution changed it all around and made the thing academic." In Lester, *Oral History,* Oral Histories of the Johnson Administration.

133. Cleveland, "The Taming of the Shrew."

134. Jenkins, "Mainland Developments Demand a Clearer U.S. Policy," 5.

135. "Situation in Communist China and United States Policy Alternatives," 1967, *DDC*, 1992, 3206, p. 5.

136. Edward Rice, "Communist China and Recommendations for United States Policy," November 6, 1964, *DDC*, 1977, 117A.

137. This was a stance the Department of Defense agreed to. As Jenkins related it, "Mort Halperin told me at lunch today that a DOD memorandum on Chirep advocating abandonment of the old formula and pointing toward a 'two China' policy had been approved all the way through McNamara, without any discernible opposition in Defense." McNamara wanted the DOD in deliberations on the China issue because "our present stand damages our relations with friends, and . . . particularly in the case of Japan such damage has defense implications." Note to Walt Rostow, "DOD interests in ChiRep," September 1, 1966, in LBJ, *Asia*, 4-0975.

138. A 1966 assessment of American objectives on Taiwan restated U.S. objectives: (1) to prevent Communist seizure of Taiwan, prevent the outbreak of hostilities, and continue friendly relations with the government; (2) to maintain access by the U.S. military to facilities there; (3) to support GRC military forces to obtain such objectives as above; (4) to encourage political evolution and internal political stability; (5) to complete the transition to sustaining economic growth; (6) to limit Chinese Communist influence by supporting the GRC in the United Nations and support it as the legal government of China; (7) to work with the GRC to weaken Communist power in Asia; (8) to discourage GRC actions and policies that might damage U.S. interests and that might confront the U.S. with 'unacceptable alternatives.' This 1966 assessment judged that the United States had been remarkably successful in achieving these objectives. The emphasis on Taiwan's importance as "probably the most intensely pro-American area

in Asia" was increasing. Of particular note was the "deployment of U.S. Air Force units to Taiwan in support of the Vietnam war . . . with none of the political problems such a deployment would cause in almost any other Asian country . . . etc." "Taiwan: U.S. Policy Problems," January 10, 1966, *DDC*, 1992, 2117, p. 1.

139. Ambassador Edwin O. Reischauer, Cable 1126, August 13, 1966, *DDC*, 1978, 69C, pp. 6–8. This view of the Taiwan tail wagging the American dog was gaining ground among American diplomats. The problem was Rusk: "Because Mr. Rusk is so firmly persuaded of the rightness of our present posture," little could be done on the UN. So the United States continued to hang on "for dear life to a position . . . which now appears to be much less persuasive." Howard Wiggins, Memo to Rostow, "As Seen from the Sidelines: The ChiRep Issue," September 21, 1966, in LBJ, *Asia*, 4-0812, 1–3.

140. DOS, "Communist China: A History of Relations." The 1966 trade recommendation to Rusk "results from the first inter-agency review of the complete China trade picture since the outbreak of the Korean War." Memo for Rostow, "Relaxation of U.S. Embargo on Trade with Communist China," August 4, 1966, *DDC*, 107.

141. Travel, passports, and journalists were by now all accepted on the ground that they undercut the arguments of those who still thought the United States was seeking to isolate China. Refusals to allow travel, for example, "actually impair U.S. national interests because their existence tends to perpetuate the belief both in the United States and abroad that the United States through its policies is responsible for the isolation of China." Report of the China Working Group to the Far East Interdepartmental Regional Ground, Harold W. Jacobson, Chairman, [n.d., 1966?] *DDC*, 1979.

142. "On December 20, 1967, in the case of Lynd vs. Rusk, the United States Court of Appeals for the District of Columbia stated that the Secretary of State was not authorized to take steps to prevent American citizens from

traveling to restricted areas if the traveler were prepared to do so without using or transporting their passports into those areas. Departmental instructions designed to implement the court's decision state that the Department would continue to designate restricted areas and validate passports for travel to them, but that passports 'henceforth would not be revoked or denied for unauthorized travel or for use of a passport for unauthorized travel.'" DOS, Communist China: A History of Relations."

143. Nowhere was "morale" more constantly and incessantly invoked than in the dispatches from Taipei. There was a constant preoccupation with what Jiang would do. Would he leave the United Nations if American policy shifted, even if tactically it was designed to keep the Chinese communists out? As one CIA memorandum on the Nationalist position in the UN stated, "Chiang Kai-shek's continuing concern over internal morale in Taiwan is reinforcing his determination to adhere rigidly to the principle that his is the only government of China. Since this principle is the basic rationale underlying the very existence of the Government of the Republic of China, Chiang might prefer to leave the United Nations if a simple majority of UN members do not support him on the China representation issue, rather than resort to complex procedural maneuvers which he would consider damaging to the prestige of his regime in Taiwan." CIA, April 16, 1964, *CIA Research Reports*, ed. Paul Kesaris (Frederick, Md.: University Publications of America, 1982).

144. "Long Range Study," IX-12.

145. CIA, "Growing Pessimism among Nationalist Chinese Leaders," May 17, 1966, *DDC*, 1996, p. 2.

146. "Long Range Study," IX-13.

147. "What the GRC did find alarming, however, was that as late as early September [1966] the U.S. had made no final decision on tactics for the forthcoming General Assembly and so far as GRC diplomats in most countries were aware, the U.S. had not made its customary demarches urging support on Chirep tactics.... [T]he question of what position the U.S. might take nevertheless hung like a dark cloud ... since the GRC believed that a reversal of U.S. tactics could nullify the GRC achievement." Ambassador Arthur W. Hummel Jr., "The 1966 ChiRep Crisis and Its Impact on Future GRC ChiRep Tactics," January 28, 1967, in LBJ, *UN*, 5-0029.

148. CIA, "Growing Pessimism among Nationalist Chinese Leaders," p. 142.

149. "Long Range Study," IX-4.

Index

Acheson, Dean, 20, 23, 50, 62, 66, 164
    anticommunism of, 30, 93
    on CCP maltreatment of American citizens, 96
    China, assessments of, 6–7, 50, 51–52, 54
    China, nonrecognition policy, 94–100, 123–24
    Chinese nationalism, provocation of, 275n115
    Guomindang and, 126, 278n25
    on Ho Chin Minh, 52, 270n21
    Korea and, 35–36, 113, 114, 115, 127
    on propaganda warfare, 111, 133
    on simplification, 26
    on Sino-Soviet split possibility, 61, 285n19
    Taiwan and, 85–86, 87, 88–90, 92, 125, 129, 279n52
"Acheson in China" (Cohen), 274–75n115
African nationalism, 41
Africa policy (U.S.), 267n81
Ambrose, Stephen, 160, 301–2n20
American expansionism, 21
American globalism, 10–12, 15, 17–22
    anticommunism as mobilizing tool for, 21–22, 33, 45–46
    British imperialism, conflicting interest with, 104–7, 282–83n99, 283nn102–4
    domestic opposition to, 21–22
    ideology of, 30–31
    See also global capitalism
"American Nationalism, the China Myth, and the Truman Doctrine" (McLean), 275n117
American Visions of Europe (Harper), 266–67n76, 266n68
"Anglo-American Relations and China Policy" (Foot), 294n22
"Anglo-Japanese Relations" (Buckley), 297n84
anticolonialism, 41
anticommunism, 7, 21–22, 93
    American globalism, mobilizing tool for, 21–22, 33, 45–46
    distorted prism of, 299n121
    extreme nationalism and, 168–69

    National Security Council, 31–35, 45–46, 54, 264n50
    rationale for opening American market, 297n83
anti-imperialism, 65, 70
antiterrorism, 22
"Appraisal of Communist Effects in Southeast Asia: 1948" (OIR Report), 270n20
Arab nationalism, 165–67
Asia
    economic market system (1950s), 155–56
    nationalism within, 41, 158–59
    socialism, 101
    U.S.-Guomindang alliance, criticism of, 121–23, 124
Asian economic order, U.S. vision of, 159–60
Asia policy (U.S.), 228–32
    containment proposals, 230–32, 313n13
    contradictions of, 48–50
    disengagement proposal, 228–29
    Japan, centrality of, 136–39, 156, 157–58, 159
    Kennan's criticism of, 70–71
    Korean War and, 83, 84, 92–93
    showdown proposal, 229–30
    trade liberalization, 158–60
    Vietnam War and, 232–33
Atlee, Clement, 114, 129
Australia, 293n135
Austrian State Treaty (1955), 294n21

Bacon (Second Secretary to China), 97, 278–79n47
Baig, O. A., 122
Ball, George, 215, 232–33, 239, 305n27, 310n113
Bandung Conference (1955), 181
Barnard, J. L., 293n4
Barrett, Edward W., 117
Belden, Jack, 13
Bevin, Ernest, 111
bipolar globalism, 145–48
    National Security Council, 37–38, 263n37
    United Kingdom, avoidance of, 266n67
    See also international communism

Bishop, Max, 299n109
Blum, Robert, 61
Bohlen, Charles, 141, 145, 174, 202, 209, 239
Bowie, Robert, 175, 192–93
Bowles, Chester, 197, 210, 317n70
Bradbury, William C., 291n109
Bradley, Omar, 88, 130, 132
Brands, H. W., 29
British Imperial Strategy and the Origins of the Cold War (Kent), 282n98
Brzezinski, Zbigniew, 23–24
Buckley, Roger, 297n84
Bundy, McGeorge, 23–24, 233, 237
Bundy, William, 23–24, 201, 218, 255, 320n132
Burma, 94, 132
Butterworth, W. Walton, 52–53, 57, 60, 68, 87, 270n21
Byroade, Henry A., 299n121

Cabot, John, 58–59, 60, 65, 66–67
Cairo Declaration (1943), 87, 277n22
Canada, 94, 98
capitalist core, 213–15
Castro, Fidel, 223
CCP (Chinese Communist Party), 56, 57, 76–77
   maltreatment of American citizens, 95, 96
   Soviet support of, 66–67
   See also communists
Central Intelligence Agency. *See* CIA
Ceylon, 94
Chambers, Whitaker, 261n3
Chang, Gordon, 298n91
Chen Jian, 281n74
Chennault, Claire, 277n12
Chiang Kai-shek. *See* Jiang Jieshih
Chile, 299–300n124
China
   "aggressor", UN identification as, 134
   American public opinion of threat risk, 306–7n52
   Cultural Revolution, 250–51
   extreme nationalism, 169
   India, border dispute with, 209–11
   Indonesian relations, 134–35
   Indo-Pakistan War, 318n81
   industrialization model, 170–71
   intellectual-peasant gap, 77
   Japanese relations, 88, 102–4, 137–38, 157–58, 214, 292n127, 293n134
   Korean War and, 114, 115–16

   national interests, 196
   propaganda warfare, 133, 300n137
   regional interests, 150, 151
   sovereignty, 293n4
   Taiwan, strategy to effect U.S. withdrawal from, 240–41
   Thailand relations, 162–63
   trade embargo against, 134–36, 159–63, 292n119, 293n134, 298n103
   See also Sino-Soviet split
"China: Evaluation of All Strategies for Conduct of Limited Offensive Operations" (NSC), 314n29
China, junior partner in international communism, 7–9, 140–42, 271–72n47
   Soviet Union, comparison to, 150–52
China, recognition of, 93–100
   international community, 87, 93–95, 287n52, 288–89n89
   UN, 255–57, 259, 288–89n89
   U.S. criteria for, 94–100, 175
China, revolutionary model, 9–10, 151–53, 195–97
   expansionism, 243–44
   loss of appeal, 247–49, 317n77
   nuclear war and, 241–43
   self-reliance, 243
   simplification of, 240–44
China, Soviet puppet, 6–7
   communism *vs.* nationalism, 50–54, 57–59
   dimensions of, 48
   dissent against, 72–82
   Korean War and, 111–15
   Stalin and, 54–57
   tragic dilemma, 63–67
China policy, containment with isolation, 3–4, 8–9, 132–39, 156–62
   criticism of, 161, 173, 180–81, 192–93
   economic dimension, 134–36
   factors in, 83–84
   global capitalism and, 100–102
   hostility of, 143–45, 160–61, 173, 177–78, 179–80
   ideological dimension, 133–34
   Japan, centrality of, 136–39, 156, 157–58, 159
   Korean War and, 83, 84
   military dimension, 132–33
   overthrow of government, 289–90n97
   Taiwan, commitment to, 110–11, 173–75, 178
   trade embargo, 134–36, 159–63, 292n119, 293n134, 298n103

China policy, containment without isolation, 227–28
  globalizing simplifications of, 238–40
  nuclear war and, 231–32
  shift toward, 198–99
  trade, 218–19
  two-China proposals, 199, 305n121, 321n137
  UN and, 199–200
China policy, modified containment with subversion, 249–55
  modernization, 249–53
  passport control, 258, 321–22nn141–142
  reconciliation, 254–55
  Taiwan and, 257–59
China policy, nonrecognition, 280–81nn74–75, 296n56
  criticism of, 87, 95–96, 98, 124, 128, 278–79n47
  rationale, 123–24
"China's Growing Isolation in the Communist Movement" (CIA), 317n77
"Chinese Communist Military Doctrine" (CIA), 242
Chinese Communists. See CCP
Chinese Nationalists. See Guomindang
"Chinese Position in North Vietnam" (CIA), 315n39
"Chinese Representation in the United Nations" (Hovet), 320n125
Chou En-lai. See Zhou Enlai
CIA (Central Intelligence Agency), 55, 281n75, 315n39, 317n61, 317n77
  on Chinese expansionism, 49, 210, 244, 313n1
  on Chinese independence, 58, 243
  on Chinese nationalism, 49, 51
  on Japan, 282n87
  Korean War analysis, 112, 114
  National Intelligence Estimate, 15–16, 141, 145–46, 151, 180, 203, 313n1
  nuclear war analysis, 241–42
  POWs and, 302n29
  Sino-Soviet split analysis, 209, 308n91, 316–17n59
  Taiwan analysis, 87, 178, 240–41, 322n143
  trade embargo analysis, 218, 281n81
Clayton, William, 23
Cleveland, Harlan, 199–200, 215
Clinton, Bill, 27
Clubb, O. Edmund, 60, 69, 97, 126, 276n127
  overthrow of CCP, efforts to, 289–90n97
  on Taiwan, 90, 124

Cohen, Warren, 274–75n115
Cold War, NSC definition of, 26
Collins, J. Laughton, 88
Commerce Department (U.S.), 175, 176–77
communism, 164
  appeal of, 222
  international vs. monolithic, 149–50
  nationalism and, 50–54, 60
  as state-driven anticapitalism, 220
  UK concern over, 105–6
"Communist and Free World Reactions to a Possible US Courses of Action" (CIA), 314n25
communist bloc, nationalism within, 235–38
"Communist China's Foreign Policy" (CIA), 313n1
communists
  propaganda warfare, 27–29, 133
  simplification of, 233–38
  See also CCP
Congress Party (India), 300n137
Congress (U.S.), 110, 155
"Consequences of U.S. Troop Withdrawal for Korea in Spring 1949" (CIA), 284n121
containment strategy, 304n15
  as defensive action, 41–42
Controlling the Waves (McGlothen), 277n18
counterinsurgency strategy, 304n15
Couve de Murville, Maurice, 239
Cuba, 40, 94, 223–24, 309n95
Cuban Missile crisis, 306n50
Cultural Revolution, 250–51

Davies, John Paton, Jr., 69, 75, 96–97, 115, 119, 265n64, 279n55
Defense Department (U.S.), 111, 120–21
de Gaulle, Charles, 255, 305n27
Democratic Republic of Vietnam, 52, 226–27, 237
Denmark, 94
developmental containment, 312n138
  factors favoring, 312n140
  Third World, 211–13, 215–19, 221
  See also modernization
Diffusion of Power (Rostow), 317–18n78
Dobson, Alan P., 283n102, 283n104
DOD. See Defense Department
domino theory, 38–40, 223–24, 266n71
DOS. See State Department
Douglas, Lewis W., 121–22
Dower, John, 136, 139, 293nn134–35
Dulles, Allen, 222

Dulles, John Foster, 3, 38, 90, 163, 167, 180, 222
  anticommunism of, 145, 148–49, 151–52
  China, assessment of, 141
  China, isolationist stance, 163, 180
  Chinese model of industrialization, fear of, 170–71
  Geneva talks, 4, 181, 182, 183–84, 185
  on Japan, 156, 157–58
  Mission Chiefs address (1955), 185–86
  negotiating style, 294n21
  offshore islands crises, 186–87, 188–90, 191
  Pacific settlement proposals, opposition to, 177, 179
  San Francisco speech (1957), 191–92
  Soviet Union and, 150, 152, 153, 154, 155, 160, 170
  Taiwan and, 174, 187–89, 193, 300–301n2
  on trade embargo, 161, 162
  wedge strategy, 142–43, 144, 150, 156, 159
"Dulles, Latin America, and Cold War Anticommunism" (Rabe), 296n62

Eastern Europe policy (U.S.), 203–4
Economic Cooperation Administration, 89
Eckes, Alfred E., Jr., 297n83
economic gap, 211, 308–9n92
economic self-determination, 167
Eden, Anthony, 104, 166, 266n67, 282n98
Egypt, 94
Eisenhower, Dwight D., 28, 41, 42, 157, 160, 165
  anticommunism of, 143–44
  bipolar globalism, 295n38
  bipolar globalism of, 145, 147
  on CCP, 5, 152
  China, assessments of, 7–8, 140
  Khruschev and, 193–94, 202
  Latin American policy, 168
  massive retaliation policy, 147–48
  modernization, 221–22
  nuclear war and, 147–48, 207
  offshore islands crises, 186–87, 191
  Pacific settlement, opposition to, 175, 179
  Soviet Union and, 3, 5, 153–54
  Taiwan policy, 174, 178, 193–94, 303n63
  wedge strategy, 144, 145
  See also China policy, containment with isolation

"Eisenhower's Foreign Economic Policy with Respect to East Asia" (Kaufman), 297n89
"Estimate of a Princeton Graduate" (Merchant), 292n125
Europe
  capitalist integration, 153
  economic rivalry from, 213
  global capitalism, resistance to, 43
  expansionism, 21
  extreme nationalism, 164–69, 172
    Asia, 158–59
    China, 169
    Latin America, 167–69, 299–300n124
    Middle East, 165–67
    See also nationalism

Fairbank, John, 266n65
Faisal, King, 165
fascism, 18
fifth columnists, 33–34
Foot, Rosemary, 294n22
Formosa. See Taiwan
Forrestal, James, 23
Fox Report, 126–27
France, 94, 153, 173, 178, 239
  Arab relations, 166, 167
  freedom, 32–33
Fulbright, J. William, 265n53
"The Future of Japan" (DOS), 310nn108–9

Gaddis, John Lewis, 60, 72, 267n78, 269n106, 304–5n18
  on ideological fervor of NSC, 29–30, 30–31
  on wedge strategy, 149–50, 286n46
Galbraith, John Kenneth, 209
de Gaulle, Charles, 255, 305n27
Geneva talks (1954), 181–85
  Chinese overtures, 184–85
  no-force position on Taiwan, 182–83
  release of prisoners, 182, 183–84, 185
Gerges, Fawaz A., 299n121
Germany, 19, 49, 269n4
global capitalism, 42–45
  capital and, 44, 268nn95–97, 268–69n99
  dollar gap, 268n87
  freedom and, 32
  isolation of China and, 100–102
  tariffs, lowering of, 43–44
  See also American globalism

Goldstein, Stephen M., 280–81n74
Gomulka, Wladyslaw, 155
Graves, H. A., 280n69, 285–86n32
Gray, Gordon, 150, 312n136
Great Britain. *See* United Kingdom
Great Depression, 18
Griffin, Allen, 277n7
Guomindang
    brutality of, 76, 77, 98–99
    Cairo Declaration and, 277n22
    criticism of, 73–75, 76, 127, 273n84
    mainland raids, 182
    offshore islands crises, 187, 303n57
    U.S. alliance, international criticism of,
        121–23, 124
    U.S. support of, 63–64, 66–67, 126–27,
        278n25, 322n147
    See also Jiang Jieshih; Republic of China

Halperin, Morton, 190, 191, 303n57,
    321n137
*Handbook on National Security Council Func-
    tions and Procedures* (DOS), 262n8
Harding, Harry, 94, 95, 121
Harper, John Lamberton, 266–67n76,
    266n68
Harriman, Averell, 23, 76, 110, 207–8, 209,
    315n30
Hartz, Louis, 11
Henderson, Loy W., 129
Hillenkoetter, Roscoe, 60–61
Hilsman, Roger, 219–20, 311n134
Hinton, William, 13
Ho Chi Minh, 52, 227 Holland, R. F.,
    282–83n99
Hoover, Herbert, Jr., 222, 302n25
hostility, 2
    modernization and, 222–23
Hovet, Thomas, Jr., 320n125
Hughes, Thomas L., 236–37, 248, 318n84
Hummel, Arthur W., Jr., 322n147
Humphrey, George M., 43, 222
Humphrey, Hubert H., 314n26
Hungary, 155
Husserl, Edmund, 27

ideological warfare. *See* propaganda
    warfare
Ikeda, Hayato, 214
Immermann, Richard, 143
"The Imperial Factor in British Strategies
    from Attlee to Macmillan" (Holland),
    282–83n99

"Implication of a Chinese Communist
    Nuclear Capability" (Rostow),
    316n53
India, 94, 178, 300n137, 318n81
    China, border dispute with, 209–11
    U.S. China policy, criticism of, 95, 98,
        121, 173
Indonesia, 121, 132, 292n116
    Chinese trade relations, 134–35
Indo-Pakistan War, 318n81
industrialization, models of, 169–71
international communism, 147, 149–50
    See also bipolar globalism
international monetary policy, problems of,
    311n115
Italy, 94

Jackson, C. D., 27–28, 222
Jackson Committee, 28, 262–63n23
Japan, 7, 19
    Chinese relations, 88, 102–4, 137–38,
        157–58, 214, 292n127, 293n134
    global economy, integration into, 43, 49,
        136–37, 139, 158, 310nn108–9
    rearmament, 136, 292n125
    Soviet relations, 157
    U.S. Asia policy, centrality to, 136–39,
        156, 157–58, 159
    U.S. China policy, criticism of, 95–96,
        121
JCS. *See* Joint Chiefs of Staff
Jenkins, Alfred, 198, 250, 254, 255, 257,
    321n137
    on Sino-Soviet split possibility, 246–47
    technological innovation, on impact of,
        319n95
Jessup, Philip, 127–28
Jiang Jieshih, 89, 161, 258–59
    anti-Jiang coup proposal, 90–91, 288n76
    raids on mainland China, 301n9
    Roosevelt and, 73, 74
    U.S. appraisal of, 126, 127, 186,
        288nn76–77
    See also Guomindang
Jinmin-Matsu disputes, 186–87, 188–91,
    265n59, 303n57
Johnson, Louis, 126
Johnson, Lyndon B., 10, 27, 226, 238, 239
    Third World, concern over, 216–17
    on Vietnam War, 248
    See also China policy, containment with-
        out isolation; China policy, modified
        containment with subversion

Johnson, U. Alexis, 182, 183, 184
Joint Chiefs of Staff (JCS), 112, 207,
    291n106, 294n21, 301n9
    anticommunist commitment, 108–9,
      132, 147, 175, 235–36
    Korean War analysis, 115
    Taiwan and, 112, 125, 126, 178, 287n71
Joint Strategic Survey Committee (JSSC),
    115

Kahn, Herman, 34
Katzenbach, Nicholas, 201
Kaufman, Burton I., 297n89
Kaysen, Karl, 216, 217, 218, 311n123
Kennan, George, 2, 103, 202, 209, 271n36
    anticommunism of, 31, 33, 34
    Asia policy, criticism of, 70–71
    China, assessments of, 51, 54–55, 56
    Chinese military expansionism, skepti-
      cism of, 107–8
    domino theory, invocation of, 38–39
    globalism, vision of, 265n58, 274n113
    on nationalism, 41, 65–66
    on propaganda warfare, 27
    Service, criticism of, 275n120
    on Sino-Soviet split possibility, 159
    on Soviet Union, 56–57
    Taiwan and, 86–87
    on Titoism, 61, 62
    on Vietnam, 52
Kennedy, John F., 1, 43, 202–3, 304–5n18,
    305n21
    on China, 195, 208
    on India, 209, 308n88
    Khrushchev and, 202–4, 207
    Laotian crisis, 205
    Latin America, counterinsurgency efforts
      in, 313n147
    Third World, concern over, 196, 211, 215,
      217, 264n47, 308–9n92
    See also China policy, containment with-
      out isolation
Kent, John, 282n98
Kenyatta, Jomo, 210
Khan, Ayub, 210
Khrushchev, Nikita, 193–94, 202–4, 206,
    207
Kirk, Alan, 94
Kissinger, Henry, 15, 23–24
Komer, Robert, 255, 256
Korean War
    armistice negotiations, 291n107
    Asia policy and, 83, 84, 92–93
    China policy, reinforcement to, 111–16

mobilization of American power to Asia,
    rationale for, 131
    POW issue, 133–34
    Zhou's warning, 285–86n32
Kuomintang. See Guomindang

Laos, 205
Latin America, 300n125
    democracy in, 264n47
    nationalism within, 40, 167–69,
      299–300n124
    U.S. counterinsurgency efforts, 313n147
Latin American policy (U.S.), 168
Lee Kuan Yew, 248, 315n44
Lin Biao, 240, 319n109
Lippmann, Walter, 78–79
Lodge, Henry Cabot, 146
Lo Jui-ching, 319n109
Long Range Study (1966), 196, 313n150,
    318n79
    Asia policy proposals, 228–32
    on China's objectives, 226, 244
    communism, multiple layers of, 237–38
    modified containment policy, advocacy
      of, 253, 254–55, 306n32
    on nation building, 309–10n98
    on Soviet-American détente, 246,
      317n71
    Taiwan analysis, 258–59
    on Third World development, 247, 248
Lost Chance in China (Service), 275n120,
    275–76n122
Lovett, Robert, 276–77n6
Lubell, Samuel, 306n52
Ludendorff, Erich, 74
Lutzker, Michael, 265n59
Lynd vs. Rusk, 321–22n142

MacArthur, Douglas, 110, 115, 126, 284n8
MacMillan, Harold, 213
"Mainland China" (Rice), 319–20n109
"Mainland Developments Demand a Clearer
    U.S. Policy" (Jenkins), 319n95
Malaya, 104
Malaysia, 132
Mansfield, Mike, 201
Mao Zedong, 14–15, 38, 60, 162, 241–42
Marshall, Charles Burton, 119, 133–34
Marshall, George, 52, 103, 109
Marshall Plan, 101
Mass Behavior in Battle and Captivity (Brad-
    bury), 291n109
massive retaliation policy, 147–48
Maxwell, Neville, 210

McCarthy, Joseph, 13
McCarthyism, 13–14, 22
McClintock, Robert, 178–79
McClure, Robert, 133
McConaughy, Walter, 96, 185, 273n84
McGlothen, Ronald, 277n18
McLean, David, 275n117
McNamara, Robert, 203, 211, 218, 226–27, 233, 234, 321n137
Melby, John F., 76–78
Memoirs (Kennan), 271n36
Memoirs (Truman), 62
Merchant, Livingston, 89, 101, 127, 290n97, 292n125
Middle East
    extreme nationalism, 165–67
    French relations, 166, 167
    UK relations, 165, 166–67
militant liberty, 264n43
"The Missing Ambassador" (Thomson), 319n103
modernization, 46–47, 220–25
    counterstrategy to communism, 212, 224
    domino theory and, 223–24
    hostility and, 222–23
    modified containment policy and, 249–53
    See also developmental containment
monolithic communism, 149–50
multilateralism, 215, 217
Murphy, Robert, 138–39
"The Myth of America's 'Lost Chance' in China" (Chen), 281n74

Nasser, Gamal Abdel, 164, 165–66
nationalism
    Africa, 41
    communism and, 50–54, 60
    communist bloc, 235–38
    Middle East, 165–67
    threat to NSC, 40–41
    UK concern over, 105
    See also extreme nationalism
National Security Council (NSC), 11, 24–25, 37–45, 88, 130, 142, 294n16
    anticommunism of, 31–35, 45–46, 54, 264n50
    bipolar globalism of, 37–38, 263n37
    China, assessment of, 140
    on Chinese industrialization, 170
    code words of, 25–26
    communist influence, classification of people subject to, 264n48

containment as defensive strategy, 41–42
domino theory, 38–40
global capitalism of, 42–45, 267–68n85
nationalism, threat of, 40–41
propaganda warfare, 27, 29
racism of, 5–6
satellite, criteria for, 55–56
Sino-Japanese trade analysis, 103, 137
Soviet Union, analysis of, 55–56, 146, 154–55
Vietnam War, response proposals to Chinese intervention in, 314n29
See also specific NSC documents
NSC 17, 263nn24–25
NSC 20/1, 34, 264n41, 264–65n51
NSC 20/4, 29, 262n21
NSC 34, 50, 54, 65
NSC 48, 107
NSC 48/1, 50, 71–72, 88, 108
NSC 48/2, 83
NSC 48/3, 284–85n16, 292n120
NSC 58/2, 55–56, 273n78, 273n80
NSC 68, 9–10, 29–30, 31, 212, 263n30
NSC 98, 268n95
NSC 138/1, 264n45
NSC 141, 37, 43, 44, 268n97, 268–69n99, 274n104
NSC 144, 268n87
NSC 166/1, 15, 140–41, 175, 267n82
NSC 5707/8, 265n62
NSC 5719, 267n81
NSC 5906/1, 267–68n85
NSC 6005/1, 268–69n99
national security world, 6, 19, 20
    language of power, 35–37
    wise men of, 23–24
    See also National Security Council
nation building, 225, 309n98
    See also developmental containment; modernization
Nehru, Jawaharlal, 52–53, 102, 164, 289n89
    China-India border dispute, 210
    on Korean War, 116, 134
    Taiwan policy, criticism of, 123
    U.S. nonrecognition policy, criticism of, 87, 124, 128
New Deal, 18, 19, 224
New Zealand, 293n135
Ngo Dinh Diem, 161
NIE (National Intelligence Estimate), 15–16, 141, 145–46, 151, 180, 203, 313n1
"The 1966 ChiRep Crisis and Its Impact on Future GRC ChiRep Tactics" (Hummel), 322n147

Ninkovich, Frank, 40
Nishimura, Kumao, 138
Nitze, Paul, 89, 125
Nixon, Richard, 177, 201
Nkrumah, Kwame, 210
North/South divide, 215–19
North Vietnam, 226–27, 237
Norway, 94, 289n89
NSC. *See* National Security Council
nuclear war, 205, 206–9, 231–32, 241–43

OCB (Operations Coordinating Board), 28, 263n23
Office of Far Eastern Affairs, 100
Office of Research and Intelligence (ORI), 52, 63, 121, 138, 190, 270n20 offshore islands crises, 186–87, 188–91, 265n59, 303n57
Ogburn, Charlton, 122
OIR (Office of Research and Intelligence), 52, 63, 121, 138, 190, 270n20
Okinawa, Japan, 136
On People's War (Lin), 240
"Open Door Speech", 219–20
Opening America's Market (Eckes), 297n83
Operations Coordinating Board (OCB), 28, 263n23
The Origins of the Cold War in Europe (Pleshakov and Zubok), 266n66, 271n37
ORI (Office of Research and Intelligence), 52, 63, 121, 138, 190, 270n20
otherness, 6

Pacific settlement proposals
    Commerce Department, 175, 176–77
    international support for, 178
    U.S. opposition to, 175–79
Pakistan, 94, 210, 318n81
Pandit, V. L., 122
Pannikar, K. M., 115–16, 128–29, 285n31
passport control, 163, 258, 321–22nn141–142
"Peacemaking in Asia" (Schonberger), 283n103
Peake, C. H., 134
Peck, Graham, 13
"Peiping's Views of Revolutionary War" (CIA), 240–41
People's Daily, 15
People's Republic of China. *See* China
Perkins, Troy, 130
Philippines, 132
Pibul Songgram, 162–63, 299n107, 299n109
Pleshakov, Constantine, 266n66, 271n37

Policy Planning Staff (PPS), 58, 61
Politics of the Anglo-American Economic Special Relationship (Dobson), 283n102, 283n104
Port Arthur (China), 141
Portugal, 94
power, language of, 35–37
POWs, 133–34
    CIA and, 302n29
PRC. *See* China
Present at the Creation (Acheson), 61, 279n52
propaganda warfare
    China, 133, 300n137
    communists, 27–29, 133
    Jiang Jieshih, 259
    Latin American nationalism and, 299–300n124
    militant liberty, 264n43
    U.S., 7, 27, 29, 69–71, 116–20, 171–72, 286nn40–41
"Proposal for an offer by the United States to the Chinese Communists for a Settlement in the Far East" (Strong), 131–32
Psychological Strategy Board (PSB), 27, 28, 133
psychological warfare. *See* propaganda warfare

Quantico report, 151
Quemoy-Matsu Crisis, 186–87, 188–91, 265n59, 303n57

Rabe, Stephen G., 296n62
racism, 5–6
Radford, Arthur, 161, 177, 186, 264n43, 295n41
radical nationalism. *See* extreme nationalism
Randall, Clarence, 156, 222
Rankin, Karl, 186
Red Star over China (Snow), 13, 73
Reischauer, Edwin O., 198, 214, 257–58, 304n14
Republic of China (ROC), 185–91
    See also Guomindang
Review of the World (CIA), 49
"Review of U.S. China Policy: A Pacific Settlement" (McClintock), 178–79
revisionism, 250
revolution, 47
revolutionary nationalism, 172
Rice, Edward, 248, 250, 257, 319n109
Richards, James, 62

Robertson, Walter, 152, 184, 186
ROC. *See* Republic of China
Rockefeller, Nelson, 222
Roosevelt, Franklin, 18–19, 73, 74
Rostow, Walt, 23–24, 156, 198–99, 214, 248,
    312n136, 317–18n78
    "Basic National Security Policy" draft,
        304–5n18
    on modernization, 212, 222–23,
        312n144
    on nuclear war, 316n53, 316–17n59
Rusk, Dean, 205, 207, 223, 305n21, 311n131
    on CCP maltreatment of American citi-
        zens, 96
    China, assessments of, 7, 48, 50, 54, 123
    China-India border dispute, 210
    China policy, firmness of, 200–201,
        238–39
    public relations guidelines for China, 249
    Taiwan and, 90–91, 92, 278n25, 278n34
Rusk, Lynd *vs.*, 321–22n142
Russell, Richard, 165–66, 205

Sartre, Jean-Paul, 35
satellite, NSC criteria for, 55–56
Saturday Evening Post, 79
Schlesinger, Arthur M., Jr., 196, 264n47,
    266n71, 305n21, 309n97
Schonberger, Howard, 283n103
Scowcroft, Brent, 23–24
Service, John S., 13, 14–15, 73–75,
    275n120, 275–76n122
Shanghai, bombing of, 98–99
Singapore, 104
"The Sino-Soviet Dispute and Its Signifi-
    cance" (CIA), 317n61
Sino-Soviet split, 204–9
    Chinese independence, 243
    ideological hostility, 204–6, 208
    nuclear war, 205, 206–9
    simplification of, 244–47
    Soviet-American détente and, 308n91
    U.S. propaganda to foment, 117, 286n40
    See also wedge strategy
Sino-Soviet Treaty (1950), 55
Smedley, Agnes, 13
Smith, Gerald, 187
Smith, Walter Bedell, 60, 175
Snow, Edgar, 4, 13, 14–15, 73, 79–82, 241
socialism, 101
Soedjatmoko, 122
Solarium Project's Task Force "A", 42, 43,
    268n92' 293n5
South Africa, 248

Soviet-American détente, 245–46, 308n91,
    317n71
Soviet Union, 3, 8, 80
    American public opinion of threat risk,
        306–7n52
    Arab relations, 165
    CCP, support of, 66–67
    China, comparison to, 150–52
    Cuban Missile crisis, 306n50
    expansionism, 152
    French relations, 153
    global interests, 150, 151
    industrialization model, 170
    Japanese relations, 157
    peace offensive, 145–47
    post-WWII, 19
    Soviet-American détente, 245–46,
        308n91, 317n71
    UK relations, 153
    wars of national liberation, support for,
        202–3
    Yugoslavia's break from, 61–62
    See also Sino-Soviet split
Soviet Union policy (U.S.), 8, 49, 153–55,
    160, 218
Sprouse, Philip, 63, 91–92, 97, 99
Stalin, Joseph, 54–57, 266n66, 271nn36–37,
    271–72n47
Stassen, Harold, 222
State Department (U.S.), 72, 76, 101, 145,
    196
    on CCP, 108, 118, 205–6
    on Chinese intellectual-peasant gap, 77
    on Cultural Revolution, 250, 251
    Guomindang, criticism of, 126–27
    *Handbook on National Security Council
        Functions and Procedures*, 262n8
    on Japan, 310nn108–9
    on Korean War, 112
    on nuclear question, 207
    OIR, 52, 63, 121, 138, 190, 270n20
    PPS, 58, 61
    propaganda warfare, 118–19
    on Sino-Japanese trade, 297n81
    Taiwan and, 78, 89, 124–25
    on trade embargo, 134
    on Vietnam War, 226
Stevenson, Adlai, 305n21
Stilwell, Joseph, 14, 73, 74, 75
Stimson, Henry, 23
"Strategic Importance of Japan" (CIA),
    282n87
"The Strategic Perspective" (Gaddis),
    267n78

Strategies of Containment (Gaddis), 304–5n18
Strong, Robert, 131–32, 288nn76–77, 289–90n97
Stuart, Leighton, 56, 64, 65, 77, 78, 275n115
China, assessments of, 51, 57, 58
Suez crisis, 165, 298n103
Sukarno, 170
Sun Li-jen, 91
The Superpowers and the Middle East (Gerges), 299n121
"Survey of American Opinion on Communist China" (Thomson), 306–7n52
Sweden, 94
Switzerland, 94
Syngman Rhee, 161

Taft, Robert, 21
Taiwan, 85–93
anti-Jiang coup proposal, 90–91, 288n76
China policy and, 110–11, 173–75, 178, 257–59
Chinese strategy to effect U.S. withdrawal from, 240–41
concessions proposal, 131–32
irredentism, threat of, 86–87
military intervention proposal, 88–90
model proposal, 303n49
self-determination proposal, 88, 91–92
two-China proposals, 89, 90, 187, 199, 305n121, 321n137
UN and, 125–26
U.S. relations, 9, 173–75, 258–59
"Taiwan: U.S. Policy Problems" (DOS), 321n138
Taiwan policy (U.S.), 120–31
CCP, denial to, 85–86
CCP occupation, denial of, 85–86
domestic opposition to, 277n7
neutralization, 120–27
no-force position, 181, 182–83
objectives, 321n138
refusal to negotiate, 127–31, 289n92
Taiwan Strait crises, 186–87, 188–91, 265n59, 303n57
Talbot, Philip, 209
Task Force "A" of Project Solarium, 42, 43, 268n92, 293n5
Taylor, Maxwell, 17, 23–24, 295n41
Taylor Study Group, 211
tension. *See* hostility
Thailand, 162–63, 299n107

Theorists of Economic Growth from David Hume to the Present (Rostow), 312n136
Third World
developmental containment of, 211–13, 215–19, 221
modernization and, 46–47
revolutionary model, loss of appeal of, 247–49
Thompson, Llewellyn, 202, 306n36
Thomson, James, C., Jr., 252–53, 315n44, 319n103, 319n117, 306–7n52
A Thousand Days (Schlesinger), 264n47, 266n71, 305n21, 309n97
Tibet, 116, 210
Tito, Josip Broz, 59–62, 155, 273n78, 273n81
Titoism, 59–62, 155
total penetration approach, 203–4
trade, as diplomatic weapon, 160
trade embargo, 134–36, 159–63, 292n119, 293n134, 298n103
Treasury Department (U.S.), 4
Truman, Harry S, 41, 42, 84, 164, 285n18, 312n138
anticommunism of, 62, 68, 93
bipolar globalism of, 7
on Korean War, 114, 267n77
on NSC, 262n7
Sino-Soviet split and, 60
Taiwan policy, 85, 88–89, 120, 127, 129, 276n5
See also China policy, containment with isolation
two-China proposals, 89, 90, 187, 199, 305n121, 321n137

United Kingdom (UK), 19
American globalism, conflicting interest with, 104–7, 282–83n99, 283nn102–4
Arab relations, 165, 166–67
bipolar globalism, avoidance of, 266n67
China, assessment of, 53
China, recognition of, 87, 94–95, 288–89n89
communism, concern over, 105–6
containment of China, advocacy of, 104–5
Guomindang, criticism of, 127
isolation of China, concerns over, 102
nationalism, concern over, 105

Soviet relations, 153
trade embargo and, 298n103
U.S. China policy, criticism of, 95, 173
U.S.-Guomindang alliance, criticism of,
121, 280n69
United Nations (UN)
China, identification as "aggressor", 134
China, recognition of, 255–57, 259,
288–89n89
Taiwan and, 125–26
The United States and China (Fairbank),
266n65
"United States Courses of Action in Korea"
(JSSC), 115
U.S.
Africa policy, 267n81
Asian economic order, vision of, 159–60
capitalist core, control of, 213–15
China, assessments of (*See* China, junior
partner in international communism;
China, revolutionary model; China,
Soviet puppet)
China, criteria for recognition of,
94–100, 175
China, hostility toward, 2–4, 5–6, 13–16
Eastern Europe policy, 203–4
expansionism, 21
Guomindang, backing of, 63–64, 66–67,
126–27, 278n25, 322n147
Guomindang, motives for cooperation
with, 188–89
Guomindang alliance, international criti-
cism of, 121–23, 124, 280n69
Guomindang brutality, complicity in,
98–99
Jiang, appraisal of, 126, 127, 186,
288nn76–77
Latin American policy, 168
national interest and, 23, 196
Pacific settlement proposals, opposition
to, 175–79
propaganda warfare, 7, 27, 29, 69–71,
116–20, 171–72, 286nn40–41
Soviet-American détente, 245–46,
308n91, 317n71
Soviet Union policy, 8, 49, 153–55, 160,
218
Taiwanese relations, 9, 173–75, 258–59

See also American globalism; Asia policy;
China policy; National Security Coun-
cil; Taiwan policy
U.S. Congress, 110, 155
"U.S. Policy toward Cuba" (*DDC*), 309n95
USSR. *See* Soviet Union

Vandenberg, Arthur, 11
Vietnam, 52, 226–27, 237
Vietnam War, 226–27, 232–33
international accommodation to U.S.,
315n44
visionary globalism. *See* American globalism

Wampler, Robert, 295n41
Wang Pingnan, 183
WanWaithayakon, Prince of Thailand, 162
Ward, Angus I., 65, 96
Webb, James, 98, 130
Weber, Max, 32
wedge strategy, 71–72, 113–14, 286n46
Dulles, 142–43, 144, 150, 156, 159
variant on, 284n13
See also Sino-Soviet split
Westernization, 46
West Germany, 43
Wiggins, Howard, 321n139
"Will China Become a Russian Satellite?"
(Snow), 79
Williams, William Appleman, 83
"Will Tito's Heretics Halt Russia?" (Snow),
79
Wittgenstein, Ludwig, 12
world capitalism. *See* global capitalism
WWII, aftermath of, 18

Yanan (China), 73
Years of Trial and Hope (Truman), 285n18
Yoshida Shigeni, 138, 292n127
Yost, Charles, 100
Young, Kenneth, 197
Yugoslavia, 61–62, 94

Zhou Enlai, 4, 60–61, 115–16, 162, 181, 241,
316n53
Geneva talks, 184–85
Korean War warning, 285–86n32
Zubok, Vladislav, 266n66, 271n37

James Peck is director of the U.S.-China Book Publication Project. For eighteen years he was a senior editor at Pantheon Books, and he was executive director of the Culture and Civilization of China publishing project for over a decade. Dr. Peck did his graduate work at Harvard and New York University. He lives in New York City with his wife and daughter.